Get Saucy

Get Saucy

MAKE DINNER A NEW WAY EVERY DAY
WITH SIMPLE SAUCES, MARINADES,
DRESSINGS, GLAZES, PESTOS, PASTA SAUCES,
SALSAS, AND MORE

GRACE PARISI

The Harvard Common Press
Boston, Massachusetts

The Harvard Common Press
535 Albany Street
Boston, Massachusetts 02118
www.harvardcommonpress.com

Printed in the United States

Library of Congress Cataloging-in-Publication Data
Parisi, Grace.
    Get saucy : make dinner a new way every day with simple sauces, marinades, dressings,
glazes, pestos, pasta sauces, salsas, and more / Grace Parisi.
        p. cm.
    Includes index.
    ISBN 1-55832-236-1 (hc : alk. paper) -- ISBN 1-55832-237-X (pb : alk. paper)
  1. Sauces. I. Title.
    TX819.A1P365 2005
    641.8'14—dc22
                                                    2004018566

Special bulk-order discounts are available on this and other Harvard Common Press
books. Companies and organizations may purchase books for premiums or resale,
or may arrange a custom edition, by contacting the Marketing Director at the
address above.

10 9 8 7 6 5 4 3 2 1

Cover and interior design by Barbara Balch

Interior photographs by StockFood, Inc.

Cover photographs: Stir-fry by David Loftus, StockFood, Inc.; cake ©Food Pix;
appetizers by Halsey Creative Services/StockFood, Inc.; salmon ©Food Pix

For my family

CONTENTS

ACKNOWLEDGMENTS

I wish to thank the following people whose support, insight, and influence, whether stated or not, made this project possible:

- To my friends at *Food & Wine* magazine, especially Dana Cowin for her enthusiasm for self-expression and growth, Tina Ujlaki for her inexhaustible food knowledge and encouragement to always be better, Marcia Kiesel for her simple elegance in the kitchen and her passion for Vietnamese food, Jim Standard for his inspiration to try something daring, and, finally, to Kate Heddings, my friend in sweets, for showing me the door

- To my editor, Pam Hoenig, for helping to organize the mess

- To Marilyn Rifkin, GM, for helping organize my thoughts

- To some of my favorite cooks for their quiet inspiration: Julia Child, Diana Sturgis, Paula Wolfert, Mark Vetri, Sandy Gluck, and Maria Sinsky

- To my brother Frank for his always ready appetite

- To my mom, Fran, who's the best home cook in the world

- To my brother Carl for his faith that this was more than a phase

- To my kids, Pia and Malcolm, for finding just about everything unappetizing and who can't wait for me to do a cake book

- And, finally, to my truly amazing, unflinching husband, Christopher, without whose trust, support, honesty, and appetite (for food and stress) this book could never have been written

INTRODUCTION

In trying to describe just what a sauce is, it's rather hard to know exactly where to begin. It could be said that a sauce is simply any pourable accompaniment served over or with food. Basically that's it, but in researching and creating these recipes, I've come to understand how wide-ranging and varied that definition can be. From Alfredo to zabaglione, a sauce can be an accompaniment, a condiment, a pesto, or a salsa, or it can be the base for stews, soups, soufflés, gratins, ice creams, frostings, and more—the applications are limitless.

A collection of recipes this comprehensive is an asset to any cook, primarily because it greatly increases your culinary supply of sauces. You can serve a pork chop, pasta, fish, chicken breast, steak—what have you—every night for months without repeating the same sauce, and have a completely new taste experience every time. Try the Cilantro-Mint Dipping Sauce (page 246) with grilled pork chops on Monday, shrimp on Tuesday, and chicken curry on Wednesday, and it will be vastly different each time.

Although some sauces—especially classic French ones—can be somewhat complicated, I've tried my absolute best to make these accessible, easy, and supermarket friendly, yet still complex in flavor. All this means is that if you can sauté, whisk, stir, or simmer, every sauce in this book will be manageable and ultimately satisfying. What's more, once you become comfortable with the basics of sauce making, you can easily expand your repertoire even further by creating your own variations.

Each chapter contains many helpful boxes and sidebars with tips and suggestions, variations, and recipes that illustrate how certain sauces can be used and integrated into other recipes. Also, the Sauce Index by Suggested Use at the back is an invaluable resource for food and sauce pairings. Simply search the index for poultry, for example, and a list of appropriate sauces follows. The same goes for beef, vegetables, pasta, ice creams, and more. What I hope you will love about this book is its everyday usefulness—it really puts you in charge. Yes, of course you are following a recipe, but you can decide how to use it. Now get going into your kitchen and try out some sauces!

COMPOUND BUTTERS, BROWN BUTTER SAUCES, BEURRE BLANC, AND HOLLANDAISE

Compound butter is really nothing more than a mixture of softened butter and aromatic seasonings. The mixture gets formed into a log and chilled, then sliced and served over something hot, where it melts into a luscious, simple sauce. It's one of the most multipurpose sauces you'll find. It's great with vegetables, especially corn on the cob, broccoli, asparagus, cauliflower, and potatoes; smeared on sandwiches, crackers, and toasted French bread slices; dolloped on steaks, chops, chicken, and fish; and stirred into pasta, noodles, and rice. I particularly love compound butters because they are incredibly easy and can be made way ahead and either refrigerated for about 1 week or frozen for 1 month.

Butter sauces are a bit more complex. These include beurre blancs, brown butter sauces, and hollandaise, plus their variations—béarnaise, Maltaise, Choron. Except for the brown butter sauces, these are emulsified sauces that result from adding butter to another liquid. In the case of beurre blanc, it is added to a mixture of vinegar and such

aromatics as shallots, ginger, or chiles. In the case of hollandaise, it is added to warm beaten egg yolks.

Like any emulsion, beurre blanc and hollandaise sauces make most people nervous—and with good reason. These sauces are temperamental and a little tricky, plus they can break easily. There are a number of ways, however, to considerably lower the risk of disappointment. One is using a double boiler to make a hollandaise. I like to use a saucepan set into a slightly larger saucepan of simmering water. This will keep the pan from getting too hot, causing the butter to melt, the eggs to scramble, and the sauce to separate or break. It's also good to start with chilled butter so that, with each addition, the sauce is cooled just enough to prevent separation (however, if, despite your precautions, the worst happens, see the tips on page 20 for fixing a broken hollandaise sauce).

Brown butter sauces are pretty uncomplicated sauces. Butter is cooked in a skillet until the milk solids turn a golden brown. This gives the sauce its characteristic nut-like flavor. You can elevate this simple sauce with the addition of various ingredients, such as capers, nuts, herbs, shallots, garlic, or chiles.

GARLIC BUTTER

MAKES ABOUT ½ CUP

THIS SIMPLE BUTTER makes incredible garlic bread. Spread some on the cut sides of a split loaf of Italian or French bread and bake until hot and the butter is melted, or thinly slice the butter over peeled and cleaned shrimp and broil until sizzling and cooked through.

    3 large garlic cloves, minced
    Salt
    ½ cup (1 stick) salted butter, softened
    1 teaspoon sweet paprika
    1 tablespoon finely chopped fresh Italian
        parsley leaves
    Generous pinch of freshly ground black
        pepper

1. On a cutting board, using the flat side of a chef's knife, mash the garlic with a pinch of salt to a paste.

2. In a medium-size bowl, using a wooden spoon, beat the butter until creamy. Add the garlic paste, paprika, parsley, and pepper and stir until smooth.

3. Spoon the butter onto a sheet of plastic wrap into a 4-inch-long log. Roll up the plastic, forming the butter into a cylinder. Twist the ends tightly to press the butter into a compact log. Refrigerate until chilled. Will keep refrigerated for about 1 week or frozen for 1 month.

ROASTED GARLIC COMPOUND BUTTER

MAKES ABOUT ½ CUP

THIS LUSCIOUS COMPOUND butter is great on meats, poultry, and fish, as well as steamed vegetables, roasted or boiled potatoes, pasta, rice, and crusty bread. It also makes a great finish to risotto or polenta.

    1 head garlic
    1 tablespoon extra-virgin olive oil
    3 fresh thyme sprigs
    Salt
    ½ cup (1 stick) salted butter, softened
    Freshly ground black pepper

1. Preheat the oven to 425°F. On a sturdy cutting board, stand the head of garlic on its side and, using a sharp knife, cut off the top third of the head of garlic. Place the bottom section on a 12-inch square of aluminum foil, cut side up, and drizzle it with the olive oil. Place the thyme sprigs on top and sprinkle lightly with salt. Bring up the sides of the foil and seal the package. Roast the garlic until tender and golden, about 1 hour. Let cool.

2. Using a toothpick or small knife, remove the garlic from the papery skins and transfer them to a medium-size bowl. Mash the garlic with the back of a wooden spoon. Discard the thyme stems but scrape the leaves into the garlic. Add the butter and stir until smooth. Season with pepper.

3. Spoon the butter onto a sheet of plastic wrap into a 4-inch-long log. Roll up the plastic, forming the butter into a cylinder. Twist the ends tightly to press the butter into a compact log. Refrigerate until chilled. Will keep refrigerated for about 1 week or frozen for 1 month.

ANCHO-GARLIC–PINE NUT COMPOUND BUTTER

MAKES ABOUT 1 CUP

GRILLED STEAK, CHOPS, chicken, shrimp, and fish are all suitable pairings for this chile butter. Since the flavors are a bit intense, choose firm-fleshed meaty fish, such as swordfish, halibut, tuna, cod, or salmon. I also like to add this butter to roasted potatoes, broccoli, cauliflower, and asparagus or slather it all over corn on the cob. Cut the flavored butter into pats and let it melt on whatever you are serving it with.

    3 large ancho chiles, stemmed
    1 cup boiling water
    2 tablespoons extra-virgin olive oil
    2 tablespoons pine nuts
    3 garlic cloves, lightly smashed
    1/2 teaspoon ground cumin
    1/2 teaspoon ground coriander
    1/2 teaspoon finely grated lemon zest
    1 teaspoon fresh lemon juice
    3/4 cup (11/2 sticks) salted butter, softened
    Cayenne pepper

1. In a small, heatproof bowl, soak the anchos in the boiling water until pliable, about 20 minutes. Drain the anchos, remove the seeds, and coarsely chop.

2. Meanwhile, heat the olive oil in a small skillet over medium-high heat until shimmering. Add the pine nuts and cook, stirring constantly, until lightly browned, about 3 minutes. Add the garlic, cumin, and coriander and cook, stirring constantly, until the garlic is softened and the pine nuts are deep golden, about 1 minute longer. Transfer to a plate to cool.

3. In a mini–food processor, combine the anchos, the pine nut mixture, and the lemon zest and juice and pulse into a paste. Add the butter and pulse until combined. Season with cayenne.

4. Spoon the butter onto a sheet of plastic wrap into an 8-inch-long log. Roll up the plastic, forming the butter into a cylinder. Twist the ends tightly to press the butter into a compact log. Refrigerate until chilled. Will keep refrigerated for about 1 week or frozen for 1 month.

ANCHOVY BUTTER

MAKES ABOUT 1/2 CUP

THIS BUTTER IS soooo good spread on crusty French bread and topped with prosciutto, arugula, and sliced tomatoes. Cut it into pats and serve it on grilled or pan-roasted steaks, chops, chicken, or fish; it's equally tasty tossed with steamed or roasted vegetables, pasta, or mashed potatoes.

6 small anchovy fillets
1 garlic clove, minced
1/2 cup (1 stick) salted butter, softened
1 teaspoon fresh lemon juice
Freshly ground black pepper

1. Rinse the anchovies and pat dry. Finely chop them, add the garlic, and, using the flat side of a chef's knife, mash them into a paste. In a medium-size bowl, beat the butter with a wooden spoon until creamy. Add the anchovy paste, lemon juice, and a generous pinch of black pepper and stir until smooth, being sure to break up any clumps.

2. Spoon the butter onto a sheet of plastic wrap into a 4-inch-long log. Roll up the plastic, forming the butter into a cylinder. Twist the ends tightly to press the butter into a compact log. Refrigerate until chilled. Will keep refrigerated for about 1 week or frozen for 1 month.

10 TASTY USES FOR COMPOUND BUTTER

1. Add it to mashed potatoes, pasta, polenta, or rice.

2. Stuff hamburgers with a slice—be sure to seal all around the edges to enclose the butter before grilling.

3. Finish a pan sauce with a spoonful just before serving.

4. Make fast, inventive variations on garlic bread—split a baguette, spread with the compound butter of your choice, and bake, broil, or grill.

5. Spread on toasted baguette slices for a quick hors d'oeuvre.

6. Add to drained cooked beans.

7. Use on sandwiches in place of butter, mayo, mustard, etc.

8. Mix with bread crumbs and use as a topping for broiled clams on the half shell.

9. Slice over steamed vegetables and broil.

10. Slice over grilled, roasted, or sautéed meat, fish, or poultry.

CAPER-SHALLOT COMPOUND BUTTER

MAKES ABOUT 2/3 CUP

YOU'LL FIND THAT this all-purpose compound butter is an indispensable refrigerator staple. It makes a great crusty French bread sandwich spread or seasoning for mashed potatoes, pasta, or rice, not to mention the obvious steak, chops, chicken, and fish.

- 2 tablespoons small capers, drained, patted dry, and chopped
- 1 tablespoon chopped shallot
- 1 tablespoon snipped fresh chives
- 1 1/2 teaspoons chopped fresh tarragon or chervil leaves
- 1/2 cup (1 stick) salted butter, softened
- Generous pinch of freshly ground black pepper

1. On a cutting board, chop the capers, shallot, chives, and tarragon together until finely chopped.

2. In a medium-size bowl, beat the butter with a wooden spoon until creamy. Add the caper-herb mixture and black pepper and stir until smooth.

3. Spoon the butter onto a sheet of plastic wrap into a 4-inch-long log. Roll up the plastic, forming the butter into a cylinder. Twist the ends tightly to press the butter into a compact log. Refrigerate until chilled. Will keep refrigerated for about 1 week or frozen for 1 month.

CHIPOTLE-CILANTRO COMPOUND BUTTER

MAKES ABOUT 1/2 CUP

SERVE THIS SMOKY, spicy chile butter on grilled meats, poultry, or a meaty fish such as swordfish, snapper, tuna, halibut, salmon, or cod, or try it tossed with roasted or steamed vegetables. I sometimes like to stir a tablespoon or so into a tomato sauce at the end to enrich it with a creamy, smoky flavor.

- 1/2 cup (1 stick) salted butter, softened
- 1 small canned chipotle packed in adobo, seeded and minced, plus 1 teaspoon of the adobo sauce
- 2 scallions (white and tender green parts), minced
- 2 tablespoons finely chopped fresh cilantro leaves
- Freshly ground black pepper

1. In a medium-size bowl, beat the butter with a wooden spoon until creamy. Add the chipotle and adobo, scallions, and cilantro, season with pepper, and beat until combined.

2. Spoon the butter onto a sheet of plastic wrap into a 4-inch-long log. Roll up the plastic, forming the butter into a cylinder. Twist the ends tightly to press the butter into a compact log. Refrigerate until chilled. Will keep refrigerated for about 1 week or frozen for 1 month.

SHRIMP BUTTER

MAKES ABOUT 1½ CUPS

THIS CLASSIC COMPOUND butter is usually made by pounding cooked shrimp, lobster, or crawfish shells with butter and pressing the mixture through a fine-mesh sieve. This method is far simpler and doesn't require so much elbow grease. Serve it with poached fish and shellfish, as well as with fettuccine or other pasta, rice, or crusty French bread. It also makes a great impromptu hors d'oeuvre spread on crackers or croutons.

> ¼ pound medium-size shrimp, shelled and deveined
>
> ½ cup (1 stick) salted butter, softened
>
> 1½ teaspoons finely chopped fresh Italian parsley leaves
>
> ½ teaspoon finely chopped fresh tarragon leaves
>
> ¼ teaspoon sweet paprika
>
> Cayenne pepper

1. Bring a medium-size saucepan of water to a boil. Add the shrimp and cook until opaque and firm, about 1 minute. Drain and let cool completely. Pat dry.

2. Coarsely chop the shrimp and transfer them to a food processor along with the butter, and pulse until combined and the shrimp is finely chopped but not pureed. Transfer to a bowl and stir in the parsley, tarragon, and paprika, and season with cayenne.

3. Spoon the butter onto a sheet of plastic wrap into a 4-inch-long log. Roll up the plastic, forming the butter into a cylinder. Twist the ends tightly to press the butter into a compact log. Refrigerate until chilled. Will keep refrigerated for about 1 week or frozen for 1 month.

COMPOUND BUTTER TIPS

- Always form your compound butter into a cylinder about 2 inches in diameter. It will make slicing it for serving much easier.

- All compound butters can be frozen for up to a month. Defrost in the microwave or at room temperature just until you can slice through it.

- You can use up little bits of leftover compound butters to enrich sauces such as Ravigote (page 169) or any of the béchamels (pages 26–30) or beurre blancs (pages 14–16).

THE ULTIMATE ROAST BEEF SANDWICH

MAKES 4 SERVINGS

THIS SANDWICH IS so good, you can serve it hot or cold, grilled or ungrilled. If you have a sandwich press, just follow the manufacturer's instructions. I happen to love using a cast-iron griddle on the bottom and a heavy skillet on top. You may need to add a few heavy cans to weigh the sandwich down slightly. Ciabatta rolls are my first choice, but a crusty baguette or 4 good-quality long rolls will do as well.

4 ciabatta rolls, split

6 tablespoons Roquefort-Shallot Compound Butter (right), softened

3/4 pound thinly sliced rare roast beef

Salt and freshly ground black pepper

1/2 small red onion, sliced paper thin

1 bunch arugula or tender watercress, stems removed

1 1/2 tablespoons unsalted butter, softened

1. Arrange the rolls cut sides up on a work surface and spread each with the Roquefort butter. Mound the roast beef on the bottom half of each roll and season with salt and pepper. Top with the onion and arugula. Replace the tops and press to flatten slightly.

2. Heat a cast-iron griddle or large skillet over medium-low heat. Lightly spread the softened butter all over the rolls and place the sandwiches on the griddle. Top with a cast-iron or heavy skillet and cook over medium-low heat until the bottom is warm and crusty, 2 to 3 minutes. Turn the sandwiches and cook until the other side is warm and crusty and the butter is melted, about 3 minutes longer. Cut each sandwich in half and serve right away.

ROQUEFORT-SHALLOT COMPOUND BUTTER

MAKES ABOUT 1 CUP

THIS COMPOUND BUTTER'S versatility makes it another must-have-on-hand item. Serve it with croutons, pita crisps, or crackers for a quick hors d'oeuvre or spread it on French bread and pop it under the broiler for a quick toasted cheese sandwich. I particularly like to spread some, softened, on a crusty roll and top with sandwich fixings, as in The Ultimate Roast Beef Sandwich (left). Stir some butter into mashed potatoes, pasta, polenta, or risotto and, of course, serve it on steaks, chops, chicken, and steamed vegetables.

> ²/₃ cup crumbled Roquefort cheese, at room temperature
> 1¹/₂ teaspoons Dijon mustard
> 2 tablespoons finely chopped shallot
> ¹/₂ cup (1 stick) salted butter, softened
> 1 tablespoon finely chopped fresh chives
> Generous pinch of freshly ground black pepper

1. In a mini–food processor, combine the Roquefort, mustard, and shallot and process into a paste. Add the butter and process until fairly smooth. Add the chives and pepper and pulse just until combined.

2. Spoon the butter onto a sheet of plastic wrap into a 6-inch-long log. Roll up the plastic, forming the butter into a cylinder. Twist the ends tightly to press the butter into a compact log. Refrigerate until chilled. Will keep refrigerated for about 1 week or frozen for 1 month.

HERBED COMPOUND BUTTER

MAKES ABOUT ²/₃ CUP

USE AS A sandwich spread, slathered on chops, steaks, chicken, fish, or shellfish, stirred into mashed potatoes, pasta, risotto, or polenta, or tossed with roasted, grilled, or steamed vegetables.

> ¹/₂ cup (1 stick) salted butter, softened
> 2 tablespoons finely chopped fresh basil leaves
> 2 tablespoons finely chopped fresh Italian parsley leaves
> 1 tablespoon finely chopped fresh chives
> 1 tablespoon finely chopped fresh tarragon or chervil leaves
> 1¹/₂ teaspoons finely chopped fresh dill
> 1 small garlic clove, minced
> Generous pinch of freshly ground black pepper

1. In a medium-size bowl, using a wooden spoon, beat the butter until creamy. Add the herbs, garlic, and pepper and stir until smooth.

2. Spoon the butter onto a sheet of plastic wrap into a 4-inch-long log. Roll up the plastic, forming the butter into a cylinder. Twist the ends tightly to press the butter into a compact log. Refrigerate until chilled. Will keep refrigerated for about 1 week or frozen for 1 month.

SCALLION-HORSERADISH
COMPOUND BUTTER

MAKES ABOUT 1/2 CUP

FRESH HORSERADISH CAN be astoundingly flavorful—it's nothing like the bottled stuff. But unlike commercial brands, fresh horseradish can vary greatly in heat. I've given a range here so that you can determine how hot you want it. Serve this aromatic compound butter on steaks or steamed or roasted vegetables, or spread it under the skin of chicken, turkey breast, or game hens before roasting.

1/2 cup (1 stick) salted butter, softened

2 scallions, minced

1 to 1 1/2 tablespoons finely grated
   horseradish, preferably fresh

Freshly ground black pepper

1. In a medium-size bowl, beat the butter with a wooden spoon until creamy. Add the scallions and horseradish, season with pepper, and beat until combined.

2. Spoon the butter onto a sheet of plastic wrap into a 4-inch-long log. Roll up the plastic, forming the butter into a cylinder. Twist the ends tightly to press the butter into a compact log. Refrigerate until chilled. Will keep refrigerated for about 1 week or frozen for 1 month.

HAZELNUT
BROWN BUTTER SAUCE

MAKES ABOUT 1/2 CUP

SERVE THIS EXQUISITE nutty browned butter sauce with poached or sautéed fish, especially skate, sole, porgy, orange roughy, or any firm mild white-fleshed fish, as well as chicken and grilled steak.

1/4 cup (1/2 stick) unsalted butter

1/4 cup chopped hazelnuts

1 small shallot, minced

2 tablespoons finely chopped fresh Italian
   parsley leaves

Salt and freshly ground black pepper

Melt the butter in a medium-size, heavy saucepan over medium-low heat until pale golden, 4 to 5 minutes. Add the hazelnuts and cook, stirring, over medium heat until golden and fragrant, 2 to 3 minutes longer. Add the shallot and parsley and cook until just softened, about 1 minute. Season with salt and pepper. This sauce can be rewarmed just before serving.

CAPER
BROWN BUTTER SAUCE

MAKES ABOUT 1/2 CUP

DON'T USE A dark-colored or nonstick saucepan for this sauce since it is nearly impossible to see when the butter browns. Stainless steel, aluminum, or enameled cast-iron works the best. Serve this super-quick, aromatic nut-brown butter sauce with grilled, poached, or sautéed fish or chicken, grilled steaks, or steamed vegetables.

1/4 cup (1/2 stick) unsalted butter
2 tablespoons small capers, drained, patted dry, and chopped
1 small shallot, minced
2 tablespoons finely chopped fresh Italian parsley leaves
1 1/2 teaspoons snipped fresh chives
Salt and freshly ground black pepper

1. Melt the butter in a medium-size, heavy saucepan over medium-low heat until golden, 5 to 6 minutes.

2. Tilt the pan and add the capers, shallot, parsley, and chives to the empty side to avoid excessive splattering. Shake the pan and cook until sizzling, about 1 minute. Season with salt and pepper and use right away.

RED CHILE
BROWN BUTTER SAUCE

MAKES ABOUT 1/2 CUP

THE ASSERTIVE FLAVORS of pure chile powder and garlic make this browned butter sauce a perfect foil for pork chops, steaks, roasted potatoes, and steamed broccoli or cauliflower.

1/4 cup (1/2 stick) unsalted butter
1 teaspoon pure chile powder, preferably ancho or New Mexico
1 small shallot, minced
1 garlic clove, minced
1 tablespoon finely chopped fresh Italian parsley leaves
1 tablespoon finely chopped fresh cilantro leaves
Salt and freshly ground black pepper

1. Melt the butter in a medium-size, heavy saucepan over medium-low heat until golden, 5 to 6 minutes.

2. Add the chile powder, shallot, and garlic and cook, stirring, until softened, about 1 minute. Stir in the parsley and cilantro. Season with salt and black pepper and use right away.

CLASSIC BEURRE BLANC

MAKES ABOUT 1/2 CUP

MEANING "WHITE BUTTER," this simple sauce is never cooked at more than a simmer after the softened butter has been incorporated. The result is a creamy, silky emulsion of shallots, vinegar, wine, and butter. If you let the sauce overheat, the butter will separate. It's not a huge problem though, more an aesthetic issue, and the sauce can be used anyway. Serve it with poached or pan-roasted fish or chicken, or steamed vegetables such as asparagus, broccoli, cauliflower, green beans, and carrots.

1 small shallot, minced
1/4 cup white wine vinegar, preferably 6 percent acidity or lower
1/4 cup dry white wine
1/2 cup (1 stick) cold unsalted butter, cut into 1/2-inch cubes
1 tablespoon finely chopped fresh Italian parsley leaves
Salt and freshly ground white pepper

1. In a medium-size, heavy saucepan, combine the shallot, vinegar, and wine and cook over medium-high heat until reduced to about 2 tablespoons, 6 to 8 minutes.

2. Let cool slightly, then, over low heat, add the butter 3 or 4 pieces at a time, whisking until almost completely emulsified before adding more. Stir in the parsley and season with salt and pepper.

3. Use right away or keep warm in a thermos or set the saucepan in a shallow pan of simmering water.

BLOOD ORANGE BEURRE BLANC

MAKES ABOUT 2/3 CUP

BLOOD ORANGES ARE usually available in the winter months, though I have occasionally seen them at other times. Their deep reddish color and slightly bitter orange flavor make for a great beurre blanc. If you can't find fresh blood oranges, look for bottled juice in specialty stores. If you still can't find it, juice oranges, tangerines, or tangelos are fine too. Serve this sauce with fish, shellfish, chicken, or pork loin.

1/2 cup blood orange juice
1/4 cup white wine vinegar, preferably 6 percent acidity or lower
1 small shallot, minced
1/2 cup (1 stick) cold unsalted butter, cut into 1/2-inch cubes
Salt and freshly ground black pepper

1. In a medium-size, heavy saucepan, combine the orange juice, vinegar, and shallot and cook over medium-high heat until reduced to 2 table-spoons, about 10 minutes.

2. Let cool slightly, then, over low heat, add the butter 3 or 4 pieces at a time, whisking until almost completely emulsified before adding more. Season with salt and pepper.

3. Use right away or keep warm in a thermos or set the saucepan in a shallow pan of simmering water.

CHIPOTLE BEURRE BLANC

MAKES ABOUT 1/2 CUP

SWEET, CREAMY BUTTER has a terrific ability to mellow even the most fiery of chiles. I love how it carries the smokiness of the chipotles. Serve this sauce with poached or pan-roasted chicken, all types of fish and shellfish, or vegetables.

1 small shallot, minced

1 small canned chipotle chile packed in adobo sauce, seeded and minced

1/4 cup white wine vinegar, preferably 6 percent acidity or lower

1/4 cup low-sodium chicken broth

1/2 cup (1 stick) cold unsalted butter, cut into 1/2-inch cubes

Salt and freshly ground black pepper

1/2 teaspoon adobo sauce (optional)

1. In a medium-size, heavy saucepan, combine the shallot, minced chipotle, vinegar, and broth and cook over medium-high heat until the liquid is reduced to about 2 tablespoons, 6 to 8 minutes.

2. Let cool slightly, then, over low heat, add the butter 3 or 4 pieces at a time, whisking until almost completely emulsified before adding more. Season with salt and pepper and add the adobo sauce, if desired.

3. Use right away or keep warm in a thermos or set the saucepan in a shallow pan of simmering water.

TOMATO-SOY BEURRE BLANC

MAKES ABOUT 3/4 CUP

NO ONE WOULD guess that ketchup is the secret ingredient in this slightly sweet, slightly tart butter sauce. Sometimes, if I have leftover ketchup-based BBQ sauces, I use one of these instead. This sauce is great on fish, shellfish, chicken, and steamed vegetables but it stands up equally well to beef, lamb, and pork.

1 small shallot, minced

1/2 small jalapeño, seeded and minced

2 tablespoons sherry vinegar

1/4 cup low-sodium chicken broth

2 tablespoons ketchup

1 1/2 tablespoons soy sauce

1 tablespoon fresh lime juice

1/2 cup (1 stick) cold unsalted butter, cut into 1/2-inch cubes

Salt and freshly ground black pepper

1. In a medium-size, heavy saucepan, combine the shallot, jalapeño, vinegar, and broth and cook over medium-high heat until reduced to about 1 tablespoon, 6 to 8 minutes. Stir in the ketchup, soy sauce, and lime juice.

2. Let cool slightly, then, over low heat, add the butter 3 or 4 pieces at a time, whisking until almost completely incorporated before adding more. Season with salt and pepper.

3. Use right away or keep warm in a thermos or set the saucepan in a shallow pan of simmering water.

SORREL BEURRE BLANC

MAKES ABOUT 1/2 CUP

SORREL ADDS A lovely tart, lemony note to rich beurre blanc. Serve it with poached or sautéed fish, poached eggs, or steamed vegetables. Baby spinach or arugula can be substituted for the sorrel, but you'll need to add 1 tablespoon fresh lemon juice to supply the tartness.

    1 small shallot, minced
    1/4 cup white wine vinegar, preferably
        6 percent acidity or lower
    1/4 cup dry white wine
    2 cups sorrel leaves, coarsely chopped
    1/2 cup (1 stick) cold unsalted butter, cut into
        1/2-inch cubes
    Salt and freshly ground white pepper

1. In a medium-size, heavy saucepan, combine the shallot, vinegar, and wine and cook over medium-high heat until reduced to about 2 tablespoons, 6 to 8 minutes. Add the sorrel and cook, stirring, until wilted.

2. Transfer the mixture to a mini–food processor and process until smooth. Strain the puree through a fine-mesh sieve, pressing and scraping hard on the solids. Return the mixture to the saucepan.

3. Over low heat, add the butter 3 or 4 pieces at a time, whisking until almost completely incorporated before adding more. Season with salt and pepper.

4. Use right away or keep warm in a thermos or set the saucepan in a shallow pan of simmering water.

SOY-GINGER BEURRE BLANC

MAKES ABOUT 2/3 CUP

IT'S EASY TO see why soy and ginger are so popular together, and not just in Asian cooking. They definitely balance each other nicely and, with the addition of butter, make the base for a delicious fusion-y sauce. Serve this with poached or pan-roasted chicken, all types of fish and shellfish, or vegetables.

    1 small shallot, minced
    1 1/2 teaspoons peeled and finely grated
        fresh ginger
    1/4 cup seasoned rice vinegar
    1/4 cup low-sodium chicken broth
    1/2 cup (1 stick) cold unsalted butter, cut into
        1/2-inch cubes
    1 tablespoon low-sodium soy sauce
    1 small scallion (white and tender green
        parts), minced
    Salt and freshly ground black pepper

1. In a medium-size, heavy saucepan, combine the shallot, ginger, vinegar, and broth and cook over medium-high heat until reduced to about 2 tablespoons, 6 to 8 minutes.

2. Let cool slightly, then, over low heat, add the butter 3 or 4 pieces at a time, whisking until almost completely incorporated before adding more. Add the soy sauce and scallion and season with salt and pepper.

3. Use right away or keep warm in a thermos or set the saucepan in a shallow pan of simmering water.

CLASSIC HOLLANDAISE SAUCE

MAKES ABOUT 1 CUP

THIS TRADITIONAL FRENCH sauce can be served with poached fish, eggs, chicken, and shellfish and boiled or roasted potatoes. It has the unwarranted reputation of being utterly complicated and oh so fancy. Actually, it's quite simple, just a very basic emulsion of eggs, an acid (in this case, lemon juice), and butter. If you're still daunted, see the blender version that follows.

2 extra-large egg yolks, at room temperature
1 tablespoon cold water
Pinch of salt
3/4 cup (1 1/2 sticks) cold unsalted butter, cut into 1/2-inch cubes
1 1/2 tablespoons fresh lemon juice
Cayenne pepper

1. Set a medium-size, heavy saucepan into a larger pan filled with 2 inches of simmering water. Put the egg yolks, water, and salt in the saucepan and whisk until warm to the touch. Add a few cubes of butter and whisk until almost completely incorporated. Whisking constantly, add the remaining butter a few pieces at a time, being sure that they are fully incorporated before adding more. Whisk in the lemon juice and season to taste with salt and cayenne.

2. Transfer the sauce to a warmed small pitcher. Use right away or keep warm by setting the pitcher directly into the pan of barely simmering water. Thin with a tablespoon of simmering water if the sauce gets too thick.

BLENDER HOLLANDAISE SAUCE

MAKES ABOUT 1 CUP

SOME PURISTS THINK using a blender is cheating, but I think it really takes the mystery (and the worry) out of making a hollandaise sauce. It's much less tricky and can be done ever so quickly. Just be sure to keep the butter hot but not sizzling, so that its heat slightly cooks the egg yolks. Serve it with poached fish, chicken, eggs, vegetables, or shellfish.

3/4 cup (1 1/2 sticks) unsalted butter
3 large egg yolks, at room temperature
1 1/2 tablespoons fresh lemon juice
Pinch of salt
Pinch of cayenne pepper

1. In a small saucepan, melt the butter and keep warm over low heat.

2. Put the egg yolks, lemon juice, salt, and cayenne in a blender and blend for about 10 seconds. With the machine running, slowly add the melted butter in a steady stream and blend until the mixture thickens, or emulsifies.

3. Transfer to a small pitcher and use right away or keep warm by setting the pitcher directly into a shallow pan of barely simmering water. Thin with a tablespoon of simmering water if the sauce is too thick.

ORANGE HOLLANDAISE

MAKES ABOUT 1½ CUPS

CREAMY ORANGE AND decadently rich, this sauce is perfectly suited for poached or sautéed fish, shellfish, or chicken, as well as steamed vegetables and poached eggs.

    ½ cup fresh orange juice
    ½ teaspoon finely grated orange zest
    1 small shallot, minced
    2 extra-large egg yolks, at room temperature
    Salt
    ¾ cup (1½ sticks) cold unsalted butter, cut into ½-inch cubes
    1½ tablespoons fresh lemon juice
    Cayenne pepper

1. In a medium-size, heavy saucepan, combine the orange juice and zest and shallot and cook over medium-high heat until reduced to about 2 tablespoons, about 5 minutes. Strain the mixture into a small metal bowl, pressing hard on the solids, and let cool slightly.

2. Set the top of a double boiler over 2 inches of simmering water. Combine the egg yolks, orange reduction, and a pinch of salt in the top of the double boiler and whisk until warm to the touch. Add a few cubes of unsalted butter and whisk until almost completely incorporated. Whisking constantly, add the remaining butter a few pieces at a time, being sure that they are fully incorporated before adding more. Whisk in the lemon juice and season with salt and cayenne.

3. Transfer the sauce to a warmed small pitcher. Use right away or keep warm by setting the pitcher directly into the pan of barely simmering water. Thin with a tablespoon of water if the sauce gets too thick.

MALTAISE (BLOOD ORANGE HOLLANDAISE)

MAKES ABOUT 1 CUP

THIS BEAUTIFUL CRIMSON sauce, a variation on Classic Hollandaise, uses the juice of blood oranges. Serve it with chicken or fish, or steamed asparagus and broccoli.

    1 recipe Classic Hollandaise Sauce (page 17)
    ¼ cup fresh blood orange juice

Prepare the hollandaise, then stir in the orange juice.

SHRIMP HOLLANDAISE

MAKES ABOUT 1¼ CUPS

THIS IS A great way to use up any leftover shrimp butter. It lends a sweet seafood flavor to the already rich hollandaise sauce and is perfect over poached or sautéed fish, shellfish, steamed vegetables, or poached eggs.

> 2 extra-large egg yolks, at room temperature
>
> 1 tablespoon cold water
>
> Pinch of salt
>
> ½ cup (1 stick) cold unsalted butter, cut into ½-inch cubes
>
> ¼ cup cold Shrimp Butter (page 9), cut into ½-inch cubes
>
> 1½ tablespoons fresh lemon juice

1. Set a medium-size, heavy saucepan into a larger pan filled with 2 inches of simmering water. Put the egg yolks, water, and salt in the saucepan and whisk until warm to the touch. Add a few cubes of the unsalted butter and whisk until almost completely incorporated. Whisking constantly, add the remaining butter a few pieces at a time, being sure that they are fully incorporated before adding more. Add the shrimp butter, a few pieces at a time, whisking until fully incorporated. Whisk in the lemon juice.

2. Transfer the sauce to a warmed small pitcher. Use right away or keep warm by setting the pitcher directly into the pan of barely simmering water. Thin with a tablespoon of water if the sauce gets too thick.

CHORON (TOMATO HOLLANDAISE)

MAKES ABOUT 1½ CUPS

WITH THE ADDITION of a puree of cooked fresh tomatoes to Classic Hollandaise Sauce or Béarnaise, you have Choron. Serve this with poached or sautéed fish or shellfish, chicken, or vegetables.

> 1 tablespoon unsalted butter
>
> 2 large ripe tomatoes, peeled, seeded, and coarsely chopped
>
> Salt and freshly ground black pepper
>
> 1 recipe Classic Hollandaise Sauce (page 17), Blender Hollandaise Sauce (page 17), or Béarnaise (page 20)

1. Melt the butter in a medium-size, heavy saucepan over medium-high heat. Add the tomatoes and cook until the liquid has evaporated and the tomatoes have broken down, about 8 minutes. Season with salt and pepper.

2. Prepare the hollandaise or béarnaise and keep warm. Whisk in the tomato puree and season with salt and pepper.

3. Transfer the sauce to a small pitcher and use right away or keep warm by setting the pitcher directly into a shallow pan of barely simmering water.

BÉARNAISE

MAKES ABOUT 1 CUP

THIS CLASSIC SAUCE is a variation on hollandaise but uses the assertive flavors of tarragon, white wine, and vinegar to give it added depth. Serve it with steaks, chicken, roast beef, fish, poached eggs, and steamed vegetables.

1/2 cup dry white wine

1/4 cup sherry vinegar, preferably 6 percent acidity or lower

2 medium-size shallots, finely chopped

One 1-ounce bunch fresh tarragon, coarsely chopped with stems

2 extra-large egg yolks, at room temperature

1 tablespoon cold water

Salt

3/4 cup (1 1/2 sticks) cold unsalted butter, cut into 1/2-inch cubes

1 1/2 tablespoons fresh lemon juice

Cayenne pepper

2 tablespoons finely chopped fresh tarragon leaves

1. In a medium-size, heavy saucepan, combine the wine, vinegar, shallots, and coarsely chopped tarragon and bring to a boil. Reduce the heat to medium heat and simmer until the liquid is reduced to about 2 tablespoons. Strain the liquid into a small heatproof bowl, pressing hard on the solids to extract as much of the liquid as possible.

2. Rinse out the saucepan and return the reduced liquid to it along with the egg yolks, water, and a pinch of salt. Set the saucepan into a larger pan filled with 2 inches of simmering water. Whisk over low heat until the eggs are warm to the

HOW TO FIX
A BROKEN HOLLANDAISE

If the heat is too high or the eggs are too hot, the sauce may "break," which simply means separate into liquids and solids. You'll know for sure if your sauce is broken because it will look slightly lumpy and curdled.

• Adding a bit of very cold water will sometimes bring the emulsion back. Simply whisk 1 tablespoon ice water into the sauce. Whisking in an ice cube until it melts or the sauce thickens works pretty well too.

• If that fails, in a separate saucepan over very low heat, whisk an egg yolk with 1 tablespoon ice water until pale and thick. At that point, begin to gradually add the broken sauce in a thin stream, whisking constantly until thick again.

touch. Add a few cubes of butter and whisk until almost completely incorporated. Whisking constantly, add the remaining butter a few pieces at a time, being sure that it is fully incorporated before adding more. Whisk in the lemon juice, season with salt and cayenne, and stir in the finely chopped tarragon leaves.

3. Transfer the sauce to a warmed small pitcher. Use right away or keep warm by setting the pitcher directly into the pan of barely simmering water. Thin with a tablespoon of simmering water if the sauce gets too thick.

HERB HOLLANDAISE

MAKES ABOUT 1 CUP

A SIMPLE HOLLANDAISE can be transformed and elevated just by adding a handful of chopped herbs. Serve this sauce with poached fish, eggs, chicken, or shellfish.

2 extra-large egg yolks, at room temperature

1 tablespoon cold water

Salt

3/4 cup (1 1/2 sticks) cold unsalted butter, cut into 1/2-inch cubes

1 1/2 tablespoons fresh lemon juice

Cayenne pepper

2 tablespoons finely chopped fresh Italian parsley leaves

1 tablespoon finely chopped fresh chives

1 teaspoon finely chopped fresh chervil or tarragon leaves

1. Set a medium-size, heavy saucepan into a larger pan filled with 2 inches of simmering water. Put the egg yolks, water, and a pinch of salt in the saucepan and whisk until warm to the touch. Add a few cubes of butter and whisk until almost completely incorporated. Whisking constantly, add the remaining butter a few pieces at a time, being sure that they are fully incorporated before adding more. Whisk in the lemon juice and season with to taste with salt and cayenne. Stir in the herbs.

2. Transfer the sauce to a warmed small pitcher. Use right away or keep warm by setting the pitcher directly into the pan of barely simmering water. Thin with a tablespoon of simmering water if the sauce gets too thick.

AVGOLEMONO

MAKES ABOUT 2 CUPS

THIS TART AND rich egg-lemon sauce tasted so exotic to me the first time I had it as a kid in a wonderful little Greek restaurant on Long Island (that was rumored to be a bordello). Maybe it was the restaurant's checkered past, or the distant childhood taste memory, but I've never forgotten it. I've tried to recreate it here and I think it's pretty darn close. Enjoy it with roasted meats, especially lamb and chicken, as well as fish, broccoli, asparagus, and artichokes. Or add a little chicken stock and dill-flavored meatballs to create a delicious soup, as in Avgolemono Soup with Greek Meatballs (right).

2 cups low-sodium chicken broth
¼ cup long-grain rice
4 large egg yolks
¼ cup plus 1 tablespoon fresh lemon juice
Salt and freshly ground white pepper

1. In a small saucepan, combine the broth and rice and simmer over low heat, covered, until the rice is very tender and beginning to break down, about 25 minutes.

2. Transfer the rice mixture to a blender and process until very smooth. With the machine is running, add the egg yolks through the feed tube, one at a time, along with the lemon juice and process until smooth.

3. Return the sauce to the saucepan, season with salt and pepper, and simmer until slightly thickened, 2 to 3 minutes. Serve hot.

AVGOLEMONO SOUP WITH GREEK MEATBALLS

MAKES 4 TO 6 SERVINGS

THIS SOUP MAKES a lovely first course or light meal when served with a salad. I love how its richness is balanced by the tartness of the lemon juice in the avgolemono sauce. Lamb is definitely the meat of choice here, but ground beef works wonderfully too.

3/4 pound ground lamb

1 scallion, minced

1 garlic clove, minced

1 tablespoon finely chopped fresh dill

2 tablespoons crumbled feta cheese

2 tablespoons dry fine bread crumbs

1 large egg white

1 teaspoon kosher salt, or more to taste

1/4 teaspoon freshly ground black pepper, or more to taste

2 cups homemade (page 161) or canned low-sodium chicken broth

2 cups Avgolemono (left)

1/2 cup cooked white rice

1. In a medium-size bowl, combine the lamb, scallion, garlic, dill, feta, bread crumbs, and egg white. Season with the salt and pepper and knead with your hands until combined. Using lightly moistened hands, roll the meat into twenty-four 1-inch meatballs and transfer them to a plastic-lined plate.

2. In a large saucepan, bring the broth to a simmer. Add the meatballs, cover, and simmer over low heat until firm, about 5 minutes. Add the avgolemono and rice, season with salt and pepper, and cook just until heated through. Serve hot.

BÉCHAMEL, CHEESE, AND CREAM SAUCES

Béchamel, a basic white sauce made with butter, flour, and milk, was the first sauce I learned how to make as a kid. I thought I was so sophisticated grating fresh nutmeg into it as it simmered in the pot. But all it tasted like was milk with salt and nutmeg. I didn't get it at all. It wasn't until I added some grated cheese that I understood. It's not about the sauce; it's about the embellishments. Cheese is the most obvious one, but only because it's fantastic! Mustard, fresh herbs, sun-dried tomatoes, and caramelized onions are just a few others that are also tasty.

Béchamel may be a little old-fashioned, but I've included a few interesting variations. They're delicious and very quick to prepare. Since you add other ingredients for seasoning, it doesn't require long simmering to draw out any hidden flavor. In the time it takes to clean and steam a head of broccoli, Smoked Gouda Béchamel or Mornay Sauce would be ready to go.

The cream-based sauces are only slightly more complicated, but no less quick. Heavy cream is flavored with mushrooms, shallots, stock, herbs, or what have you, and simmered until thick and rich, which usually takes no more than 10 to 15 minutes.

BASIC BÉCHAMEL

MAKES ABOUT 4 CUPS

NO SAUCE IS more versatile than the basic béchamel or white sauce (though tomato sauce is a close second). It's the base for dozens of classic French sauces, baked pastas, soufflés, and custards.

¼ cup (½ stick) unsalted butter
¼ cup all-purpose flour
1 quart whole milk
Salt and freshly ground white pepper
Freshly grated nutmeg

In a large saucepan, melt the butter over medium heat. When the foam subsides, add the flour and cook, stirring constantly, until foamy, 2 to 3 minutes. All at once, add the milk, whisking constantly, and bring to a boil over medium heat. Reduce the heat to low and simmer until thickened, about 10 minutes. Season with salt, white pepper, and nutmeg. Will keep in the refrigerator up to 3 days. While it is still warm, press a sheet of plastic wrap directly on top of the sauce, then refrigerate. This should keep a skin from forming on top. Reheat gently before serving.

THICK BÉCHAMEL

MAKES ABOUT 4 CUPS

THIS BÉCHAMEL USES more butter and flour for a thicker, sturdier sauce, as well as milk and half-and-half for added richness. It makes a terrific base for Mornay Sauce (page 32) and other cheesy sauces used specifically for topping and broiling vegetables. It's also perfect for Greek moussaka and pastitsio.

½ cup (1 stick) unsalted butter
½ cup all-purpose flour
2 cups whole or 2 percent milk
2 cups half-and-half
Salt and freshly ground white pepper
Freshly grated nutmeg

In a large saucepan over medium heat, melt the butter. Add the flour and cook, stirring constantly, until pale gold and nutty, 3 to 4 minutes. All at once, add the milk and half-and-half, whisking constantly, and bring to a boil. Reduce the heat to very low and simmer until thickened, about 10 minutes. Season with salt, white pepper, and nutmeg. Will keep in the refrigerator up to 3 days. While it is still warm, press a sheet of plastic wrap directly on top of the sauce, then refrigerate. This should keep a skin from forming on top. Reheat gently before using.

SPINACH AND RICOTTA LASAGNA

MAKES 6 SERVINGS

THIS RECIPE COMBINES some of my favorite things—ricotta, rich and nutmeg-y béchamel, pasta, and spinach–pine nut pesto.

> 1 cup fresh ricotta cheese
> 8 ounces mozzarella cheese, coarsely shredded
> Salt and freshly ground black pepper
> 3½ cups Basic Béchamel (left)
> Nine 3 x 7-inch sheets no-boil lasagna
> 1 cup Spinach-Pignoli Pesto with Raisins (page 107)
> ¼ cup freshly grated parmesan cheese

1. Preheat the oven to 375°F. In a medium-size bowl, combine the ricotta and mozzarella and season with salt and pepper.

2. Spread ¾ cup of the béchamel over the bottom of a 9-inch-square baking dish. Arrange 3 of the noodles in the dish, slightly overlapping them and breaking 1 of the noodles to patch any open spots. Using a tablespoon, dollop half of the cheese mixture in small lumps all over the noodles. Dollop half of the pesto over the cheese, and cover with ¾ cup of the béchamel. Repeat with 3 more noodles, the remaining cheese, the remaining pesto, and another ¾ cup of the béchamel. Top with the last 3 noodles and pour the remaining 1¼ cups béchamel all over the top and down the sides. Sprinkle the parmesan on top and cover.

3. Bake until bubbling and the noodles are softened, about 1 hour. Uncover and bake until the top is golden and puffed, about 15 minutes longer. Let rest for 15 minutes before cutting.

MUSTARD BÉCHAMEL

MAKES 1¼ CUPS

DIJON AND WHOLE-GRAIN mustards and egg yolks enrich basic béchamel as well as add a beautiful golden color. Serve with steamed vegetables or roasted meats, fish, or poultry.

1 cup Basic Béchamel (page 26), warmed
1 tablespoon Dijon mustard
1½ teaspoons whole-grain mustard
1 large egg yolk
1½ teaspoons fresh lemon juice
Salt and freshly ground white pepper
2 tablespoons snipped fresh chives

1. In a medium-size saucepan, combine the béchamel and mustards and whisk until smooth.

2. In a small bowl, whisk together the egg yolk, lemon juice, and ½ cup of the warmed béchamel. Add this mixture to the saucepan, whisking constantly, and simmer gently over medium-low heat until thickened, about 4 minutes. Season with salt and pepper and stir in the chives. Will keep in the refrigerator up to 2 days. While it is still warm, press a sheet of plastic wrap directly on top of the sauce, then refrigerate. This should keep a skin from forming on top. Reheat gently before using.

SOUBISE (ONION SAUCE)

MAKES ABOUT 2½ CUPS

IN THIS CLASSIC French sauce, named after an eighteenth-century prince, a puree of sautéed onions adds a sweet flavor and silky texture to a simple béchamel. Using onions like Vidalia or Walla Walla will make the sauce exceptionally sweet. Sweating the onions under a sheet of waxed paper is a nifty trick I learned from my friend and idol Paula Wolfert. It keeps the moisture in while allowing the onions to cook slowly. Serve it with roasted meats or poultry.

2 tablespoons unsalted butter
1 large Spanish onion (1¼ pounds), cut in half and thinly sliced into half-moons
Pinch of salt
2 cups Basic Béchamel (page 26), warmed
½ cup heavy cream
Freshly ground white pepper

1. Melt the butter in a large, heavy saucepan over medium-low heat. When the foam subsides, add the onion and salt. Loosely cover the onion directly with a circle of wax paper and cook, stirring occasionally, until softened but not browned, about 15 minutes.

2. Transfer the onion to a food processor or blender and process until finely chopped. Add about ½ cup of the béchamel and process until smooth. Return the onion mixture to the saucepan, add the remaining 1½ cups béchamel and the cream, and simmer until slightly reduced,

7 to 8 minutes. Taste for salt and season with pepper. Will keep, tightly covered, in the refrigerator for up to 3 days. While it is still warm, press a sheet of plastic wrap directly on top of the sauce, then refrigerate. This should keep a skin from forming on top. Reheat gently before serving.

BÉCHAMEL WITH SHALLOTS AND MORELS

MAKES ABOUT 2½ CUPS

THE SWEETNESS OF sautéed shallots and the rich, earthy quality of morels take this rich sauce to an even higher level. Morels go extremely well with beef—and this sauce would be suited for any roasted beef, especially filet mignon. The honeycomb structure of morels causes them to trap lots of dirt and sand. After soaking them, be sure to remove any grit.

½ ounce dried morels (about 1 cup)

2 cups boiling water

2 tablespoons unsalted butter

2 medium-size shallots, finely chopped

¼ cup Madeira or dry Marsala

1 teaspoon chopped fresh thyme leaves

2 cups Thick Béchamel (page 26), warmed

Salt and freshly ground black pepper

1. In a medium-size bowl, cover the morels with the boiling water and let sit until softened, about 15 minutes. Using a slotted spoon, transfer the morels to a plate. Reserve the soaking water. Fill a medium-size bowl with water and, working with one morel at a time, gently shake them in the water to dislodge any grit. Drain the morels, discarding the rinsing water, and thinly slice. Let the morel soaking water settle, then slowly pour it into a heatproof glass measuring cup, stopping when you reach the grit at the bottom.

2. In a medium-size saucepan, melt the butter over medium heat. When the foam subsides, add the shallots and cook, stirring, until softened, about 3 minutes. Add the morels and cook, stirring, for 2 minutes. Add the Madeira and cook until nearly evaporated, 2 to 3 minutes. Add the thyme, béchamel, and ½ cup of the mushroom soaking water and simmer until reduced to about 2½ cups. Season with salt and pepper. This sauce is best used right away, but it can be refrigerated for up to 2 days. While it is still warm, press a sheet of plastic wrap directly on top of the sauce, then refrigerate. This should keep a skin from forming on top. Reheat gently before using.

TIPS FOR BÉCHAMEL SUCCESS

- Be sure to use a good whisk, one that gets into the corners of your saucepan.

- When adding milk to the roux, gradually add it in a stream, whisking constantly to avoid any lumps.

- If the sauce is lumpy, strain it through a sieve before adding the remaining ingredients.

- If not used right away, to prevent a skin from forming on the surface of the sauce, press a piece of plastic wrap directly onto the sauce. Or rub a tablespoon of butter over the surface. The butter will melt and form a layer. Whisk it in before serving.

- Be sure to season well with salt and pepper. Béchamel can be very bland otherwise.

- For a lowfat version that has a decent consistency, substitute evaporated skim milk for the whole milk.

- Heat that is too high may cause the milk to scorch or cheese to break down and separate. Medium heat will ensure the best results.

SUN-DRIED TOMATO BÉCHAMEL

MAKES ABOUT 2½ CUPS

I LOVE THE simplicity of this sauce. It's thicker and more substantial than Tomato Cream Sauce (page 86), so it stands up very well to baking or broiling. Use anywhere a basic béchamel is called for, or with poached fish or chicken.

¼ cup oil-packed sun-dried tomatoes
1 small onion, finely chopped
Pinch of sugar
½ cup half-and-half or light cream

1½ cups Basic Béchamel (page 26), warmed
Salt and freshly ground black pepper
1 tablespoon finely chopped fresh basil leaves

1. Drain the tomatoes, reserving 1 tablespoon of the oil separately, and coarsely chop. Heat the reserved oil in a medium-size saucepan over medium heat. Add the onion and the sugar and cook, stirring, until softened, about 5 minutes.

2. Scrape the onion into a mini–food processor, add the sun-dried tomatoes, and process until finely chopped. Add the half-and-half and process until smooth. Add the béchamel and process until combined. Return the sauce to the saucepan, season with salt and pepper, and bring to a simmer over medium heat. Will keep in the refrigerator for up to 3 days. While it is still warm, press a sheet of plastic wrap directly on top of the sauce, then refrigerate. This should keep a skin from forming on top. Reheat gently before using.

3. Just before serving, stir in the basil.

TANGY HERBED WHITE SAUCE

MAKES ABOUT 1⅓ CUPS

A SQUEEZE OF lemon juice, some Dijon mustard, and chopped fresh herbs make this variation on béchamel a perfect accompaniment for fish, poached eggs, or steamed vegetables.

2 tablespoons crème fraîche or heavy cream
1½ teaspoons Dijon mustard
1 tablespoon fresh lemon juice
1 cup Basic Béchamel (page 26)
1 tablespoon finely chopped fresh Italian parsley leaves
1 tablespoon finely chopped fresh chives
½ tablespoon finely chopped fresh tarragon leaves
Salt and freshly ground white pepper

1. In a small bowl, whisk the crème fraîche, mustard, and lemon juice together.

2. Warm the béchamel in a medium-size saucepan over medium-low heat. Whisk in the crème fraîche mixture and simmer until heated through. Stir in the herbs and season with salt and pepper. This sauce is best used right away.

QUATTRO FORMAGGI (FOUR-CHEESE SAUCE)

MAKES ABOUT 2 CUPS

THIS SAUCE IS so incredibly rich, a little really goes a long way. Serve with pasta, especially tortellini or fettuccine, or stir a bit into fresh-cooked polenta.

1 tablespoon unsalted butter
1 large shallot, minced
1 cup low-sodium chicken broth
1 cup heavy cream
½ cup mascarpone
½ cup shredded fontina cheese
¼ cup crumbled Gorgonzola dolce
¼ cup freshly grated parmesan cheese
Pinch of freshly grated nutmeg
Salt and freshly ground white pepper

Melt the butter in a medium-size saucepan over medium heat. Add the shallot and cook, stirring, until softened, about 3 minutes. Add the broth and cream and simmer until reduced to 1¼ cups, about 15 minutes. Over low heat, add the mascarpone and cook, stirring, until smooth. Add the fontina, Gorgonzola, and parmesan, stirring to combine, and cook just until melted. Add the nutmeg and season with salt and pepper. This sauce is best used right away.

SMOKED GOUDA BÉCHAMEL

MAKES ABOUT 2½ CUPS

I LOVE THE flavor smoked Gouda adds to foods. It's a great melting cheese with a silky though slightly granular texture. *Pimenton* is a smoked sweet or hot paprika from Spain. It's become pretty trendy in new restaurants, so you'll find it at most gourmet markets. This sauce is very well suited for pasta, steamed vegetables, poached eggs, or baked macaroni and cheese, especially if you add diced smoked ham, steamed vegetables, or sautéed mushrooms. After the sauce goes on, pop the dish under the broiler until golden and nutty.

1½ cups Basic Béchamel (page 26), warmed

¼ cup heavy cream

4 ounces smoked Gouda, rind removed and shredded (about 1 packed cup)

½ teaspoon *pimenton*

Salt and freshly ground black pepper

In a medium-size saucepan, combine the béchamel and cream and bring to a simmer over medium heat. Add the Gouda and *pimenton,* season with salt and pepper, and simmer until the cheese is melted, stirring to fully incorporate it. Will keep in the refrigerator for up to 3 days. While it is still warm, press a sheet of plastic wrap directly on top of the sauce, then refrigerate. This should keep a skin from forming on top. Reheat gently before using.

MORNAY SAUCE (CHEESE SAUCE)

MAKES ABOUT 2½ CUPS

IN THIS CLASSIC French sauce, named after an eighteenth-century duke, the Duc de Mornay, flavorful cheeses are added to basic béchamel to create a rich white cheese sauce. It is perfect in gratins or in casseroles that need a bit of baking or broiling, or simply spooned over roasted meats, vegetables, fish, or fowl.

1½ cups Basic Béchamel (page 26), warmed

½ cup heavy cream

¼ cup freshly grated parmesan cheese

¼ cup shredded Gruyère cheese

Salt and freshly ground white pepper

1 tablespoon unsalted butter

Combine the béchamel and cream in a medium-size saucepan and bring to a simmer over medium heat. Stir in the cheeses and simmer just until melted. Season with salt and pepper and whisk in the butter. Will keep in the refrigerator for up to 3 days. While it is still warm, press a sheet of plastic wrap directly on top of the sauce, then refrigerate. This should keep a skin from forming on top. Reheat gently before serving.

FONTINA CREAM SAUCE

MAKES ABOUT 1½ CUPS

FONTINA, IMPORTED FROM Italy, has a very distinct flavor. A slightly pungent cheese with a creamy, buttery texture, it melts nicely and is well suited for many different applications. Serve this sauce with pasta, stirred into polenta or mashed potatoes, or with steamed vegetables and meats.

    1 cup heavy cream
    1½ tablespoons tomato paste
    1 cup shredded fontina cheese (4 ounces)
    Salt and freshly ground white pepper

Bring the cream to a boil in a medium-size saucepan. Reduce the heat to medium-low and simmer until reduced by one-third, about 10 minutes. Whisk in the tomato paste. Stir in the fontina and simmer over low heat just until melted. Season with salt and pepper. This is best used right away, but will keep, covered, in the refrigerator for up to 2 days. While it is still warm, press a sheet of plastic wrap directly on top of the sauce, then refrigerate. This should keep a skin from forming on top. Reheat gently before serving.

GORGONZOLA CREAM SAUCE WITH CARAMELIZED ONIONS

MAKES ABOUT 1½ CUPS

THIS RICH SAUCE flavored with sweet caramelized onions and Gorgonzola goes well with pasta or roasted poultry, beef, or game. Soft, pungent, and creamy, Gorgonzola is Italy's prized blue-veined cheese. The type that I prefer for this recipe is Gorgonzola dolce, which simply means it hasn't been aged.

    2 tablespoons unsalted butter
    1 large Spanish onion, cut in half and thinly
        sliced into half-moons
    Pinch of sugar
    ¼ cup dry white wine
    1½ cups heavy cream
    4 ounces Gorgonzola dolce, broken into pieces
    Salt and freshly ground black pepper

1. Melt the butter in a large, heavy saucepan over low heat. Add the onion and sugar, cover, and cook until very soft, stirring occasionally, about 20 minutes. Uncover and cook over medium heat, stirring occasionally, until golden and caramelized, 15 to 20 minutes longer.

2. Stir in the wine and cook until nearly evaporated, 2 to 3 minutes. Add the cream, bring to a boil, reduce the heat to medium, and simmer until slightly thickened and reduced, about 10 minutes. Add the Gorgonzola, season with salt and pepper, and simmer, stirring, until melted and fully incorporated. This sauce is best used right away.

CHEDDAR CHEESE SAUCE

MAKES ABOUT 3½ CUPS

USE THIS SAUCE for any and all macaroni and cheeses. It's pretty rich.

- 3 tablespoons unsalted butter
- 3 tablespoons all-purpose flour
- 2½ cups half-and-half or whole milk
- Pinch of freshly grated nutmeg
- Salt and freshly ground black pepper
- 8 ounces sharp cheddar cheese, cut into ½-inch pieces
- 4 ounces colby or other creamy melting cheese, cut into ½-inch pieces
- 1 tablespoon Dijon mustard

Melt the butter in a large saucepan over medium heat. When the foam subsides, add the flour and cook, stirring constantly, for 2 minutes. Add the half-and-half, whisking, and cook until thickened, about 3 minutes. Add the nutmeg and season with salt and pepper. Add the cheeses and cook over low heat, stirring, until the cheese has melted. Stir in the mustard. Will keep in the refrigerator for up to 3 days. While it is still warm, press a sheet of plastic wrap directly on top of the sauce, then refrigerate. This should keep a skin from forming on top. Reheat gently before using.

BÉCHAMEL WITH MANCHEGO CHEESE AND ALMONDS

MAKES ABOUT 1½ CUPS

TOASTED ALMONDS, STEEPED in half-and-half, and the tangy aged sheep's milk cheese from Spain called manchego add another dimension to Thick Béchamel. Serve this delicate sauce with poached or sautéed fish or poultry or steamed vegetables.

- ½ cup blanched whole almonds
- ¾ cup half-and-half
- 1 tablespoon unsalted butter
- 1 medium-size shallot, minced
- 1 cup Thick or Basic Béchamel (page 26)
- ½ cup shredded manchego cheese (2 ounces)
- Salt and freshly ground black pepper

1. Preheat the oven to 350°F. Put the almonds in a pie plate and toast until fragrant and golden, about 8 minutes. Let cool.

2. Place the almonds and half-and-half in a blender or food processor and pulse until finely chopped but not ground.

3. Transfer the almond milk to a medium-size saucepan and bring to a boil. Remove from the heat and let steep, covered, for 30 minutes. Strain the liquid through a fine-mesh sieve set over a bowl, pressing hard on the almonds to extract as much of the milk as possible. There should be about ½ cup.

CLASSIC MACARONI AND CHEESE
MAKES 6 TO 8 SERVINGS

IF YOU CAN'T afford the extra calories, this fabulous mac and cheese is definitely not for you (at least not more than every other week. . .). And it's not worth skimping on the cheese, or worse, using lowfat or fat-free cheese.

1 pound elbow macaroni

1 recipe Cheddar Cheese Sauce (left), warm

8 ounces sharp cheddar cheese, cut into 1/2-inch pieces

4 ounces colby or other creamy melting cheese, cut into 1/2-inch pieces

2 tablespoons unsalted butter

3/4 cup plain dry bread crumbs

Salt and freshly ground black pepper

1. Preheat the oven to 350°F, and generously butter a 2-quart shallow baking dish.

2. Cook the pasta in salted boiling water until *al dente*. Drain well, shaking out any excess water. Return the pasta to the pot along with the cheese sauce and cheese and stir until evenly combined. Pour the mixture into the prepared dish. In a small, microwave-safe bowl, melt the butter. Add the bread crumbs, season with salt and pepper, and stir until evenly moistened. Sprinkle the crumbs evenly over the macaroni.

3. Bake until bubbling and golden, about 45 minutes. Let rest for 15 minutes before serving. The recipe can be prepared through step 2 and refrigerated overnight. Return to room temperature before baking.

4. Rinse out the saucepan and melt the butter over medium heat. Add the shallot and cook, stirring, until softened, about 3 minutes. Add the béchamel and almond milk and simmer over medium-low heat until thickened. Add the cheese, season with salt and pepper, and simmer until the cheese is melted. This sauce is best used right away, but it can be refrigerated for up to 4 days. While it is still warm, press a sheet of plastic wrap directly on top of the sauce, then refrigerate. This should keep a skin from forming on top. Reheat gently before using.

MASCARPONE CREAM SAUCE

MAKES ABOUT 1¼ CUPS

SWEET MASCARPONE IS Italy's answer to cream cheese, though it has a much more delicate flavor and silky texture. Like cream cheese, it is used in sweet as well as savory dishes. Serve this simple sauce with cooked green vegetables or roasted root vegetables, fold it into mashed potatoes or cooked polenta, or toss with pasta.

- 1 tablespoon unsalted butter
- 1 large leek (white and tender green parts), washed well and finely chopped
- ¾ cup mascarpone
- ½ cup heavy cream
- Salt and freshly ground white pepper
- 2 tablespoons snipped fresh chives

1. Melt the butter in a medium-size saucepan over medium heat. When the foam subsides, add the leek and cook, stirring, until softened, about 4 minutes. Add the mascarpone and cook, stirring, until melted. Add the cream, season with salt and pepper, and simmer until slightly reduced.

2. Just before serving, stir in the chives. This sauce is best used right away.

WILD MUSHROOM MASCARPONE CREAM SAUCE

MAKES ABOUT 1½ CUPS

THIS VARIATION ON Mascarpone Cream Sauce (left) uses dried porcini mushrooms to infuse an intense wild mushroom flavor. For even more mushroom flavor, I've added some of the soaking liquid. Serve with roasted meats, poultry, or game, as well as pasta, eggs, or polenta.

- ¼ cup dried porcini mushrooms (about ⅓ ounce)
- 1 cup boiling water
- 1 tablespoon unsalted butter
- 1 medium-size leek (white and tender green parts), washed well and finely chopped
- 1 teaspoon finely chopped fresh thyme leaves
- ½ cup mascarpone
- ½ cup heavy cream
- Salt and freshly ground black pepper
- 2 tablespoons snipped fresh chives

1. In a small, heatproof bowl, soak the mushrooms in the boiling water until completely softened, about 20 minutes. Drain the mushrooms, reserving the soaking liquid. Briefly dip the mushrooms in clean water to dislodge any grit, then finely chop them. Let the soaking liquid settle, then slowly pour it into a clean cup, stopping when you get to the grit.

2. Melt the butter in a medium-size saucepan over medium heat. When the foam subsides, add the leek, chopped porcini, and thyme and cook,

stirring, until softened, about 3 minutes. Add ½ cup of the porcini soaking water and simmer until nearly evaporated, 10 to 12 minutes. Add the mascarpone and cook, stirring, until melted. Add the cream, season with salt and pepper, and simmer over low heat until slightly reduced, about 5 minutes. Refigerate for up to 2 days. Reheat gently before serving.

3. Just before serving, stir in the chives.

CREAMED VEGGIES YOUR WAY

Spread a layer of any of the following sauces over 1 head of steamed broccoli or cauliflower or 1½ pounds steamed asparagus in a large baking dish and bake in a preheated 375°F oven until bubbling for a delicious gratin.

- Béchamel with Manchego Cheese and Almonds (page 34)
- Fontina Cream Sauce (page 33)
- Mornay Sauce (page 32)
- Mustard Béchamel (page 28)
- Smoked Gouda Béchamel (page 32)
- Soubise (page 28)

ANCHO CHILE CREAM SAUCE

MAKES ABOUT 1½ CUPS

THE SOMEWHAT BITTER, earthy flavors of dried ancho chiles are mellowed by sweet cream and blanched garlic. I love this sauce with grilled or roasted beef, especially rib-eye and sirloin, but it goes equally well with roasted pork, lamb, or chicken or even as a sauce for enchiladas.

2 cups water
4 garlic cloves, peeled
3 medium-size ancho chiles, stemmed and seeded
1 cup low-sodium chicken broth
2 sprigs fresh thyme
1 cup heavy cream
¼ teaspoon sweet paprika
Pinch of sugar
Salt

1. Bring the water to a boil in a small saucepan. Add the garlic and simmer until softened, about 10 minutes. Using a slotted spoon, transfer the garlic to a small bowl. Off the heat, add the anchos to the boiling water and let sit until softened, about 15 minutes.

2. Drain the anchos, reserving the water, and transfer them to a blender along with the garlic and pulse until finely chopped. Add ½ cup of the reserved ancho soaking liquid and process until smooth. Strain the puree through a fine-mesh sieve, scraping with a rubber spatula, to remove as much of the skin as possible.

3. In a small saucepan, combine the ancho puree, broth, and thyme and bring to a boil. Reduce the heat to medium and simmer until reduced by half, about 20 minutes. Add the cream, paprika, and sugar and simmer until thickened slightly and reduced to 1½ cups, about 10 minutes. Season with salt and discard the thyme sprigs. Will keep, tightly covered, in the refrigerator for up to 4 days. Reheat gently before serving.

TANGY MUSTARD CREAM SAUCE

MAKES ABOUT 1½ CUPS

SWEET CREAM AND sautéed shallots balance the tartness of this whole-grain mustard sauce. Serve it with steaks, roasted chicken, pork or veal chops, and lots of mashed potatoes. It's also great with poached chicken and boiled potatoes.

1 tablespoon unsalted butter

1 large shallot, minced

3/4 cup dry white wine

Bouquet garni containing 3 sprigs fresh parsley, 2 sprigs fresh thyme, and 1 small bay leaf, tied in cheesecloth

1½ cups Rich Chicken Stock (page 161)

1 cup heavy cream

2 tablespoons whole-grain mustard

2 tablespoons Dijon mustard

Salt and freshly ground black pepper

1 tablespoon chopped fresh tarragon leaves (optional)

1. Melt the butter in a medium-size saucepan over medium heat. Add the shallot and cook, stirring, until softened, about 4 minutes. Add the wine and bouquet garni and simmer until reduced to 1¼ cup, about 10 minutes.

2. Add the stock and simmer until reduced to ¾ cup, about 25 minutes.

3. Remove the bouquet garni, add the cream and both mustards and simmer until thickened and reduced to 1½ cups, about 20 minutes longer. Will keep, tightly covered, in the refrigerator up to 3 days. Reheat gently before serving.

4. Season with salt and pepper and stir in the tarragon, if using.

CURRIED CHANTERELLE CREAM SAUCE

MAKES ABOUT 1½ CUPS

A PINCH OF aromatic curry powder is just enough to transform this rich mushroom cream sauce into something entirely exotic. It's great with roasted poultry, steamed vegetables, rice, potatoes, polenta, or sautéed mild white-fleshed fish such as snapper, striped bass, or grouper. You can also try making this with shiitake, oyster, and/or cremini mushrooms.

1 tablespoon unsalted butter

1/2 pound chanterelles, cleaned and cut into 1/2-inch pieces

1 teaspoon pure olive oil

2 medium-size shallots, minced

1 teaspoon Madras curry powder

1 cup low-sodium chicken broth

2 sprigs fresh thyme

1 cup heavy cream

Salt and freshly ground black pepper

1 tablespoon snipped fresh chives

1. Melt the butter in a large saucepan over medium-high heat. When the foam subsides, add the chanterelles and cook, stirring occasionally, until the liquid is evaporated and the mushrooms are golden brown, about 10 minutes.

2. Add the oil, shallots, and curry powder and cook, stirring, until the shallots are softened, about 3 minutes. Add the broth and thyme and bring to a boil. Reduce the heat to medium and simmer until reduced by three-quarters, about 10 minutes.

3. Add the cream and simmer over low heat until slightly thickened and reduced to 1½ cups, about 10 minutes longer. Remove and discard the thyme sprigs, then season with salt and pepper and stir in the chives. Will keep, tightly covered, in the refrigerator for up to 3 days. Reheat gently before serving.

ARUGULA CREAM SAUCE

MAKES ABOUT 1 CUP

PEPPERY ARUGULA ADDS a fresh, slightly grassy flavor to the cream in this rich sauce, as well as a bright green color. Sorrel, which is very tart and lemony, can be substituted for the arugula for a more elegant sauce, though it turns a drab green color when cooked. Omit the lemon juice if you use sorrel. This sauce goes nicely with fish, game, or poultry.

3 tablespoons unsalted butter

2 scallions (white and tender green parts), minced

1 large bunch (6 ounces) arugula, stems trimmed and finely chopped

1 cup heavy cream

1 tablespoon fresh lemon juice

1 teaspoon finely grated lemon zest

Salt and freshly ground black pepper

1 tablespoon finely chopped fresh Italian parsley leaves

1. Melt 1 tablespoon of the butter in a medium-size saucepan over medium heat. When the foam subsides, add the scallions and cook, stirring, until softened but not browned, 2 to 3 minutes. Add the arugula and cook just until wilted. Add the cream and lemon juice and zest and bring to a boil. Reduce the heat to medium and simmer until thickened and slightly reduced, about 5 minutes.

2. Transfer the sauce to a blender and process until smooth. Return the sauce to the saucepan and season with salt and pepper. Stir in the remaining 2 tablespoons butter and the parsley and heat until the butter is incorporated. This is best used right away.

SEAFOOD CREAM SAUCE

MAKES ABOUT 1¾ CUPS

THE SHELLFISH I like to use in this bisque-like sauce are shrimp and bay scallops, but crawfish, lump crabmeat, and lobster are great choices as well. Serve it with pasta or rice, or even grilled steak for an extremely rich surf and turf, but I like to serve it with fried or grilled polenta cakes. Cooking the shrimp shells in the broth really intensifies the shrimp flavor.

1 tablespoon unsalted butter

1 large shallot, minced

½ pound medium-size shrimp, shelled and deveined (shells reserved)

1½ teaspoons tomato paste

¼ cup dry vermouth

2 cups water

1 cup heavy cream

¼ pound bay scallops or sea scallops, quartered

Salt and freshly ground black pepper

1 tablespoon finely chopped fresh chervil leaves (optional)

1. In a medium-size saucepan, melt the butter over medium-high heat. Add the shallot and cook, stirring, until softened, about 4 minutes.

Add the reserved shrimp shells and cook, stirring, until they turn bright pink, 2 to 3 minutes. Add the tomato paste, stirring until the shells are coated. Add the vermouth and cook, stirring, until nearly evaporated, about 2 minutes. Add the water and bring to a boil. Reduce the heat to medium-low and simmer until richly flavored and reduced to 1 cup, about 20 minutes.

2. Strain the shrimp stock through a fine-mesh sieve, pressing hard on the solids, into a clean, medium-size saucepan and simmer over medium heat until reduced to ½ cup, about 10 minutes. Add the cream and simmer until reduced to ⅔ cup, about 30 minutes.

3. Cut the shrimp into ½-inch pieces and add them to the sauce along with the scallops and simmer over medium heat until opaque and cooked through, about 5 minutes. Season with salt and pepper and stir in the chervil, if using. This sauce is best used right away.

BREAD SAUCE

MAKES ABOUT 2 CUPS

SLIGHTLY LESS REFINED, though no less rich and tasty, than béchamel, this white sauce is thickened with fresh bread crumbs. Traditionally, this sauce is served in England with roasted poultry, but I think it works equally well with lamb or beef. Use dense, good-quality white sandwich bread with the crusts removed.

    2 cups half-and-half or whole milk
    1 medium-size onion, halved
    1 imported bay leaf
    Scant 1/4 teaspoon allspice berries
    Pinch of ground mace or freshly grated nutmeg
    4 slices white bread, crusts removed and
        torn into pieces
    1/4 cup heavy cream
    1 tablespoon unsalted butter
    Salt and freshly ground white pepper

1. In a medium-size saucepan, combine the half-and-half, onion, bay leaf, allspice, and mace and bring to a boil. Reduce the heat to low and simmer until the onion is tender, about 20 minutes. Strain the milk, reserving the onion; discard the bay leaf and allspice.

2. Place the onion and half of the half-and-half in a blender and process until smooth. Return the mixture to the saucepan, add the bread and remaining milk, and simmer over medium heat until thickened, about 10 minutes. Stir in the cream and butter, whisking until melted. Season with salt and pepper. This is best used right away.

CRÈME FRAÎCHE

MAKES 1 1/2 CUPS

CONSIDERING HOW EXPENSIVE it is to buy crème fraîche in gourmet shops, it's a wonder more people don't just make it at home. It's dead simple and so much more cost effective. Plus, since buttermilk is only sold in quarts, there'll be plenty left over to make Ranch Dressing (page 289) or Lowfat Goat Cheese–Buttermilk Dressing (page 288).

    1 tablespoon cultured buttermilk
    1 1/2 cups heavy cream, preferably not ultra-
        pasteurized

1. In a small saucepan, combine the buttermilk and heavy cream and heat very gently over medium-low heat until lukewarm, about 85°F on an instant-read thermometer.

2. Pour the mixture into a clean, heatproof glass measure, cover with aluminum foil or plastic wrap, and let sit at room temperature for 24 hours.

3. Transfer the crème fraîche to the refrigerator and chill until thickened. Will keep, tightly covered, in the refrigerator for up to 3 days.

PASTA SAUCES

As an Italian-American growing up with a large extended family not far away, pasta has always been a big part of my family tradition. With my parents' move out to the suburbs, we were definitely more Americanized than some of my relatives, so pasta became more of a quick weeknight supper or a special Sunday treat. Several of the recipes here are from my family, specifically my mother and grandmother, both incredible cooks.

While many of the sauces from other chapters in this book make wonderful pasta sauces, the sauces here are either classic, or not suited for other applications, or both, in the case of Carbonara (page 44).

The tomato-based sauces in this chapter could probably have been shuffled around to other chapters, but the ones included here are true pasta classics, especially Arrabbiata, Bolognese, Puttanesca, Tomato Sauce with Tuna, and Vodka Sauce. They really have few other applications.

I've also included several thinner creamy sauces here as opposed to in the chapter devoted to béchamel, since their consistency suits them well to nicely coat the pasta.

ALFREDO

MAKES ABOUT 1¼ CUPS, ENOUGH FOR

1 POUND PASTA (4 TO 6 SERVINGS)

WITH AS MANY versions of this classic dish as I've seen and tasted, I've discovered that the simpler it is, the better. Don't be fooled by the gloppy, overly rich version perpetrated by certain chain restaurants. Classic Alfredo is rather light and delicately flavored with sweet cream, nutty parmesan, and a pinch of nutmeg. Use with fettuccine.

1 cup heavy cream

¼ cup (½ stick) unsalted butter

Pinch of freshly grated nutmeg

½ cup freshly grated parmesan cheese, plus more for serving

Salt and freshly ground black pepper

In a small saucepan, combine the cream, butter, and nutmeg and bring to a boil. Reduce the heat to medium, add the parmesan, season with salt and pepper, and cook just until melted. This sauce is best used right away.

CARBONARA

MAKES 4 SERVINGS

THOUGH TECHNICALLY A sauce, carbonara is wholly dependent upon the addition of piping hot spaghetti to complete the dish. Since the eggs are cooked by the heat of the pasta, it's crucial to have your eggs at room temperature and to work as quickly as possible. Toss with spaghetti until well coated.

4 large eggs, lightly beaten

½ cup freshly grated parmesan cheese, plus more for serving

¼ cup mascarpone or heavy cream

¼ cup finely chopped fresh Italian parsley leaves

Generous pinch of freshly ground black pepper

6 ounces sliced pancetta or bacon, cut into ½-inch pieces

12 ounces spaghetti

Salt

1. In a large bowl, combine the eggs, parmesan, mascarpone, parsley, and pepper.

10 CLASSIC SPAGHETTI SAUCES

2. In a large skillet, cook the pancetta over medium-high heat until crisp and browned. Using a slotted spoon, transfer the pancetta to a small bowl. Pour off and discard all but 1 tablespoon of the fat from the skillet and set aside.

3. In salted boiling water, cook the spaghetti until *al dente*. Drain the pasta, reserving ¼ cup of the cooking water. Add the pasta to the skillet and cook over high heat for 1 minute, tossing until coated with the fat. Working quickly, transfer the pasta to the bowl with the egg mixture, along with 2 tablespoons of the reserved cooking liquid, and toss until creamy and the pasta is well coated, adding more of the cooking liquid if needed. Season with salt and more pepper and add the pancetta. Serve right away, passing additional cheese at the table.

ANCHOVY CREAM SAUCE

MAKES ABOUT 1¼ CUPS, ENOUGH FOR
1 POUND PASTA (4 TO 6 SERVINGS)

THE SALTY, ASSERTIVE flavor of anchovies is mellowed by sweet cream and parmesan cheese in this sauce. There are a few brands that I really like to use. Look for imported Italian, French, or Portuguese anchovies, packed in glass jars. For a lighter flavor, soak the anchovies in milk or warm water for 20 minutes, then drain. Use this with penne, bow ties, fusilli, or fettuccine.

  2 tablespoons unsalted butter
  6 anchovy fillets, mashed
  2 garlic cloves, minced
  ¼ cup dry white wine
  1 cup heavy cream
  2 tablespoons freshly grated parmesan cheese
  Salt
  Cayenne pepper

Melt the butter in a medium-size saucepan over medium heat. Add the anchovies and garlic and cook, stirring, until the anchovies begin to dissolve, about 2 minutes. Add the wine and cook until reduced by two-thirds, about 5 minutes. Stir in the cream and simmer until slightly reduced, about 5 minutes. Stir in the parmesan and season with salt and cayenne. This sauce is best used right away.

FRESH PECORINO TRUFFLE CREAM SAUCE

MAKES 1½ CUPS, ENOUGH FOR 1 POUND PASTA

(6 SERVINGS)

FRESH TRUFFLES ADD an exquisitely musty, earthy flavor to foods, but I find it difficult to justify the cost when cooking for my family. Good-quality white truffle oil, found in tiny bottles in gourmet markets, is a great alternative. Fresh Pecorino cheese from Sardinia or Tuscany has a sweet, nutty flavor, much like parmesan, as opposed to Pecorino Romano, which is very sharp and pungent. This sauce is great on pasta, especially long-strand pasta, but I also love it over poached eggs or grilled steaks; however, then it needs to be cooked a bit longer, until slightly thicker.

1 tablespoon unsalted butter

1 medium-size leek (white and tender green parts), washed well and finely chopped

1 cup heavy cream

½ cup freshly grated Pecorino Sardo or Toscano, or parmesan cheese

1 teaspoon white truffle oil, or more to taste

Freshly ground white pepper

Melt the butter in a medium-size saucepan over medium heat. Add the leek and cook, stirring a few times, until softened, about 4 minutes. Add the cream and simmer until reduced by half, about 10 minutes. Add the cheese and simmer, stirring occasionally, until slightly thickened, 2 to 3 minutes. Stir in the truffle oil and season with white pepper. This sauce is best used right away.

TIPS FOR MAKING SUCCESSFUL PASTA SAUCES

- Pasta shapes like penne, rotini, and farfalle are good choices for hearty, chunky sauces.

- Thin-strand pastas such as spaghetti, linguine, fettuccine, and bucatini are best with slightly smoother, less chunky sauces.

- Flat-strand pastas such as fettuccine and pappardelle are best with creamy sauces because the folds trap the sauce.

- Cook the pasta for 1 minute in a small amount of the tomato sauce before transferring it to a serving platter. This will allow the sauce to permeate the pasta and prevent it from getting watery. Spoon more sauce on top before serving.

ROASTED GARLIC CREAM SAUCE

MAKES ABOUT 1⅓ CUPS, ENOUGH FOR
1 POUND PASTA (4 TO 6 SERVINGS)

OVEN ROASTING GIVES the garlic a sweet, mellow flavor that pairs extremely well with cream and pasta. I like to serve this sauce with fettuccine because the noodles trap the delicious sauce in its folds, but it also works well with farfalle (bow ties) or penne.

- 1 head garlic, cut in half horizontally
- 1 tablespoon extra-virgin olive oil
- 1½ teaspoons fresh thyme leaves
- Generous pinch of freshly ground black pepper
- 1 cup heavy cream
- ¼ cup freshly grated Asiago or parmesan cheese
- Salt

1. Preheat the oven to 350°F. Place the garlic, cut sides up, in a small glass or ceramic baking dish and drizzle with the olive oil. Sprinkle with the thyme and pepper. Cover the dish with aluminum foil and bake until the garlic is meltingly tender and golden, about 1 hour. Let cool.

2. Using a small fork or toothpick, remove the garlic from the skins, transfer them to a small saucepan, and mash until fairly smooth. Stir in the cream and simmer over medium-low heat until reduced slightly, 8 to 10 minutes. Stir in the cheese and season with salt and pepper. Will keep, tightly covered, in the refrigerator for up to 2 days. Reheat gently.

SWEET PEA CREAM SAUCE WITH MORELS

MAKES ABOUT 1½ CUPS, ENOUGH FOR
1 POUND PASTA (6 SERVINGS)

SWEET PEAS, ALONG with morels, herald springtime. I love this sauce over a pasta such as fettuccine, bow ties, or orecchiette, or on polenta or stirred into risotto. The cooked bacon can be crumbled and used as a garnish or eaten by the chef as a special "cook's treat!" If you can't find morels, chanterelles or oyster mushrooms are a fine substitute.

- 1¾ cups Rich Chicken Stock (page 161)
- ¾ pound fresh peas, shelled
- 4 ounces thick-sliced bacon
- 6 ounces small fresh morels, rinsed, drained, and halved lengthwise
- ½ cup heavy cream
- Salt and freshly ground black pepper
- 2 tablespoons finely chopped fresh garlic chives or 2 scallions, minced

1. In a medium-size saucepan, bring the stock to a boil. Add the peas and cook over medium-high heat until just tender, about 10 minutes. Transfer the stock and peas to a blender and process until smooth.

2. Cook the bacon in a medium-size skillet over medium-high heat until browned and crisp, about 7 minutes. Drain on paper towels. Pour off all but 1 tablespoon of the fat. Add the morels and cook until they release their liquid, about 4 minutes. Raise the heat to high, add the cream, and season with salt and pepper. Cook until slightly reduced, about 2 minutes. Stir in the pea puree and cook until just heated through. Stir in the chives and serve immediately.

ROASTED PEPPER CREAM SAUCE

MAKES 1¾ CUPS, ENOUGH FOR
1 POUND PASTA (4 TO 6 SERVINGS)

THIS SAUCE CAN be served with grilled or roasted meat or poultry as well as pasta; fettuccine, bow ties, penne, and rotini all work well. I find that roasting peppers in a hot oven, as opposed to over an open flame, gives them a creamier texture and a more intense, sweet flavor.

3 large red or yellow bell peppers

2 tablespoons plus 1 teaspoon extra-virgin olive oil

1 medium-size onion, finely chopped

2 garlic cloves, thinly sliced

2 tablespoons Marsala

½ cup low-sodium chicken broth

½ cup heavy cream

Salt

Cayenne pepper

1 tablespoon unsalted butter

1. Preheat the oven to 425°F and position a rack in the upper third of the oven. Rub the peppers with 1 teaspoon of the oil and place them in a sturdy roasting pan. Roast the peppers, uncov-ered, until collapsed and browned, about 30 minutes. Transfer the peppers to a bowl, cover with plastic wrap, and let steam for 15 minutes. When cool enough to handle, peel the peppers and remove the core, seeds, and any tough inner ribs. Coarsely chop the peppers.

2. In a large saucepan, heat the remaining 2 tablespoons oil over medium heat until shimmering. Add the onion, garlic, and roasted peppers and cook, stirring occasionally, until softened, about 5 minutes. Add the Marsala and cook, stirring a few times, until evaporated, about 1 minute. Add the broth and simmer over low heat until the onion and peppers are very tender and the stock is nearly evaporated, about 10 minutes.

3. Transfer the mixture to a blender and process until fairly smooth, scraping down the sides of the bowl. Add the cream and process until smooth. Return the sauce to the saucepan and simmer over medium heat until slightly reduced, about 5 minutes. Season with salt and cayenne and stir in the butter until melted. Will keep, tightly covered, in the refrigerator up to 2 days. Reheat gently.

SUN-DRIED TOMATO GORGONZOLA SAUCE

MAKES ABOUT 1 CUP, ENOUGH FOR
1 POUND PASTA (4 TO 6 SERVINGS)

CREAMY, BUTTERY GORGONZOLA dolce, Italian blue cheese, is paired with pancetta, sun-dried tomatoes, and cream in this rich and decadent pasta sauce. Long pastas work well here—pappardelle, fettuccine, or spaghetti are the best for trapping this luscious sauce.

1 tablespoon extra-virgin olive oil

4 ounces sliced pancetta, coarsely chopped

1 large shallot, minced

1/2 cup drained oil-packed sun-dried tomatoes, chopped

1/2 cup low-sodium chicken broth

1/2 cup heavy cream

4 ounces imported Gorgonzola dolce, in pieces

Salt and freshly ground black pepper

1. In a medium-size saucepan, heat the oil over medium-high heat until shimmering. Add the pancetta and cook until browned and crisp. Using a slotted spoon, remove the pancetta to a plate, leaving the fat in the pan. Add the shallot and cook, stirring, until softened, about 3 minutes. Add the sun-dried tomatoes, broth, and cream and bring to a boil. Reduce the heat to medium and simmer until the liquid is slightly reduced, 8 to 10 minutes.

2. Transfer the mixture to a blender and process until smooth. Return the sauce to the saucepan,

add the Gorgonzola, and simmer, stirring, over medium-low heat just until melted. Season with salt and pepper, stir in the pancetta, and serve immediately.

PRIMAVERA SAUCE

MAKES ABOUT 2 1/2 TO 3 CUPS, ENOUGH FOR
1 POUND PASTA (6 SERVINGS)

NAMED FOR THE fresh vegetables of springtime, this sauce traditionally contained little more than asparagus, baby peas, and leeks, along with cream, butter, and a bit of ham. Over time, though, pasta primavera has come to include zucchini, carrots, yellow squash, red peppers, green beans, and broccoli. I prefer the simpler version, but feel free to improvise with whatever vegetables you have. Also, you can omit the prosciutto for a totally vegetarian sauce. Serve this with penne, rotini, fettuccine, or spaghetti.

1 pound pencil-thin asparagus, bottoms trimmed and cut into 1-inch pieces

1/2 cup fresh or frozen baby peas

1 tablespoon unsalted butter

1 tablespoon extra-virgin olive oil

4 ounces prosciutto, in one 1/4-inch-thick piece, cut into 1/4-inch cubes

2 small leeks (white and tender green parts), cut in half lengthwise, washed well, and thinly sliced crosswise

1 1/2 cups heavy cream

1/3 cup freshly grated parmesan cheese

Salt and freshly ground black pepper

1. Bring a medium-size saucepan of salted water to a boil. Add the asparagus and cook until crisp-tender, about 3 minutes. Using a slotted spoon, transfer the asparagus to a plate. Return the water to a boil, add the peas (fresh only), and cook until tender, 5 to 6 minutes. Drain the peas and add them to the asparagus.

2. In a large saucepan, melt the butter in the olive oil over medium heat. Add the prosciutto and cook until warmed through but not browned. Add the leeks and cook, stirring, until softened, about 4 minutes. Add the cream and bring to a boil. Reduce the heat to low and simmer until thickened, about 8 minutes. Add the asparagus and peas and simmer until heated through. Stir in the parmesan, season with salt and pepper, and use right away.

WILD MUSHROOM RAGU

MAKES 2 CUPS, ENOUGH FOR 12 OUNCES PASTA

(4 SERVINGS)

WILD MUSHROOMS AND cream is an exquisite pairing in any configuration—whether in soups, risottos, or stews—but when paired with pasta, it is truly sublime; fettuccine and pappardelle are wonderful with this, but penne, rotini, and bow ties also work well. As stated elsewhere in this book, my favorites are chanterelles, morels, oyster mushrooms, shiitakes, and fresh porcini, but feel free to use whatever you like. Chanterelles and morels tend to be very dirty, so be sure to rinse and dry them well just before using them.

1 teaspoon extra-virgin olive oil

4 ounces sliced pancetta or bacon, cut into 1/2-inch pieces

1 1/4 pounds mixed wild mushrooms, trimmed and thinly sliced

1 large shallot, minced

1 teaspoon fresh thyme leaves

1/4 cup Madeira or Marsala

3/4 cup heavy cream

Salt and freshly ground black pepper

1. Heat the olive oil in a large, deep skillet over medium-high heat until shimmering. Add the pancetta and cook, stirring occasionally, until crisp and golden, about 5 minutes. Using a slotted spoon, transfer the pancetta to a bowl, leaving the fat in the skillet.

2. Add the mushrooms to the skillet and cook until softened and beginning to brown, 8 to 10 minutes. Add the shallot and thyme and cook, stirring a few times, until softened. Add the Madeira and cook, scraping up any browned bits stuck to the bottom of the pan, until nearly evaporated, about 2 minutes. Add the cream, season with salt and pepper, and simmer until slightly thickened, 2 to 3 minutes. Will keep, tightly covered, in the refrigerator for up to 2 days. Reheat gently.

3. Just before serving, stir in the pancetta.

SICILIAN CAULIFLOWER SAUCE

MAKES 2½ TO 3 CUPS, ENOUGH FOR
1 POUND PASTA (6 SERVINGS)

THIS CLASSIC PASTA sauce from Sicily combines the sweet and salty flavors of raisins and anchovies with pine nuts and cauliflower and is usually served with orecchiette—little ears—pasta, but bow ties, medium-size shells, and penne are fine also. Customarily, dried bread crumbs that have been fried in olive oil until golden and crisp replace parmesan cheese as a finishing touch. I like to soak the raisins in cognac or brandy, but most Sicilians would use Marsala or simply plain water.

1/3 cup raisins or currants

2 tablespoons cognac or brandy

1/4 cup warm water

1 large head cauliflower, cut into 1-inch florets and stems discarded

1/4 cup (½ stick) unsalted butter

2 tablespoons extra-virgin olive oil

1/3 cup pine nuts

1 large Spanish onion, thinly sliced lengthwise

Pinch of sugar

4 to 5 large anchovies, rinsed and finely chopped

3/4 cup low-sodium chicken broth

Salt and freshly ground black pepper

1. Combine the raisins, cognac, and water in a small bowl and set aside.

2. Bring a large pot of salted water to a boil. Add the cauliflower and cook until tender, 5 to 6 minutes. Drain the cauliflower, shaking off the excess water.

3. In a large, deep skillet, melt the butter in the olive oil over medium heat. Add the pine nuts and cook, stirring or shaking frequently, until golden, 3 to 4 minutes. Using a slotted spoon, transfer them to a plate. Add the onion and sugar and cook, stirring occasionally, until softened and beginning to caramelize, 8 to 10 minutes. Add the anchovies and cook, stirring, just until combined. Add the cauliflower and cook over high heat, stirring occasionally, until lightly browned, 5 to 6 minutes. Add the broth and raisins and their soaking liquid and season with salt and pepper. Simmer over medium heat until the liquid is reduced by about half, 5 to 6 minutes.

4. Using a wooden spoon or potato masher, mash about two-thirds of the cauliflower. Stir in the pine nuts and serve immediately.

BRAISED ZUCCHINI SAUCE

MAKES 2 CUPS, ENOUGH FOR 12 OUNCES PASTA

(4 SERVINGS)

SHREDDED ZUCCHINI, COOKED with onions, garlic, and wine, makes up the base of this rustic, peasant-like sauce. Grate the zucchini lengthwise, on the largest holes of a box grater or, even better, julienne them on a mandoline. I like to serve it with a long pasta such as thin linguine or spaghetti and lots of grated parmesan, Asiago, or Pecorino Sardo.

2 pounds small, young zucchini, ends trimmed and halved crosswise

1½ teaspoons kosher salt

¼ cup extra-virgin olive oil

1 medium-size onion, thinly sliced lengthwise

2 large garlic cloves, thinly sliced

¼ to ½ teaspoon red pepper flakes, to your taste

¼ cup dry white wine

1 tablespoon fresh lemon juice

1 teaspoon finely grated lemon zest

2 tablespoons finely chopped fresh marjoram or oregano leaves

1. Using a box grater, shred the zucchini lengthwise on the largest holes, stopping when you get to the seedy center. Discard the centers. Toss the shredded zucchini with the salt, transfer to a colander set in the sink, and let sit for 20 minutes. Using your hands, squeeze out as much excess water as possible without completely smashing the zucchini.

2. In a large, deep skillet, heat the olive oil over medium-high heat until shimmering. Add the onion and garlic and cook until softened and browned, 5 to 6 minutes. Add the zucchini and red pepper flakes and cook, stirring occasionally, until softened and just beginning to brown, about 10 minutes. Add the wine, reduce the heat to medium, and cook until the zucchini is just beginning to break down. Stir in the lemon juice and zest and marjoram. Taste and season with salt, if necessary. This sauce is best used right away.

BROCCOLI–BLACK OLIVE SAUCE

MAKES 2½ TO 3 CUPS, ENOUGH FOR

12 OUNCES PASTA (4 SERVINGS)

THIS SIMPLE SAUCE from Sicily is a favorite of mine. I love the assertive flavors of briny, salty olives, anchovies, garlic, lemon, and broccoli. I like to use a combination of brined and oil-cured olives, such as picholine and Sicilian green olives, niçoise and Kalamata black olives, and oil-cured Moroccan black olives. If you omit the anchovies, it makes a substantial vegetarian meal. Serve with penne, rotini, fettuccine, or spaghetti, topped with parmesan cheese.

1 large bunch broccoli, cut into 1-inch florets and stems peeled and thinly sliced

¼ cup extra-virgin olive oil

2 large garlic cloves, thinly sliced

4 large anchovies, rinsed and finely chopped

1/4 teaspoon red pepper flakes

Salt and freshly ground black pepper

1 1/2 cups low-sodium chicken broth or water

1/2 cup pitted and coarsely chopped olives

1 1/2 tablespoons fresh lemon juice

1. Bring a large saucepan of salted water to a boil. Add the broccoli and cook until barely tender, about 5 minutes. Drain the broccoli, shaking off any excess water.

2. Heat the oil in a large, deep skillet over medium heat until shimmering. Add the garlic, anchovies, and red pepper flakes and cook until lightly golden and the anchovies begin to melt, about 2 minutes. Add the broccoli, season with salt and black pepper, and cook over high heat until browned around the edges, about 5 minutes. Add the broth and cook, mashing half of the broccoli with a wooden spoon or potato masher, until the liquid is reduced by two-thirds, about 10 minutes. Stir in the olives and lemon juice. This sauce is best used right away.

VODKA SAUCE

MAKES 3 CUPS, ENOUGH FOR 1 POUND PASTA

(6 SERVINGS)

PENNE À LA VODKA is a standard at just about every Italian-American restaurant I've been to. One of my favorites, though I've only had it once, is at Rao's in the Bronx. There they combine vodka, cream, and tomatoes to make a delectable, rich pasta sauce that is traditionally served with penne. Here I've used pancetta, an Italian bacon that is cured rather than smoked. I love how it gently infuses the sauce with a slight gamy and tangy flavor without overpowering it the way a smoked bacon would. If pancetta proves difficult to find, bacon is a perfectly fine substitute, though it will give the sauce a decidedly smoky flavor. Look for a bacon that is mildly smoked.

1 teaspoon extra-virgin olive oil

4 ounces thickly sliced pancetta, cut into 1/4-inch dice

1/2 small onion, minced

1 large garlic clove, minced

1/4 teaspoon red pepper flakes

Pinch of dried oregano, crumbled

1/4 cup vodka

One 35-ounce can peeled whole Italian tomatoes, with their juices, finely chopped

Pinch of sugar

Salt and freshly ground black pepper

1/2 cup heavy cream

1 tablespoon tomato paste

1. In a large, deep skillet, heat the oil over medium-high heat until shimmering. Add the pancetta and cook, stirring frequently, until browned and crisp and most of the fat is rendered, about 5 minutes. Add the onion, garlic, red pepper flakes, and oregano and cook, stirring, until softened, about 3 minutes. Add the vodka and cook until evaporated, scraping up any browned bits that are stuck to the pan. Add the tomatoes and sugar, season with salt and pepper, and simmer over medium heat until thickened and slightly reduced, about 20 minutes.

2. In a small bowl, whisk the cream with the tomato paste. Add the cream to the sauce and simmer over low heat, stirring occasionally until thickened and slightly reduced, about 10 minutes longer. Will keep, tightly covered, in the refrigerator for up to 4 days or in the freezer for a month.

ARRABBIATA

MAKES ABOUT 2½ CUPS, ENOUGH FOR
12 OUNCES PASTA (4 SERVINGS)

I LIKE MY arrabbiata on the spicy side, but have given a range in the amount of hot pepper flakes. The low end is mild and the high end is pretty perky. Pancetta is an Italian cured pork product much like bacon but without the smoky flavor. Bacon will do in a pinch, but the flavor will be much more prominent. Serve this with penne, rotini, or spaghetti.

2 pounds vine-ripened tomatoes or one 28-ounce can diced tomatoes, with their juices

1 tablespoon extra-virgin olive oil

4 ounces sliced pancetta, finely diced

½ small onion, minced

1 large garlic clove, minced

¼ to ½ teaspoon red pepper flakes, to your taste

Pinch of sugar

Salt and freshly ground black pepper

1. If using fresh tomatoes, bring a medium-size saucepan of water to a boil. Fill in a medium-size bowl with ice water. Using a sharp paring knife, make a shallow X in the bottom of each tomato. Put the tomatoes in the boiling water for 15 to 20 seconds; remove them using a slotted spoon and plunge them immediately into the ice water to cool. Whether using fresh or canned, peel, if necessary, core, seed, and coarsely chop the tomatoes.

2. Heat the oil in a large saucepan over medium-high heat. Add the pancetta, onion, and garlic and cook, stirring occasionally, until the pancetta just begins to turn pink and the onion is translucent, about 5 minutes. Add the red pepper and cook, stirring, until the pancetta begins to brown. Add the tomatoes along with their juices and the sugar. Season with salt and black pepper and bring to a boil. Reduce the heat to medium-low and cook, partially covered, until the sauce is thickened, about 30 minutes. Will keep, tightly covered, in the refrigerator for up to 4 days or in the freezer for a month.

BAKED PASTA WITH WILD MUSHROOMS AND SMOKED HAM

MAKES 6 SERVINGS

THIS RUSTIC BAKED pasta dish is truly greater than the sum of its parts—meaty wild mushrooms, smoky ham, creamy cheeses, and richly flavored tomato sauce. The exact choice of sauce is yours—try Classic Marinara (page 74), Arrabbiata (left), American-Style Tomato Sauce (page 73), Saffron-Scented Tomato Sauce (page 91), or Smoky Pan-Blackened Tomato Sauce (page 87); each one will bring something a little different to the dish. Any combination of wild mushrooms will do quite nicely. I like chanterelles, morels, oyster mushrooms, shiitakes, or fresh porcini, but feel free to use whatever moves you. If using portobello mushrooms, be sure to scrape out the dark gills on the underside of the cap to prevent the sauce from becoming murky and to remove the stems. Chanterelles and morels tend to be very dirty, so be sure to rinse and dry them well just before using them.

12 ounces penne rigate

2 tablespoons extra-virgin olive oil

12 ounces mixed wild mushrooms, trimmed and thickly sliced

1 shallot, finely chopped

Salt and freshly ground black pepper

2 1/2 cups tomato sauce of your choice (see above)

1/2 pound good-quality smoked ham, finely diced

1/2 cup mascarpone cheese

1 cup shredded mozzarella cheese

1 cup shredded Italian fontina cheese

1/4 cup freshly grated parmesan cheese

1. Preheat the oven to 400°F, and lightly butter a 2-quart glass or ceramic baking dish.

2. Cook the pasta in salted boiling water until *al dente*. Drain the pasta, reserving 1/2 cup of the cooking water separately, and transfer the pasta to a large bowl.

3. In a large skillet, heat the oil over medium-high heat until shimmering. Add the mushrooms and cook, stirring occasionally, until softened and beginning to brown, 8 to 10 minutes. Add the shallot, season with salt and pepper, and cook, stirring, until softened, about 4 minutes. Add the mushroom mixture to the pasta along with the tomato sauce, ham, mascarpone, and reserved pasta cooking water and combine well.

4. Spread half of the pasta mixture in an even layer in the prepared baking dish. Sprinkle with 1/2 cup each of the mozzarella and fontina and cover with the remaining pasta. Sprinkle with the remaining 1/2 cup each of mozzarella and fontina cheeses and all of the parmesan. Bake, uncovered, until bubbling and crusty on top, about 30 minutes. Let rest 10 minutes before serving.

UNCOOKED ARRABBIATA

MAKES ABOUT 2½ CUPS, ENOUGH FOR
12 OUNCES PASTA (4 SERVINGS)

SUMMERTIME, WHEN TOMATOES are at their absolute best, is the only time I make this version of the spicy tomato sauce. Since it's uncooked, prosciutto replaces the more familiar pancetta. Look for ripe, juicy heirloom or beefsteak tomatoes and small fresh red or green chiles, such as serrano or Thai bird. Be sure to cook your pasta after the sauce is assembled so that the heat of the pasta warms the tomatoes as it's tossed together. Try this with penne, rotini, bow ties, spaghetti, linguine, or fettuccine.

1½ pounds ripe tomatoes
4 ounces thinly sliced prosciutto, cut into ¼-inch-wide strips
1 large garlic clove, minced
1 small fresh chile, seeded and minced
2 tablespoons extra-virgin olive oil
Salt and freshly ground black pepper

1. Bring a large saucepan of water to a boil. Fill a medium-size bowl with ice water. Using a sharp paring knife, make a small X in the bottom of each tomato. Plunge the tomatoes in the boiling water for 30 seconds. Using a slotted spoon, transfer the tomatoes to the ice water bath to cool for 1 minute. Drain, then peel, core, and cut each tomato in half crosswise.

2. Working over a strainer set over a large pasta

19 SUPER QUICK PASTA SAUCES

bowl, pry the seeds from the tomatoes, using your fingers. Press the tomato pulp to release the juices, then discard the seeds. Coarsely chop the tomatoes and add them to the strained juices along with the prosciutto, garlic, and chile. Stir in the oil and season with salt and pepper. This is best served right away.

FRESH TOMATO AND RICOTTA SAUCE

MAKES ABOUT 2½ CUPS, ENOUGH FOR
12 OUNCES PASTA (4 SERVINGS)

THE SWEETNESS OF fresh ricotta combines with the tart juices of ripe tomatoes to make a creamy, fresh sauce. The heat of freshly cooked pasta is enough to warm the sauce. I prefer to use the fresh ricotta available in Italian markets or cheese shops. Serve this with farfalle, fettuccine, linguine, or rotini.

- 8 ounces fresh ricotta cheese
- 1 small garlic clove, minced
- 1 teaspoon finely grated lemon zest
- 1 teaspoon seeded and minced red or green chile
- 1 pound ripe tomatoes, coarsely chopped
- Salt and freshly ground black pepper

Put the ricotta, garlic, lemon zest, and chile in a mini–food processor and process until smooth. Transfer the mixture to a medium-size bowl, add the tomatoes and any accumulated tomato juices, and season with salt and pepper. Alternatively,

press the ricotta through a fine-mesh sieve and stir in the remaining ingredients. Toss with hot pasta and serve immediately.

PUTTANESCA

MAKES 3 CUPS, ENOUGH FOR 1 POUND PASTA
(6 SERVINGS)

QUICK AND EASY to make, puttanesca combines garlic, anchovies, olives, and capers with fresh or canned tomatoes and is briefly cooked. The olives I like most here are brined black olives, such as Kalamata or gaeta, both of which can be found already pitted in most delis. This sauce is great with pastas like penne and spaghetti, and is also delicious with grilled tuna or swordfish steaks—which is how my grandmother served it.

- ¼ cup extra-virgin olive oil
- 6 large anchovies, rinsed and finely chopped
- 2 large garlic cloves, minced
- ¼ teaspoon red pepper flakes
- One 28-ounce can peeled whole tomatoes, with their juices, coarsely chopped
- ¼ cup sliced pitted olives
- 1 tablespoon capers, rinsed and chopped
- 2 tablespoons coarsely chopped fresh basil leaves
- Salt and freshly ground black pepper

Heat the oil in a large saucepan over medium heat until shimmering. Add the anchovies, garlic, and red pepper flakes and cook, stirring and mashing, until softened and the anchovies begin to disintegrate, about 2 minutes. Add the tomatoes and cook over high heat just until slightly reduced, about 5 minutes. Add the olives and capers and simmer over medium-low heat, stirring occasionally, until slightly thickened, about 10 minutes. Stir in the basil and season with salt and black pepper. This sauce is best used right away.

13 PASTA SAUCES THAT FREEZE WELL

1. American-Style Meat Sauce (page 60)
2. American-Style Tomato Sauce (page 73)
3. Arrabbiata (page 54)
4. Bolognese Sauce (page 60)
5. Catalan Tomato, Pepper, and Eggplant Sauce (page 75)
6. Classic Marinara (page 74)
7. Hearty Italian Meat Sauce (right)
8. North African Tomato Sauce with Chickpeas and Sweet Spices (page 78)
9. Pizzaiola (page 73)
10. Provençal Fennel Tomato Sauce (page 76)
11. Puttanesca (page 57)
12. Smoky Pan-Blackened Tomato Sauce (page 87)
13. Vodka Sauce (page 53)

HEARTY ITALIAN MEAT SAUCE

MAKES ABOUT 16 CUPS, ENOUGH FOR
1½ TO 2 POUNDS PASTA (10 TO 12 SERVINGS)

FOR MOST OF the week my grandmother cooked modest, almost meatless dishes. But when Sunday came around, she went wild with this rich, hearty meat sauce. Sometimes she would add pork chops, veal shanks, beef short ribs, or Italian braciola, slices of flank steak stuffed with seasoned bread crumbs and cheese and rolled. Meatballs and sausage are added nearer the end so they don't overcook. Serve this tossed with rigatoni, spaghetti, or penne or in lasagna.

SAUCE:

¼ cup extra-virgin olive oil

1 pound boneless veal shoulder, trimmed of fat and cut into 1-inch cubes

1 pound boneless pork shoulder, trimmed of fat and cut into 1-inch cubes

1 pound sweet or hot Italian sausage or a combination

1 large onion, finely chopped

4 large garlic cloves, minced

Two 28-ounce cans peeled whole tomatoes, with their juices, coarsely chopped

One 28-ounce can tomato puree

One 6-ounce can tomato paste

3 cups water

2 tablespoons sugar

3 imported bay leaves

½ teaspoon dried oregano, crumbled

Salt and freshly ground black pepper

MEATBALLS:

1 teaspoon olive oil

1 medium-size onion, minced

1 large garlic clove, minced

1 teaspoon dried thyme

1/2 teaspoon dried rosemary, crushed

1/4 cup milk

3 slices firm white sandwich bread, torn into pieces

1 large egg, beaten

2 tablespoons freshly grated parmesan cheese

2 tablespoons finely chopped fresh Italian parsley leaves

1 teaspoon salt

1/2 teaspoon freshly ground black pepper

1/2 pound ground beef

1/2 pound ground veal

Vegetable oil for frying

All-purpose flour

1. To make the tomato sauce, heat the oil in a large, heavy casserole over medium-high heat until shimmering. Add the veal and pork in batches and brown on all sides, 8 to 10 minutes per batch. Using a slotted spoon, transfer the meat to a platter as it browns. Add the sausages to the pot and cook, turning occasionally, until browned but not cooked through, about 8 minutes. Transfer the sausages to the platter.

2. Add the onion and garlic to the pot and cook, stirring, until the onion is translucent. Return the browned veal and pork to the pot along with the tomatoes and their juices, the tomato puree and paste, water, sugar, bay leaves, and oregano. Season with salt and pepper and bring to a boil. Reduce the heat to low and cook, partially

covered, until the meat is tender and the sauce is slightly thickened, about 1½ hours.

3. Meanwhile, make the meatballs. Heat the oil in a small skillet over medium heat. Add the onion, garlic, thyme, and rosemary and cook, stirring, until the onion is translucent. Transfer to a large bowl and let cool. Add the milk, then the bread, and let soak until moistened. Add the egg, cheese, parsley, salt, and pepper and knead until combined. Add the ground beef and veal and knead until evenly mixed. Divide the meat into 12 portions and, using lightly moistened hands, roll into balls.

4. Heat ½ inch of the vegetable oil in a large skillet over medium-high heat until shimmering. Dust the meatballs with flour, tapping off any excess, and add them to the skillet. Cook, turning occasionally, until browned all over, about 3 minutes. Add the meatballs to the sauce along with the browned sausages and simmer, uncovered, until cooked through, about 30 minutes. Will keep, tightly covered, in the refrigerator for up to 4 days or in the freezer for a month.

AMERICAN-STYLE MEAT SAUCE

MAKES ABOUT 4 CUPS, ENOUGH FOR
1 POUND PASTA (6 SERVINGS)

THIS ALL-PURPOSE MEAT sauce is great on pasta or in lasagna or other baked pasta dishes. By using extra-lean ground beef, there's hardly any fat that needs to be poured off. Americans tend to add more sauce to their pastas than Italians do. One pound of pasta will be generously sauced by this recipe.

   2 tablespoons extra-virgin olive oil
   1 small onion, finely chopped
   2 garlic cloves, minced
   12 ounces extra-lean ground beef
   One 28-ounce can tomato puree
   2 tablespoons tomato paste
   1 3/4 cups water
   Pinch of sugar
   1/2 teaspoon dried oregano, crumbled
   1/2 teaspoon dried thyme
   1 bay leaf
   Salt and freshly ground black pepper

1. Heat the oil in a large saucepan over medium-high heat until shimmering. Add the onion and garlic and cook, stirring occasionally, until lightly browned, 5 to 6 minutes. Add the ground beef and cook, breaking up the meat with a wooden spoon, until no longer pink, about 10 minutes. Spoon off the excess fat, if desired.

2. Add the tomato puree, tomato paste, water, sugar, and herbs. Season with salt and pepper and bring to a boil. Reduce the heat to low, cover partially, and simmer until thickened, about 45 minutes. Taste again for salt and pepper. Will keep, tightly covered, in the refrigerator for up to 4 days or in the freezer for a month.

BOLOGNESE SAUCE

MAKES ABOUT 4 CUPS, ENOUGH FOR
1 POUND PASTA (6 SERVINGS)

THIS RECIPE COMES from my brother Carl, who was a great chef and big inspiration. With its subtle infusion of wine and pancetta, not to mention three types of ground meat, I think it's the absolute best Bolognese sauce I've ever had. Some Bolognese sauces add milk along with the tomatoes, but this one adds rich cream at the end to really round out the flavors. Serve this with spaghetti or another strand pasta, as well as penne, rotini, ziti, or farfalle.

   1/4 cup extra-virgin olive oil
   1 large onion, finely diced
   1 medium-size carrot, finely diced
   1 medium-size celery rib, finely diced
   1/4 pound sliced pancetta, finely diced
   1/2 pound ground beef
   1/2 pound ground veal
   1/2 pound ground pork
   2 large garlic cloves, minced
   3/4 cup dry white wine
   One 28-ounce can diced tomatoes,
      with their juices

1 cup low-sodium chicken broth

1/2 teaspoon dried thyme

1 imported bay leaf

Generous pinch each of salt and freshly
ground black pepper

1/4 cup heavy cream

2 tablespoons finely chopped fresh Italian
parsley leaves

1. In a large, heavy saucepan, heat 1 tablespoon
of the oil over medium heat. Add the onion,
carrot, celery, and pancetta and cook, stirring
occasionally, until softened but not browned,
about 8 minutes. Transfer the mixture to a bowl.

2. Add the remaining 3 tablespoons oil to the
saucepan and heat over medium-high heat until
shimmering. Add the ground beef, veal, and
pork and cook, breaking it into pieces, until just
firm but not cooked through, about 5 minutes.
Increase the heat to high, add the garlic, and
cook, stirring a few times, just until fragrant.
Add the wine and cook until nearly evaporated.
Add the tomatoes, broth, thyme, bay leaf, and
salt and pepper. Reduce the heat to medium-low
and cook, partially covered, until thickened,
about 1 hour. Stir in the cream and parsley and
taste again for salt and pepper. Will keep, covered, in the refrigerator for up to 4 days or in
the freezer for a month.

VEAL AND WILD MUSHROOM RAGU

MAKES ABOUT 4 CUPS, ENOUGH FOR
1 POUND PASTA (6 SERVINGS)

IN THIS CLASSIC ragu from the northern part
of Italy, succulent pieces of veal, seasoned with
rosemary and lemon zest, are slowly cooked with
dried wild mushrooms. I like the pungent flavor
of porcini mushrooms, but you can use morels,
chanterelles, or any other dried wild mushroom.
Serve this with pappardelle—wide noodles—and
thin shavings of good-quality parmesan cheese.

2 pounds boneless veal shoulder, trimmed of
fat and cut into scant 1/2-inch pieces

1/4 cup extra-virgin olive oil

Six 1-inch-wide strips lemon zest, removed
with a vegetable peeler

1 large sprig fresh rosemary, broken
into 1-inch pieces

Generous pinch each of salt and freshly
ground black pepper

1 ounce dried porcini mushrooms

1 cup boiling water

2 large carrots, finely diced

1 medium-size onion, finely diced

2 garlic cloves, minced

2 tablespoons all-purpose flour

1 1/2 cups dry white wine

1 1/2 cups low-sodium chicken broth

1 tablespoon fresh lemon juice

1 tablespoon finely chopped fresh Italian
parsley leaves

1. In a large bowl, combine the veal, 1 tablespoon of the oil, the lemon zest, rosemary, salt,

and pepper and let marinate for 30 minutes at room temperature or up to 2 hours in the refrigerator.

2. Meanwhile, in a small, heatproof bowl, soak the mushrooms in the boiling water until completely hydrated, about 20 minutes. Drain the mushrooms, reserving the soaking liquid. Briefly dip the mushrooms in clean water to dislodge any grit, then finely chop them. Let the soaking liquid settle, then slowly pour it into a clean cup, stopping when you get to the grit.

3. Heat 1 tablespoon of the oil in a large, deep skillet until shimmering over high heat. Add one-third of the veal, along with the lemon zest and rosemary, and cook until browned and crusty all over. Transfer the veal to a plate, then add the remaining 2 tablespoons oil to the skillet and brown the remaining meat, transferring it to the plate as it browns.

4. Add the chopped mushrooms, carrots, onion, and garlic to the skillet and cook, stirring occasionally, over medium-low heat until softened, 6 to 8 minutes. Sprinkle the flour over the vegetables, tossing until evenly coated. Add the wine and cook, scraping up any browned bits stuck to the pan, until slightly reduced.

5. Return the veal to the pan along with the broth and reserved mushroom soaking liquid and bring to a boil. Reduce the heat to medium-low and simmer until the sauce is thickened and the veal is meltingly tender, about 45 minutes. Season with salt and pepper, stir in the lemon juice and parsley, and discard the rosemary stems. Will keep, tightly covered, in the refrigerator for up to 4 days or in the freezer for a month.

TUSCAN HARE RAGU
MAKES ABOUT 4 CUPS, ENOUGH FOR
1 POUND PASTA (6 SERVINGS)

PAPPARDELLE—A WIDE ITALIAN noodle variety—is traditionally paired with this classic ragu from Tuscany, but it is also good with fettuccine, orrechiete, farfalle, and penne. Rabbit is becoming more widely available in the freezer section of most large supermarkets. Don't worry about cutting it up into perfectly neat pieces since the meat ends up getting pulled off the bones. Two large veal shanks or 1 small chicken make a perfectly acceptable alternative.

1/4 cup extra-virgin olive oil

4 strips bacon, cut into 1/4-inch pieces

One 2 1/2- to 3-pound rabbit, cut into 8 pieces

Salt and freshly ground black pepper

3 medium-size carrots, 1 finely chopped, 2 cut into 1-inch-thick rounds

1 small onion, finely chopped

1 celery rib, finely chopped

2 large garlic cloves, coarsely chopped

2 tablespoons all-purpose flour

1 cup dry white wine

2 cups low-sodium chicken broth

1 cup water

1 tablespoon tomato paste

1/2 teaspoon dried thyme

1 imported bay leaf

Pinch of sugar

1 cup pearl onions, peeled

2 tablespoons unsalted butter

10 ounces small white button mushrooms

LASAGNA BOLOGNESE

MAKES 6 SERVINGS

THIS CLASSIC LASAGNA, from northern Italy, uses creamy béchamel, a milk-based sauce, in place of the more familiar ricotta and mozzarella, and ragu Bolognese, a delicate tomato-meat sauce. I usually prefer fresh lasagna noodles to dried, but both work well here. Serve any remaining Bolognese on the side.

3/4 pound lasagna noodles (about 15), preferably imported

3 cups Bolognese Sauce (page 60)

3 1/2 cups Thick Béchamel (page 26)

1 cup freshly grated parmesan cheese

1. Preheat the oven to 400°F, and bring a large pot of salted water to a boil. Add the lasagna noodles and cook, stirring occasionally, until *al dente.* Drain and rinse well under cold running water. Arrange the noodles on a kitchen towel and cover with plastic wrap.

2. Spread 1 cup of the Bolognese Sauce over the bottom of a 2-quart glass or ceramic baking dish. Set aside the best third of the noodles for the top layer. Arrange one-third of the noodles in the baking dish in a slightly overlapping layer. Spread one-third of the béchamel on the pasta and top with 1 cup of the Bolognese. Sprinkle with 1/3 cup of the parmesan. Top with another layer of noodles and repeat with half of the remaining béchamel, 1 cup of the Bolognese, and 1/3 cup of the parmesan. Top with the remaining noodles. Spread the remaining béchamel on top and sprinkle with the remaining 1/3 cup parmesan.

3. Bake the lasagna until bubbling and the top is golden and crisp, about 45 minutes. Let rest 15 minutes before cutting into squares. Will keep, tightly covered, in the refrigerator for up to 2 days.

1. Heat 2 tablespoons of the oil in a large, deep skillet over medium-high heat until shimmering. Add the bacon and cook, stirring, until browned and crisp. Using a slotted spoon, transfer the bacon to a plate. Season the rabbit with salt and pepper, add it to the skillet, and cook over medium heat until browned all over, about 10 minutes. Transfer the rabbit to a platter.

2. Add the chopped carrot to the skillet along with the onion, celery, and garlic and cook, stirring a few times, until softened and browned, about 5 minutes. Sprinkle on the flour and cook for 1 minute. Add the wine and cook until thickened, scraping up any browned bits stuck to the pan, about 2 minutes.

3. Return the rabbit to the skillet along with the broth, water, tomato paste, thyme, bay leaf, and sugar. Season with salt and pepper and bring to a boil. Reduce the heat to medium-low and cook, partially covered, stirring occasionally, until the meat is tender and the sauce is slightly thickened, about 1 hour.

4. Transfer the rabbit to a platter. When cool enough to handle, pull the meat from the bones and cut or shred it into bite-size pieces. Strain the sauce through a fine-mesh sieve, pressing hard on the solids to extract as much of the gravy as possible. Return the sauce to the skillet along with the rabbit.

5. Meanwhile, steam the carrot pieces and pearl onions together until tender, about 7 minutes. Melt 1 tablespoon of the butter in 1 tablespoon of the olive oil in a large skillet over medium-high heat. Add the carrots and onions and cook until golden all over, about 6 minutes. Using a slotted spoon, transfer the carrots and onions to the sauce.

6. Melt the remaining 1 tablespoon butter in the remaining 1 tablespoon olive oil in the skillet over high heat. Add the mushrooms and cook, stirring occasionally, until golden all over, about 8 minutes. Using a slotted spoon, transfer the mushrooms to the sauce along with the bacon and simmer for 5 minutes to allow the flavors to blend. Season with salt and pepper. Will keep, tightly covered, in the refrigerator for up to 4 days or in the freezer for a month.

PORT CHICKEN LIVER RAGU

MAKES ABOUT 2½ CUPS, ENOUGH FOR
1 POUND PASTA (6 SERVINGS)

SALSA DI FEGATINI is a classic northern Italian sauce that features sautéed chicken livers, pancetta or prosciutto, and Marsala. I like the flavor of tawny or ruby port, in which the livers marinate briefly. The sauce is customarily served with pappardelle, a long pasta that is wider than fettuccine, but it's also wonderful with fettuccine or tagliatelle.

- 1 pound chicken livers, trimmed and cut into 1-inch pieces
- 3/4 cup tawny port
- 2 ounces sliced pancetta or bacon
- 1 tablespoon extra-virgin olive oil
- Salt and freshly ground black pepper
- 1/2 cup finely chopped shallots (about 4 medium-size)
- 1 cup low-sodium chicken broth
- Pinch of freshly grated nutmeg
- 1 tablespoon all-purpose flour mixed with 1½ tablespoons water
- 1 tablespoon finely chopped fresh tarragon or chervil leaves

1. In a medium-size bowl, toss the chicken livers with the port and marinate at room temperature for 30 minutes or in the refrigerator for up to 2 hours. Drain the livers, reserving the port separately, and pat them dry with paper towels.

2. In a large skillet, cook the pancetta in the oil over medium-high heat until browned and crisp.

Using a slotted spoon, transfer the pancetta to a cutting board and coarsely chop. Season the chicken livers with salt and pepper. Add them to the skillet and cook over medium-high heat, turning once, until browned and crusty on the outside but not cooked through, about 3 minutes. Transfer the chicken livers to a plate and keep warm.

3. Add the shallots to the skillet and cook over medium heat, stirring a few times, until softened, 3 to 4 minutes. Add the reserved port and cook until thick and syrupy, scraping up any browned bits stuck to the pan. Add the broth and nutmeg and bring to a boil. Whisk the flour mixture into the skillet and simmer until the sauce thickens. Return the chicken livers to the skillet and cook until heated through. Season with salt and pepper.

4. Just before serving, stir in the chopped pancetta and tarragon. This sauce is best used right away.

FRESH TOMATO SEAFOOD SAUCE

MAKES ABOUT 5 TO 6 CUPS, ENOUGH

FOR 1 POUND PASTA (6 SERVINGS)

FULL OF SEAFOOD—shrimp, scallops, squid, clams, and mussels—this quick-cooked pasta sauce works best with spaghetti, linguine, or other long pasta shapes. Because parmesan and other grating cheeses are so assertive and would overwhelm the delicate seafood flavor, this type of pasta sauce is never served with cheese.

1/4 cup extra-virgin olive oil

2 garlic cloves, thinly sliced

2 dozen cockles or Manila clams, scrubbed

2 dozen mussels, scrubbed and debearded

1 pound plum tomatoes, seeded and coarsely chopped

1/2 pound medium-size shrimp, peeled and deveined

1/2 pound cleaned small squid, bodies cut into 1/2-inch-wide rings and tentacles cut in half

1/4 pound bay scallops, or sea scallops, quartered

Salt and freshly ground black pepper

2 tablespoons finely chopped fresh Italian parsley leaves

Heat the olive oil in a large, deep skillet over high heat until shimmering. Add the garlic and cook, stirring, until lightly golden. Add the cockles and mussels and cook, stirring a few times, until they just begin to open, 4 to 5 minutes. Add the tomatoes, shrimp, squid, and scallops, season with salt and pepper, and cook just until the seafood is cooked through and the shells are opened, about 5 minutes longer. Discard any clams or mussels that will not open. Stir in the parsley and serve right away.

WHITE WINE SEAFOOD SAUCE

MAKES ABOUT 5 TO 6 CUPS, ENOUGH
FOR 1 POUND PASTA (6 SERVINGS)

THIS ELEGANT SEAFOOD pasta sauce combines all the basics of a white clam sauce (wine, olive oil, garlic, and tender clams) with the more luxurious seafood (scallops, shrimp, calamari, and mussels). Grated cheese is never served with this type of pasta sauce since its assertiveness would overwhelm the delicate flavor of the seafood. I like to cook the pasta—either spaghetti or linguine—in the sauce for 2 to 3 minutes so that it absorbs some of the flavor.

- 1/4 cup extra-virgin olive oil
- 2 garlic cloves, thinly sliced
- 2 dozen cockles or Manila clams, scrubbed
- 2 dozen mussels, scrubbed and debearded
- 1/2 cup dry white wine
- 1/2 cup water
- 1/2 pound medium-size shrimp, peeled and deveined
- 1/2 pound cleaned small squid, bodies cut into 1/4-inch-wide rings and tentacles cut in half
- 1/2 pound bay scallops, or sea scallops, quartered
- Salt and freshly ground black pepper
- 2 tablespoons finely chopped fresh Italian parsley leaves
- 1 teaspoon finely chopped fresh oregano leaves
- 1/2 teaspoon hot chile oil

1. Heat the oil in a large, deep skillet with a tight-fitting lid over high heat until shimmering.

Add the garlic and cook, stirring frequently, until golden, about 1 minute. Add the clams and mussels and cook, stirring, for 2 minutes. Add the wine and water, cover, and cook until most of the shells are opened, 4 to 5 minutes.

2. Add the remaining seafood, season with salt and pepper, and cook, stirring, until cooked through, 3 to 4 minutes longer.

3. Just before serving, stir in the parsley, oregano, and hot chile oil. Serve immediately.

PIQUANT TOMATO-CLAM SAUCE

MAKES 2 1/2 CUPS, ENOUGH FOR
12 OUNCES PASTA (4 SERVINGS)

A SPICY, PIQUANT variation on the familiar White Clam Sauce (right), except with the addition of fresh tomatoes, capers, and green olives. I like the briny flavor of Sicilian green olives—it echoes that of the clams. Cook the pasta—spaghetti, linguine, and bucatini are best—in the sauce for 1 to 2 minutes so that it absorbs some of the flavor.

- 18 littleneck clams, scrubbed and soaked in water for 1 hour
- 1/2 cup dry white wine
- 1/2 cup water
- 2 tablespoons extra-virgin olive oil
- 1 large garlic clove, thinly sliced
- 1/4 to 1/2 teaspoon red pepper flakes, to your taste

4 large plum tomatoes, seeded and coarsely chopped

1/4 cup pitted and sliced green olives

1 tablespoon capers, drained and chopped

Salt and freshly ground black pepper

1 tablespoon finely chopped fresh Italian parsley leaves

1. In a large saucepan, combine the clams, wine, and water. Cover and cook over high heat until the shells open, 6 to 8 minutes. Drain the clams, reserving the liquid separately. Remove the clams from their shells, discarding any clams that will not open. Briefly dip the clams in a bowl of water to remove any grit. Pat dry and coarsely chop. Pass the reserved clam juice through a coffee filter to remove any grit. Alternatively, let the liquid sit so the grit settles to the bottom, then slowly pour it into another container, stopping when you get to the grit.

2. Heat the oil in a large, deep skillet over high heat until shimmering. Add the garlic and cook, stirring, until lightly golden. Add the red pepper flakes and cook for 10 seconds. Add the tomatoes, olives, and capers and cook until the tomatoes just begin to break down, stirring a few times, about 5 minutes. Add 2/3 cup of the reserved clam juice and bring to a boil. Add the clams and cook just until heated through. Season with salt and pepper and stir in the parsley. This sauce is best used right away.

WHITE CLAM SAUCE

THERE IS NOTHING like the salty, sweet, and briny flavors that fresh clams impart to this sauce. I avoid canned clams altogether. Even though parmesan cheese is customarily not served with seafood, I sometimes make an exception with this sauce. Fruity extra-virgin olive oil adds another dimension to this quick and simple sauce. I like to finish cooking the pasta—linguine or spaghetti— in the sauce for the last 2 to 3 minutes to absorb some of the delicious sauce.

3 dozen littleneck or small cherrystone clams, scrubbed and soaked in water for 1 hour

3/4 cup dry white wine

1/2 cup water

1/4 cup plus 2 tablespoons fruity extra-virgin olive oil

2 large garlic cloves, minced

1/4 to 1/2 teaspoon red pepper flakes, to your taste

Salt and freshly ground black pepper

2 tablespoons finely chopped fresh Italian parsley leaves

1. In a large saucepan, combine the drained clams, wine, and water. Cover and cook over high heat, stirring occasionally, until the shells open, about 8 minutes. Drain the clams, reserving the liquid separately, discard any clams whose shells won't open, and remove the clams from the remaining shells. Briefly dip the clams in a bowl

of water to remove any grit. Pat dry and coarsely chop. Pass the reserved clam juice through a coffee filter to remove any grit. Alternatively, let the liquid sit so the grit settles to the bottom, then slowly pour it into another container, stopping when you get to the grit.

2. Heat the oil in a large, deep skillet over high heat until shimmering. Add the garlic and cook, stirring, until lightly golden. Add the red pepper flakes and reserved clam juice, and cook until reduced by half, 8 to 10 minutes. Add the clams, season lightly with salt and black pepper, and cook just until heated through. Just before serving, stir in the parsley. This is best used right away.

TOMATO SAUCE WITH TUNA

MAKES ABOUT 2½ CUPS, ENOUGH FOR
1 POUND PASTA (4 TO 6 SERVINGS)

ANOTHER CLASSIC tomato-based pasta sauce from southern Italy, this one uses canned tuna, packed in extra-virgin olive oil, imported from Italy, along with anchovies and garlic. Traditionally, it is served with perciatelli or bucatini, but you can serve it with any shape you like.

    2 pounds vine-ripened tomatoes or one
        28-ounce can peeled whole tomatoes,
        chopped
    3 tablespoons extra-virgin olive oil
    4 anchovies, rinsed and chopped
    2 large garlic cloves, lightly smashed

¼ teaspoon red pepper flakes
Pinch of sugar
Salt and freshly ground black pepper
One 6-ounce can or jar olive oil–packed
    tuna, imported from Italy, drained and
    lightly flaked

1. If using fresh tomatoes, bring a medium-size saucepan of water to a boil. Fill a medium-size bowl with ice water. Using a sharp paring knife, make a shallow X in the bottom of each tomato. Put the tomatoes in the boiling water for 15 to 20 seconds, remove with a slotted spoon, and plunge them immediately into the ice water to cool. Whether fresh or canned, peel, if necessary, core, seed, and coarsely chop the tomatoes.

2. Heat the oil in a large saucepan over medium-high heat until shimmering. Add the anchovies and garlic and cook, stirring, until the garlic is golden and the anchovies dissolve, about 3 minutes. Add the tomatoes and their juices, red pepper flakes, and sugar, season with salt and black pepper, and cook, stirring occasionally, until the juices have nearly evaporated and the garlic is tender, about 5 minutes. Remove the garlic from the sauce, mash it with a spoon, return it to the sauce along with the tuna, and cook, stirring, just until heated through. Will keep, tightly covered, in the refrigerator for up to 2 days. Reheat gently.

COLD SESAME SAUCE

MAKES ABOUT 1 CUP, ENOUGH
FOR 1 POUND PASTA (4 TO 6 SERVINGS)

ALTHOUGH COLD NOODLES with sesame sauce is standard fare in nearly every Chinese-American restaurant, it is rare to find a really good one. Either too thin or too thick, with an overwhelming flavor of sesame oil, the sauce inevitably disappoints. Serve this tossed with 1 pound cooked and chilled Chinese egg noodles or spaghetti, or with chilled poached chicken or shrimp.

2 tablespoons sesame seeds, preferably unhulled
1/3 cup smooth peanut butter, preferably natural
1/3 cup warm low-sodium chicken broth
1 tablespoon rice vinegar
2 tablespoons low-sodium soy sauce
1 teaspoon chili garlic sauce
1/2 teaspoon peeled and finely grated fresh ginger
1 small garlic clove, thinly sliced
2 scallions (white part only), thinly sliced
1/8 teaspoon toasted sesame oil
Pinch of salt
Pinch of freshly ground black pepper

1. In a small skillet, toast the sesame seeds over medium heat, shaking the pan, until lightly golden, about 2 minutes. Transfer the sesame seeds to a coffee grinder, let cool, then grind until a fine powder.

2. Transfer the ground sesame seeds to a blender or food processor, add the peanut butter, broth, vinegar, soy sauce, chili garlic sauce, ginger, and garlic, and process until smooth. Add the scallions, sesame oil, salt, and pepper and pulse until finely chopped. Will keep, tightly covered, in the refrigerator for up to 4 days.

CRISP-FRIED ALMOND AND GARLIC SAUCE

MAKES ABOUT 1/2 CUP, ENOUGH
FOR 1 POUND PASTA (4 TO 6 SERVINGS)

THIS NUTTY, LIGHT sauce is a sophisticated version of *aglio e olio*, classic garlic and oil. I've added a generous pinch of anise seeds to give the sauce a faint licorice tone, but you can use whole cumin, fennel, or caraway seeds; cracked coriander seeds; or cracked peppercorns. Serve this sauce with long pasta or fish, chicken, or veal.

1/4 cup fruity extra-virgin olive oil
1/3 cup sliced almonds
3 large garlic cloves, thinly sliced
1/2 teaspoon anise seeds
2 tablespoons finely chopped fresh Italian parsley leaves
Salt and freshly ground black pepper

In a medium-size skillet, heat the oil over medium-high heat until shimmering. Add the almonds and garlic and cook, stirring until golden, about 2 minutes. Add the anise seeds and cook just until fragrant, about 30 seconds longer, stirring constantly. Transfer to a small heatproof bowl, stir in the parsley and season with salt and pepper. This is best used right away.

TOMATO SAUCES

Being Italian, I assumed that tomatoes were a part of my ethnic culinary heritage forever, but they weren't. In fact, Europe had never seen a tomato before the sixteenth century. Tomatoes were native to South America, and it is believed that Spain's conquest of Mexico was responsible for their arrival in Europe. The Spanish Moors in particular were thought to have brought tomatoes to the Italians, who called them *pomodoro* (from *pomi di mori* or Moor's apples), and the French, who originally named them *pommes d'amoure* (which translates to "love apples," but phonetically "Moor's apples"). Oddly enough, it was Thomas Jefferson who brought the tomato back to the New World and ensured its popularity and place in American culinary history after his travels in France.

It's amazing how pervasive the tomato has become in world cuisines. The recipes here represent the foods of many different cultures, from the New World to the Old World and back. There is North African Tomato Sauce with Chickpeas and Sweet Spices; Catalan Tomato, Pepper, and Eggplant Sauce (also called Samfaina); Italian Pizzaiola; and American-Style Tomato Sauce. Traditional Mole Negro Sauce from Mexico should really begin the chapter, since that part of the world is where it all began in the first place.

When looking for fresh tomatoes, always choose firm but not ripe ones. They should yield a little when gently pressed. Peeling and seeding, which can seem daunting and tedious, is the best way to use fresh tomatoes. Quite simply, using a small, sharp knife, score the bottom with a shallow X, dip them in boiling water for a few seconds, then quickly transfer to a bowl of ice water. The skin slips off easily. Next, set a strainer over a bowl, halve the tomatoes across the middle, and scoop out the seeds into the strainer. Press any pulp and juices through the strainer, and discard the seeds. Chop the tomatoes and add them to the juice in the bowl. Done!

For canned tomatoes, I love imported San Marzano tomatoes from Italy. For best flavor, look for brands that don't contain citric acid. Several American brands are quite good too. Ones that come in enamel-lined cans are especially tasty.

Whether you use fresh or canned depends entirely on your mood and time constraints. Fresh will take a few minutes longer and, honestly, the longer you cook the sauce, the less it matters whether the tomatoes are fresh or not. In any case, this is one of my favorite chapters because tomato sauce is the first sauce I have strong memories of my mom and grandmothers making, many years ago.

AMERICAN-STYLE TOMATO SAUCE

MAKES ABOUT 3½ CUPS, ENOUGH FOR
1 POUND PASTA (6 SERVINGS)

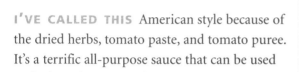

I'VE CALLED THIS American style because of the dried herbs, tomato paste, and tomato puree. It's a terrific all-purpose sauce that can be used as the base for many other sauces or dishes, like baked pastas, stewed chicken, or other meats.

2 tablespoons extra-virgin olive oil

2 garlic cloves, minced

1 small onion, finely chopped

One 28-ounce can tomato puree

2 tablespoons tomato paste

1 cup water

Pinch of sugar

½ teaspoon dried oregano, crumbled

½ teaspoon dried thyme

1 bay leaf

Salt and freshly ground black pepper

1 tablespoon unsalted butter

1. Heat the oil in a large saucepan over medium-high heat until shimmering. Add the garlic and onion and cook, stirring a few times, until lightly browned, 5 to 6 minutes. Add the tomato puree, tomato paste, water, sugar, and herbs. Season with salt and pepper and bring to a boil. Reduce the heat to low, cover partially, and simmer until thickened, about 45 minutes.

2. Stir in the butter and taste again for salt and pepper. Will keep, tightly covered, in the refrigerator for up to 5 days or in the freezer for a month.

PIZZAIOLA

MAKES ABOUT 2 CUPS, ENOUGH FOR
12 OUNCES PASTA (4 SERVINGS)

PIZZAIOLA REFERS TO the ingredients used in making pizzas—namely oregano, garlic, and tomatoes. This sauce is also great on pasta—penne, spaghetti, farfalle, fettuccine, and orecchiette—and grilled steaks or pork chops.

¼ cup extra-virgin olive oil

2 garlic cloves, minced

1 small onion, finely chopped

One 28-ounce can peeled whole tomatoes, with their juices, chopped

1 tablespoon tomato paste

Pinch of sugar

1 teaspoon dried oregano, crumbled

1 bay leaf

Salt and freshly ground black pepper

Heat the oil in a large saucepan over medium-high heat until shimmering. Add the garlic and onion and cook, stirring occasionally, until lightly browned, 5 to 6 minutes. Add the chopped tomatoes, tomato paste, sugar, oregano, and bay leaf, season with salt and pepper, and bring to a boil. Reduce the heat to low, cover partially, and simmer until thickened, about 30 minutes. Will keep, tightly covered, in the refrigerator for up to 5 days or in the freezer for a month.

CLASSIC MARINARA

MAKES 2½ TO 3 CUPS, ENOUGH FOR
12 OUNCES PASTA (4 SERVINGS)

THIS QUICKLY COOKED light tomato sauce was a staple in my house as a kid. It was served over pasta, with fried breaded veal cutlets, in lasagna, and with stuffed peppers, as well as a base for other dishes where a simple sauce was needed. Serve with all types of pasta.

- 2 pounds vine-ripened tomatoes or one 28-ounce can peeled whole tomatoes, drained (juices reserved)
- 2 tablespoons extra-virgin olive oil
- 1 large garlic clove, lightly smashed
- Pinch of red pepper flakes
- Pinch of sugar
- Salt and freshly ground black pepper
- 1 tablespoon finely chopped fresh basil leaves

1. If using fresh tomatoes, bring a medium-size saucepan of water to a boil. Fill a medium-size bowl with ice water. Using a sharp paring knife, make a shallow X in the bottom of each tomato. Blanch the tomatoes in the boiling water for 15 to 20 seconds, remove with a slotted spoon, and plunge them immediately into the ice water to cool. Whether using fresh or canned, peel, if necessary, core, seed, and coarsely chop the tomatoes.

2. Heat the oil in a medium-size saucepan over medium-high heat until shimmering. Add the garlic and cook, stirring, until golden and fragrant, 2 to 3 minutes. Add the red pepper flakes and cook for 10 seconds. Add the tomatoes and their juices (including the reserved juice, if using canned) and the sugar. Season with salt and black pepper and simmer over medium heat, stirring frequently, until slightly thickened, 15 to 20 minutes.

3. Using a fork, mash the garlic against the side of the saucepan. Stir in the basil. Will keep, tightly covered, in the refrigerator for up to 5 days or in the freezer for a month.

MY TOP 6 TOMATO SAUCES FOR LASAGNA

1. American-Style Meat Sauce (page 60)
2. American-Style Tomato Sauce (page 73)
3. Classic Marinara (left)
4. Hearty Italian Meat Sauce (page 58)
5. Tomato Cream Sauce (page 86)
6. Vodka Sauce (page 53)

CATALAN CITRUS TOMATO SAUCE

MAKES ABOUT 2½ CUPS

CATALAN COOKING USES many of the same ingredients as those of Provence, and in interesting combinations, such as citrus, especially orange, with tomato. This brightly flavored citrus-infused tomato sauce calls for Saffron-Scented Tomato Sauce or Tomato-Mint Sauce in the ingredient list. If you're short on time, a good-quality tomato puree or any leftover tomato sauce can be used in its place. Serve this sauce with any roasted meat or poultry or with poached fish or shellfish.

    ¼ cup extra-virgin olive oil
    1 medium-size Spanish onion, minced
    4 large garlic cloves, minced
    ¼ cup Madeira or Marsala
    1 recipe Saffron-Scented Tomato Sauce
        (page 91) or Tomato-Mint Sauce (page 89),
        pureed
    Finely grated zest and juice of 1 medium-
        size orange
    Finely grated zest and juice of
        1 small lemon
    Salt and freshly ground black pepper
    Pinch of cayenne pepper
    2 tablespoons finely chopped fresh Italian
        parsley leaves

1. Heat the oil in a large saucepan over low heat until shimmering. Add the onion and garlic and cook, stirring occasionally, until very soft, about 15 minutes.

2. Increase the heat to high, add the Madeira, and cook until evaporated. Add the tomato sauce and citrus zests and juices. Season with salt and black pepper, add the cayenne, and bring to a boil. Simmer, uncovered, over low heat, until slightly thickened, about 20 minutes. Stir in the parsley before serving. Will keep, tightly covered, in the refrigerator for up to 5 days.

CATALAN TOMATO, PEPPER, AND EGGPLANT SAUCE (SAMFAINA)

MAKES ABOUT 4 CUPS

TENDER, CREAMY EGGPLANT and sweet, tangy peppers add depth to this simple, rustic tomato sauce from Spain. Serve it with grilled or roasted meats or on grilled peasant bread. Smoked Spanish paprika, *pimenton*, is sold in gourmet shops and comes in either hot or sweet.

    1 medium-size eggplant (about 1 pound),
        peeled and cut into ½-inch cubes
    1 teaspoon kosher salt
    2 pounds ripe tomatoes or one 28-ounce can
        peeled whole tomatoes
    ¼ cup extra-virgin olive oil
    1 medium-size Spanish onion, finely chopped
    1 medium-size red bell pepper, seeded and
        cut into ½-inch pieces
    1½ teaspoons *pimenton dulce*
    ½ to ¾ cup low-sodium chicken broth, as
        needed
    Salt and freshly ground black pepper

1. Toss the eggplant with the kosher salt and let drain in a colander for 45 minutes. Gently squeeze out some of the excess liquid.

2. If using fresh tomatoes, bring a medium-size saucepan of water to a boil. Fill a medium-size bowl with ice water. Using a sharp paring knife, make a shallow X in the bottom of each tomato. Blanch the tomatoes in the boiling water for 15 to 20 seconds, remove with a slotted spoon and plunge them immediately into the ice water to cool. Whether using fresh or canned, peel, if necessary, core, seed, and coarsely chop the tomatoes.

3. Heat the oil in a large, deep skillet over medium-high heat until shimmering. Add the onion and cook, stirring a few times, until softened but not browned, about 5 minutes. Add the bell pepper and cook, stirring occasionally, until crisp-tender and the onion begins to brown, 7 to 8 minutes. Add the eggplant and *pimenton dulce*, reduce the heat to medium, and cook until softened, about 5 minutes. Add the tomatoes and ½ cup of the broth. Reduce the heat to low, season with salt and pepper, and simmer until the sauce thickens and the vegetables are tender, about 25 minutes. Add the remaining ¼ cup stock if the pan dries out. Will keep, tightly covered, in the refrigerator for up to 4 days.

PROVENÇAL FENNEL TOMATO SAUCE

MAKES ABOUT 3½ CUPS

THIS THICK AND chunky tomato sauce features several typical Provençal ingredients—fennel, herbes de Provence (a mixture of thyme, rosemary, lavender, marjoram, and savory), orange, and capers. It's perfectly suited for pasta (one pound of rigatoni, penne, ziti, farfalle, or fettuccine), as well as grilled and roasted meats. But I especially like to poach snapper fillets, shrimp, or chicken breasts in it.

    1 large red bell pepper
    2 tablespoons extra-virgin olive oil
    2 tablespoons unsalted butter
    1 large fennel bulb, cored, trimmed, and
        thinly sliced, feathery fronds reserved
    2 leeks (white and tender green parts),
        thinly sliced and washed well
    2 medium-size shallots, finely chopped
    ¼ cup dry red wine
    One 28-ounce can diced tomatoes, with
        their juices
    2 tablespoons capers, rinsed and chopped
    Finely grated zest of 1 orange
    1½ teaspoons dried herbes de Provence
    Salt and freshly ground black pepper
    1 tablespoon chopped fresh basil leaves

1. Rub the pepper very lightly with ½ teaspoon of the oil and broil or roast over a gas flame, turning, until blackened all over. Transfer the pepper to a bowl, cover with plastic wrap, and let steam for 15 minutes. When cool enough to

handle, peel, core, and remove the seeds and any tough inner ribs. Cut the pepper into thin strips.

2. In a large saucepan, melt the butter in the remaining oil over medium-high heat. Add the sliced fennel and cook, stirring occasionally, until softened, about 10 minutes. Add the leeks, shallots, and roasted red pepper and cook, stirring, until softened, about 5 minutes. Add the wine, scraping up any browned bits stuck to the bottom of the pan, and cook until evaporated, about 2 minutes. Add the tomatoes with their juices, capers, orange zest, and herbes de Provence and season with salt and pepper. Reduce the heat to low, cover partially, and cook until thickened slightly, about 20 minutes.

3. Coarsely chop 2 tablespoons of the feathery fronds and stir it into the sauce along with the basil. Will keep, tightly covered, in the refrigerator for up to 5 days or in the freezer for a month.

4 SUPER SAUCES FOR ENCHILADAS

1. Ancho Chile Cream Sauce (page 37)

2. Green Chile Tomato Sauce (right)

3. Mexican Tomato Sauce with Sofrito (page 81)

4. Red Chile Tomato Sauce (page 84)

GREEN CHILE TOMATO SAUCE

MAKES ABOUT 3 CUPS

ROASTED FRESH GREEN chiles—poblanos, Anaheims, New Mexican—add a unique smoky, slightly bitter flavor to this rustic tomato sauce. If you can't find any of the above chiles, large jalapeños are a good substitute, though they can be quite hot. Taste them after roasting to check their heat level. Use this sauce in any Latin American preparation, such as huevos rancheros, enchiladas, or fajitas, or with grilled or roasted meats.

> 2 pounds ripe tomatoes or one 28-ounce can peeled whole tomatoes, drained (juices reserved)
>
> 3 large green chiles
>
> 3 tablespoons vegetable oil
>
> 1 medium-size onion, finely chopped
>
> 1 large garlic clove, minced
>
> Salt and freshly ground black pepper
>
> 1 tablespoon unsalted butter

1. If using fresh tomatoes, bring a medium-size saucepan of water to a boil. Fill a medium-size bowl with ice water. Using a sharp paring knife, make a shallow X in the bottom of each tomato. Blanch the tomatoes in the boiling water for 15 to 20 seconds, remove with a slotted spoon, and plunge them immediately into the ice water to cool. Whether using fresh or canned, peel, if necessary, core, seed, and finely chop the tomatoes.

2. Lightly rub the chiles with ½ teaspoon of the

oil and roast over a gas flame or under a broiler until blackened all over, turning occasionally. Transfer the chiles to a bowl, cover with plastic wrap, and let steam until collapsed and cool. Peel, core, seed, and finely chop the chiles.

3. Heat the remaining oil in a large saucepan over medium-high heat until shimmering. Add the onion, garlic, and roasted chiles and cook, stirring frequently, until softened, about 5 minutes. Add the tomatoes with their juices (including the reserved juice if using canned), season with salt and pepper, and cook over medium heat until thickened, about 20 minutes. Will keep, tightly covered, in the refrigerator for up to 5 days or in the freezer for a month.

4. Defrost, if necessary, reheat, and stir in the butter right before serving.

NORTH AFRICAN TOMATO SAUCE WITH CHICKPEAS AND SWEET SPICES

MAKES ABOUT 4 CUPS

FOLLOW THE ANCIENT spice route and you'll find that many cultures combine sweet spices such as cinnamon, nutmeg, and allspice with savory ingredients. The sauce is perfectly suited to accompany lamb kebabs and couscous, but goes equally well with grilled meats and poultry or even pasta (rigatoni, penne, farfalle, rotini, or orecchiette). Or use it to braise succulent pieces of lamb, as in the North African Lamb Stew with Chickpeas and Raisins (right).

2 tablespoons extra-virgin olive oil

1 medium-size onion, finely chopped

1 large garlic clove, minced

1/2 teaspoon ground cumin

1/4 teaspoon ground cinnamon

Pinch of freshly grated nutmeg

Pinch of ground allspice

2 tablespoons tomato paste

One 28-ounce can diced tomatoes, with their juices

1 cup low-sodium beef broth

Salt

Cayenne pepper

1 cup canned chickpeas, rinsed and drained

1/4 cup golden raisins

2 tablespoons finely chopped fresh Italian parsley leaves

1. Heat the oil in a large saucepan over medium-high heat until shimmering. Add the onion and cook, stirring occasionally, until lightly browned, 6 to 8 minutes. Add the garlic, cumin, cinnamon, nutmeg, and allspice and cook until fragrant, about 1 minute. Add the tomato paste, reduce the heat to medium, and cook, stirring, until the onion is lightly caramelized, about 2 minutes. Add the tomatoes and broth, season with salt and cayenne, and bring to a boil. Reduce the heat to medium-low and simmer until slightly thickened, about 20 minutes.

2. Add the chickpeas and raisins and simmer until heated through and the sauce is slightly reduced, about 5 minutes. Taste for salt and cayenne and stir in the parsley. Will keep, tightly covered, in the refrigerator for up to 5 days or in the freezer for a month.

NORTH AFRICAN LAMB STEW WITH CHICKPEAS AND RAISINS

MAKES 6 SERVINGS

TENDER, SUCCULENT PIECES of lamb are slowly simmered in this rich, fragrant sauce. Serve it over couscous, rice, orzo, polenta, or wide egg noodles.

1/4 cup extra-virgin olive oil

2 1/4 pounds boneless lean lamb shoulder, trimmed of fat and cut into 1-inch pieces

Salt and freshly ground black pepper

1/2 cup dry red wine

1 tablespoon all-purpose flour

1 recipe North African Tomato Sauce with Chickpeas and Sweet Spices (left)

2 cups low-sodium beef broth

Pinch of sugar

2 large carrots, cut into 1-inch-thick rounds

1. Heat 1 tablespoon of the oil in a large enameled cast-iron casserole or Dutch oven over medium-high heat until shimmering. Season the lamb with salt and pepper, add one-third to the casserole, and cook until browned and crusty on all sides, about 8 minutes. Transfer the lamb to a plate and brown the remaining meat in the remaining 3 tablespoons oil in two more batches, transferring it to the plate as it browns.

2. Return the meat to the casserole. Add the wine and cook, scraping up any browned bits stuck to the pan, until the liquid is evaporated, 3 to 4 minutes. Sprinkle the flour over the meat and toss to coat. Add the tomato sauce, broth, and sugar, season with salt and pepper, and bring to a boil. Reduce the heat to low, partially cover, and cook, stirring occasionally, until the meat is just tender, about 1 hour. Add the carrots and simmer until the meat and carrots are tender, about 1 hour longer. Will keep, tightly covered, in the refrigerator for up to 4 days or in the freezer for a month.

TOMATO, ANCHO, AND PUMPKIN SEED SAUCE (PEPIAN)

MAKES 4 1/2 TO 5 CUPS

PEPIAN, A MEAT or poultry stew made with pumpkin seeds, nuts, tomatoes, and chiles, somewhat resembles mole, but without the chocolate. Traveling around Guatemala a number of years ago, I had the opportunity to sample this version, made with pumpkin seeds, almonds, anchos, and orange juice. Brown the meat (chicken, beef, goat, or pork) and simmer it in the sauce until tender.

- 1/2 cup raw shelled pumpkin seeds
- 1/4 cup blanched whole almonds
- 2 pounds vine-ripened tomatoes or one 28-ounce can peeled whole tomatoes, drained (juices reserved)
- 2 ancho chiles
- 1 large red bell pepper, seeded and coarsely chopped
- 1 medium-size onion, coarsely chopped
- 2 large garlic cloves, chopped
- 1/4 teaspoon ground cinnamon
- 1/4 teaspoon ground cloves or allspice
- Salt and freshly ground black pepper
- 1/4 cup peanut or other mild-flavored vegetable oil
- 1 cup low-sodium chicken broth
- 1/4 cup orange juice
- 2 tablespoons fresh lime juice

1. Preheat the oven to 350°F. Put the pumpkin seeds in a pie plate and toast until golden and beginning to pop, about 5 minutes. Put the almonds in the pie plate and toast until golden, 8 to 10 minutes. Let cool, then combine in a food processor and pulse until finely ground.

2. If using fresh tomatoes, bring a medium-size saucepan of water to a boil. Fill a medium-size bowl with ice water. Using a sharp paring knife, make a shallow X in the bottom of each tomato. Blanch the tomatoes in the boiling water for 15 to 20 seconds, remove with a slotted spoon, and plunge them immediately into the ice water to cool. Whether using fresh or canned, peel, if necessary, core, seed, and coarsely chop the tomatoes. Reserve the blanching water and return to a boil.

3. Using kitchen scissors, cut the anchos into large pieces. Heat a cast-iron griddle or skillet until hot to the touch. Place the anchos on the hot griddle and press with a metal spatula until pliable, about 15 seconds per side. Put the chiles in a heatproof bowl, cover with 1 cup of the boiling water and let soak until softened, about 30 minutes.

4. Transfer the chiles with their soaking water to a blender along with the tomatoes, red bell pepper, onion, and garlic and process to a smooth paste. Add the ground nuts, cinnamon, and cloves and pulse to combine. Season with salt and pepper.

5. Heat the oil in a large saucepan over low heat until shimmering. Add the tomato mixture, cover partially, and cook, stirring, until thickened and has the consistency of thin porridge, about 20 minutes.

6. Add the broth, orange juice, and lime juice and simmer, partially covered, until thickened, about 45 minutes. Will keep, tightly covered, in the refrigerator for up to 5 days or in the freezer for a month.

MEXICAN TOMATO SAUCE WITH SOFRITO

MAKES 3½ CUPS

SOFRITO **IN SPANISH** cooking is simply a mixture of aromatic vegetables much like a French *mirepoix*—onion, carrot, and celery, which are sautéed and used to season sauces and stews. In Latin American cooking, the mixture usually consists of onion, garlic, and peppers. I like the assertive, slightly bitter flavor of poblano chiles, but jalapeños are a good substitute. Use this chunky sauce with grilled or roasted meats, poultry, and fish or with cheese and scrambled eggs rolled in tortillas.

- 2 tablespoons vegetable oil
- 1 large onion, finely chopped
- 2 large garlic cloves, minced
- 1 medium-size red or small green bell pepper, seeded and finely chopped
- 1 large poblano chile, seeded and finely chopped
- 1 small canned chipotle chile packed in adobo sauce, seeded and minced
- 1 teaspoon ground cumin
- ½ teaspoon ground coriander
- ¼ teaspoon dried oregano, preferably Mexican, crumbled
- Salt and freshly ground black pepper
- One 28-ounce can peeled whole tomatoes, with their juices, chopped
- 2 tablespoons finely chopped fresh cilantro leaves

1. Heat the oil in a large saucepan over medium-high heat until shimmering. Add the onion, garlic, red bell pepper, and poblano and cook until softened, about 8 minutes, stirring frequently.

2. Add the cumin, coriander, and oregano, season with salt and black pepper, and cook until fragrant, about 1 minute. Stir in the tomatoes and cook over medium-low heat until thickened, 15 to 20 minutes. Stir in the cilantro. Will keep, tightly covered, in the refrigerator for up to 5 days or in the freezer for a month.

TRADITIONAL MOLE NEGRO SAUCE

MAKES ABOUT 8 CUPS

MOLE, **A DERIVATION** of the Nahuatl word *molli*, simply means "a sauce made with chiles." With so many different chiles and so many different regions in Mexico, it's difficult to say just how many variations there really are. Nearly every region—and every household—boasts its own version. *Mole negro,* Mexico's prized sauce, is a delicate blend of dried chiles, the variety of which depends upon the region, almonds, peanuts, sweet spices, dried fruit, tomatoes, and unsweetened chocolate. It is traditionally served with turkey, but can also be paired with game hens, chicken, pork, or veal. Brown the meat and simmer it in the sauce until tender, adding more broth as necessary. Pasilla chiles have a subtle smoky, raisin-like flavor, similar to that of the ancho and mulato chiles. The mulato chile also has a chocolaty undertone, making it a great choice for mole. This delicious mole came from my good friends Laura Annunziata and her husband, Arnoldo Borja. This makes enough to cook 4 large chickens, cut into pieces. It freezes extremely well.

1 medium-size vine-ripened tomato
4 ancho chiles, seeded
4 dried pasilla chiles, seeded
4 dried mulato chiles, seeded
1 dried chipotle chile (optional), seeded
1 large Spanish onion, chopped
4 large garlic cloves, chopped
2 slices firm-textured white bread, toasted
3/4 cup blanched whole almonds
1/2 cup dry-roasted unsalted peanuts
1/2 cup dark raisins or dried apricots
2 tablespoons sesame seeds
1 teaspoon dried oregano, preferably Mexican, crumbled
1/2 teaspoon dried thyme
1 teaspoon ground coriander
1/2 teaspoon ground cinnamon
1/8 teaspoon ground cloves or allspice
1/4 cup vegetable oil
2 ounces unsweetened chocolate, chopped
2 cups low-sodium chicken broth
Salt and freshly ground black pepper

1. Bring a medium-size saucepan of water to a boil. Fill a medium-size bowl with ice water. Using a sharp paring knife, make a shallow X in the bottom of the tomato. Blanch the tomato in the boiling water for 15 to 20 seconds, remove with a slotted spoon, and plunge it immediately into the ice water to cool. Peel, core, seed, and coarsely chop the tomato. Reserve the blanching water and keep warm.

2. Using kitchen scissors, cut the dried chiles into large pieces. Heat a cast-iron griddle or skillet until hot to the touch. Place the chile pieces on the hot griddle, in batches, and press with a metal spatula until pliable, about 15 seconds per side. Put the chiles in a heatproof bowl; cover with the hot blanching water and let soak until softened, about 30 minutes.

3. Transfer the chiles with 2 cups of their soaking water to a blender along with the tomatoes, onion, and garlic and process until fairly smooth. Using a rubber spatula or wooden spoon, scrape the mixture through a fine-mesh sieve, pressing hard on the solids to remove any skin or seeds. Transfer the chile mixture to a medium-size bowl. Add the bread, almonds, peanuts, raisins, 1 tablespoon of the sesame seeds, oregano, thyme, coriander, cinnamon, and cloves, combine well, transfer to the blender in batches, and process into a thick paste. Add additional blanching water, if necessary, to loosen up.

4. Heat the oil in a large saucepan over medium-low heat until shimmering. Add the chile paste and cook, stirring occasionally, until it is thick, pasty, and has the consistency of loose mashed potatoes. Be careful of the sputtering that you don't get burned. Add the chocolate and stir until melted. Stir in the broth and cook until the sauce has the consistency of thin sour cream, about 25 minutes more. Season with salt and pepper and stir in the remaining 1 tablespoon sesame seeds. Will keep, tightly covered, in the refrigerator for up to 5 days or in the freezer for a month.

TIPS FOR PUTTING TOGETHER A STEW OR BRAISE

- Before you start, thoroughly pat dry the meat, poultry, or seafood, then season with salt and pepper.

- Heat the oil, generally about 1 tablespoon per pound of meat, until shimmering. Be sure the pan is hot enough so the meat immediately sizzles. Begin at medium-high heat, but lower the temperature if the pan begins to burn.

- Don't overcrowd the pan. Cooking the meat in batches will ensure even browning, which is key to a successful stew. If the pan is crowded, the meat will release a lot of liquid very quickly and steam instead of sauté. Some liquid is expected; just cook long enough for the juices to evaporate and the meat to brown.

- Once the meat is thoroughly browned and crusty, usually between 8 and 15 minutes, depending on size of the pieces and moisture content, transfer it to a large plate and continue with the remaining meat, adding additional oil as needed.

- If the pan juices are very caramelized and stuck to the bottom before all of the meat is browned, add about ½ cup water to the empty pan and scrape up the browned bits (this is called deglazing). Pour the juices into a cup—this is instant stock and will enrich your stew! Wipe out the pan, heat fresh oil, and continue to brown the remaining meat.

- Once the meat is browned, pour off any excess oil. Add a bit of fresh oil before adding chopped aromatics like onion, garlic, carrots, etc., and cook, stirring, over medium heat until softened.

- Return all of the meat to the pan, then add the sauce of your choice and any accumulated meat juices from the platter. Add any deglazed pan juices, bay leaves, a bouquet garni, or other seasonings and bring to a gentle boil. Cover and cook over low heat on the stove or in a low oven (300°F) until the meat is tender, anywhere from 1 to 4 hours, depending upon the size and type of meats. Larger cuts, such as lamb shanks, pork shoulder, veal shanks, and beef (brisket, oxtail, short ribs), can take 3 to 4 hours. Dark-meat chicken and turkey and seafood will take about 1 hour, whereas stew meat (1- to 2-inch pieces) should be somewhere in the middle, 1½ to 2 hours.

RED CHILE TOMATO SAUCE (CHILE COLORADO)

MAKES ABOUT 3 1/2 CUPS

GUAJILLO CHILES ARE most commonly used in red chile sauce because of their distinctive fruity flavor and bright red color. I like the slight smokiness of anchos, so I've added a few for depth. Use this fairly mild chile sauce as a base for enchiladas, *carne adobo* (beef, pork, lamb, or goat stew with chiles), or Pork Colorado (right). New Mexican chiles can be substituted for the guajillo, and mulato chiles can be substituted for the ancho. For a hotter chile sauce, add 1 or 2 dried chipotles or moritas along with the anchos.

- 2 medium-size vine-ripened tomatoes
- 4 dried guajillo chiles
- 2 dried ancho chiles
- 3 cups boiling water
- 1 large onion, coarsely chopped
- 2 garlic cloves, coarsely chopped
- 1/2 teaspoon dried oregano, preferably Mexican, crumbled
- 1/4 teaspoon dried thyme
- 1/2 small bay leaf
- Pinch of ground cinnamon
- Pinch of ground cloves
- 1/4 cup peanut oil or other mild-flavored vegetable oil
- 2 cups low-sodium chicken broth
- Pinch of sugar
- Salt

1. Bring a medium-size saucepan of water to a boil. Fill a medium-size bowl with ice water. Using a sharp paring knife, make a shallow X in the bottom of each tomato. Blanch the tomatoes in the boiling water for 15 to 20 seconds, remove with a slotted spoon, and plunge them immediately into the ice water to cool. Peel, core, seed, and coarsely chop the tomatoes. Reserve the blanching water and return to a boil.

2. Using kitchen scissors, cut the guajillos and anchos into large pieces. Heat a cast-iron griddle or skillet until hot to the touch. Place them on the hot griddle and press with a metal spatula until pliable, about 15 seconds per side. Put the chiles in a heatproof bowl; cover with the boiling water and let soak until softened, about 30 minutes.

3. Drain the chiles, reserving the soaking water. Place them in a blender, add the tomatoes, onion, garlic, oregano, thyme, bay leaf, cinnamon, and cloves and process until coarsely chopped. Add 1 cup of the chile soaking water and process into a smooth paste. Pass the puree through a fine-mesh sieve, pressing hard on the solids to remove any bits of skin and seeds.

4. Heat the oil in a large saucepan over medium heat until shimmering. Add the chile paste and cook, stirring, until sizzling and very thick, about 10 minutes. Add the broth and sugar, season with salt, and simmer until slightly reduced, about 20 minutes. Will keep, tightly covered, in the refrigerator for up to 5 days or in the freezer for a month.

PORK COLORADO
(PORK IN RED CHILE SAUCE)

MAKES 6 SERVINGS

SERVE THIS SIMPLE pork chile with rice and tortillas, chopped cilantro, and sliced fresh chiles.

2 pounds boneless pork shoulder, trimmed of fat and cut into 1-inch pieces

2 teaspoons salt, or more to taste

2 tablespoons lard or vegetable oil

1 small onion, finely chopped

1 garlic clove, minced

1½ cups Red Chile Tomato Sauce (left)

Pinch of sugar

Freshly ground black pepper

1. Put the pork in a large saucepan, add enough water to barely cover and the 2 teaspoons salt, and bring to a boil. Reduce the heat to medium-low and simmer, partially covered, until the pork is barely tender, about 30 minutes. Drain the pork, reserving the broth separately. Skim any excess fat from the surface of the broth. Wipe out the saucepan.

2. Return the saucepan to medium-high heat and melt the lard. Add the pork and cook, stirring occasionally, until lightly browned on all sides. Add the onion and garlic and cook, stirring, until softened, about 4 minutes. Add the tomato sauce, 1½ cups of the reserved pork broth, and the sugar. Season with salt and pepper and bring to a boil. Reduce the heat to low and simmer, uncovered, until the pork is very tender and the sauce is slightly thickened, about 1 hour longer, adding more of the broth if necessary. Will keep, tightly covered, in the refrigerator for up to 4 days or in the freezer for a month.

GREEN OLIVE AND CAPER BERRY TOMATO SAUCE

MAKES ABOUT 3½ CUPS

THE LEMON ZEST accentuates the tartness of the olives and caper berries, while the butter mellows and rounds out the sauce. Caper berries aren't really berries at all, but what's left of a blossom after the petals fall off. They are packed in brine in jars and available at most gourmet markets or ethnic food stores. Discard any caper berries with tough, seedy interiors. If you can't find caper berries, substitute capers, which are about one-sixth the size and taste similar. Serve this sauce as a condiment with grilled steaks, swordfish, and salmon, or as a medium for braising pork chops or chicken breasts.

2 tablespoons unsalted butter

2 tablespoons extra-virgin olive oil

2 leeks (white and tender green parts), split lengthwise, washed well, and thinly sliced

One 28-ounce can peeled whole tomatoes, with their juices, chopped

1 teaspoon finely grated lemon zest

1 imported bay leaf

Salt and freshly ground black pepper

½ cup pitted and sliced green olives, such as picholine or Sicilian

¼ cup caper berries, stemmed and quartered

1 tablespoon finely chopped fresh tarragon leaves

1. In a large saucepan, melt the butter in the oil over medium heat. Add the leeks and cook, stirring, until softened but not browned, 2 to 3 minutes. Add the tomatoes, lemon zest, and bay leaf, season with salt and pepper, and bring to a boil. Reduce the heat to medium-low and simmer, stirring occasionally, until slightly thickened, about 15 minutes.

2. Add the olives and caper berries and simmer 10 minutes longer. Taste for salt and pepper and stir in the tarragon. Discard the bay leaf. Will keep, tightly covered, in the refrigerator for up to 4 days or in the freezer for a month.

TOMATO CREAM SAUCE

MAKES ABOUT 2½ CUPS

THIS VERSATILE CREAM sauce goes well with pasta (especially fettuccine, pappardelle, penne, ziti, and farfalle), poached eggs, and poached fish or chicken.

1½ pounds ripe tomatoes

2 tablespoons unsalted butter

1 large shallot, minced

Salt

Cayenne pepper

¾ cup heavy cream

1 tablespoon tomato paste

1 tablespoon finely chopped fresh tarragon or chervil leaves

1. Bring a medium-size saucepan of water to a boil. Fill a medium-size bowl with ice water. Using a sharp paring knife, make a shallow X in the bottom of each tomato. Blanch the tomatoes in the boiling water for 15 to 20 seconds, remove with a slotted spoon, and plunge them immediately into the ice water to cool. Peel, core, seed, and coarsely chop the tomatoes.

2. Melt the butter in a medium-size saucepan over medium heat. When the foam subsides, add the shallot and cook, stirring, until softened but not browned, about 3 minutes. Add the tomatoes, season with salt and cayenne, and simmer until softened and the liquid has evaporated, about 20 minutes.

3. Add the cream and tomato paste and cook over medium-high heat until slightly reduced, about 5 minutes.

4. Transfer the sauce to a blender and process until smooth. Return the sauce to the saucepan, season with salt and cayenne, gently reheat to a simmer, and stir in the tarragon. Will keep, tightly covered, in the refrigerator for up to 3 days.

SMOKY PAN-BLACKENED TOMATO SAUCE

MAKES ABOUT 2½ CUPS

I LOVE THE simplicity of this quick tomato sauce. Use it on all kinds of pasta, especially fettuccine, linguine, and farfalle, or in lasagna, spread over pizza, or as a sauce for braising or poaching meats and fish. Cast-iron grill pans are wonderful for infusing a smoky, charred flavor without lighting a fire or letting small pieces fall through the grates. If you don't have one, broil

the tomatoes and garlic on a shelf nearest the heat source. *Pimenton dulce,* or smoked sweet Spanish paprika, is available at gourmet markets.

6 large garlic cloves, unpeeled
2 pounds ripe plum tomatoes, quartered lengthwise and seeded
One 3-inch sprig fresh rosemary
¼ cup extra-virgin olive oil
1 teaspoon *pimenton dulce* (optional)
1 tablespoon balsamic vinegar
1 tablespoon fresh lemon juice
Salt and freshly ground black pepper

1. Preheat a cast-iron grill pan over medium heat. In a medium-size bowl, combine the garlic cloves, tomatoes, rosemary, and 1 tablespoon of the oil. Add the garlic cloves to the grill pan and cook, turning occasionally, until softened and the skins are blackened in spots. Transfer to a small bowl to cool. Peel the garlic.

2. Meanwhile, place the rosemary and tomatoes on the grill pan, skin side down, and cook until softened and the skins are blackened, 6 to 7 minutes. Transfer to the medium-size bowl, cover with plastic wrap, and let sit for 10 minutes.

3. Remove the leaves from the rosemary sprig and transfer them to a blender along with the peeled garlic, *pimenton dulce,* vinegar, and lemon juice and pulse until chopped. Add the tomatoes with any accumulated juices and process until smooth. With the machine running, add the remaining 3 tablespoons olive oil in a thin stream and process until the mixture thickens. Season with salt and pepper and reheat gently before using. Will keep, tightly covered, in the refrigerator for up to 3 days.

BEST TOMATO SAUCES TO USE AS THE BASIS FOR A STEW OR BRAISE

After each recipe title you'll find listed the kind and amount of meat, poultry, and/or seafood appropriate to cook in that sauce. For all these recipes, if using them in a stew or braise, be sure to check it while cooking and add a bit of water or broth as necessary to prevent scorching.

- Spicy Coconut Curry Tomato Sauce (page 226): about 2 pounds chicken parts, lamb, goat, or beef stew meat, meatballs, or shelled and deveined large shrimp

- Thai Red Curry Coconut Sauce (page 227): about 2 pounds chicken parts or beef stew meat, or shelled and deveined large shrimp

- West African Spiced Curry Tomato Sauce (page 230): about 2 pounds chicken parts, lamb, veal, goat, or beef stew meat, meatballs, shelled and deveined large shrimp, 4 lamb shanks, or mixed root vegetables

- American-Style Tomato Sauce (page 73): about 3 pounds boneless pork shoulder, beef, veal, goat, or lamb stew meat, chicken parts, or meatballs

- Green Chile Tomato Sauce (page 77): about 3 pounds boneless pork shoulder, beef, goat, or lamb stew meat, chicken parts, or meatballs

- Red Chile Tomato Sauce (page 84): 3½ to 4 pounds boneless pork shoulder, beef, goat, veal, or lamb stew meat, chicken parts, or meatballs

- Tomato, Ancho, and Pumpkin Seed Sauce (Pepian) (page 80): about 6 pounds boneless pork shoulder, beef, goat, or lamb stew meat, chicken parts, or turkey drumsticks

- Traditional Mole Negro Sauce (page 81): about 8 pounds boneless pork shoulder, beef, goat, or lamb stew meat, chicken parts, or turkey drumsticks

- Green Olive and Caper Berry Tomato Sauce (page 86): about 3 pounds boneless pork shoulder, beef, goat, or lamb stew meat, chicken parts, or meatballs

- North African Tomato Sauce with Chickpeas and Sweet Spices (page 78): about 3 pounds boneless pork shoulder, beef, goat, or lamb stew meat, chicken parts, meatballs, or 4 lamb or veal shanks

TOMATO SAUCE WITH OLIVES, RAISINS, AND PIGNOLI

MAKES ABOUT 3 CUPS

COMMON IN SICILIAN cooking, raisins are combined with savory ingredients, such as tomatoes, olives, and toasted pine nuts, as in this thick, chunky robust sauce. Serve with grilled lamb chops, swordfish, and rib-eye steaks or roasted chicken.

2 tablespoons extra-virgin olive oil

1 large onion, chopped

1 garlic clove, minced

1 teaspoon sugar

One 28-ounce can peeled whole tomatoes, drained and coarsely chopped

1 tablespoon red wine vinegar

1/2 cup pitted and sliced green olives, preferably Sicilian

1/4 cup raisins

Salt and freshly ground black pepper

1/4 cup pine nuts

1 tablespoon finely chopped fresh basil leaves

1 tablespoon unsalted butter

1. Heat the oil in a large saucepan over medium heat until shimmering. Add the onion, garlic, and sugar and cook, stirring, until softened and just beginning to brown, 6 to 8 minutes. Add the drained tomatoes and vinegar and bring to a boil. Add the olives and raisins, reduce the heat, and simmer until the sauce thickens and the liquid is evaporated, about 15 minutes. Season with salt and pepper.

2. Meanwhile, toast the pine nuts in a small skillet over medium-high heat, stirring or shaking constantly, until golden brown, 3 to 4 minutes. Transfer them immediately to a plate to stop the cooking and let them cool.

3. Just before serving, stir the pine nuts, basil, and butter into the hot sauce. Will keep, tightly covered, in the refrigerator for up to 3 days.

TOMATO-MINT SAUCE

MAKES ABOUT 2 1/2 CUPS

THIS CHUNKY, FRESH tomato sauce is especially good on grilled swordfish, lamb chops, or steak. Plum tomatoes are slightly less juicy than vine-ripened tomatoes and therefore well suited to this sauce and are available (and fairly decent) all year long.

2 pounds ripe tomatoes

1/4 cup extra-virgin olive oil

2 large scallions, finely chopped

1 garlic clove, minced

Pinch of red pepper flakes

Salt and freshly ground black pepper

2 tablespoons finely chopped fresh spearmint leaves

1. Bring a large saucepan of water to a boil. Fill a medium-size bowl with ice water. Using a sharp paring knife, make a shallow X in the bottom of each tomato. Blanch the tomatoes in the boiling water for 15 to 20 seconds, remove with a slotted

MUSSELS MARINIERE

MAKES 6 SERVINGS

I LIKE USING cultivated mussels for this recipe because they require much less scrubbing and they are almost completely grit free. This makes a great first course for six or a hearty meal for four if you serve a salad alongside.

Six 3/4-inch-thick slices Tuscan or peasant bread
1/4 cup extra-virgin olive oil
5 garlic cloves, 4 lightly smashed, 1 halved
4 pounds mussels, scrubbed and debearded
2 cups Saffron-Scented Tomato Sauce (right)
1/4 teaspoon red pepper flakes

1. Preheat the oven to 350°F. Lightly brush the bread on both sides with 2 tablespoons of the oil and arrange them on a large baking sheet. Bake until golden and crisp, about 15 minutes, turning them halfway through. Rub the halved garlic clove on one side of each of the toasts.

2. Heat the remaining 2 tablespoons oil in a large soup pot over high heat. Add smashed garlic cloves and cook, stirring, until golden, about 2 minutes. Add the mussels and toss to coat with the oil. Add the tomato sauce and red pepper flakes, cover, and cook, stirring occasionally, until nearly all of the shells have opened, 5 to 8 minutes. Discard any mussels whose shells will not open.

3. Place a toast in each of 6 large, deep bowls, spoon the mussels and sauce on top, and serve immediately.

spoon, and plunge them immediately into the ice water to cool. Peel, core, seed, and coarsely chop the tomatoes.

2. Heat the oil in a large saucepan over high heat until shimmering. Add the scallions and garlic and cook, stirring, until softened, about 1 minute. Add the red pepper flakes and tomatoes, season with salt and black pepper, and cook until the liquid is evaporated and the sauce thickens, about 10 minutes.

3. Just before using, stir in the mint and taste again for salt and black pepper. Will keep, tightly covered, in the refrigerator for up to 2 days.

SAFFRON-SCENTED TOMATO SAUCE

MAKES ABOUT 2½ CUPS

I LOVE THE combination of saffron and tomato with seafood—the basic flavors of bouillabaisse, a Provençal fish stew. This sauce goes well with grilled or poached fish but I also like to poach mussels in it and serve it with lots of garlic-rubbed toasted bread. Saffron threads, part of the crocus flower, are far superior to powdered saffron, which often contains paprika, and a little really goes a long way—a good thing since it's quite expensive.

Scant ¼ teaspoon saffron threads, crushed

½ cup dry white wine

2 tablespoons unsalted butter

2 tablespoons extra-virgin olive oil

2 medium-size shallots, minced

One 28-ounce can peeled whole tomatoes, with their juices, finely chopped

1 cup low-sodium chicken broth

1 imported bay leaf

1 large sprig fresh thyme

½ teaspoon dried herbes de Provence

Pinch of sugar

Salt

Cayenne pepper

1. In a small bowl, crush the saffron with the back of a spoon into a coarse powder. Add the wine and let sit for 5 minutes.

2. Melt the butter in the oil in a large saucepan over medium-high heat. Add the shallots and cook, stirring occasionally, until lightly browned, 3 to 4 minutes. Add the saffron-infused wine and cook until reduced by two-thirds, about 5 minutes. Add the tomatoes, broth, bay leaf, thyme, herbes de Provence, and sugar, season with salt and cayenne, reduce the heat to medium-low, and simmer, stirring occasionally, until slightly thickened, 25 minutes.

3. Discard the bay leaf and thyme. Puree the sauce in a blender for a smoother texture, if desired. Will keep, tightly covered, in the refrigerator for up to 5 days or in the freezer for 1 month.

PESTOS

Until fairly recently, the combination of basil, garlic, oil, and parmesan stood exclusively for pesto. The classic definition of a pesto is a mixture of herbs and seasonings pounded in a mortar with a pestle to be used with pasta or in vegetable soup (pistou) but those parameters are quickly changing. Gremolata, a classic Italian herb mixture traditionally stirred into braised veal shanks (osso buco), is like pesto minus the oil and cheese. Many pestos can be made in a food processor, which opens the door to a whole host of new ideas. Sun-dried tomatoes, roasted peppers, herbs and olives, nuts, and chiles are just some of the ingredients you can try in pesto-style preparations. And pesto is not just for pasta anymore—use it as a condiment, a kicky addition to meatball, burger, and/or meatloaf mixtures, stirred into mayonnaise for a sandwich spread, even added to fondue.

CLASSIC PESTO GENOVESE

MAKES ABOUT 1 CUP

I LIKE USING a mix of parmesan and Pecorino Romano cheeses for a more complex flavor. The little bit of butter at the end rounds out the flavors and mellows the garlic.

1/4 cup pine nuts

2 cups loosely packed fresh basil leaves, torn

2 tablespoons tightly packed fresh Italian parsley leaves

2 garlic cloves, coarsely chopped

1/2 cup extra-virgin olive oil

1/4 cup freshly grated parmesan cheese

2 tablespoons freshly grated Pecorino Romano cheese

1 tablespoon unsalted butter, softened

Salt and freshly ground black pepper

1. Toast the pine nuts in a small, dry skillet over medium heat, stirring or shaking frequently until golden, 3 to 4 minutes. Transfer immediately to a plate to stop the cooking and let cool.

2. In a large mortar using a pestle, pound together the basil, parsley, garlic, and pine nuts a little at a time, adding more when there's room. When the pesto is roughly pounded, add the oil in a thin stream, pounding and stirring until all has been added. Stir in the cheeses and butter and season with salt and pepper. Will keep, tightly covered, in the refrigerator for up to 4 days.

Food Processor Method: Combine the basil, parsley, garlic, and pine nuts in a food processor or blender and pulse until finely chopped. With the machine running, add the oil in a thin stream and process until fairly smooth. Add the cheeses and butter and process until smooth. Season with salt and pepper.

TIPS FOR SUCCESSFUL PESTO

- Be sure that the herbs are washed and well dried before making pesto. Water will make it difficult to pound or puree the leaves.

- Season the finished pesto generously with salt and pepper to bring out the flavor of the herbs.

- Make sure all toasted nuts have been cooled to room temperature before pounding or processing. Warm nuts will make the pesto soggy.

- Pounding in a mortar will yield a more rustic pesto; using the food processor a more uniform pesto.

PESTO TRAPANESE

MAKES ABOUT 1 CUP

PESTO TRAPANESE, FROM Trapani in Sicily, is very similar to Classic Pesto Genovese (left), but with the addition of tomato and the use of Pecorino, a sheep's milk cheese that is a bit more assertive than parmesan, which is made from cow's milk. The tomato dulls the vibrant green of the basil a bit, but adds flavor and moisture. Use it as you would any other pesto.

- 1/4 cup pine nuts
- 2 cups loosely packed fresh basil leaves
- 2 tablespoons tightly packed fresh Italian parsley leaves
- 2 garlic cloves, coarsely chopped
- 1 plum tomato, peeled, seeded, and coarsely chopped
- 1/2 cup extra-virgin olive oil
- 1/4 cup freshly grated Pecorino Romano cheese
- Salt and freshly ground black pepper

1. Toast the pine nuts in a small, dry skillet over medium heat, shaking or stirring frequently, until golden, 3 to 4 minutes. Transfer to a plate immediately to stop the cooking and let cool.

2. Combine the basil, parsley, garlic, and pine nuts in a food processor or blender and pulse until finely chopped. Add the tomato and pulse until finely chopped. With the machine running, add the oil in a thin stream and process until fairly smooth. Add the cheese and process until smooth. Season with salt and pepper. Will keep, tightly covered, in the refrigerator for up to 3 days.

PISTOU

MAKES ABOUT 1 CUP

THE ONLY MAJOR difference between pistou and pesto is the country of origin. Pistou is from the Provence region of France while pesto is Italian. Both are garlic and basil sauces, both use extra-virgin olive oil, parmesan cheese, and pine nuts. Pistou is also the name of a vegetable-based soup served with the sauce at the table. This pistou is a little looser than Classic Pesto Genovese (left). Use it as you would any pesto.

- 2 cups loosely packed fresh basil leaves
- 2 garlic cloves, coarsely chopped
- 2 tablespoons pine nuts
- 1/2 cup extra-virgin olive oil
- 1/4 cup freshly grated parmesan cheese
- Salt and freshly ground black pepper

Combine the basil, garlic, and pine nuts in a food processor or blender and pulse until finely chopped. With the machine running, add the oil in a thin stream and process until smooth. Add the cheese and pulse until combined. Season with salt and pepper. Will keep, tightly covered, in the refrigerator for up to 4 days.

HERB PESTO WITH FRIED BREAD CRUMBS

MAKES ABOUT 1 CUP

SPRINKLE THIS BREAD crumb "pesto" over pasta. Don't toss the pasta after adding it, or it will lose its delicious crunch. It's also great on grilled steak.

- ¼ cup plus 2 tablespoons extra-virgin olive oil
- 1 cup cubed (¼-inch) crustless Italian bread
- 1 large garlic clove, smashed
- ½ cup tightly packed fresh basil leaves
- ¼ cup tightly packed fresh Italian parsley leaves
- ¼ cup freshly grated parmesan cheese
- Salt and freshly ground black pepper

1. Heat 2 tablespoons of the oil in a large skillet over medium heat until shimmering. Add the bread cubes and garlic and cook, stirring frequently, until golden and crisp, 5 to 6 minutes. Transfer the bread and garlic to a plate and let cool.

2. In a mini–food processor, combine the basil, parsley, and cooled garlic clove and pulse until finely chopped. Add the parmesan and pulse just until combined. With the machine running, add the remaining ¼ cup oil in a thin stream and process until fairly smooth. Add the bread cubes and pulse until coarsely chopped. Season with salt and pepper. This is best used right away.

15 BEST PESTOS FOR TOSSING WITH PASTA

MIXED HERB PESTO ENRICHED WITH EGG YOLKS

MAKES 2/3 CUP

COOKED EGG YOLK adds richness and body to this herby pesto. It's wonderful with pastas like penne, rotini, and long pastas such as spaghetti or bucatini.

1 large garlic clove, smashed

Large pinch of salt

1/2 cup tightly packed fresh basil leaves

1/4 cup tightly packed fresh Italian parsley leaves

2 tablespoons tightly packed fresh mint leaves

2 tablespoons snipped fresh chives

1 large hard-cooked egg yolk, pushed through a fine-mesh sieve

1 tablespoon white wine vinegar

1/4 cup extra-virgin olive oil

1/4 cup freshly grated parmesan cheese

Freshly ground black pepper

In a large mortar using a pestle, pound the garlic and salt together into a paste. Add the herbs, a little at a time, adding more when there's room and pounding them into a coarse paste. Stir in the egg yolk and vinegar. In a thin stream, add the oil, pounding and stirring until fairly smooth. Stir in the cheese, taste for salt, and season with pepper. Will keep, tightly covered, in the refrigerator for up to 3 days.

Food Processor Method: Pulse the garlic and salt together until finely chopped. Add the herbs and pulse until finely chopped. Add the egg and vinegar. With the machine running, add the oil in a thin stream and process until fairly smooth. Pulse in the cheese, taste for salt, and season with pepper.

SUMMER HERB PESTO

MAKES 1 CUP

DURING THE HEIGHT of the summer, when my herb garden tends to look like a jungle, I like to run out there and pluck whatever's in abundance—usually a little bit of everything. This recipe is more of a guide than anything else. By all means, let your mood and garden dictate.

1/2 cup extra-virgin olive oil

1/4 cup pine nuts

1 large garlic clove, smashed

1 1/2 cups loosely packed mixed fresh herbs, such as basil, parsley, mint, cilantro, tarragon, chives, chervil, lovage, thyme, and/or rosemary (the majority being soft, fragrant herbs like basil, parsley, and mint)

1/4 cup freshly grated parmesan cheese

Salt and freshly ground black pepper

1. Heat 1 teaspoon of the oil in a small skillet over medium heat. Add the pine nuts and cook, stirring constantly until golden, 2 to 3 minutes. Transfer the nuts to a plate and let cool.

2. In a large mortar using a pestle, pound the garlic and herbs together, a little at a time, adding more when there's room. Add the pine nuts and pound until roughly chopped. Add the remaining oil in a thin stream, pounding and stirring to a coarse puree. Stir in the parmesan and season with salt and pepper. Will keep, tightly covered, in the refrigerator for up to 3 days.

Food Processor Method: Combine the garlic and herbs in a food processor and pulse until coarsely chopped. Add the pine nuts and pulse until finely chopped. With the machine running, add the remaining oil in a thin stream and process until fairly smooth. Add the parmesan and season with salt and pepper.

TIPS FOR FREEZING PESTO

- I have always found that pesto freezes extremely well if you leave out the cheese (though I'm not exactly sure why). You can always add the cheese later.

- Freeze pesto in ice cube trays. Once completely frozen, transfer the cubes to a resealable bag and use them as needed. This keeps the pesto especially fresh because you're only thawing what you need. Another benefit is that the cubes thaw rather quickly.

PIGNOLI-HERB SAUCE

MAKES ABOUT 2/3 CUP

SIMILAR TO PESTO, only slightly looser and nuttier and without cheese, this sauce is great on pasta, steamed veggies, potatoes, tomato salads, and grilled veggies, meats, poultry, and seafood.

1/2 cup extra-virgin olive oil

1/4 cup pine nuts

2 small garlic cloves, coarsely chopped

1/4 cup loosely packed fresh basil leaves, torn

1/4 cup loosely packed fresh Italian parsley leaves

20 small fresh mint leaves

1 tablespoon snipped fresh chives

Salt and freshly ground black pepper

1. Heat 1 teaspoon of the oil in a small skillet over medium heat. Add the pine nuts and cook, stirring constantly, until golden, about 3 minutes. Drain on paper towels and let cool.

2. Pulse the garlic and herbs together in a mini–food processor until finely chopped. Add the pine nuts and pulse until the mixture is roughly pureed. While the machine is running, add the remaining oil in a thin stream and process into a coarse puree. Season with salt and pepper.

TOASTED BREAD CRUMB, ROSEMARY, AND PARMESAN PESTO

MAKES ABOUT 2/3 CUP

SICILIANS SERVE TOASTED bread crumbs on spaghetti in place of grated cheese when the sauce is seafood based. This pesto is a slightly more complex variation. It does call for cheese, so I wouldn't use it with seafood, but it is great with pasta *aglio e olio* (spaghetti with garlic and oil) or on grilled rib-eye steaks, roasted vegetables, or braised veal shanks.

> 2 large slices good-quality white sandwich bread
> 1 teaspoon minced fresh rosemary leaves
> 3 tablespoons pure olive oil
> 2 tablespoons freshly grated parmesan cheese
> Salt and freshly ground black pepper

1. Lightly toast the bread and let sit until cool and slightly dried out. Tear the bread into small pieces, transfer to a food processor, and pulse to coarse crumbs.

2. In a medium-size bowl, combine the bread crumbs, rosemary, and 2 tablespoons of the oil and stir until moistened.

3. Heat a medium-size skillet over medium heat until hot to the touch. Add the bread crumbs and cook, stirring constantly, until golden and crisp, 5 to 6 minutes. Transfer the bread crumbs to a bowl and let cool. Stir in the parmesan and remaining 1 tablespoon oil and season with salt and pepper. This is best used right away.

MINT, PARSLEY, AND SCALLION PESTO

MAKES ABOUT 3/4 CUP

TOSS THIS MINTY pesto with boiled potatoes or pastas like penne or rotini, or dollop on grilled steaks or pork chops.

> 1/2 cup tightly packed fresh Italian parsley leaves
> 1/4 cup tightly packed fresh mint leaves
> 2 medium-size scallions, thinly sliced
> 1/4 cup shelled roasted, salted sunflower seeds
> 6 tablespoons extra-virgin olive oil
> 1 tablespoon fresh lemon juice
> 1/2 teaspoon finely grated lemon zest
> Salt and freshly ground black pepper

In a large mortar, using a pestle, pound the parsley, mint, and scallions together a little at a time, adding more when there's room. Add the sunflower seeds and pound until roughly chopped. Add the oil in a thin stream, pounding and stirring to a coarse puree. Stir in the lemon juice and zest and season with salt and pepper. Will keep, tightly covered, in the refrigerator for up to 3 days.

Food Processor Method: combine the herbs and scallions in a food processor and pulse until coarsely chopped. Add the sunflower seeds and pulse until finely chopped. With the machine running, add the oil in a thin stream and process until fairly smooth. Pulse in the lemon juice and zest and season with salt and pepper.

PESTO-STUFFED CHICKEN

MAKES 4 SERVINGS

MANY OF THE pestos contained in this book can be stuffed under the skin of chicken breasts, but sage is such a classic seasoning for poultry that it's my personal favorite. Chill the pesto for easier stuffing. Browning the chicken in a skillet and finishing it in the oven creates moist, evenly cooked meat with an exceptionally crispy skin. This recipe also works well with some of the other pestos in this chapter, including the following: Spinach-Pignoli Pesto with Raisins (page 107); Herb Pesto with Fried Bread Crumbs (page 96); Artichoke Pesto with Almonds and White Wine (page 108); Olive, Caper, and Mint Pesto (page 102); Wild Mushroom and Herb Pesto (page 110); and Sun-Dried Tomato Pesto (page 113).

4 bone-in chicken breast halves (about 8 ounces each)

¼ cup Fried Sage and Caper Pesto with Fresh Pecorino (right; or another pesto listed in headnote), chilled

Salt and freshly ground black pepper

1 tablespoon extra-virgin olive oil

1 tablespoon fresh lemon juice

½ cup low-sodium chicken broth

1. Preheat the oven to 425°F. Make a pocket under the skin of each chicken breast: Slip a finger under the skin at the point where the wing was attached and separate the skin from the breast, leaving it attached all around the edges. Divide the pesto into fourths and roll each into a 2-inch-long log. Slip the pesto under the skin and gently press it to flatten and spread it out. Season the chicken with salt and pepper.

2. Heat the oil in a large, ovenproof skillet over medium-high heat until shimmering. Add the chicken, skin side down, and cook until golden, about 5 minutes. Turn the chicken and roast in the oven until cooked through, about 15 minutes. Transfer the chicken to a plate.

3. Spoon off the excess fat from the skillet and set it over medium heat. Add the lemon juice and broth and cook, scraping up any browned bits stuck to the bottom of the pan, until reduced to ¼ cup, about 5 minutes. Pour the pan juices into a bowl and serve alongside the chicken.

FRIED SAGE AND CAPER PESTO WITH FRESH PECORINO

MAKES ABOUT 1/2 CUP

FRYING SAGE LEAVES mellows their intense flavor and adds a nutty crispness to this pesto. Use it with pasta, with grilled or roasted meats, or as a spread for grilled bread with tomatoes and mozzarella.

> 1/4 cup extra-virgin olive oil
>
> 1 cup lightly packed fresh sage leaves
>
> 1 medium-size garlic clove, smashed
>
> Pinch of salt
>
> 1/4 cup tightly packed fresh Italian parsley leaves
>
> 2 tablespoons small capers, drained
>
> 1/4 cup freshly grated Pecorino Tuscano or Sardo cheese
>
> Freshly ground black pepper

1. Heat the oil in a small skillet over medium-high heat until shimmering. Add the sage leaves in several batches and fry until crisp, about 15 seconds. Drain on paper towels. Let the oil cool.

2. In a large mortar using a pestle, pound the garlic and salt into a paste. Add the parsley and capers and pound until coarsely pureed. Add the crisp sage leaves and pound until fine. Add 2 tablespoons of the sage oil in a thin stream, pounding and stirring, until fairly smooth. Add the cheese, taste for salt, and season with pepper. Will keep, tightly covered, in the refrigerator for up to 2 days.

Food Processor Method: Pulse the garlic and salt together in a mini–food processor until finely chopped. Add the parsley and capers and pulse until finely chopped. Add the fried sage leaves and pulse until finely chopped. With the machine running, add 2 tablespoons of the sage oil in a thin stream and process until fairly smooth. Add the cheese and pulse until combined. Taste for salt and season with pepper.

MORE TIPS FOR FREEZING PESTO

- If you intend to freeze the pesto from the start, make sure that the herbs are not soggy with water. Too much water will cause ice crystals to form when the pesto is in the freezer, which will weaken its flavor and texture.

- Pesto will freeze even better if there's slightly more oil in the mix. The fat envelops the herbs, protecting them from potential freezer burn. If you intend to freeze the pesto from the start, add a few more tablespoons oil or, even better, a few tablespoons of butter.

MINT AND ALMOND PESTO

MAKES ABOUT ¾ CUP

I LIKE TO serve this refreshing mint sauce with grilled lamb, either a butterflied boneless leg of lamb or thick, meaty chops. It's also surprisingly good with pasta and potatoes, hot or cold, and fresh summer tomato salads.

  ½ cup blanched whole almonds

  1 large garlic clove, smashed

  Large pinch of salt

  ½ cup loosely packed fresh mint leaves

  ¼ cup loosely packed fresh Italian parsley leaves

  ¼ cup extra-virgin olive oil

  1 teaspoon fresh lemon juice

  ½ teaspoon finely grated lemon zest

  Freshly ground black pepper

1. Preheat the oven to 350°F. Spread the almonds in a pie plate and toast until golden and fragrant, about 10 minutes. Transfer to a plate to cool, then coarsely chop.

2. In a large mortar using a pestle, pound the garlic with the salt until pasty. Add the mint and parsley and pound into a coarse paste. Add the toasted almonds and pound until broken into small pieces. Add the oil in a thin stream, pounding and stirring into a chunky puree. Stir in the lemon juice and zest and season with salt and pepper. Will keep for 2 days in the refrigerator.

Food Processor Method: Combine the garlic, salt, mint, and parsley in a food processor and pulse until coarsely chopped. Add the almonds and pulse until coarsely chopped. While the machine is running, add the oil in a thin stream through the feed tube and process to a coarse paste. Stir in the lemon juice and zest and season with salt and pepper.

OLIVE, CAPER, AND MINT PESTO

MAKES ABOUT 1 CUP

I LIKE USING a mix of oil- and brine-cured olives for a more complex pesto. Look for plump, juicy olives sold loose, available at specialty stores or at the deli counter, rather than the jarred variety.

  2 tablespoons tightly packed fresh mint leaves

  2 tablespoons small capers, rinsed

  1 large garlic clove, smashed

  ½ teaspoon finely grated lemon zest

  Pinch of red pepper flakes

  ¼ cup extra-virgin olive oil

  1 cup pitted mixed olives, such as Moroccan, Kalamata, Cerignola, Sicilian, and/or niçoise

  Salt and freshly ground black pepper

In a food processor, combine the mint, capers, garlic, lemon zest, and red pepper flakes. While the machine is running, add the oil in a thin stream and process until finely chopped. Add the olives and pulse until roughly chopped. Season with salt and pepper. Will keep, tightly covered, in the refrigerator for up to 4 days.

PARSLEY PESTO ENRICHED WITH EGG YOLKS

MAKES ABOUT 2/3 CUP

THE ADDITION OF hard-cooked egg yolks yields a creamier, richer pesto. Use as you would any classic pesto.

¼ cup pine nuts

¼ cup extra-virgin olive oil

1 large garlic clove, smashed

2 anchovy fillets, coarsely chopped

Large pinch of salt

1 cup tightly packed fresh Italian parsley leaves

2 tablespoons tightly packed fresh tarragon leaves

1 tablespoon fresh lemon juice

1 large hard-cooked egg yolk, pushed through a fine-mesh sieve

Freshly ground black pepper

1. Heat 1 teaspoon of the oil in a small skillet over medium heat. Add the pine nuts and cook, stirring constantly, until golden, about 3 minutes. Drain on paper towels and let cool.

2. In a large mortar using a pestle, pound the garlic, anchovies, and salt together into a paste. Add the parsley, tarragon, and pine nuts a little at a time, adding more as there is room, and pound into a coarse paste. Stir in the lemon juice and egg yolk. Add the remaining oil in a thin stream, pounding and stirring, until fairly smooth. Taste for salt and season with pepper. Will keep, tightly covered, in the refrigerator for up to 4 days.

Food Processor Method: Pulse the garlic, anchovies, and salt together until finely chopped. Add the herbs and pine nuts and pulse until finely chopped. Pulse in the lemon juice and egg yolk. While the machine is running, add the oil in a thin stream and process until fairly smooth. Taste for salt and season with pepper.

PESTO—WHY STOP AT PASTA?

- Stir into mayonnaise for a sandwich spread.

- Stir into cream cheese or goat cheese for a spread for toasted slices of French bread, bagels, etc.

- Add to ground meat for meatballs or burgers.

- Add to marinades.

- Whisk into vinaigrettes.

- Knead into bread dough.

- Use as a pizza topping.

- Stir into softened goat cheese and milk for a crudité dip.

- Add to potato or pasta salads.

- Stir into soups.

- Stir into softened butter for an instant compound butter (you can freeze this almost indefinitely).

PARSLEY SAUCE
(SALSA VERDE)

MAKES 1 CUP

SALSA VERDE IS ubiquitous throughout Latin America. There are probably more variations on this sauce than any other one. I happen to love the licorice-y flavors of tarragon and chervil, but sometimes chervil is difficult to find. If you have trouble just double the tarragon. Serve this with grilled meats, fish, and poultry.

- 1/2 cup finely chopped fresh Italian parsley leaves
- 1 tablespoon finely chopped fresh chervil leaves
- 1 tablespoon finely chopped fresh tarragon leaves
- 1 tablespoon finely chopped fresh basil leaves
- 1 tablespoon chopped capers
- 2 anchovy fillets, mashed
- 2 garlic cloves, minced
- 1 small shallot, minced
- 1/2 cup pure olive oil
- Salt and freshly ground black pepper

In a mortar using a pestle, pound the parsley, chervil, tarragon, basil, capers, anchovies, garlic, and shallot together into a coarse paste. Stir in the oil and season with salt and pepper. Will keep, tightly covered, in the refrigerator for up to 3 days.

SALSINA VERDE

MAKES 1 CUP

SALSINA VERDE IS an Italian version of salsa verde. The oregano, anchovies, and capers give it an entirely Mediterranean flavor. It's great with meats, poultry, fish, and grilled vegetables and with a long pasta like spaghetti or linguine.

- 6 tablespoons extra-virgin olive oil
- 6 plump anchovy fillets, rinsed
- 1 teaspoon minced garlic
- 1 cup tightly packed fresh Italian parsley leaves
- 3 tablespoons small capers, rinsed
- 1 tablespoon fresh oregano leaves
- 1 teaspoon fresh thyme leaves
- 1 teaspoon fresh lemon juice
- Salt and freshly ground black pepper

1. Heat the oil in a small skillet over medium heat until shimmering. Add the anchovies and garlic and cook, stirring, until the garlic is golden and the anchovies begin to fall apart, about 1 minute. Scrape the mixture into a small bowl and let cool.

2. In a large mortar using a pestle, pound the parsley, capers, oregano, and thyme together a little at a time, adding more when there's room, until lightly crushed. Add the anchovy mixture in a thin stream, pounding until coarsely pureed. Stir in the lemon juice and season with salt and pepper. Will keep, tightly covered, in the refrigerator for up to 4 days.

CHIMICHURRI

MAKES ABOUT 1³/4 CUPS

THIS TANGY BRAZILIAN herb sauce is a traditional accompaniment to mixed grilled meats—*churrasco*—but it's also terrific with fish, vegetables, and potatoes.

- 1 cup pure olive oil
- 2 garlic cloves, minced
- 1 serrano chile, thinly sliced (don't remove the seeds)
- 1¹/2 tablespoons red pepper flakes
- ³/4 cup finely chopped fresh Italian parsley (leaves from about 1 bunch)
- 1/4 cup finely chopped fresh oregano leaves
- 1/4 cup finely chopped fresh cilantro leaves
- 1 medium-size shallot, minced
- 2 tablespoons red wine vinegar
- Salt and freshly ground black pepper

1. In a small skillet, heat the oil with the garlic, chile, and red pepper flakes just until warm, about 1 minute. Transfer to a bowl and let cool.

2. Add the parsley, oregano, cilantro, shallot, and vinegar and season with salt and pepper. Will keep, tightly covered, in the refrigerator for up to 2 days.

ANCHOVY-PARSLEY PESTO

MAKES ABOUT ³/4 CUP

I LOVE THIS intense pesto with pasta as well as spread on grilled bread and topped with thick slices of tomato or mozzarella (or both!).

- 1/4 cup extra-virgin olive oil
- 1/4 cup sliced almonds or pine nuts
- One 2-ounce can oil-packed flat anchovies, drained and coarsely chopped
- 1 large garlic clove, smashed
- 1/4 teaspoon red pepper flakes
- Pinch of salt
- 1 cup tightly packed fresh Italian parsley leaves
- 1/4 cup freshly grated Pecorino Tuscano or parmesan cheese
- 1 tablespoon fresh lemon juice
- 1 tablespoon unsalted butter, softened

1. Heat ¹/2 teaspoon of the oil in a small skillet over medium heat. Add the nuts and cook, stirring constantly, until golden, 2 to 3 minutes. Drain on paper towels and let cool.

2. In a large mortar using a pestle, pound together the anchovies, garlic, red pepper flakes, and salt. While pounding, add the parsley, a little at a time, adding more when there's room. Add the pine nuts and pound until finely chopped. Add the remaining oil in a thin stream, pounding and stirring until incorporated. Stir in the cheese, lemon juice, and butter and taste for salt. Will keep, tightly covered, in the refrigerator for up to 4 days.

Food Processor Method: put the anchovies, garlic, and red pepper flakes in a mini–food processor and pulse until finely chopped. Add the parsley and almonds and process until finely chopped. With the machine running, add the remaining oil in a thin stream and process until fairly smooth. Add the cheese, lemon juice, and butter and process until smooth. Taste for salt.

ANCHOIADE

MAKES ABOUT 1 CUP

THIS CLASSIC RECIPE from Provence is used with vegetables and poached chicken, but I also love it with boiled potatoes, pastas such as penne, rotini, and spaghetti, and sautéed spinach and broccoli rabe. The parsley helps balance the intensity of the garlic and anchovies.

6 large garlic cloves, smashed

Two 2-ounce cans oil-packed flat anchovies, drained and chopped

2 tablespoons finely chopped fresh Italian parsley leaves

1½ tablespoons red wine vinegar

½ cup extra-virgin olive oil

Freshly ground black pepper

In a mortar using a pestle, pound the garlic with the anchovies into a paste. Stir in the parsley and vinegar. Add the oil in a thin stream, pounding and stirring until incorporated. Season with pepper. Will keep, tightly covered, in the refrigerator for up to 4 days.

CREAMY ARUGULA PESTO

MAKES ABOUT 2/3 CUP

THIS PESTO MAKES a great sandwich spread. It's relatively low in fat but very substantial.

1 small garlic clove, smashed

Pinch of salt

¼ cup farmer's cheese

1 cup tightly packed arugula leaves, chopped

2 tablespoons extra-virgin olive oil

2 tablespoons freshly grated parmesan cheese

2 teaspoons fresh lemon juice

Freshly ground black pepper

In a mini–food processor, pulse the garlic and salt together until finely chopped. Add the farmer's cheese and process until smooth, scraping down the sides of the bowl as needed. Add the arugula and pulse until finely chopped. While the machine is running, add the oil in a thin stream and process until fairly smooth. Add the parmesan and lemon juice and process just until combined. Season with salt and pepper. Will keep, tightly covered, in the refrigerator for up to 3 days.

SPINACH-PIGNOLI PESTO WITH RAISINS

MAKES 1 CUP

THIS PESTO IS great spread on grilled bread, stirred into beef or pork stews, or served on grilled pork chops, lamb chops, or beefsteaks.

1/4 cup extra-virgin olive oil

1/4 cup pine nuts

One 10-ounce bag curly spinach, stems and inner ribs removed

1 garlic clove, smashed

1 anchovy fillet, coarsely chopped

Salt

1/4 cup freshly grated parmesan or Pecorino Toscano cheese

1 teaspoon fresh lemon juice

2 tablespoons raisins, coarsely chopped

Freshly ground black pepper

1. Heat 1 teaspoon of the oil in a small skillet over medium heat. Add the pine nuts and cook, stirring constantly, until golden, about 3 minutes. Drain on paper towels and let cool.

2. Bring a large saucepan of water to a boil. Add the spinach and cook just until wilted but not tender, about 10 seconds. Drain and plunge into a bowl of ice water. Drain again and pat somewhat dry. Finely chop the spinach.

3. Pulse the garlic and anchovy together in a mini–food processor until finely chopped. Add the spinach and pine nuts and pulse until roughly pureed. While the machine is running, add the remaining oil in a thin stream and process until fairly smooth. Pulse in the cheese and lemon juice. Add the raisins and pulse just until combined. Season with salt and pepper. Will keep, tightly covered, in the refrigerator for up to 3 days.

10 BEST PESTOS TO SPREAD ON CROSTINI

SWEET PEA PESTO WITH CHIVE OIL

MAKES ABOUT 3/4 CUP

I USUALLY WAIT for the fresh tender young peas of spring to make this recipe. When I can't, good-quality frozen baby peas are a remarkably good substitution. I like to spread this pesto on toasted baguette slices, drizzled with a bit more of the chive oil and sprinkled with coarse sea salt or crumbled bacon for a delicious appetizer.

1/2 cup coarsely snipped fresh chives

2 tablespoons water

1/2 cup peanut or other mild-flavored vegetable oil

Salt

1 pound fresh peas, shelled (1 cup), or 1 cup frozen baby peas, thawed

1 tablespoon extra-virgin olive oil

1 small shallot, minced

1 tablespoon fresh lemon juice

Freshly ground white pepper

1 teaspoon finely chopped fresh tarragon leaves

1. In a mini–food processor or blender, combine the chives and water and process until fairly smooth. While the machine is running, add the peanut oil in a thin stream and process until smooth. Transfer the mixture to a jar and let sit for 1 hour, shaking the jar from time to time. Strain the mixture through a fine-mesh sieve, pressing hard on the solids. Season with salt.

2. If using fresh peas, bring a medium-size saucepan of salted water to a boil. Add the peas and cook until tender and bright green, about 5 minutes. Drain.

3. Heat the olive oil in a small skillet over medium heat. Add the shallot and cook, stirring, until softened but not browned, about 3 minutes. Add the peas and cook just until heated through.

4. Transfer the mixture to a food processor along with the lemon juice and pulse until finely chopped. Scrape down the sides of the bowl and process until fairly smooth. With the machine running, add 1/4 cup of the chive oil in a thin stream and process until smooth. Season with salt and white pepper and stir in the tarragon. Will keep, tightly covered, in the refrigerator for up to 3 days.

ARTICHOKE PESTO WITH ALMONDS AND WHITE WINE

MAKES ABOUT 3/4 CUP

SERVE THIS YUMMY pesto on grilled bread with tomatoes or cheese for a fast hors d'oeuvre or with pasta or potatoes. I also love adding a few tablespoons to ground lamb for meatballs or burgers.

2 large globe artichokes (10 to 12 ounces each)

1/2 lemon

3 tablespoons plus 1 teaspoon extra-virgin olive oil

1/4 cup slivered almonds

1 large garlic clove, thickly sliced

Salt and freshly ground black pepper

1/4 cup dry white wine

1. Trim the artichoke stems to 1 inch of the base. Snap off the bottom 4 to 5 rows of leaves, revealing lighter green leaves. Using a sharp chef's or serrated knife, cut off the top about 1½ inches from the base. Cut each artichoke into quarters. Rub the cut sides with the lemon half to prevent discoloration.

2. Meanwhile, bring a medium-size saucepan of water to a boil. Add the artichoke bottoms and cook over medium heat until just tender, about 15 minutes. Drain the artichokes, shaking out any excess water. Using a spoon, scoop out the hairy chokes and discard any tough leaves. Thickly slice the artichoke hearts.

3. Heat 1 teaspoon of the oil in a medium-size skillet over medium heat. Add the almonds and cook, stirring, until golden, 2 to 3 minutes. Transfer the almonds to a plate. Add the remaining 3 tablespoons oil to the skillet. Add the artichokes and cook over medium heat, stirring occasionally, until lightly golden, about 5 minutes. Add the garlic, season with salt and pepper, and cook, stirring, until the garlic is lightly golden, about 3 minutes longer. Add the wine and simmer until nearly evaporated, about 3 minutes longer.

4. Scrape the mixture into a food processor along with the almonds and pulse until coarsely pureed. Taste for salt and pepper again. This is best used right away.

ROASTED RED PEPPER PESTO WITH PECORINO PEPATO

MAKES 1 CUP

PECORINO PEPATO IS a semiaged sheep's milk cheese from Italy that contains green peppercorns. It has a buttery yet sharp and tangy flavor with a delicate hit of pepper. If you can't find it, parmesan and cracked peppercorns are a fine alternative. This pesto makes a great sandwich spread as well as a seasoning for burger and meatball mixtures and a sauce for grilled meats and poultry.

2 large red bell peppers

Vegetable oil

6 tablespoons extra-virgin olive oil

1 large garlic clove, smashed

2 anchovy fillets, rinsed

1/4 cup finely crumbled pecorino pepato

Salt

1. Lightly rub the peppers all over with vegetable oil and roast over a gas flame or under a broiler, turning, until blackened all over. Transfer the peppers to a bowl, cover with plastic wrap, and let sit for 20 minutes. Peel, core, seed, and cut the peppers into wide strips.

2. Heat 2 tablespoons of the olive oil in a medium-size skillet over medium-high heat until shimmering. Add the bell pepper strips and cook, stirring frequently, until very tender, lightly browned, and rather dry, about 5 minutes. Add the garlic and anchovies and cook for 1 minute. Transfer to a bowl and let cool.

3. Coarsely chop the pepper mixture in a food processor. With the machine running, add the remaining ¼ cup olive oil in a thin stream and process until coarsely pureed. Add the cheese and pulse just until combined. Season with salt. Will keep, tightly covered, in the refrigerator for up to 1 week.

GINGER, GARLIC, AND LEMONGRASS PESTO

MAKES ABOUT ¼ CUP

I LIKE TO add a teaspoon or so of this aromatic mixture to piping hot soba or udon noodle soup for an energizing and restorative light meal.

> One 2 x 1-inch piece fresh ginger, peeled and thinly sliced
>
> 2 large garlic cloves, smashed
>
> 1 stalk lemongrass, tender inner bulb from the bottom 4 inches, finely chopped
>
> ¼ teaspoon sugar
>
> 1 teaspoon Asian fish sauce
>
> 1 teaspoon fresh lime juice

Using a mortar with pestle, pound the ginger, garlic, lemongrass, and sugar together into a coarse paste. Add the fish sauce and lime juice, stirring and pounding until fairly smooth. Will keep, tightly covered, in the refrigerator for up to 3 days.

WILD MUSHROOM AND HERB PESTO

MAKES ABOUT 1½ CUPS

WILD MUSHROOMS ARE a big favorite of mine. I love them in just about any configuration! Their versatility allows for endless pairing possibilities. Try this pesto with scrambled eggs, grilled rib-eye steaks, wide egg noodles, or tortellini; stirred into mashed potatoes or a pan gravy; or on garlicky toasted baguette slices with shavings of fresh Pecorino from Tuscany or Sardinia.

> ½ pound mixed fresh wild mushrooms, such as chanterelle, morel, oyster, shiitake, cremini, and/or porcini
>
> ½ pound white button mushrooms
>
> 2 tablespoons unsalted butter
>
> ¼ cup extra-virgin olive oil
>
> 1 large shallot, minced
>
> 1½ teaspoons fresh thyme leaves
>
> ½ teaspoon minced fresh rosemary leaves
>
> 2 tablespoons dry white vermouth
>
> ¼ cup heavy cream
>
> Salt and freshly ground black pepper
>
> 2 tablespoons freshly grated parmesan cheese

1. Clean and trim the mushrooms: Brush away any dirt or grit and trim the stems. If using shiitakes, remove the stems altogether. Rinse the mushrooms briefly under cold running water to remove as much grit as possible. Shake off any excess water and transfer the mushrooms to a towel to dry. Roughly chop the mushrooms into ½-inch pieces.

2. In a large skillet, melt the butter in the oil over medium heat. Add the shallot and cook, stirring, until softened. Add the mushrooms and cook over medium-high heat, stirring frequently, until all of the liquid has evaporated and the mushrooms are browned, about 12 minutes. Add the thyme, rosemary, and vermouth and cook, stirring, until the liquid is evaporated. Add the cream, season with salt and pepper, and cook until the cream is nearly evaporated. Let cool.

3. Transfer the mixture to a food processor and pulse into a coarse puree. Add the parmesan and pulse just until combined. Will keep, tightly covered, in the refrigerator for up to 4 days. Return to room temperature before using.

14 GREAT PESTOS TO SEASON THE MEAT MIXTURE FOR BURGERS, MEATBALLS, OR MEATLOAF

1. Ancho Chili and Roasted Garlic Pesto with Piñons (page 116)

2. Artichoke Pesto with Almonds and White Wine (page 108)

3. Charred Garlic-Jalapeño Pesto with Queso Fresco (page 119)

4. Chèvre and Piquillo Pepper Pesto (page 119)

5. Classic Pesto Genovese (page 94)

6. Crispy Shallot Pesto (page 113)

7. Fried Sage and Caper Pesto with Fresh Pecorino (page 101)

8. Green Chile and Scallion Pesto (page 117)

9. Olive, Caper, and Mint Pesto (page 102)

10. Roasted Red Pepper Pesto with Pecorino Pepato (page 109)

11. Scallion-Macadamia Pesto (page 116)

12. Spinach-Pignoli Pesto with Raisins (page 107)

13. Sun-Dried Tomato Pesto (page 113)

14. Wild Mushroom and Herb Pesto (left)

CANNELLONI WITH SHALLOT-RICOTTA FILLING

MAKES 6 SERVINGS

MY GRANDMOTHER ALWAYS made Italian crepes, called *crespelles*, for her cannelloni, which is also known as manicotti. The dough is so tender and light, it practically melts in your mouth. I like to flavor the ricotta filling with Crispy Shallot Pesto because it adds a delicate oniony flavor, but plain sautéed shallots would be fine too. This recipe makes about 20 *crespelles*; any extras can be filled with jam, baked, and dusted with confectioners' sugar for dessert. They also freeze well.

CRESPELLES:

1 cup all-purpose flour

1/2 teaspoon salt

4 large eggs

1/4 cup pure olive oil, plus more for cooking

1 3/4 cups whole milk

1 pound fresh ricotta cheese

1 recipe Crispy Shallot Pesto (right)

2 tablespoons finely chopped fresh Italian parsley leaves

Salt and freshly ground black pepper

2 large eggs

1 recipe Tomato Cream Sauce (page 86)

2 tablespoons freshly grated parmesan cheese

1. Combine the *crespelle* ingredients in a blender and process until smooth. Cover and let rest for 20 minutes.

2. Heat a 6- or 7-inch skillet or crepe pan over medium-high heat until hot. Brush lightly with oil. Spoon about 3 tablespoons of the batter into the hot pan, tilting and swirling to coat the bottom of the pan completely with it. Cook until brown around the edges and just set, about 30 seconds. Loosen the *crespelle* from the pan, flip, and cook about 10 seconds longer. Transfer the *crespelle* to a plate and repeat with the remaining batter, brushing the pan with oil as needed. Let the *crespelles* cool.

3. In a medium-size bowl, combine the ricotta, pesto, and parsley and season with salt and pepper. Add the eggs and stir until combined.

4. Preheat the oven to 350°F. Spread 1/2 cup of the sauce over the bottom of a 2-quart glass or ceramic baking dish. Arrange 12 of the *crespelles* on a work surface, brown side up. Divide the filling evenly and spoon into the centers of each *crespelle*. Fold in the sides and roll the dough into a cylinder. Place the cannelloni in the baking dish, seam side down, and cover with 1 cup of the sauce. Sprinkle with the parmesan and bake until bubbling and lightly browned, about 30 minutes. Serve the remaining sauce alongside.

SUN-DRIED TOMATO PESTO

MAKES ABOUT 1¼ CUPS

MY FAVORITE BRAND of sun-dried tomato is California Brand. I like to use this pesto with pasta, grilled meats and poultry, or with crackers or bruschetta. Ricotta salata is a salted and pressed cake of ricotta. Feta makes a good substitute.

1 cup loosely packed oil-packed sun-dried tomatoes, drained, ¼ cup of the oil reserved

¼ cup sliced almonds

2 large garlic cloves, thickly sliced

½ teaspoon dried oregano, crumbled

½ teaspoon dried rosemary, crumbled

1 tablespoon red wine vinegar

⅓ cup finely crumbled ricotta salata or feta cheese

Salt

Cayenne pepper

1. Heat 1 teaspoon of the reserved tomato oil in a small skillet over medium heat. Add the almonds and cook, stirring constantly, until golden, 2 to 3 minutes. Transfer to a plate and let cool completely. Add another teaspoon of the oil to the skillet and the garlic and cook, stirring, over medium heat until softened and lightly golden, about 2 minutes. Add the oregano and rosemary and cook for 30 seconds.

2. Combine the sun-dried tomatoes, vinegar, garlic, almonds, and remaining reserved tomato oil in a food processor and pulse until coarsely pureed. Add the ricotta salata and pulse just until combined. Season with salt and cayenne. Will keep, tightly covered, in the refrigerator for up to 4 days.

CRISPY SHALLOT PESTO

MAKES ½ CUP

THIS VARIATION ON *aglio e olio* (garlic and oil) is chunkier, heartier, and less pungent than the traditional preparation. Toss it with pasta, use it as a condiment for grilled or roasted meats and vegetables, or mix it with crème fraîche for a super-fancy French onion dip. It's also great as a seasoning for ricotta-stuffed shells or cannelloni, as in Cannelloni with Shallot-Ricotta Filling (page 112). The leftover shallot oil is a great medium for sautéing vegetables or tossing with potatoes before you roast them.

¾ cup pure olive oil

4 large shallots, thinly sliced (about 1½ loosely packed cups)

¼ cup freshly grated grana padano or parmesan cheese

1 tablespoon finely chopped fresh Italian parsley leaves

½ teaspoon finely grated lemon zest

Salt and freshly ground black pepper

1. Heat the oil in a medium-size skillet over medium heat until shimmering. Add the shallots and cook, stirring frequently, until golden and crisp, 10 to 12 minutes. Using a slotted spoon, transfer the shallots to a paper towel–lined plate in a single layer to drain. Let cool, then coarsely chop. Strain the oil through a fine-mesh sieve to remove any sediment and let cool.

2. Transfer the shallots to a small bowl and stir in the cheese, parsley, and lemon zest. Add 2 tablespoons of the shallot oil to make a loose mixture and season with salt and pepper. Will keep, tightly covered, in the refrigerator for up to 4 days.

OVEN-DRIED TOMATO AND GARLIC PESTO

MAKES ABOUT 1½ CUPS

ROASTING TOMATOES IN a very low oven slightly dehydrates them, which intensifies their flavor. I like to oven-dry an especially large batch of tomatoes and freeze them in jars with olive oil for the winter. This pesto makes a great sandwich spread, pasta sauce, or seasoning for stews or soups.

3 pounds ripe plum tomatoes, cored

1 large head garlic, cloves separated but not peeled

1 large sprig fresh rosemary, cut into 1-inch lengths

2 large sprigs fresh thyme

4 plump anchovy fillets, finely chopped

¼ cup extra-virgin olive oil

2 tablespoons red wine vinegar

1 tablespoon finely chopped fresh Italian parsley leaves

Salt and freshly ground black pepper

1. Bring a large saucepan of water to a boil. Fill a medium-size bowl with ice water. Using a sharp knife, make a shallow X in the bottom of each tomato. Blanch the tomatoes in the boiling water, a few at a time for about 30 seconds, remove them with a slotted spoon, and plunge them immediately into the ice water to cool. Peel the tomatoes, halve them lengthwise, and scoop out the seeds.

2. Preheat the oven to 275°F and lightly oil a large, rimmed baking sheet. Arrange the tomatoes cut side down on the baking sheet and scatter the garlic, rosemary, and thyme all around. Roast until the tomatoes begin to look a little dry, about 1 hour. Carefully turn the tomatoes over and roast until the tomatoes look slightly leathery and the garlic is golden, about 1 hour longer. Turn the oven off, prop open the door with the handle of a wooden spoon, and let the tomatoes dry and cool for 1 hour longer. Discard the rosemary and thyme.

3. Coarsely chop the tomatoes. Peel the garlic, transfer it to a large mortar along with the anchovies, and pound into a paste. Add the tomatoes and oil and pound into a coarse paste. Stir in the vinegar and parsley and season with salt and pepper. Will keep, tightly covered, in the refrigerator for up to 1 week.

SPICY GARLIC-HAZELNUT SAUCE

MAKES ABOUT 1 CUP

THIS PIQUANT PESTO-LIKE sauce from Spain, called *picada*, is traditionally served with grilled meats and sausages, but I like to serve it with roasted chicken and fish.

1/2 cup pure olive oil

1/2 cup hazelnuts, chopped

1 slice firm white sandwich bread, torn

2 garlic cloves, coarsely chopped

1 tablespoon chopped fresh mint leaves

1/2 teaspoon red pepper flakes

2 tablespoons white wine vinegar

Salt

1. In a small skillet, heat 2 tablespoons of the oil over medium-high heat. Add the hazelnuts and cook, stirring, until golden, 3 to 4 minutes. Using a slotted spoon, transfer the nuts to a plate to cool. Add the bread to the skillet and cook, stirring, until golden and crisp, about 4 minutes. Transfer to the plate to cool.

2. Transfer the nuts and bread to a food processor, add the garlic, mint, and red pepper and pulse until finely chopped. Add the vinegar and pulse to a coarse, thick paste. While the machine is running, gradually add the remaining 6 tablespoons oil in a thin stream through the feed tube and process until smooth. Season with salt. This is best used right away, but will keep in the refrigerator for 2 days.

LEMON-WALNUT PESTO

MAKES ABOUT 1 1/4 CUPS

TOASTED WALNUTS GROUND with lemon zest and fruity olive oil make an interesting Mediterranean twist on cold sesame sauce when served with spaghetti or linguine. I like to use almonds or pecans occasionally for a slightly sweeter pesto. Although it's not necessary, when I have extra time, I gently rub the walnuts to remove some of the papery skin. Toss with pasta or serve with grilled or roasted lamb, veal chops, poultry, or fish.

1 cup walnut halves

1 teaspoon finely grated lemon zest

1/4 teaspoon red pepper flakes

1/2 teaspoon coarsely chopped fresh thyme leaves

Scant 1/4 teaspoon coarsely chopped fresh rosemary leaves

1/4 cup fruity extra-virgin olive oil

1 teaspoon fresh lemon juice

Salt

Preheat the oven to 350°F. Spread the walnuts in a pie plate and toast until golden and fragrant, 8 to 9 minutes. Let cool, then transfer to a food processor along with the lemon zest, red pepper, thyme, and rosemary and pulse until finely chopped. While the machine is running, add the oil in a thin stream and process until fairly smooth. Stir in the lemon juice and season with salt. Will keep in the refrigerator for up to 2 days.

SCALLION-MACADAMIA PESTO

MAKES ¾ CUP

SWEET, NUTTY MACADAMIAS are a great foil for the intense onion flavor of the scallions. I love serving this pesto with grilled fish, but it also makes a great sandwich spread with fresh, juicy summer tomatoes.

1 small garlic clove, smashed

2 tablespoons coarsely chopped fresh cilantro leaves

1 bunch tender thin scallions, ends trimmed and cut into ½-inch pieces

¼ cup extra-virgin olive oil

¼ cup coarsely chopped roasted, salted macadamia nuts

1 tablespoon fresh lime juice

Salt and freshly ground black pepper

In a food processor, pulse the garlic and cilantro together until finely chopped. Add the scallions and pulse until finely chopped, scraping down the sides of the bowl as needed. While the machine is running, add the oil in a thin stream and process into a coarse paste. Add the macadamia nuts and pulse until finely chopped. Pulse in the lime juice and season with salt and pepper. Will keep, tightly covered, in the refrigerator for up to 3 days.

ANCHO CHILE AND ROASTED GARLIC PESTO WITH PIÑONS

MAKES ABOUT ⅔ CUP

PIÑONS, ALSO KNOWN as pine nuts, figure very prominently in the cooking of the Southwest, especially in Native American cuisines. *Queso fresco* is a mild, semidry cheese from Mexico that resembles farmer's cheese or feta. If you can't find *queso fresco*, either will do. Try spreading some of this pesto on softened corn tortillas before filling them for enchiladas or fajitas.

2 dried ancho chiles

Boiling water

4 large garlic cloves, left unpeeled

¼ cup pine nuts

⅛ teaspoon dried oregano, preferably Mexican

2 tablespoons peanut or other mild-flavored vegetable oil

1 tablespoon heavy cream

⅓ cup crumbled *queso fresco*

Salt and freshly ground black pepper

Cayenne pepper

1. Remove the stems from the ancho chiles. Using scissors, cut the chiles down one side and remove the seeds. Heat a cast-iron skillet or griddle over medium heat until hot to the touch. Add the chiles, flatten with a metal spatula, and heat just until pliable, about 20 seconds per side. Transfer the anchos to a heatproof bowl, cover with boiling water, and let sit until softened, about 20 minutes. Drain the chiles, reserving ½ cup of the soaking liquid. Chop the chiles.

2. Meanwhile, add the garlic to the skillet and cook over low heat until softened and blackened in spots, about 15 minutes. Let cool, then peel the garlic. Add the pine nuts to the skillet and cook over low heat, stirring or shaking frequently, until golden, 3 to 4 minutes. Remove immediately to a plate to stop the cooking and let cool.

3. Put the softened chiles, garlic, pine nuts, oregano, and 2 tablespoons of the reserved chile soaking liquid in a mini–food processor. Pulse until finely chopped, scraping down the sides of the bowl as needed. While the machine is running, add the oil and process until the mixture is finely chopped. Add the heavy cream and *queso fresco*, pulse to combine, and season with salt, black pepper, and cayenne. Will keep, tightly covered, in the refrigerator for up to 4 days.

GREEN CHILE AND SCALLION PESTO

MAKES 3/4 CUP

I LOVE TO spread this pesto on tortillas before filling them with roasted meat or chicken. It is also great mixed into burgers or meatballs or stirred into soup.

  2 tablespoons shelled raw pumpkin seeds
  3 large mild fresh green chiles, such as Anaheim or New Mexico
  Vegetable oil
  4 scallions, cut into 1-inch pieces
  1 small garlic clove, smashed
  2 tablespoons coarsely chopped fresh cilantro leaves

  2 tablespoons extra-virgin olive oil
  2 teaspoons fresh lime juice
  Salt and freshly ground black pepper

1. Toast the pumpkin seeds in a dry skillet over medium heat, shaking the pan frequently, until lightly browned and beginning to pop, about 4 minutes. Transfer to a plate and let cool.

2. Lightly rub the chiles all over with vegetable oil. Roast the chiles over a gas flame or under a broiler until blistered all over. Transfer the peppers to a bowl, cover with plastic wrap, and let cool. Peel, core, and seed the chiles. Pat dry with paper towels.

3. In a mini–food processor, combine the pumpkin seeds, scallions, garlic, cilantro, olive oil, and lime juice and process until finely chopped. Add the chiles and pulse to a coarse puree. Season with salt and pepper. Will keep, tightly covered, in the refrigerator for up to 3 days.

CREATE YOUR OWN CROUTONS

Preheat the oven to 350°F. Slice a baguette (or French or Italian bread) thinly, about ¼- to ⅓-inch thick. Brush both sides lightly with olive oil and arrange them in a single layer on a baking sheet. Bake in the center of the oven until lightly browned and crisp, 12 to 15 minutes, depending on the size of your bread.

ROASTED POTATOES AND ONIONS
WITH CHÈVRE AND PIQUILLO PEPPER PESTO
MAKES 6 SERVINGS

THE PESTO COATS the crisp roasted potatoes with a creamy glaze.

1¼ pounds russet potatoes, peeled and cut into 1-inch cubes

1 medium-size red onion, cut into ¾-inch wedges through the root

2 tablespoons extra-virgin olive oil

Salt

Cayenne pepper

¼ cup Chèvre and Piquillo Pepper Pesto (right), plus more
     for serving, at room temperature

1. Preheat the oven to 425°F and lightly oil a large, rimmed baking sheet, preferably nonstick.

2. In a large bowl, toss the potatoes, onion, and oil together until coated and season with salt and cayenne. Spread the vegetables in a single layer on the baking sheet and roast until golden and crisp, about 30 minutes, gently tossing once or twice.

3. Return the vegetables to the bowl, add the pesto, and toss to coat. Spread the vegetables on the baking sheet again and return to the oven until glazed and browned, about 10 minutes. Serve hot with additional pesto on the side.

ROASTED POTATOES AND ONIONS WITH OTHER PESTOS

IF YOU'RE LOOKING for some variety, this recipe also tastes great with these other pestos:

- Anchovy-Parsley Pesto (page 105)
- Chimichurri (page 105)
- Classic Pesto Genovese (page 94)
- Green Chile and Scallion Pesto (page 117)
- Olive, Caper, and Mint Pesto (page 102)
- Oven-Dried Tomato and Garlic Pesto (page 114)
- Pignoli-Herb Sauce (page 98)
- Roasted Red Pepper Pesto with Pecorino Pepato (page 109)
- Romesco (page 120)
- Sun-Dried Tomato Pesto (page 113)
- Wild Mushroom and Herb Pesto (page 110)

CHÈVRE AND PIQUILLO PEPPER PESTO

MAKES ABOUT 1⅓ CUPS

PIQUILLO PEPPERS, WHICH are smoky and sweet, come from Spain. You can find them in jars or tins at gourmet markets or some supermarkets; if you can't find them, use the same amount of pimentos, plus 1 teaspoon paprika. Serve this pesto with grilled bread and tomatoes, with pasta, or add it to burgers and meatballs.

1 tablespoon extra-virgin olive oil

2 tablespoons pine nuts

1 small garlic clove, smashed

1 small shallot, minced

1 tablespoon fresh lemon juice

Pinch of sugar

½ cup crumbled semiaged goat cheese, such as Boucheron

One 7-ounce jar piquillo peppers, drained

Salt

Cayenne pepper

1. Heat ½ teaspoon of the oil in a small skillet over medium heat. Add the pine nuts and cook, stirring until golden, 2 to 3 minutes. Transfer the nuts to a plate to cool.

2. In a food processor, combine the garlic, shallot, lemon juice, and sugar and pulse until finely chopped. Add the pine nuts and pulse until finely chopped. Add the cheese and remaining oil and process until smooth. Add the peppers and pulse until you have a fine puree. Season with salt and cayenne. Will keep, tightly covered, in the refrigerator for up to 4 days.

CHARRED GARLIC-JALAPEÑO PESTO WITH QUESO FRESCO

MAKES ABOUT 3/4 CUP

I LIKE TO spread this pesto on warm corn tortillas, then add grilled chicken or pork, black beans, and chopped tomatoes. It makes a great seasoning when added to meatballs, as in Albondigas in Red Chile Tomato Sauce (page 121), or stirred into rice, sautéed ground beef, or chicken soup. Farmer's cheese or feta can be substituted if you have trouble finding *queso fresco*.

4 large red or green jalapeños

3 tablespoons peanut or other mild-flavored vegetable oil

4 large garlic cloves, unpeeled

2 scallions (white and tender green parts)

¼ cup tightly packed coarsely chopped fresh cilantro leaves

⅓ cup crumbled *queso fresco*

Salt and freshly ground black pepper

1. Heat a cast-iron skillet over medium heat until hot to the touch. Lightly rub the jalapeños with some of the oil. Add them to the skillet along with the garlic and scallions and cook until softened and charred all over, about 15 minutes for the garlic and jalapeños and 5 minutes for the scallions. Transfer the jalapeños to a bowl, cover with plastic wrap, and let cool. Peel and seed the jalapeños and peel the garlic.

2. Transfer the jalapeños, garlic, and scallions to a food processor and pulse until finely chopped. While the machine is running, add the remaining oil in a thin stream and process until coarsely pureed. Add the cilantro and *queso fresco* and pulse just until combined. Season with salt and pepper. Will keep, tightly covered, in the refrigerator for up to 4 days.

A PESTO IN EVERY POT

Try stirring a teaspoon of any of the following pestos into a serving of chicken noodle or chicken and rice soup or vegetable soup for a bright pop of flavor:

1. Ancho Chile and Roasted Garlic Pesto with Piñons (page 116)

2. Anchovy-Parsley Pesto (page 105)

3. Charred Garlic-Jalapeño Pesto with Queso Fresco (page 119)

4. Classic Pesto Genovese (page 94)

5. Ginger, Garlic, and Lemongrass Pesto (page 110)

6. Green Chile and Scallion Pesto (page 117)

7. Mint, Parsley, and Scallion Pesto (page 99)

8. Pistou (page 95)

ROMESCO

MAKES ABOUT 1 CUP

THOUGH TRULY AN uncomplicated and rustic sauce, this Romesco requires a little patience in sautéing the ingredients separately. In Spain it is traditionally served with seafood, but I also love it with grilled vegetables, steaks, lamb, and pork.

1 small red bell pepper or fresh pimento
1/2 cup extra-virgin olive oil
1/4 cup blanched whole almonds
1/2 cup cubed (1/4-inch) firm-textured crustless white bread
2 garlic cloves, smashed
2 plum tomatoes, peeled, seeded, and coarsely chopped
2 tablespoons sherry vinegar
Salt and cayenne pepper

1. Lightly rub the pepper all over with oil. Roast the pepper over a gas flame or under a broiler until charred all over. Transfer to a bowl, cover with plastic wrap, and let cool. Peel, core, seed, and cut the pepper into wide strips.

2. Heat 1 tablespoon of the oil in a medium-size skillet over medium heat until shimmering. Add the almonds and cook, stirring frequently, until golden, about 5 minutes. Transfer the almonds to a bowl and let cool.

3. Heat 1 tablespoon of the oil in the skillet over medium heat. Add the bread cubes and cook, stirring frequently, until golden and crisp. Transfer to a plate.

ALBONDIGAS IN RED CHILE TOMATO SAUCE

MAKES 8 SERVINGS

NEARLY EVERY CUISINE has some form of meatball. I love them all, but Mexican meatballs—*albondigas*—are among my favorites. I like to season the meat with Charred Garlic-Jalapeño Pesto with Queso Fresco for a deeper flavor, but a simple *sofrito* (page 81) is perfectly fine. I usually make a double batch of these meatballs, because they all seem to mysteriously disappear. Alternatively, I like to serve them as hors d'oeuvres, with chunky fresh salsas, such as Charred Garlic–Tomatillo Salsa (page 321) or Green Tomato Salsa (page 320), in which case they should be a bit smaller and cooked all the way through in step 2.

4 slices firm-textured white sandwich bread, crusts removed

1/4 cup milk or water

2 large eggs, beaten

1 recipe Charred Garlic-Jalapeño Pesto with Queso Fresco (page 119), Ancho Chile and Roasted Garlic Pesto with Piñons (page 116), or Green Chile and Scallion Pesto (page 117)

1/2 teaspoon dried oregano, preferably Mexican, crumbled

2 teaspoons salt

1/2 teaspoon freshly ground black pepper

3/4 pound ground beef

3/4 pound ground pork

3/4 cup all-purpose flour

Vegetable oil for frying

1 1/2 cups Red Chile Tomato Sauce (page 84)

1/2 cup low-sodium chicken broth (optional)

Warm tortillas and *queso fresco* for serving

1. In a medium-size bowl, crumble the bread into the milk and let set until absorbed. Using your hands, knead the mixture into a paste. Add the eggs, pesto, oregano, salt, and pepper and knead until combined. Add the beef and pork and knead until evenly combined. Divide the mixture into 2 tablespoonful portions and, with lightly moistened hands, roll the portions into balls.

2. Heat 1/4 inch vegetable oil in a large cast-iron skillet over medium heat until shimmering. Put the flour in a pie plate. Dredge the meatballs in the flour, tapping off any excess, and add half of them to the skillet. Cook, turning occasionally, until browned all over, about 5 minutes. Transfer to a plate and fry the remaining meatballs, adding more oil as needed.

3. Pour off the oil in the skillet, add the tomato sauce and meatballs, and simmer over low heat until the sauce is reduced and thickened and the meatballs are coated nicely, about 15 minutes. Add some broth if the sauce gets too thick.

4. Serve the meatballs with warm tortillas and *queso fresco*.

4. Heat 1 tablespoon of the oil in the skillet. Add the bell pepper and garlic and cook, stirring frequently, until very tender, lightly browned, and rather dry, about 5 minutes. Add the tomatoes and cook for 1 minute. Transfer to a plate.

5. In a large mortar, pound the pepper mixture with the almonds into a coarse paste. Add the bread cubes, along with a bit of the oil, and pound into a thick paste. Add the remaining oil in a thin stream, pounding and stirring until a thick emulsion forms. Stir in the vinegar a few teaspoons at a time. Season with salt and pepper. Will keep, tightly covered, in the refrigerator for up to 4 days.

CLASSIC GREMOLATA

MAKES ABOUT ¼ CUP

THIS CONDIMENT IS a classic accompaniment to osso buco, veal shanks braised with carrots, onion, celery, wine, and tomato, which gets sprinkled on at the table. The combination of parsley and lemon is a refreshing counterpoint to the richly flavored veal. Try it on any braised meat, poultry, or vegetable stew as well as soup, rice, or mashed potatoes.

    1 large garlic clove, minced
    1½ teaspoons finely grated lemon zest
    3 tablespoons finely chopped fresh Italian
        parsley leaves
    1 teaspoon fresh lemon juice
    Salt

Combine the garlic, lemon zest, and parsley on a cutting board and chop together until combined and minced. Transfer the mixture to a small bowl, stir in the lemon juice, and season with salt. This is best used right away.

MINT GREMOLATA

MAKES ABOUT ⅓ CUP

I LIKE SERVING this with braised lamb shanks or stew and roast leg of lamb as a fresh-tasting twist on the classic lamb-mint combination. Prepare it shortly before serving to prevent the mint from turning brown.

    2 large garlic cloves, minced
    2 teaspoons finely grated lemon zest
    2 tablespoons finely chopped fresh Italian
        parsley leaves
    3 tablespoons finely chopped fresh mint
        leaves
    2 teaspoons fresh lemon juice
    Salt

On a cutting board, combine the garlic, lemon zest, parsley, and mint and chop until minced together. Transfer the mixture to a small bowl, stir in the lemon juice, and season with salt. This is best used right away.

SKORDALIA I

MAKES 1½ CUPS

THIS RICH, GARLICKY sauce from Greece is thickened with potatoes, though I've had it made with almonds and bread as well. It's usually served chilled over fried or grilled fish or boiled vegetables. It also makes a great dip for fresh vegetables.

4 small waxy or 2 small baking potatoes (about ¾ pound)
3 large garlic cloves, smashed
Generous pinch of salt
1 cup extra-virgin olive oil
¼ cup fresh lemon juice
Freshly ground black pepper
Warm water as needed

1. Put the potatoes in a small saucepan and cover with cold water. Bring to a boil and let continue to boil until tender, about 20 minutes. Drain the potatoes and let cool slightly. Peel the potatoes and cut into large pieces.

2. Using a large mortar, pound the garlic and salt together into a smooth paste. Add the warm potatoes, a few pieces at a time, and pound until fairly smooth. While pounding and stirring, add the oil in a thin stream, thinning it out with a bit of the lemon juice if the sauce gets too thick. When all of the oil and lemon juice have been added, taste for salt and season with pepper. Thin with a bit of warm water if the sauce is too thick to stir. Serve warm or at room temperature. Will keep, tightly covered, in the refrigerator for up to 3 days. Bring to room temperature before serving.

SKORDALIA II

MAKES ABOUT 1½ CUPS

THIS VARIATION ON the potato-based sauce is made with almonds and bread. I've geared this one for the blender or food processor, though it can easily be pounded in a mortar with a pestle as well.

3 large garlic cloves, smashed
½ cup blanched whole almonds, coarsely chopped
2 cups cubes (¼-inch) firm-textured, crustless white bread
2 tablespoons fresh lemon juice
¼ cup water, plus more for thinning
1 cup extra-virgin olive oil
Salt and freshly ground black pepper

Combine the garlic and almonds in a blender or food processor and pulse until roughly chopped. Add the bread cubes, lemon juice, and water and process until chopped. With the machine running, add the oil in a thin stream and process until fairly smooth. Season with salt and pepper and thin with additional water if the sauce is too thick (it should have the consistency of thick yogurt). Before serving, refrigerate until chilled, up to 3 days.

GRAVIES AND PAN SAUCES

I f you're looking for a nearly effortless way to dress up a piece of meat, a pan sauce or gravy is it. Fast, versatile, and open for all sorts of variations, these preparations can elevate a sad little chicken breast or lonely pork medallion to a much higher status with just a few ingredients. The essential elements of a pan sauce are the skillet used to sauté a piece of meat and some type of liquid.

Specifically, with a pan sauce, the meat or poultry (or whatever) is gently sautéed in a skillet in a small amount of fat, then removed to a plate. As a result of the sautéing, the bottom of the skillet is nicely coated with bits of the meat protein. These bits are actually the base for a delicious pan sauce. Added to the skillet are some aromatics, such as a little minced shallot, onion, or garlic, which are lightly sautéed. Next, a liquid is added, usually wine or vinegar—this is called deglazing. Using a wooden spoon to scrape up the bits stuck to the pan will release their flavor into the sauce. Then stock is added and, once the sauce simmers for a few minutes to reduce slightly, cream or butter is swirled in to enrich the flavor and give the sauce body—this is called mounting. Last, the sauce is strained into a gravy boat and seasoned, and is ready for serving.

With a gravy, the steps are slightly different. Here, meat or poultry is roasted, generally in the form of a roast or whole bird, in a large pan surrounded by aromatic vegetables, such as onions, carrots,

garlic, and celery. Once the roast is cooked, it's transferred to a platter or cutting board to rest. This allows the meat juices to be reabsorbed into the meat, making a very succulent roast while allowing you enough time to make the gravy. The pan drippings are poured into a heatproof bowl and the fat skimmed off. In some cases some fat is returned to the pan and an equal amount of flour, usually 2 tablespoons, is whisked into it to create a roux, which is what will thicken your gravy. The roasting pan is set over one or two burners and the roux is cooked for a minute or two. Then stock, about 2 cups, is added and any bits stuck to the bottom and sides of the pan are scraped up and released into the liquid. The gravy is strained into a saucepan, seasoned, and simmered until thickened.

Another way to make a gravy, which I find equally good, is, without making a roux, to pour the pan drippings into a heatproof bowl and skim off the fat. Then a small amount of flour is stirred into an equal amount of softened butter to make a paste—called a *beurre manié*. The roasting pan is placed over the burners, stock is added, and the browned bits are scraped up. Next the gravy is strained into a saucepan and simmered. The flour paste is whisked into the stock and simmered until thickened. A substitute for the butter-flour paste is a slurry made from some liquid and flour, cornstarch, or arrowroot.

CLASSIC GIBLET GRAVY

MAKES ABOUT 2 1/2 CUPS

GIBLET GRAVY IS one of those classic work-horse recipes that can be made every time you roast a chicken or turkey—provided there are gizzards and hearts with the birds. Don't use the liver, however, because the flavor is a little too strong and it makes the gravy kind of murky. But don't throw it out, either; I like to sauté it while I'm preparing dinner as a special chef's treat.

The heart, neck and gizzards from 1 turkey or 2 chickens

4 cups Rich Turkey Stock (page 162) or Rich Chicken Stock (page 161)

2 tablespoons all-purpose flour

Roasted chicken or turkey plus roasting pan drippings

Salt and freshly ground pepper

1. In a medium-size saucepan, combine the heart, neck and gizzards with the stock and bring to a boil. Reduce the heat and simmer over low heat until tender, about 45 minutes. Discard the neck. Finely chop the hearts and gizzards and reserve the stock and meat separately.

2. Remove the roasted turkey or chickens from the roasting pan and transfer to a platter or cutting board. Pour off the pan juices into a heat-proof bowl and skim the fat, reserving 2 tablespoons of it in a small bowl (or soften 2 tablespoons of butter). Stir the flour into the fat.

3. Place the roasting pan over 2 burners on medium heat. Add the stock and cook, scraping

---

KEEPING YOUR GRAVY LUMP FREE

- When adding a slurry (the mixture of liquid and thickener such as flour, cornstarch, arrow-root, etc.), be sure to add it to the hot liquid while whisking constantly. This will keep the mixture moving and it won't have time to settle into lumps. If you do happen to get lumps, strain the gravy through a fine-mesh sieve, pressing on the floury lumps to break them up. Return the gravy to the saucepan and simmer until thickened.

- If using a *beurre manié* (kneaded butter), make sure the butter and flour are sufficiently softened so that the mixture dissolves quickly. Add it while constantly whisking to prevent lumps from forming.

- If making a pan gravy by whisking flour into the pan drippings, be sure to add the liquid while whisking constantly.

- Never add your dry thickener directly to the gravy without thinning it with a liquid or butter.

up the browned bits stuck to the bottom and sides of the pan. Strain the liquids into the saucepan and add the reserved, strained pan juices. Bring to a boil and let boil until reduced to 2½ cups. Whisk the flour mixture into the stock and simmer over medium heat until thickened and no floury taste remains, about 5 minutes. Season with salt and pepper, stir in the giblets, and serve.

BASIC GRAVY FOR ROAST CHICKEN, VEAL AND PORK ROAST, AND ROAST BEEF

MAKES 1 CUP CHICKEN GRAVY OR
2 CUPS VEAL, PORK, OR BEEF GRAVY

USE THESE BASIC proportions for a simple but flavorful pan gravy. The methods are the same for chicken, veal, pork, or beef, though the amounts will differ due to the size differences of chickens, veal roasts, pork roasts, and beef roasts. Simply refer to the parentheses for the variations. The only caveat about the variations is that the veal, pork, and beef roasts should be able to serve about 6 or 8 people. And by all means, add herbs, sautéed mushrooms, a pat of leftover compound butter, or what have you to make your gravy a little more special.

> 1 roasted chicken plus roasting pan and drippings (or veal roast, pork roast, or roast beef)
> 1 tablespoon all-purpose flour (2 tablespoons for veal, pork, or beef)

1 cup chicken stock (or 2 cups veal or beef stock for veal, pork, and beef)
Salt and freshly ground pepper

1. Transfer the roast to a platter or cutting board and pour the pan juices into a small saucepan. Skim off the fat and return 1 tablespoon of the fat (for chicken and 2 tablespoons for veal, pork or beef) to the pan. Set the pan over 2 burners on medium heat. Whisk in flour and cook for 1 minute, whisking constantly.

2. Add the stock and cook, scraping up any browned bits stuck to the bottom of the pan. Strain into the small saucepan and simmer over medium heat until thickened. Season with salt and pepper, stir in any accumulated meat juices from the platter or cutting board and serve.

BALSAMIC PAN SAUCE

MAKES ABOUT ½ CUP
(4 SERVINGS)

JUST A FEW tablespoons of Balsamic-Prune Glaze (page 210) and chicken stock stirred into some pan drippings make a terrific pan sauce that is as perfect with beef as it is with chicken, pork, duck, or venison. White Pekin duck breast, tender and flavorful, is used to illustrate this delicious sweet-tart pan sauce. It's available in good butcher shops or gourmet markets and by mail order through Culver Duck Farms of Long Island.

If using chicken, beef, or pork, cook over

medium to medium-high heat on both sides in a small bit of oil until browned and cooked through, generally 10 to 12 minutes for chicken breasts, 1½-inch-thick pork tenderloin medallions, and 1-inch-thick steaks and boneless chops.

4 White Pekin duck breast halves (about 8 ounces each)

Salt and freshly ground black pepper

2 tablespoons minced shallots

½ cup low-sodium chicken or beef broth

3 tablespoons Balsamic-Prune Glaze (page 210)

1. Using a sharp paring knife, score the duck skin in a crosshatch pattern about ¼ inch deep. Be sure not to cut through the skin into the meat. Season with salt and pepper. Heat a large skillet over medium heat. Add the duck breasts skin side down and cook until the skin is deep golden and most of the fat is rendered, about 12 minutes. Pour or spoon off the fat as it accumulates in the pan. Turn the duck and cook until browned, about 6 minutes longer. Transfer the duck to a warmed plate and cover loosely with foil to keep warm.

2. Pour off all but 1 tablespoon of fat from the skillet. Add the shallot and cook over medium heat until softened, about 3 minutes. Add the broth and glaze and cook over medium-high heat until reduced by half, about 5 minutes, scraping up any browned bits stuck to the skillet. Season with salt and pepper. Pour the sauce over the breasts and serve.

CALVADOS-CIDER PAN SAUCE

MAKES ABOUT ½ CUP

(4 SERVINGS)

CALVADOS, A FRAGRANT and lovely French apple brandy, is cooked with apple cider to create a flavorful fruity sauce that pairs extremely well with pork, veal, or poultry. I've used pork tenderloin medallions here, but boneless chicken breasts or thighs are great, as well as boneless pork loin medallions and veal loin medallions.

1 teaspoon all-purpose flour, plus more for dusting

1 tablespoon water

2 tablespoons unsalted butter

1 tablespoon extra-virgin olive oil

1 pork tenderloin (about 1 pound), trimmed of any fat and silverskin, cut into 1½-inch-thick medallions, and lightly pounded

Salt and freshly ground black pepper

2 tablespoons minced shallots

¼ cup Calvados

½ cup apple cider

½ cup low-sodium chicken broth or Veal Stock (page 164)

1 teaspoon finely chopped fresh tarragon leaves (optional)

1. In a small bowl, stir the flour and water together to make a slurry. Set aside.

2. In a large, heavy skillet, melt 1 tablespoon of the butter with the olive oil over medium-high heat. Season the pork on both sides with salt and

TURKEY WITH ROASTED SHALLOT–TERIYAKI GRAVY

MAKES ABOUT 4 CUPS

WHOLE SHALLOTS, ROASTED with the turkey, add sweetness to this richly flavored pan sauce. Roast a large chicken, pork loin, or two racks of lamb and halve all of the ingredients—the times will vary.

1/2 cup low-sodium soy sauce

1/4 cup mirin

1/4 cup sake

2 tablespoons rice vinegar

2 tablespoons firmly packed light brown sugar

1 tablespoon peeled and grated fresh ginger

1 teaspoon cornstarch dissolved in 1 tablespoon water

One 16-pound turkey, preferably fresh

1 1/2 pounds large shallots, peeled

Salt and freshly ground black pepper

6 tablespoons (3/4 stick) unsalted butter, softened

1/4 cup extra-virgin olive oil

1 cup water

2 cups Rich Turkey Stock (page 162)

2 tablespoons all-purpose flour

1. Preheat the oven to 500°F. In a saucepan, combine the soy sauce, mirin, sake, vinegar, brown sugar, and ginger. Add the cornstarch slurry and bring to a boil over high heat. Cook on high, stirring, until glossy and slightly thickened, 3 minutes. Transfer the teriyaki sauce to a bowl.

2. Set the turkey in a large roasting pan; scatter the shallots around it. Season the turkey cavities and skin with salt and pepper. In a small bowl, blend 4 tablespoons (1/2 stick) of the butter with the oil and brush some over the turkey. Roast the turkey until golden, about 30 minutes. Baste with the butter mixture and add the water to the roasting pan. Reduce the oven temperature to 325°F and roast the turkey for 1 hour, basting twice with the remaining butter mixture; loosely cover the bird with aluminum foil if the breast browns too quickly.

3. Baste the turkey with some of the sauce, then roast the turkey for 1½ hours longer, basting with the sauce from the bowl every 30 minutes; the turkey is done when the skin is lacquered and an instant-read thermometer inserted in an inner thigh registers 170°F. Transfer to a carving board; let rest for 45 minutes.

4. Meanwhile, strain the pan juices into a bowl, skim off the fat, and reserve the shallots. Set the roasting pan over 1 burner. Add the shallots to the pan and cook over high heat, stirring, until browned, about 3 minutes. Add the pan juices, stock, and the reserved teriyaki sauce. Bring to a boil, scraping up any browned bits from the bottom of the pan.

5. Strain the pan sauce through a fine-mesh sieve into a medium-size saucepan, reserving the shallots. Boil the sauce over high heat until reduced by a third, about 30 minutes. In a small bowl, mix the remaining 2 tablespoons butter with the flour until smooth. Whisk the flour paste into the sauce, then boil, whisking constantly, until the gravy thickens, about 5 minutes. Add the shallots, season with salt and pepper, and transfer to a warmed gravy boat. Carve the turkey and serve with the shallot gravy.

pepper and dust lightly with flour, tapping off any excess. Add the pork to the skillet and cook until golden and crusty, about 6 minutes. Turn the pork, reduce the heat to medium, and cook until browned and cooked through, 5 to 6 minutes longer. Transfer the pork to a warmed plate and cover loosely with foil to keep warm.

3. Pour off any fat in the skillet. Melt the remaining 1 tablespoon butter over medium heat. Add the shallot and cook, stirring, until softened, about 3 minutes. Add the Calvados and cook until nearly evaporated. Add the cider and broth and cook over medium-high heat until reduced by half, scraping up any browned bits stuck to the skillet, about 5 minutes. Strain the sauce through a fine-mesh sieve into a heatproof bowl.

4. Wipe out the skillet and return the sauce to it along with the flour slurry. Simmer over medium heat, whisking constantly, until thickened and no floury taste remains, about 2 minutes longer. Stir in the tarragon and season with salt and pepper. Return the pork to the sauce along with any accumulated juices, simmer just until warmed through, and serve immediately.

CREAMY GINGER-SOY PAN SAUCE

MAKES ABOUT 1/2 CUP

(4 SERVINGS)

USE THIS GINGERY East-West pan sauce with boneless chicken breasts, 1-inch-thick boneless veal chops or pork loin medallions, or 1½-inch-thick pork tenderloin medallions. They all should cook in about 12 minutes. For a more intense ginger flavor, don't strain the sauce at the end.

2 tablespoons unsalted butter

1 tablespoon vegetable oil

4 boneless, skin-on chicken breast halves

Salt and freshly ground black pepper

All-purpose flour

2 tablespoons minced shallots

1 tablespoon peeled and minced fresh ginger

1/4 cup sake or dry vermouth

1/2 cup low-sodium chicken broth or Veal Stock (page 164)

1/4 cup heavy cream

1 tablespoon low-sodium soy sauce

1. In a large, heavy skillet, melt 1 tablespoon of the butter with the oil over medium-high heat. Season the chicken on both sides with salt and pepper and dust lightly with flour, tapping off any excess. Add the chicken to the skillet, skin side down, and cook until golden and crusty, about 6 minutes. Turn the chicken, reduce the heat to medium, and cook until browned and cooked through, 5 to 6 minutes longer. Transfer the chicken to a warmed plate and cover loosely with foil to keep warm.

2. Pour off any fat in the skillet. Melt the remaining 1 tablespoon butter over medium heat. Add the shallot and ginger and cook, stirring a few times, until softened and fragrant, about 3 minutes. Add the sake and cook until nearly evaporated. Add the broth and cook over medium-high heat, scraping up any browned bits stuck to the skillet, until reduced by half, about 5 minutes. Add the cream and bring to a boil. Simmer over low heat just until thickened, 2 to 3 minutes longer. Stir in the soy sauce and any accumulated chicken juices.

3. Strain the sauce through a fine-mesh sieve into a warmed gravy boat, season with salt and pepper, and serve on the side.

CREAMY GREEN PEPPERCORN SAUCE

MAKES ABOUT 1/2 CUP

(4 SERVINGS)

THIS LOVELY CREAM sauce is dotted with little green peppercorns and is a wonderful accompaniment to pork chops or tenderloin medallions, boneless chicken breasts or thighs, veal chops, and, my favorite, steaks, especially rib-eye, New York strip, or filet mignon, which I've used here to illustrate the technique.

2 tablespoons unsalted butter

1 tablespoon extra-virgin olive oil

Two 10- to 12-ounce boneless steaks (1 inch thick)

Salt and freshly ground black pepper

2 tablespoons minced shallots

1/4 cup cognac, Armagnac, or brandy

1/2 cup low-sodium beef broth

1/4 cup heavy cream

1 tablespoon drained green peppercorns, lightly crushed

1 tablespoon finely chopped fresh Italian parsley leaves

1. In a large, heavy skillet melt 1 tablespoon of the butter in the oil over medium heat. Season the steaks with salt and pepper, add them to the skillet, and cook, turning occasionally, until browned and crusty on the outside, about 15 minutes for medium-rare meat. Transfer the beef to a warm plate and cover loosely with foil to keep warm.

2. Pour out any fat in the skillet. Melt the remaining 1 tablespoon butter over medium heat. Add the shallot and cook, stirring a few times, until softened, about 3 minutes. Add the cognac and cook until evaporated, scraping up any browned bits stuck to the skillet. Add the broth and any accumulated beef juices and simmer until reduced to 1/3 cup, 3 to 4 minutes.

3. Strain the sauce through a fine-mesh sieve into a heatproof bowl. Wipe out the skillet and return the sauce to it along with the cream and green peppercorns and simmer over low heat until thickened and slightly reduced, 4 to 5 minutes longer. Season with salt and pepper and stir in the parsley. Pour the sauce over the beef and serve.

CREAMY SHERRY VINEGAR PAN SAUCE

MAKES ABOUT 1/2 CUP

(4 SERVINGS)

SHERRY VINEGAR GIVES this pan sauce a little zest. Use 6- to 8- ounce boneless chicken breasts, 1-inch-thick boneless veal chops or pork loin medallions, or 1½-inch-thick pork tenderloin medallions. They all should cook in about 12 minutes.

3 tablespoons unsalted butter

1 tablespoon extra-virgin olive oil

4 boneless, skin-on chicken breast halves

Salt and freshly ground black pepper

All-purpose flour

2 tablespoons minced shallots

1/4 cup sherry vinegar

1/2 cup low-sodium chicken broth

Pinch of sugar

1/4 cup heavy cream

1 tablespoon finely chopped fresh Italian parsley leaves

1. In a medium-size skillet, melt 1 tablespoon of the butter with the oil over medium-high heat. Season the chicken on both sides with salt and pepper and dust lightly with flour, tapping off any excess. Add the chicken to the skillet, skin side down, and cook until golden and crusty, about 6 minutes. Turn the chicken, reduce the heat to medium, and cook until browned and cooked through, 5 to 6 minutes longer. Transfer the chicken to a warmed plate and cover loosely with foil to keep warm.

2. Pour off any fat in the skillet. Melt 1 tablespoon of the butter over medium heat. Add the shallot and cook, stirring a few times, until softened, about 3 minutes. Add the vinegar, broth, and sugar and cook, scraping up any browned bits stuck to the skillet, until reduced by half, about 5 minutes. Add the cream and any accumulated chicken juices and bring to a boil. Simmer over low heat just until thickened, 3 to 4 minutes longer. Swirl in the remaining 1 tablespoon butter.

3. Strain the sauce through a fine-mesh sieve into a warmed gravy boat, stir in the parsley, season with salt and pepper, and serve on the side.

DRIED CHERRY–PORT REDUCTION PAN SAUCE

MAKES ABOUT ½ CUP

(4 SERVINGS)

IT'S HARD TO beat a slightly sweet, fruity pan sauce with filet mignon or sautéed duck breast. Dried sour cherries have just the right balance of sweet and sour and, when combined with port and chicken stock, complement just about any sautéed meat. I've used pork tenderloin medallions here, but duck breast (its fatty skin rendered and crisped—see Balsamic Pan Sauce on page 128 for the cooking method), beef, veal, venison, pork loin medallions, or boneless chicken breasts or thighs can be used as well.

⅓ cup dried sour cherries

½ cup ruby port

1 tablespoon unsalted butter

1 tablespoon extra-virgin olive oil

1 pork tenderloin, trimmed of any fat or silver skin, cut into 1½-inch-thick medallions, and lightly pounded

Salt and freshly ground black pepper

All-purpose flour

½ cup low-sodium chicken or beef broth

1. In a small saucepan, combine the cherries and port and bring just to a simmer. Cover and let sit off the heat until plumped, about 10 minutes. Set a small sieve over a bowl and strain the cherries, pressing hard, to extract as much of the liquid as possible. Coarsely chop the cherries and reserve both the port and cherries separately.

2. In a medium-size skillet, melt 1 tablespoon of the butter with the oil over medium-high heat. Season the pork on both sides with salt and pepper and dust lightly with flour, tapping off any excess. Add the pork to the skillet and cook until golden and crusty, about 5 minutes. Turn the pork, reduce the heat to medium, and cook until browned and cooked through, 5 to 6 minutes longer. Transfer the pork to a warmed plate and cover loosely with foil to keep warm.

3. Pour off any fat in the skillet. Add the port to the skillet and cook, scraping up any browned bits stuck to the skillet, until nearly evaporated. Add the broth and simmer until slightly reduced, 2 to 3 minutes.

4. Strain the sauce through a fine-mesh sieve into a warm gravy boat, season with salt and pepper, and add the cherries. Pour over the meat and serve.

HORSERADISH-CREAM PAN SAUCE

MAKES ABOUT ½ CUP

(4 SERVINGS)

HORSERADISH AND CREAM nearly always means beef, but this luscious sauce is equally good with pork, chicken, lamb, or venison. Fresh horseradish, when available, imparts such a sharp, floral deliciousness that it's almost a shame to use the bottled kind. Its heat level can vary greatly, so do add it gradually to taste.

2 tablespoons unsalted butter

1 tablespoon extra-virgin olive oil

Two 10- to 12-ounce boneless steaks (1 inch thick)

Salt and freshly ground black pepper

2 tablespoons minced shallots

¼ cup cognac, Armagnac, or brandy

¾ cup low-sodium beef broth

¼ cup heavy cream

1½ tablespoons finely grated horseradish, preferably fresh

1. In a large, heavy skillet, melt 1 tablespoon of the butter in the oil over medium heat. Season

TIPS FOR TASTY GRAVIES AND PAN SAUCES

- When making gravy, add a small amount of water to the roasting pan about halfway through cooking the meat to prevent the bottom from burning and so that there are some yummy pan juices.

- When making a pan sauce, be sure that the skillet doesn't get so hot that the bottom blackens. If the bits stuck to the bottom are burned, the pan sauce will taste bitter.

- Have all the ingredients ready and measured out when making a pan sauce.

- Be sure to pour any accumulated meat juices back into the finished sauce. These juices will add great meat flavor.

- When adding wine, cognac, or other alcohol to a very hot skillet, don't pour it directly from the bottle. Instead measure it into a small glass. The alcohol in the skillet could ignite and the flames travel into the bottle along the stream.

- When igniting the alcohol, always tilt the pan away from you or use a very long match to avoid any burns, and watch out for any drooping sleeves or dangling long hair.

- When adding butter to a pan sauce, be sure the heat is just high enough to gently melt the butter. If it boils once the butter is added, the sauce may separate. If that does happen, don't worry. The sauce is still delicious, so don't throw it away.

the steaks with salt and pepper, add them to the skillet, and cook, turning occasionally, until browned and crusty on the outside, about 15 minutes for medium-rare meat. Transfer the beef to a warmed plate and cover loosely with foil to keep warm.

2. Pour out any fat in the skillet. Melt the remaining 1 tablespoon butter over medium heat. Add the shallot and cook until softened, stirring a few time, about 3 minutes. Add the cognac and cook until evaporated, scraping up any browned bits stuck to the skillet. Add the broth and cook over high heat until reduced by half, 6 to 7 minutes.

3. Strain the sauce through a fine-mesh sieve into a heatproof bowl. Wipe out the skillet, return the sauce to it along with the cream and any accumulated beef juices, and simmer over low heat until thickened and slightly reduced, 2 to 3 minutes longer. Stir in the horseradish, season with salt and pepper, pour over the meat, and serve.

MADEIRA-RAISIN PAN SAUCE

MAKES ABOUT 1/2 CUP (4 SERVINGS)

VIRTUALLY ANY LEFTOVER barbecue sauce or glaze can be added to pan drippings to make a terrific, complex-flavored pan sauce in minutes. Here Madeira-Raisin Glaze, with its hint of rosemary, brown sugar, and Madeira, complements game, poultry, veal, beef, and pork. I've used pork tenderloin medallions here, but duck breast (its fatty skin rendered and crisped); beefsteaks such as filet mignon, strip steak, or rib-eye; veal or pork loin medallions; or boneless chicken breasts or thighs also work well.

> 2 tablespoons unsalted butter
>
> 1 tablespoon extra-virgin olive oil
>
> 1 pork tenderloin (about 1 pound), trimmed of any fat or silver skin, cut into 1 1/2-inch-thick medallions, and lightly pounded
>
> Salt and freshly ground black pepper
>
> All-purpose flour
>
> 1/4 cup Madeira
>
> 3/4 cup low-sodium chicken or beef broth
>
> 3 tablespoons Madeira-Raisin Glaze (page 213)

1. In a medium-size skillet, melt 1 tablespoon of the butter with the oil over medium-high heat. Season the pork on both sides with salt and pepper and dust lightly with flour, tapping off any excess. Add the pork to the skillet and cook until golden and crusty, about 6 minutes. Turn the

pork, reduce the heat to medium, and cook until browned and cooked through, 5 to 6 minutes longer. Transfer the pork to a warmed plate and cover loosely with foil to keep warm.

2. Pour off any fat in the skillet. Add the Madeira and cook over medium heat, scraping up any browned bits stuck to the skillet, until nearly evaporated. Add the broth and glaze and cook until thickened and slightly reduced, about 5 minutes. Season with salt and pepper and swirl in the remaining 1 tablespoon butter.

3. Strain the sauce through a fine-mesh sieve, wipe out the skillet, and return the sauce to it. Return the pork to the sauce along with any accumulated juices, simmer just until warmed through, and serve immediately.

LEMONGRASS–GINGER CREAM PAN SAUCE

MAKES 1/2 CUP

(4 SERVINGS)

THIS FRAGRANT PAN sauce is great with seafood as well as pork, chicken, and beef. I've used sea scallops here because when they're sautéed, the pan drippings are deliciously sweet. Look for diver scallops or dry scallops (not dried scallops). For a more refined sauce, strain out the lemongrass, shallots, and ginger.

2 tablespoons unsalted butter

1 tablespoon vegetable oil

1 1/2 pounds sea scallops

Salt and freshly ground black pepper

2 tablespoons minced shallots

1 tablespoon minced lemongrass
  (only the tender inner bulb)

1 tablespoon peeled and minced fresh ginger

1/4 cup dry vermouth

2/3 cup heavy cream

1. In a large, heavy skillet, melt 1 tablespoon of the butter with the oil over high heat. Season the scallops with salt and pepper, add them to the skillet, and cook until golden and crusty, about 3 minutes. Turn the scallops and cook until lightly browned and cooked through, about 2 minutes longer. Transfer the scallops to a warmed plate and cover loosely with foil to keep warm.

2. Pour off any fat in the skillet. Melt the remaining 1 tablespoon butter over medium heat. Add the shallot, lemongrass, and ginger and cook, stirring a few times, until softened and fragrant, about 3 minutes. Add the vermouth and cook until nearly evaporated. Add the cream and simmer over low heat, scraping up any browned bits stuck to the pan, just until thickened, about 5 minutes. Season with salt and pepper.

3. Return the scallops to the pan and turn to coat with the sauce. Transfer to plates and serve.

MOREL PAN SAUCE WITH COGNAC AND CREAM

MAKES ABOUT 1 CUP

(4 SERVINGS)

WHEN FRESH MORELS are in season, this sauce is the best! I must say, though, that dried morels are awesome in their own right. They lend a kind of earthy, smoky, musty quality that makes this sauce a classic accompaniment for sautéed filet mignon or roasted whole beef tenderloin. I've used dried morels and medallions to illustrate this sauce, but if you plan on roasting a whole tenderloin, double the amounts below, use a roasting pan instead of a skillet through step one, and then switch to a saucepan.

1/2 cup dried morels, rinsed

1 cup boiling water

2 tablespoons unsalted butter

1 tablespoon extra-virgin olive oil

Four 1 1/2-inch-thick filet mignon, lightly pounded and tied

Salt and freshly ground black pepper

All-purpose flour

2 tablespoons minced shallots

1/2 teaspoon fresh thyme leaves

1/4 cup cognac

3/4 cup low-sodium beef broth

1/4 cup heavy cream

1. In a heatproof bowl, cover the dried morels with the boiling water and let sit until softened, about 15 minutes. Using a slotted spoon, lift the morels out of the liquid. Swirl each morel, one at a time, in the soaking liquid to dislodge any grit.

Let the grit settle to the bottom, then slowly pour the soaking liquid into a bowl, stopping when you get to the sediment. Thinly slice the morels.

2. In a medium-size skillet, melt 1 tablespoon of the butter in the oil over medium heat. Season the beef with salt and pepper and dust lightly with flour, tapping off any excess. Add the beef to the skillet and cook, turning occasionally, until browned and crusty on the outside, about 15 minutes for medium-rare meat. Transfer the beef to a warmed plate and cover loosely with foil to keep warm.

3. Pour out any fat in the skillet. Melt the remaining 1 tablespoon butter over medium heat. Add the morels, shallot, and thyme and cook until softened, stirring a few times, about 3 minutes. Add the cognac and cook until evaporated, scraping up any browned bits stuck to the skillet. Add the broth and 1/4 cup of the mushroom soaking liquid and cook over medium-high heat until reduced to 1/2 cup, about 10 minutes. Add the cream and any accumulated beef juices and simmer over low heat until thickened and slightly reduced, about 5 minutes longer. Season with salt and pepper.

4. Before serving, cut the strings on the filets. Pour the sauce over the steaks and serve.

MUSTARD-DILL PAN SAUCE

MAKES ABOUT 2/3 CUP

(4 SERVINGS)

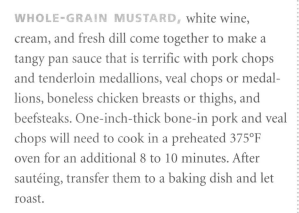

WHOLE-GRAIN MUSTARD, white wine, cream, and fresh dill come together to make a tangy pan sauce that is terrific with pork chops and tenderloin medallions, veal chops or medallions, boneless chicken breasts or thighs, and beefsteaks. One-inch-thick bone-in pork and veal chops will need to cook in a preheated 375°F oven for an additional 8 to 10 minutes. After sautéing, transfer them to a baking dish and let roast.

2 tablespoons unsalted butter

1 tablespoon vegetable oil

4 boneless, skin-on chicken breast halves

Salt and freshly ground black pepper

All-purpose flour

2 tablespoons minced shallots

1/2 cup dry white wine

3/4 cup low-sodium chicken broth or
     Veal Stock (page 164)

Pinch of sugar

1/4 cup heavy cream

1 tablespoon whole-grain mustard

1 tablespoon finely chopped fresh dill

1. In a large, heavy skillet, melt 1 tablespoon of the butter with the oil over medium-high heat. Season the chicken on both sides with salt and pepper and dust lightly with flour, tapping off any excess. Add the chicken to the skillet, skin side down, and cook until golden and crusty,

about 6 minutes. Turn the chicken, reduce the heat to medium, and cook until browned and cooked through, 5 to 6 minutes longer. Transfer the chicken to a warmed plate and cover loosely with foil to keep warm.

2. Pour off any fat in the skillet. Melt the remaining 1 tablespoon butter over medium heat. Add the shallot and cook, stirring a few times, until softened and fragrant, about 3 minutes. Add the wine and cook over high heat, scraping up any browned bits stuck to the skillet, until nearly evaporated. Add the broth and sugar, and cook over medium-high heat until reduced by half, about 6 minutes. Add the cream and bring to a boil. Simmer over low heat just until thickened, 2 to 3 minutes longer. Stir in the mustard, dill, and any accumulated meat juices and season with salt and pepper. Pour the sauce over the meat and serve.

KEEPING GRAVY WARM AT THE TABLE

Short of putting your gravy in a fondue pot or chafing dish, it's best to keep the gravy warm on the stove, refilling the gravy boat at the table as needed. Just be sure to heat the gravy on the lowest setting to avoid scorching or over-reducing.

STIR-FRY SAUCES

Although stir-fries have existed for a long time, these kinds of sauces are relatively new on the scene. Commercially bottled finishing and stir-fry sauces occupy an enormous amount of shelf space at supermarkets, gourmet markets, and Internet food purveyors. It seems that every big-name chef has a line of them. However, once they make it from restaurant kitchen to production line, the results rarely match the original efforts and intentions of the chef. I find these sauces to be so easy to prepare at home that the energy and money wasted on trying to find a decent commercial one are just too high.

If you think about it, these sauces are very similar to pan sauces. They rely on the ingredients, obviously, but also the cooking implement—here a wok or skillet. But unlike pan sauces, whose ingredients are added to the skillet in a distinct order, the ingredients for a stir-fry sauce are previously assembled, then added to the wok or skillet all at once. Like a pan sauce preparation, meals using stir-fry sauces can be put together incredibly fast.

I admit to ordering in Chinese food (and pizza, Indian, and Thai) occasionally—even cooks need a break from the stove once in a while—and it's never that great. What always gets me is the amount of fat and cornstarch in the sauces—not to mention the sheer volume of sauce itself. Why do they have to be so gloppy, fatty, and abundant? The stir-fry sauces in this chapter do have fat and cornstarch but are

considerably lighter and brighter in flavor than anything you're able to buy. And most make enough to serve 4 to 6 people, using about 1 pound of meat plus vegetables and rice.

The majority of the recipes in this chapter are Asian in character, calling for Asian ingredients. However, none of them are terribly esoteric and I've offered substitutes wherever possible, but I'm pretty confident that supermarkets all over the country are providing a wider range of ethnic and gourmet items than ever before. Certainly what they lack can be purchased at specialty stores or online. For more information, see Internet and Mail-Order Suppliers, page 387.

CLASSIC CHINESE
BROWN SAUCE

MAKES ABOUT 3/4 CUP

WHEN IT'S GOOD, this simple, flavorful gravy can be absolutely divine, but when it's bad, well, words can barely describe it. Use it for a mild-flavored stir-fry of beef, chicken, pork, tofu, and/or vegetables or as a sauce with Chinese omelets.

1/2 cup low-sodium chicken broth

2 tablespoons low-sodium soy sauce

1 tablespoon oyster sauce

1 tablespoon Chinese cooking wine or
    dry sherry

2 teaspoons sugar

1 teaspoon ketchup

1 scallion (white and tender green parts),
    minced

1 teaspoon cornstarch dissolved in
    1 tablespoon water

In a small saucepan, combine all the ingredients and bring to a boil. Reduce the heat to medium and simmer until thickened and glossy, about 2 minutes.

CHINESE-STYLE
GARLIC SAUCE

MAKES ABOUT 1/2 CUP

THIS SIMPLE GARLIC sauce is a standard in Szechuan cuisine. It can be used with stir-fried vegetables, chicken, beef, pork, or seafood.

1/2 cup low-sodium chicken broth

3 tablespoons low-sodium soy sauce

1 tablespoon Chinese cooking wine or
    dry sherry

1 1/2 teaspoons sugar

1 teaspoon cornstarch dissolved in
    1 tablespoon water

1 tablespoon peanut oil

4 small dried red chiles

3 large garlic cloves, minced

1. In a small bowl, combine the broth, soy sauce, cooking wine, sugar, and cornstarch.

2. Heat the oil in a small skillet over high heat. Add the chiles and cook until browned, 1 to 2 minutes. Add the garlic and cook just until fragrant, 30 seconds. Stir the broth mixture, add it to the pan, and bring to a boil. Reduce the heat to medium and simmer until thickened and glossy, about 1 minute longer.

CHICKEN WITH MUSHROOMS, SCALLIONS, AND BLACK BEAN SAUCE

MAKES 6 SERVINGS

BONELESS, SKINLESS CHICKEN thighs are stir-fried with mushrooms and scallions and finished with black bean sauce.

> 1/4 cup peanut oil
>
> 1 1/4 pounds boneless, skinless chicken thighs, cut into 2-inch pieces
>
> Salt and freshly ground black pepper
>
> 3/4 pound shiitake mushrooms, stems discarded and caps thickly sliced
>
> 4 scallions, cut into 2-inch lengths
>
> 1 recipe Chinese Black Bean Sauce (right)

1. Heat 2 tablespoons of the oil in a large nonstick skillet over high heat until smoking. Season the chicken lightly with salt and pepper, add it to the skillet, and cook until browned on all sides, about 5 minutes. Transfer the chicken to a plate.

2. Heat the remaining 2 tablespoons oil until smoking. Add the mushrooms and scallions and cook until tender and browned in spots, about 5 minutes. Return the chicken to the skillet and cook until sizzling. Add the sauce and cook, stirring, just until heated and bubbling, about 1 minute longer. Serve hot over rice.

CHINESE BLACK BEAN SAUCE

MAKES ABOUT 1 CUP

FERMENTED BLACK BEANS can be found in Asian markets. They tend to be a little dirty and salty, so be sure to rinse them thoroughly and pat them dry. Use this stir-fry sauce with beef, pork, vegetables, tofu, seafood, or chicken, like in Chicken with Mushrooms, Scallions, and Black Bean Sauce (left). Sometimes, for a super quick spicy black bean sauce, I substitute 1 tablespoon prepared black bean garlic sauce for the fermented black beans and garlic.

3/4 cup low-sodium chicken broth

2 tablespoons low-sodium soy sauce

1 tablespoon Chinese cooking wine or dry sherry

1 1/2 teaspoons cornstarch dissolved in 1 tablespoon water

Pinch of sugar

1/4 cup fermented black beans, rinsed

2 large garlic cloves, minced

2 scallions (white and tender green parts), chopped

1 tablespoon peeled and minced fresh ginger

1 tablespoon peanut oil

1. In a small measuring cup, combine the broth, soy sauce, cooking wine, cornstarch slurry, and sugar.

2. On a cutting board, coarsely chop the black beans with the garlic, scallions, and ginger.

3. Heat the oil in a small saucepan or skillet over high heat until smoking. Add the black bean mixture and cook just until fragrant, about 1 minute. Stir the stock mixture, add it to the saucepan, and bring to a boil. Reduce the heat to medium and simmer until thickened and glossy, 1 to 2 minutes longer.

INGREDIENT AMOUNTS

Each stir-fry can serve 4 to 6 people. The amounts of the ingredients are roughly as follows:

- Meat/seafood/poultry: 3/4 to 1 1/4 pounds when combined with vegetables, 2 pounds alone

- Garlic: 1 to 2 cloves, chopped

- Fresh ginger: 1 teaspoon to 1 tablespoon, to your taste, peeled and minced

- Vegetables: 1/2 to 1 pound when combined with meat, poultry, or seafood, otherwise, 1 1/2 to 2 pounds alone

- Oil: 1/4 cup (use a cooking oil that is neutral in flavor, such as vegetable, peanut, grapeseed, or safflower oil. You want the flavor to come from the meat, vegetables, and sauce. I prefer peanut oil because you can get it very hot without burning and ruining its flavor.)

- Tofu: 8 ounces when combined with vegetables, otherwise, 1 pound alone (firm or extra-firm)

Before you start cooking, be sure to have all of your ingredients measured and in separate bowls near at hand for easier flow. Have everything measured and ready to go. Make sure the stir-fry sauce is combined and ready to go. Cut vegetables and meat about the same size, generally about 1 inch. This will ensure quick, uniform cooking times and eliminate the need for knives at the dinner table. Heat the wok until it is very, very hot; five minutes over high heat should be enough for the average home stove. (If you're using a nonstick skillet, heat the oil and pan together.) Add the oil and let it heat up until you see a little puff of smoke. It should happen almost immediately if the wok or pan is hot enough. Immediately start adding ingredients in individual batches. For example, start with the onions or bell peppers and cook, stirring, until crisp-tender, usually about 3 minutes or so. Then scoop them out onto a plate. Reheat the wok, then add the mushrooms or other vegetables and cook until just about done, transferring it to the plate once it's done. Return the wok to high heat, add more oil, then add the meat and cook, stirring until nearly done, 2 to 3 minutes. Then add the aromatics such as ginger, garlic, and chiles so they don't burn and cook until fragrant and the meat is just about done. Return all of the ingredients to the wok and cook, stirring until very hot, usually about 1 minute. Give the stir-fry sauce a quick stir, add it to the wok and cook, stirring until heated through and bubbling, only about 1 minute or so.

- **Chicken breast, greens (such as bok choy, Chinese broccoli, or watercress), garlic, and fresh ginger with:**
  Chinese Black Bean Sauce (page 145)
  Chinese-Style Garlic Sauce (page 143)
  Classic Chinese Brown Sauce (page 143)
  Coconut-Peanut Stir-Fry Sauce (page 148)
  Fried Ginger Stir-Fry Sauce (page 148)
  Ginger-Lemongrass Stir-Fry Sauce (page 149)
  Green Curry Stir-Fry Sauce (page 150)
  Sesame-Ginger Stir-Fry Sauce (page 153)
  Sweet Chile-Garlic Stir-Fry Sauce (page 156)
  Thai Basil–Nam Pla Stir-Fry Sauce (page 156)

- **Sliced pork, red bell pepper, garlic, and fresh ginger with:**
  Chinese Black Bean Sauce (page 145)
  Chinese-Style Garlic Sauce (page 143)
  Classic Chinese Brown Sauce (page 143)
  Fried Ginger Stir-Fry Sauce (page 148)
  Ginger-Lemongrass Stir-Fry Sauce (page 149)
  Ginger-Orange Stir-Fry Sauce (page 149)
  Oyster Stir-Fry Sauce (page 152)
  Sesame-Ginger Stir-Fry Sauce (page 153)
  Spicy Pineapple Stir-Fry Sauce (page 153)
  Sweet-and-Sour Stir-Fry Sauce (page 157)
  Sweet Chile-Garlic Stir-Fry Sauce (page 156)
  Thai Basil–Nam Pla Stir-Fry Sauce (page 156)

- **Beef, oyster mushrooms, scallions, and canned sliced water chestnuts with:**
  Chinese Black Bean Sauce (page 145)
  Chinese-Style Garlic Sauce (page 143)
  Fried Ginger Stir-Fry Sauce (page 148)
  Ginger-Lemongrass Stir-Fry Sauce (page 149)
  Oyster Stir-Fry Sauce (page 152)
  Piquant Orange Stir-Fry Sauce (page 152)
  Sesame-Ginger Stir-Fry Sauce (page 153)
  Star Anise–Hoisin Stir-Fry Sauce (page 155)
  Sweet-and-Sour Stir-Fry Sauce (page 157)
  Sweet Chile-Garlic Stir-Fry Sauce (page 156)
  Thai Basil–Nam Pla Stir-Fry Sauce (page 156)

- **Peeled and deveined shrimp, snow peas, garlic, fresh ginger, and canned sliced bamboo shoots with:**
  Chinese Black Bean Sauce (page 145)
  Chinese-Style Garlic Sauce (page 143)
  Fried Ginger Stir-Fry Sauce (page 148)
  Ginger-Lemongrass Stir-Fry Sauce (page 149)
  Green Curry Stir-Fry Sauce (page 150)
  Oyster Stir-Fry Sauce (page 152)
  Sesame-Ginger Stir-Fry Sauce (page 153)
  Sweet Chile-Garlic Stir-Fry Sauce (page 156)
  Thai Basil–Nam Pla Stir-Fry Sauce (page 156)

- **Ground pork, green beans, sliced fresh basil leaves, garlic, fresh ginger, and thinly sliced chiles with:**
  Chinese Black Bean Sauce (page 145)
  Chinese-Style Garlic Sauce (page 143)
  Classic Chinese Brown Sauce (page 143)
  Fried Ginger Stir-Fry Sauce (page 148)
  Ginger-Lemongrass Stir-Fry Sauce (page 149)
  Oyster Stir-Fry Sauce (page 152)
  Sesame-Ginger Stir-Fry Sauce (page 153)
  Sweet Chile-Garlic Stir-Fry Sauce (page 156)
  Thai Basil–Nam Pla Stir-Fry Sauce (page 156)

- **Tofu, bell peppers, celery, bok choy or Chinese broccoli, and mushrooms with:**
  Chinese Black Bean Sauce (page 145)
  Chinese-Style Garlic Sauce (page 143)
  Classic Chinese Brown Sauce (page 143)
  Fried Ginger Stir-Fry Sauce (page 148)
  Oyster Stir-Fry Sauce (page 152)
  Sesame-Ginger Stir-Fry Sauce (page 153)
  Sweet Chile-Garlic Stir-Fry Sauce (page 156)
  Thai Basil–Nam Pla Stir-Fry Sauce (page 156)

COCONUT-PEANUT
STIR-FRY SAUCE

MAKES ABOUT 1 CUP

FAST AND LIGHT, this last-minute sauce is a perfect Southeast Asian accent to stir-fried beef, chicken, or pork, pan-roasted potatoes, and stir-fried vegetables such as green beans, snap peas, broccoli, and cauliflower.

> 3 tablespoons smooth peanut butter (preferably natural)
>
> 1/2 teaspoon store-bought or homemade Thai red curry paste (page 219)
>
> 1 teaspoon peeled and finely grated fresh ginger
>
> 1/3 cup well-stirred canned unsweetened coconut milk
>
> 1/3 cup low-sodium chicken broth
>
> 1 tablespoon fresh lime juice
>
> Pinch of sugar
>
> Salt

In a small bowl, combine the peanut butter, curry paste, and ginger. Gradually whisk in the coconut milk and broth until smooth. Stir in the lime juice and sugar and season with salt.

FRIED GINGER
STIR-FRY SAUCE

MAKES ABOUT 1 CUP

FRAGRANT WITH SWEET-SPICY ginger, this sauce is suitable for meat, poultry, pork, seafood, and vegetables. Chili garlic sauce is available in Asian markets and many supermarkets; Lee Kum Kee and Lan Chi both make very good ones.

> 1/2 cup low-sodium chicken broth
>
> 1/4 cup low-sodium soy sauce
>
> 1 tablespoon Chinese cooking wine or dry sherry
>
> 1 tablespoon sugar
>
> 1 teaspoon chili garlic sauce
>
> 1 teaspoon cornstarch dissolved in 1 tablespoon water
>
> 1 tablespoon peanut oil
>
> One 2-inch piece fresh ginger, peeled and cut into fine matchsticks

1. In a small bowl, combine the broth, soy sauce, cooking wine, sugar, chili garlic sauce, and cornstarch.

2. Heat the oil in a small skillet over high heat until shimmering. Add the ginger and cook, stirring, until fragrant and lightly browned, about 1 minute. Stir the broth mixture, add it to the pan, and bring to a boil. Reduce the heat to medium and simmer until thickened and glossy, about 1 minute longer.

GINGER-LEMONGRASS STIR-FRY SAUCE

MAKES ABOUT 3/4 CUP

THIS DELICIOUS ALL-PURPOSE sauce combines a light caramel flavor with the aromatic flavors of ginger, lemongrass, and fish sauce. Use it with stir-fried chicken, seafood, beef, and pork.

- 1/4 cup Asian fish sauce
- 1/4 cup fresh lime juice
- 1 stalk lemongrass, tough outer leaves and top two-thirds discarded and inner bulb minced
- 2 scallions (white and tender green parts), minced
- 1 tablespoon peeled and finely grated fresh ginger
- 1 Thai bird chile or 1/2 finger chile, seeded and finely chopped
- 1/2 cup sugar
- 2 tablespoons water

1. In a small bowl, combine the fish sauce, lime juice, lemongrass, scallions, ginger, and chile.

2. In a small saucepan, combine the sugar and water and cook over medium-high heat, stirring just until the sugar dissolves. Wipe down any sugar crystals from the side of the saucepan with a wet brush. Cook, without stirring, until a light honey-colored caramel forms, swirling the pan as the sugar begins to brown, about 5 minutes.

3. Off the heat, add the fish sauce mixture and stir until combined. Return to medium-high heat and simmer, stirring just until the caramel dissolves, 1 to 2 minutes. Transfer to a heatproof bowl.

GINGER-ORANGE STIR-FRY SAUCE

MAKES ABOUT 3/4 CUP

THIS LIGHT AND fresh-tasting sauce is a great complement to stir-fried chicken, shrimp, or pork.

- 1/2 cup fresh orange juice
- 1 tablespoon fresh lime juice
- 1 1/2 teaspoons peeled and finely grated fresh ginger
- 1 scallion (white and tender green parts), minced
- 1 tablespoon ketchup
- 1 teaspoon cornstarch dissolved in 1 tablespoon water
- Salt and freshly ground black pepper

In a small saucepan, combine the orange and lime juices, ginger, scallion, ketchup, and cornstarch. Season with salt and pepper and bring to a boil. Reduce the heat to medium and simmer until thickened and glossy, about 1 minute.

GREEN CURRY STIR-FRY SAUCE

MAKES ABOUT 1 CUP

SERVE THIS SUPER quick, spicy coconut sauce with stir-fried chicken, seafood, eggplant, tofu, noodles, or potatoes.

2/3 cup unsweetened coconut milk

1 teaspoon store-bought or homemade Thai green curry paste (page 222)

1 tablespoon sugar

1 teaspoon peeled and finely grated fresh ginger

1 scallion (white and tender green parts), minced

1 1/2 tablespoons Asian fish sauce

1 tablespoon fresh lime juice

1/2 teaspoon cornstarch dissolved in 1 tablespoon water

1 tablespoon finely chopped fresh cilantro leaves

1 tablespoon finely chopped fresh basil leaves, preferably Thai

In a small saucepan, whisk 2 tablespoons of the coconut milk with the curry paste, sugar, and ginger until smooth. Add the remaining coconut milk, the scallion, the fish sauce, lime juice, and cornstarch and bring to a boil. Reduce the heat to medium and simmer until thickened slightly, about 1 minute longer. Let cool slightly, then stir in the cilantro and basil.

LEMON-GARLIC STIR-FRY SAUCE

MAKES ABOUT 1/2 CUP

THIS MEDITERRANEAN-FLAVORED lemon-garlic sauce is well suited for stir-fried chicken, pork, and seafood served with pasta or rice. Omit the herbs and use peanut oil for a more Asian-style lemon sauce.

1/4 cup low-sodium chicken broth

2 tablespoons fresh lemon juice

1 teaspoon cornstarch dissolved in 1 tablespoon water

Pinch of sugar

2 tablespoons extra-virgin olive oil

2 large garlic cloves, minced

1 teaspoon minced fresh thyme leaves

1/2 teaspoon minced fresh rosemary leaves

1/2 teaspoon freshly ground black pepper

1/2 teaspoon finely grated lemon zest

Salt

1. In a small bowl, combine the broth, lemon juice, cornstarch, and sugar.

2. Heat the oil in a small saucepan until shimmering over medium heat. Add the garlic and cook just until fragrant and lightly browned, about 1 minute. Add the thyme, rosemary, pepper, and lemon zest, stirring for a few seconds. Stir the lemon juice mixture, add it to the saucepan, and bring to a boil. Reduce the heat to medium and simmer until thickened and glossy, about 1 minute longer. Season with salt.

STIR-FRIED VEGETABLES AND UDON

MAKES 4 SERVINGS

THICK, CHEWY WHEAT noodles, called udon, are a staple in Japanese cooking. They are available fresh or frozen in Asian markets and some supermarkets. You can substitute cooked dried rice noodles if udon are difficult to find, and the vegetables are just suggestions. Try zucchini, broccoli, asparagus, or any number of vegetables.

> Two 7-ounce pouches jumbo udon
>
> 2 tablespoons peanut oil
>
> 1 small Thai bird chile or 1/2 finger chile, thinly sliced
>
> 1 garlic clove, minced
>
> 4 thin scallions, cut into 2-inch pieces
>
> 1 small head bok choy (about 8 ounces), root end trimmed and
> cut into 1-inch lengths
>
> Salt and freshly ground black pepper
>
> Stir-fry sauce of your choice: try Chinese Black Bean Sauce (page 145),
> Chinese-Style Garlic Sauce (page 143), Fried Ginger Stir-Fry Sauce
> (page 148), Oyster Stir-Fry Sauce (page 152), Sesame-Ginger Stir-Fry
> Sauce (page 153), Star Anise–Hoisin Stir-Fry Sauce (page 155),
> Classic Chinese Brown Sauce (page 143), or Green Curry Stir-Fry
> Sauce (left)

1. Bring a medium-size saucepan of salted water to a boil. Add the udon and cook, stirring, just until softened, about 2 minutes. Drain, shaking well.

2. Heat a wok or large skillet over high heat until very hot to the touch. Add 1 tablespoon of the oil and heat until shimmering. Add the chile and garlic and cook for 10 seconds, stirring constantly. Add the scallions and stir-fry until softened and brown in spots, 2 to 3 minutes. Transfer the scallions to a plate.

3. Return the pan to high heat. Add the remaining 1 tablespoon oil and heat until shimmering. Add the bok choy, season lightly with salt and pepper, and stir-fry until crisp-tender, 3 to 4 minutes. Add the udon and scallions and stir-fry until heated through. Add the stir-fry sauce and cook just until heated and bubbling. Serve immediately.

OYSTER STIR-FRY SAUCE

MAKES ABOUT 3/4 CUP

HERE IS ANOTHER classic sauce in Chinese cuisine. Use this versatile all-purpose sauce with stir-fried chicken, pork, beef, seafood, broccoli, green beans, and/or tofu. When purchasing oyster sauce in Asian markets or supermarkets, look for brands that have real oyster essence and not flavoring, and try to avoid caramel coloring as much as possible.

1/2 cup low-sodium chicken broth

3 tablespoons oyster sauce

2 tablespoons low-sodium soy sauce

1 1/2 teaspoons Chinese cooking wine or dry sherry

1 teaspoon cornstarch dissolved in 1 tablespoon water

1 tablespoon peanut oil

1 garlic clove, minced

1 scallion (white and tender green parts), minced

1. In a small bowl, combine the broth, oyster sauce, soy sauce, cooking wine, and cornstarch.

2. Heat the oil in a small saucepan over high heat until shimmering. Add the garlic and scallion and cook until fragrant, about 1 minute. Stir the oyster sauce mixture, add it to the pan, and bring to a boil. Reduce the heat to medium and simmer until thickened and glossy, about 1 minute longer.

PIQUANT ORANGE STIR-FRY SAUCE

MAKES ABOUT 3/4 CUP

THIS IS A great way to use up leftover Piquant Orange Marmalade Glaze. Use it on stir-fried chicken, pork, or beef with broccoli.

1/4 cup Piquant Orange Marmalade Glaze (page 215)

1/2 cup low-sodium chicken broth

1 tablespoon fresh lemon juice

1 tablespoon ketchup

1 teaspoon sugar

1 teaspoon cornstarch dissolved in 1 tablespoon water

Salt

In a small saucepan, combine the glaze, broth, lemon juice, ketchup, sugar, and cornstarch and season with salt. Bring to a boil, reduce the heat to medium, and simmer until thickened and glossy, about 1 minute.

SESAME-GINGER
STIR-FRY SAUCE

MAKES ABOUT ¾ CUP

THIS FRAGRANT MULTIPURPOSE stir-fry sauce goes well with just about anything. Use it on shrimp, pork, chicken, beef, vegetables, and noodles. Chinese cooking wine, called shaoxing wine, is available in Asian markets and some liquor stores.

> ½ cup low-sodium chicken broth
>
> 3 tablespoons low-sodium soy sauce
>
> 1 tablespoon Chinese cooking wine or dry sherry
>
> 1 tablespoon sugar
>
> 1 teaspoon cornstarch dissolved in 1 tablespoon water
>
> ½ teaspoon distilled white vinegar
>
> 1 tablespoon peanut oil
>
> 3 tablespoons peeled and minced fresh ginger
>
> ½ teaspoon red pepper flakes
>
> 1 teaspoon toasted sesame oil

1. In a small bowl, combine the broth, soy sauce, cooking wine, sugar, cornstarch, and vinegar.

2. In a small saucepan, heat the oil until shimmering over high heat. Add the ginger and red pepper flakes and cook until fragrant, about 1 minute. Stir the broth mixture, add it to the pan, and bring to a boil. Reduce the heat to medium and simmer until thickened and glossy, about 1 minute longer. Off the heat, stir in the sesame oil.

SPICY PINEAPPLE
STIR-FRY SAUCE

MAKES ABOUT ¾ CUP

CANNED PINEAPPLE PACKED in its own natural juice makes a great base for this simple stir-fry sauce. Use it on beef, pork, chicken, or seafood.

> 2 tablespoons finely chopped canned pineapple plus ½ cup of the pineapple juice
>
> ¼ cup low-sodium chicken broth
>
> 1 tablespoon fresh lime juice
>
> 1 teaspoon sugar
>
> 1 teaspoon cornstarch dissolved in 1 tablespoon water
>
> 1 tablespoon vegetable oil
>
> 1 serrano chile or jalapeño, minced (leave the seeds in)
>
> 1 scallion (white and tender green parts), minced
>
> 1 small garlic clove, minced
>
> Salt and freshly ground black pepper

1. In a small bowl, combine the chopped pineapple and juice with the broth, lime juice, sugar, and cornstarch.

2. In a small saucepan, heat the oil over high heat until shimmering. Add the chile, scallion, and garlic and cook until fragrant, about 1 minute. Stir the pineapple mixture, add it to the pan, and bring to a boil. Reduce the heat to medium and simmer until thickened and glossy, about 1 minute. Season with salt and pepper.

STIR-FRIED BEEF WITH SCALLIONS AND MUSHROOMS

MAKES 6 SERVINGS

TENDER SLICES OF sirloin are stir-fried with garlic, scallions, and oyster mushrooms, then finished with any of the above sauces.

1/4 cup peanut oil

3/4 pound oyster mushrooms, stems trimmed

4 scallions, cut into 2-inch lengths

One 3/4-pound sirloin, 1 inch thick, cut into 1/3-inch-thick x 4-inch-long slices

Salt and freshly ground black pepper

1 garlic clove, minced

Stir-fry sauce of your choice: try Chinese Black Bean Sauce (page 145), Chinese-Style Garlic Sauce (page 143), Fried Ginger Stir-Fry Sauce (page 148), Oyster Stir-Fry Sauce (page 152), Sesame-Ginger Stir-Fry Sauce (page 153), Star Anise–Hoisin Stir-Fry Sauce (right), or Classic Chinese Brown Sauce (page 143)

1. Heat a wok or large skillet over high heat until very hot to the touch. Add 2 tablespoons of the oil and heat until shimmering. Add the oyster mushrooms and scallions and stir-fry until tender and browned in spots, about 5 minutes. Transfer the mixture to a plate.

2. Return the wok or skillet to high heat and add the remaining 2 tablespoons oil. Season the beef lightly with salt and pepper. Add the beef to the pan in a single layer and cook, turning once until browned, about 2 minutes. Add the garlic and cook, tossing it with the meat, just until fragrant, about 30 seconds.

3. Return the mushrooms and scallions to the pan and stir until heated through. Add the stir-fry sauce and cook, stirring, just until heated and bubbling, about 1 minute longer. Serve immediately over rice.

STAR ANISE–HOISIN STIR-FRY SAUCE

MAKES ABOUT 3/4 CUP

THE MILD LICORICE flavor of star anise makes this slightly sweet sauce a great foil for stir-fried beef or pork. Hoisin sauce, a Chinese barbecue sauce, and star anise can be found in most supermarkets or Asian grocers.

1/4 cup hoisin sauce

1/2 cup low-sodium chicken broth

1 tablespoon low-sodium soy sauce

1/2 teaspoon cornstarch dissolved in 1 teaspoon water

1 tablespoon peanut oil

4 small dried red chiles

2 whole star anise

1 large garlic clove, minced

1 1/2 teaspoons peeled and minced fresh ginger

Salt and freshly ground black pepper

1. In a small bowl, combine the hoisin sauce, broth, soy sauce, and cornstarch.

2. In a small saucepan, heat the oil over high heat until shimmering. Add the chiles and star anise and cook until the chiles are browned, about 1 minute. Add the garlic and ginger and cook just until fragrant, about 1 minute. Stir the hoisin mixture, add it to the pan, and bring to a boil. Reduce the heat to medium and simmer until thickened and glossy, about 1 minute longer. Season with salt and pepper.

TANGERINE STIR-FRY SAUCE

MAKES ABOUT 2/3 CUP

THE BRIGHT FLAVORS of tangerine juice, jalapeño, and dry sherry make this finishing sauce a perfect accent to stir-fried pork, beef, chicken, or seafood.

1/2 cup fresh tangerine juice

1/4 teaspoon finely grated tangerine zest

2 tablespoons dry sherry

1 tablespoon fresh lime juice

1/2 teaspoon cornstarch dissolved in 1 teaspoon water

1 tablespoon extra-virgin olive oil

1/2 jalapeño, seeded and thinly sliced

1 garlic clove, minced

Salt and freshly ground black pepper

1. In a small bowl, combine the tangerine juice and zest, sherry, lime juice, and cornstarch.

2. Heat the oil in a small saucepan over high heat until shimmering. Add the jalapeño and garlic and cook until fragrant, about 1 minute. Stir the tangerine juice mixture, add it to the pan, and simmer until thickened and glossy, about 1 minute longer. Season with salt and pepper.

SWEET CHILE-GARLIC STIR-FRY SAUCE

MAKES ABOUT 1 CUP

SWEET, SPICY, AND garlicky, this all-purpose stir-fry sauce is great with chicken, pork, beef, or shrimp with vegetables. Chili garlic sauce is available in Asian markets and many supermarkets; Lee Kum Kee and Lan Chi both make very good ones.

   1/2 cup low-sodium chicken broth
   1 1/2 tablespoons low-sodium soy sauce
   1 tablespoon Chinese cooking wine or dry sherry
   1 1/2 teaspoons chili garlic sauce
   1 1/2 tablespoons sugar
   1 tablespoon ketchup
   1 teaspoon cornstarch dissolved in 1 tablespoon water

In a small saucepan, combine all the ingredients and bring to a boil. Reduce the heat to medium and simmer until thickened and glossy, about 1 minute.

THAI BASIL–NAM PLA STIR-FRY SAUCE

MAKES ABOUT 3/4 CUP

THE INTENSE, AROMATIC flavors of this sauce make it a perfect accent for stir-fried chicken, seafood, beef, and vegetables.

   1 Thai bird chile, with seeds, thinly sliced
   1 garlic clove, minced
   1 tablespoon sugar
   3 tablespoons Asian fish sauce
   1/2 cup low-sodium chicken broth
   1 1/2 tablespoons fresh lime juice
   1 1/2 teaspoons cornstarch dissolved in 1 tablespoon water
   1 tablespoon torn fresh basil leaves, preferably Thai
   1 tablespoon coarsely chopped fresh cilantro leaves

1. In a mortar using a pestle, pound the chile with the garlic and sugar to a paste. Stir in the fish sauce, broth, lime juice, and cornstarch.

2. Transfer the mixture to a small saucepan and simmer over medium heat until thickened, 3 to 4 minutes. Let cool slightly, then stir in the basil and cilantro.

SWEET-AND-SOUR STIR-FRY SAUCE

MAKES ABOUT 1 CUP

I AM ALWAYS amazed that so many people still order this sauce, usually a scary orange-red color and overly cornstarch-y, in Chinese restaurants. In this version, a tiny bit of ketchup, combined with soy sauce, orange juice, and rice vinegar, gives it the right balance of flavors without the radioactive glow. Use it on stir-fried pork, beef, chicken, vegetables, seafood, or tofu.

1/3 cup orange juice

1/4 cup low-sodium chicken broth

2 tablespoons rice vinegar

2 tablespoons sugar

2 tablespoons low-sodium soy sauce

1 1/2 tablespoons ketchup

1 tablespoon Chinese cooking wine or dry sherry

2 teaspoons cornstarch dissolved in 1 tablespoon water

1 tablespoon peanut oil

2 garlic cloves, minced

1 1/2 teaspoons peeled and minced fresh ginger

2 large scallions (white and tender green parts), minced

1. In a small bowl, combine the orange juice, broth, vinegar, sugar, soy sauce, ketchup, cooking wine, and cornstarch.

2. Heat the oil in a small saucepan over high heat until shimmering. Add the garlic, ginger, and scallions and cook until fragrant, about 30 seconds. Stir the orange juice mixture, add it to the pan, and bring to a boil. Reduce the heat to medium and simmer until thickened and glossy, about 1 minute longer.

CLASSIC STOCK-BASED SAUCES

Probably more so than anything else, stock-based sauces have come to represent archetypal French cooking. They fall loosely into two categories, veloutés and demi-glaces. Veloutés are similar to béchamels in that they start with a roux—cooked flour and butter—but they use stock, mainly veal, chicken, or fish, in place of the milk. Demi-glace is a deeply flavored brown sauce made from a meat stock, usually from beef or veal bones and aromatic vegetables, and is cooked for a long time to concentrate the flavor.

Both demi-glace and velouté, sometimes called "mother sauces," are the bases for countless classic French variations. In the velouté camp are Sauce Supreme (flavored with cream and mushrooms), Bercy (a white wine fish velouté), and Ravigote (veal velouté flavored with herbed compound butter), all of which I've included here. In addition, there are Aurore (a tomato velouté), Mariniere (a mussel-flavored fish velouté), Bonnefoy (veal velouté flavored with white wine and shallot), Chivry (chicken velouté with herbs), Normande (white wine fish velouté), Poulette (enriched with egg yolks), and Hongroise (flavored with paprika).

On the demi-glace side, you'll find in this chapter Madeira Sauce, which is flavored with Madeira, Périgueux (flavored with black truffles), Chasseur (flavored with mushrooms), Lyonnaise (flavored with onions), and Bordelaise (flavored with red wine and beef marrow). Others include Moelle (another beef marrow sauce), Espagnole

(flavored with tomato), Chateaubriand (with mushrooms and herbs), Poivrade (flavored with pepper and vinegar), Diane (flavored with pepper and cream), Romaine (flavored with sugar, vinegar, and raisins), and Zingara (flavored with tomato puree, mushrooms, and black truffle).

With so many variations, it was impossible to include all of them. The ones you find here are the best representatives of each style and have the widest range of applications.

These traditional, old-fashioned sauces can take hours and hours to make—an important process that helps develop deep flavor and enrich the sauce. Demi-glace, made in vast quantity by a single person dedicated to doing nothing else, is mostly a restaurant preparation. Since spare time at home is becoming increasingly limited I've slightly modified and updated the following recipes, so that they require considerably less time but have splendid results.

Whichever you choose to make, demi-glace or velouté, always start with homemade stock. Canned or frozen varieties, even the low-sodium ones, are too salty and flavorless when boiled down. They lack in depth.

A great time-saver is to make double batches of demi-glace and freeze it in ½-cup containers. (It'll keep in the freezer for several months.) When you need demi-glace for a recipe, just pull it out of the freezer and you're good to go.

BASIC CHICKEN STOCK

MAKES ABOUT 2 QUARTS

THIS GREAT ALL-PURPOSE stock is so versatile and simple to make you won't want to use canned broth ever again. It will keep, covered, for up to 4 days in the refrigerator and up to 3 months in the freezer. I like to store it in 2-cup containers in the freezer so I can defrost small amounts.

    6 pounds chicken parts, such as legs, wings,
        and backs, rinsed
    1 medium-size onion, left unpeeled and
        quartered
    1 large carrot, cut into 2-inch pieces
    1 celery rib, cut into 2-inch pieces
    Bouquet garni tied in cheesecloth (3 fresh
        thyme sprigs, 5 fresh parsley sprigs, 1 bay
        leaf, and 1/2 teaspoon black peppercorns)
    2 1/2 quarts water
    Salt

1. Put all the ingredients in a large soup pot and bring to a boil. Skim any scum that rises to the surface. Reduce the heat to medium-low and simmer, partially covered, until the stock is flavorful and slightly reduced, about 1½ hours.

2. Strain the stock, pressing hard on the solids to extract as much of the liquid as possible. Skim off as much fat as possible and season lightly with salt. You can also remove the fat by refrigerating the stock overnight; all the fat will float to the top and harden, and you will be able to spoon it off easily and completely.

RICH CHICKEN STOCK

MAKES 1 1/2 QUARTS

THE CHICKEN AND aromatic vegetables in this stock are browned in the oven before going into the pot. It makes the stock darker and richer tasting than Basic Chicken Stock (left).

    6 pounds chicken parts, such as legs, wings,
        or backs, rinsed
    Salt and freshly ground black pepper
    2 medium-size onions, left unpeeled and
        quartered
    2 large carrots, cut into 2-inch pieces
    1 celery rib, cut into 2-inch pieces
    Bouquet garni tied in cheesecloth
        (3 fresh thyme sprigs, 5 fresh parsley
        sprigs, 1 bay leaf, and 1/2 teaspoon black
        peppercorns)
    3 quarts water

1. Preheat the oven to 425°F. Arrange the chicken parts in a large roasting pan and season with salt and pepper. Scatter the onions, carrots, and celery around the chicken and roast until the chicken is golden and the vegetables are lightly browned, about 30 minutes. Transfer the chicken and vegetables to a large soup pot along with the bouquet garni.

2. Set the roasting pan over a burner on medium-high heat until sizzling. Add 2 cups of the water and cook, scraping up any browned bits stuck to the pan. Scrape the contents of the roasting pan into the soup pot along with the remaining water and bring to a boil. Skim any scum that rises to the surface. Partially cover and simmer over medium heat until the stock is flavorful and reduced by a third, about 1½ hours.

3. Strain the stock into a large, heatproof bowl, pressing hard on the solids to extract as much of the liquid as possible and let the fat rise to the surface. Skim off as much fat as possible. Wipe out the pot. Strain the stock back into the soup pot through several layers of cheesecloth and simmer until reduced to 1½ quarts, about 1 hour more. Let cool completely, then refrigerate until chilled. Spoon the fat from the surface and, using a paper towel, blot any congealed fat from the surface. This will keep, covered, in the refrigerator for up to 4 days and in the freezer for 3 months. I recommend freezing it in 2-cup containers.

RICH TURKEY STOCK

MAKES ABOUT 2½ QUARTS

AROUND THANKSGIVING, MANY super-markets carry turkey parts in their butcher shops for (what seems to me) the sole purpose of making stock ahead of time. Please, save yourself the stress of making it on Thanksgiving day!

6 pounds turkey parts, such as necks, wings, drumsticks, and thighs

Salt

2 medium-size onions, left unpeeled and quartered

2 large carrots, cut into 2-inch pieces

1 large celery rib, cut into 2-inch pieces

Bouquet garni tied in cheesecloth (3 fresh thyme sprigs, 5 fresh parsley sprigs, 1 bay leaf, and ½ teaspoon black peppercorns)

4 quarts water

1. Preheat the oven to 425°F. Arrange the turkey parts in a large roasting pan and season with salt. Scatter the onions, carrots, and celery around the turkey and roast until the turkey is golden and the vegetables are lightly browned, about 30 minutes.

2. Transfer the turkey and vegetables to a large soup pot along with the bouquet garni. Set the roasting pan over a burner on medium-high heat until sizzling. Add 2 cups of the water and cook, scraping up any browned bits stuck to the pan. Scrape the contents of the roasting pan into the soup pot along with the remaining water and bring to a boil. Skim any scum that rises to the surface. Partially cover and simmer over medium heat until the stock is flavorful and reduced by a third, about 1½ hours.

3. Strain the stock into a large, heatproof bowl, pressing hard on the solids to extract as much of the liquid as possible and let the fat rise to the surface. Skim off as much fat as possible. Wipe out the pot. Strain the stock back into the soup pot through several layers of cheesecloth and simmer until reduced to 2½ quarts, about 1 hour more. Let cool completely, then refrigerate until chilled. Spoon the fat from the surface and, using a paper towel, blot any congealed fat from the surface. This will keep, covered, in the refrigerator for up to 4 days or in the freezer for 3 months. I recommend freezing it in 2-cup containers.

RICH BEEF STOCK

MAKES ABOUT 2 QUARTS

FOR THIS STOCK, I sometimes use shinbones that the butcher has cut into 4-inch lengths, shoulder blade bones, tail bones, cows' feet—whatever is available. If I'm making stew or trimming a whole filet mignon, I'll save the scraps as well. My freezer is often filled with baggies labeled "beef/chicken/fish/veal bones for stock" or "meat scraps for stock." Bones work the best for stock because they get nicely caramelized when roasted and yield a lovely gelatinous stock.

2 tablespoons olive oil

8 shallots, root ends trimmed

2 large carrots, cut into 2-inch pieces

6 pounds beef bones and trimmings

Bouquet garni tied in cheesecloth
   (6 sprigs each fresh thyme and parsley,
   2 bay leaves, and 1/2 teaspoon black
   peppercorns)

2 tablespoons tomato paste

4 quarts water

1 cup mushroom trimmings (optional)

1. Preheat the oven to 425°F. In a large roasting pan, combine the olive oil, shallots, and carrots and toss to coat. Add the beef bones and scraps and roast until browned and the vegetables are lightly caramelized, about 45 minutes, tossing once or twice for even browning.

2. Transfer the beef and vegetables to a large soup pot along with the bouquet garni. Pour off the fat in the roasting pan and set the pan over a burner on medium heat until sizzling. Add the tomato paste and cook until lightly caramelized, about 1 minute. Add 2 cups of the water and cook, scraping up any browned bits stuck to the pan. Scrape the contents of the roasting pan into the soup pot along with the remaining water and mushroom trimmings, if using, and bring to a boil. Skim any scum that rises to the surface. Partially cover and simmer over low heat until the stock is flavorful and reduced slightly, about 3 hours.

3. Strain the stock into a large, heatproof bowl, pressing hard on the solids to extract as much liquid as possible. Let cool, then refrigerate until chilled. Spoon the fat from the surface and, using a paper towel, blot any congealed fat from the surface. Will keep, tightly covered, in the refrigerator for up to 4 days or in the freezer for 3 months. I recommend freezing it in 2-cup containers.

VEAL STOCK

MAKES 1½ QUARTS

BEFORE OSSO BUCO (veal shank) became so popular and thus expensive, I'd use them for making veal stock. Now I ask the butcher to sell me less desirable cuts, like neck bones, calves' feet, and scraps or trimmings for veal stock.

> 5 pounds veal bones and trimmings
>
> 3 quarts water
>
> Salt and freshly ground black pepper
>
> 2 medium-size onions, left unpeeled and quartered
>
> 2 large carrots, cut into 2-inch pieces
>
> 1 celery rib, cut into 2-inch pieces
>
> Bouquet garni tied in cheesecloth (3 fresh thyme sprigs, 5 fresh parsley sprigs, 1 bay leaf, and ½ teaspoon black peppercorns)

1. Put the veal bones and trimmings into a large soup pot along with the water, salt and pepper, vegetables, and bouquet garni and bring to a boil. Skim the scum that rises to the surface for 10 minutes. Simmer over medium heat until the stock is flavorful and reduced by half, about 3 hours.

2. Strain the stock through a fine-mesh sieve or several layers of cheesecloth into a large, heatproof bowl, pressing hard on the solids to extract as much of the liquid as possible. Let the fat rise to the surface and skim off as much fat as possible. Let cool completely, then refrigerate until cold. Using a paper towel, blot any congealed fat from the surface. Will keep, tightly covered, in the refrigerator for up to 4 days and in the freezer for 3 months. I recommend freezing it in 2-cup containers.

FISH STOCK

MAKES ABOUT 1½ QUARTS

THE BONES OF cleaned and filleted fish are called frames. Sometimes fish markets keep them on hand for customers making stock. If not, buy 1 or 2 whole fish and ask your fishmonger to filet them for you and pack up the bones. Avoid using the bones from oily, strong-flavored fish like salmon, mackerel, or bluefish for stock; use those from any of the mild, firm-fleshed white fish, such as bass, grouper, snapper, and sole.

> 2 pounds fish heads, frames, or trimmings, rinsed well
>
> 1 onion, thinly sliced
>
> 1 carrot, thinly sliced
>
> 1 celery rib, thinly sliced
>
> 1 leek (white and tender green parts), washed well and thinly sliced
>
> Bouquet garni tied in cheesecloth (3 fresh thyme sprigs, 5 fresh parsley sprigs, 1 bay leaf, and ½ teaspoon black peppercorns)
>
> Two ¼-inch-thick lemon slices
>
> 1 cup dry white wine
>
> 1½ quarts water

1. Put all the ingredients into a large soup pot and bring to a simmer over low heat. Skim any scum that rises to the surface and continue skimming until no more scum rises. Simmer the stock over low heat for 30 minutes.

2. Strain the stock through a fine-mesh sieve or several layers of cheesecloth into a heatproof bowl. Will keep, tightly covered, in the refrigerator up to 2 days or in the freezer for 3 months. I recommend freezing it in 2-cup containers.

DEMI-GLACE

MAKES ABOUT 2 CUPS

THIS RICHLY FLAVORED brown sauce is the basis for so many of the classic French sauces. It starts with a rich stock of roasted bones and trimmings, usually beef or veal, some aromatics, and flour and is slowly simmered until greatly reduced. Use this sauce as it is with roast beef and wide egg noodles, or as a jumping off point for other sauces such as Madeira Sauce (right), Perigord (page 166), Chasseur (page 166), Bordelaise (page 168), and Lyonnaise (page 167). It will keep in the refrigerator for up to 4 days.

1/4 cup (1/2 stick) unsalted butter
1 large onion, finely chopped
1 large carrot, finely chopped
1 celery rib, finely chopped
1/4 cup all-purpose flour
1/2 cup dry white wine
1 tablespoon tomato paste
1 1/2 quarts Rich Beef Stock (page 163)
Bouquet garni tied in cheesecloth
    (2 fresh thyme sprigs, 6 fresh parsley
    sprigs, 1 bay leaf, and 1/2 teaspoon black
    peppercorns)
Salt

1. Melt the butter in a large saucepan over medium-high heat. Add the onion, carrot, and celery and cook, stirring occasionally, until golden and tender, 8 to 10 minutes. Add the flour, stirring to coat the vegetables, and cook for 2 minutes. Add the wine, scraping up any browned bits from the bottom, and cook until evaporated. Stir in the tomato paste, then add the stock and bouquet garni and bring to a boil. Position the saucepan so that it is sitting half on the burner. Simmer over low heat until slightly thickened and reduced by half, about 1 hour, skimming the scum that rises to the surface from time to time.

2. Strain the sauce through a fine-mesh sieve or several layers of cheesecloth into a heatproof bowl, pressing hard on the solids. Let the fat rise to the surface and skim off as much as possible. Return the sauce to the saucepan and simmer over medium heat until reduced to 2 cups, about 10 minutes longer. Season with salt.

MADEIRA SAUCE

MAKES ABOUT 1 1/2 CUPS

WITH THE ADDITION of Madeira, this rich, sweet brown sauce, sometimes referred to as Espagnole, is another of the demi-glace variations. Serve with roasted beef, lamb, or pork.

2 cups Demi-Glace (left)
3 tablespoons Madeira
Salt and freshly ground black pepper

In a medium-size saucepan, simmer the demi-glace over medium heat until reduced to 1 1/2 cups, about 15 minutes. Add the Madeira and bring to a boil. Season with salt and pepper and serve hot. Will keep in the refrigerator for 4 days, or in the freezer for up to 3 months.

PERIGORD
(BLACK TRUFFLE–FLAVORED
BROWN SAUCE)

MAKES ABOUT 1¼ CUPS

BLACK TRUFFLES ADD an earthy quality to
this classic French sauce. You can find them
preserved in a brine solution in gourmet shops.
Serve with roasted or grilled beef, poultry, or
game.

- 1 cup Demi-Glace (page 165)
- 1 tablespoon Madeira or dry sherry
- 2 tablespoons finely chopped canned
  black truffles plus 1 tablespoon of the
  brining liquid
- Salt

In a small saucepan, combine the demi-glace,
Madeira, and truffles and brining liquid and
simmer over medium heat until heated through.
Season with salt. Serve hot. Will keep, tightly covered, in the refrigerator for 4 days, or in the freezer
for up to 3 months.

CHASSEUR
(MUSHROOM DEMI-GLACE)

MAKES ABOUT 1½ CUPS

THIS DEMI-GLACE variation is absolutely
divine with roasted or sautéed chicken, capon,
pheasant, and game hens, as well as roasted beef,
venison, veal, and pork. I like to use a mix of
wild mushrooms with white mushrooms.

- 1 tablespoon unsalted butter
- 1 tablespoon extra-virgin olive oil
- 1½ cups thinly sliced mushrooms
- ½ small shallot, minced
- 1 large vine-ripened tomato, peeled,
  seeded, and finely chopped
- ½ cup dry white wine, dry sherry, or Madeira
- ½ cup water
- ½ teaspoon finely chopped fresh thyme
  leaves
- 1 cup Demi-Glace (page 165)
- Salt and freshly ground black pepper

Melt the butter with the oil in a medium-size
saucepan over medium-high heat. Add the mushrooms and cook until softened and just beginning
to brown, about 7 minutes. Add the shallot and
cook until softened. Add the tomato, wine, water,
and thyme and bring to a boil. Simmer over low
heat until the tomatoes are broken down and the
liquid is nearly evaporated, about 10 minutes.
Add the demi-glace and simmer until slightly
reduced, about 10 minutes. Season with salt and
pepper and serve hot. Will keep, tightly covered,
in the refrigerator for 4 days, or in the freezer for
up to 3 months.

LYONNAISE (ONION-FLAVORED BROWN SAUCE)

MAKES ABOUT 2 CUPS

THIS VARIATION ON demi-glace uses lightly caramelized onions and a reduction of white wine and vinegar to create a sweet-tart rich sauce. Traditionally, it's served with grilled or roasted meats, but it is also superb with poultry, game, noodles, mashed potatoes, and polenta.

2 tablespoons unsalted butter
1 medium-size Spanish onion, finely diced
1 teaspoon sugar
1/2 cup dry white wine
1/4 cup white wine vinegar
1 cup Demi-Glace (page 165)
Salt and freshly ground black pepper

In a medium-size, heavy saucepan, melt the butter over low heat. When the foam subsides, add the onion and sugar, cover, and cook until softened, about 5 minutes, stirring a few times. Remove the lid and cook over medium heat until very soft and lightly caramelized, about 10 minutes longer. Add the wine and vinegar and cook until reduced to a few tablespoons. Add the demi-glace and simmer until slightly reduced, about 5 minutes longer. Season with salt and pepper and serve hot. Will keep, tightly covered, in the refrigerator for 4 days, or in the freezer for up to 3 months.

VELOUTÉ

MAKES ABOUT 1 1/2 CUPS

VELOUTÉ IS VERY similar to Béchamel (page 26) in that it is thickened with a roux. The difference is that it is made with veal, fish, or chicken stock. Serve this sauce with poached, roasted, or sautéed chicken, capon, or other birds, as well as poached eggs and poached or sautéed fish or shellfish. The method of setting the saucepan half on the burner forces the impurities to rise to the surface on the cooler side of the pan, which when skimmed makes for a clean, silky sauce.

2 tablespoons unsalted butter
3 tablespoons all-purpose flour
2 cups Veal Stock (page 164), Rich Chicken Stock (page 161), or Fish Stock (page 164)
1/4 cup heavy cream
Salt and freshly ground white pepper

1. Melt the butter in a medium-size saucepan over medium heat. Whisk in the flour and cook, whisking constantly, until lightly browned, 4 to 5 minutes. While whisking, add the stock and bring to a boil, whisking occasionally.

2. Position the saucepan so that it is sitting half on the burner. Simmer over low heat until slightly thickened and reduced by a third, about 30 minutes, skimming the scum that rises to the surface from time to time. Add the cream, season with salt and pepper, and serve hot. Will keep, tightly covered, in the refrigerator for 4 days, or in the freezer for up to 3 months.

BORDELAISE (RED WINE BROWN SAUCE)

MAKES ABOUT 1½ CUPS

BORDELAISE SAUCE IS a wine-enriched demi-glace, finished with a few tablespoons of gently poached beef or veal marrow. You can usually find marrow bones at your butcher shop or supermarket. If you can't get them, it's perfectly delicious without the marrow. This sauce is traditionally served with grilled or pan-fried steaks but it's also great with noodles, mashed potatoes, and polenta.

>   One 4-inch-long shinbone
>   1 cup dry red wine
>   1 shallot, minced
>   1½ cups Demi-Glace (page 165)
>   Salt and freshly ground black pepper

1. Place the marrow bone in a small saucepan, cover with cold water, and bring to a boil. Simmer over medium heat for 5 minutes. Drain and let cool slightly. Tap the bone once or twice on a work surface to dislodge the marrow and gently push it out through the larger hole. Cut the marrow into ¼-inch pieces and reserve 2 tablespoons for the sauce.

2. In a medium-size saucepan, combine the wine and shallot and simmer over medium-high heat until reduced to ⅓ cup, about 15 minutes.

3. Strain the wine through a fine-mesh sieve into a heatproof bowl. Wipe out the saucepan and return the wine to it along with the demi-glace and simmer until slightly reduced, about 10 minutes. Add the reserved diced marrow and simmer for 2 minutes. Season with salt and pepper and serve hot. Will keep, tightly covered, in the refrigerator for 4 days, or in the freezer for up to 3 months.

SAUCE SUPREME (CREAM AND MUSHROOM-ENRICHED VELOUTÉ)

MAKES ABOUT 1¾ CUPS

ANOTHER OF THE velouté variations, this one uses a velouté made with chicken stock, mushrooms, cream, and a flavored butter and is traditionally served with poached chicken. I often poach the chicken in Rich Chicken Stock and then use it for the velouté for added flavor. Serve with poached or roasted chicken, game hens, capon, or mild poultry.

>   1½ cups Basic Chicken Stock (page 161)
>   1 cup sliced mushrooms
>   1½ cups Velouté (Page 167) made with Rich Chicken Stock (page 161)
>   ¼ cup heavy cream
>   2 tablespoons Herbed Compound Butter (page 11) or unsalted butter, softened
>   Salt and freshly ground black pepper

1. In a small saucepan, combine the chicken stock and mushrooms and simmer over medium heat until the liquid is reduced to ½ cup, about 30 minutes.

2. Strain through a fine-mesh sieve into a heat-proof bowl and discard the mushrooms. Wipe out the saucepan and return the reduced chicken stock to it along with the velouté, bring to a boil, and continue to boil until reduced to 1½ cups, about 15 minutes. Gradually add the cream and boil over high heat until reduced slightly, about 5 minutes.

3. Over low heat, whisk in the butter, season with salt and pepper, and serve hot. Will keep, tightly covered, in the refrigerator for 4 days, or in the freezer for up to 3 months.

BERCY
(WHITE WINE FISH VELOUTÉ)

MAKES ABOUT 1 1/2 CUPS

THIS SIMPLE YET elegant classic French sauce is a velouté that is made with fish stock and white wine and finished with herbed butter. It is classically served with poached fish.

> 1 tablespoon unsalted butter
> 2 tablespoons minced shallots
> 1/2 cup dry white wine
> 1 1/2 cups Velouté (page 167) made with fish stock
> 2 tablespoons Herbed Compound Butter (page 11) or Caper-Shallot Compound Butter (page 8)
> 1 teaspoon fresh lemon juice
> Salt and freshly ground black pepper

1. In a medium-size saucepan, melt the butter over medium heat, then add the shallots and cook until softened, stirring a few time, about 3 minutes. Add the wine and simmer over medium heat until reduced to 2 tablespoons, about 10 minutes. Add the velouté and bring to a simmer.

2. Strain the sauce through a fine-mesh sieve into a heatproof bowl. Wipe out the saucepan and return the sauce to it. Whisk in the herbed butter, add the lemon juice, season with salt and pepper, and serve hot.

RAVIGOTE
(TANGY WINE-HERB VELOUTÉ)

MAKES ABOUT 1 1/2 CUPS

SIMPLY PUT, THIS classic sauce is a white wine–infused velouté that uses veal stock and an herb butter stirred in at the end. Use any of the herbed compound butters, such as Caper-Shallot Compound Butter (page 8), Herbed Compound Butter (page 11), or, for an interesting twist, try Scallion-Horseradish Compound Butter (page 12) or Chipotle-Cilantro Compound Butter (page 8). Serve with veal, chicken, capon, or pork.

> 1/4 cup plus 2 tablespoons dry white wine
> 1 tablespoon white wine vinegar
> 1 1/2 cups Velouté (page 167) made with veal stock
> 2 tablespoons herbed compound butter of your choice
> Salt and freshly ground black pepper

1. In a medium-size saucepan, simmer the wine and vinegar over medium heat until reduced to 2 tablespoons, about 10 minutes. Add the velouté and continue to simmer until reduced slightly, about 5 minutes.

2. Off the heat, whisk in the herbed butter, season with salt and pepper, and serve hot. Will keep, tightly covered, in the refrigerator for 4 days, or in the freezer for up to 3 months.

SAUCE NEWBURG

MAKES ABOUT 2 CUPS

ORIGINALLY CREATED IN New York City's once-famous restaurant Delmonico's, this creamy sauce was served with poached lobster. It was simply a fish velouté enriched with more cream and egg yolks. Here, I've gilded it further by starting with Sauce Americaine (right) to give it a more intense lobster flavor. Serve it over a grilled Porterhouse or strip steak for a luxe surf and turf, or over risotto, polenta, or fettuccine. The sauce can be thinned into a delicious soup with a little stock, diluted clam broth, or water and served with oyster crackers as lobster bisque.

> 1 1/2 cups Sauce Americaine (right)
> 1/4 cup heavy cream
> 2 large egg yolks
> Salt
> Cayenne pepper

1. In a medium-size saucepan, bring the sauce to a simmer.

2. In a small bowl, whisk the cream with the egg yolks. While whisking, add about 1/2 cup of the hot sauce to the cream mixture. Whisk the cream mixture into the saucepan and simmer over very low heat until slightly thickened, 2 to 3 minutes. Season with salt and cayenne and serve hot. Best used right away, but can be refrigerated, tightly covered, for up to 2 days. Reheat very gently.

SAUCE AMERICAINE

MAKES ABOUT 2 CUPS

THIS CLASSIC LOBSTER-BASED sauce uses lobster shells, brandy, and dry vermouth to flavor a fish stock. In the classic French method, a live lobster is cut into pieces and sautéed to extract flavor from the shells as well as cook the meat. I no longer do it that way—no more executive chefs breathing down my neck! Here, the lobster is cooked in boiling water and the shells are cut into pieces after the meat has been removed. The meat can be returned to the sauce and served with additional shellfish, poached fish, rice, pasta, polenta, even grits. The addition of cream and egg yolks makes this Sauce Newburg (left).

> 1 live lobster (about 1 1/2 pounds)
> 4 to 5 tablespoons unsalted butter, softened
> 1 medium-size carrot, finely chopped
> 1 large shallot, finely chopped
> 1 1/2 tablespoons tomato paste
> 1/4 cup brandy
> 1/4 cup dry vermouth
> 3 cups Fish Stock (page 164)

Bouquet garni tied in cheesecloth
(3 fresh thyme sprigs, 5 fresh parsley
sprigs, 1 bay leaf, and 1/2 teaspoon black
peppercorns)
3 tablespoons all-purpose flour
Salt and freshly ground black pepper

1. Bring a large pot of water to a boil. Add the lobster and cook, partially covered, for 8 minutes. Remove the lobster from the water and let cool slightly. Twist off the tail and, using a spoon, remove and reserve the greenish tomalley (liver) and the red roe, if it's a female. In a small bowl, stir the tomalley and roe with 1 tablespoon of the butter. Don't worry if there is no roe and the tomalley inadvertently gets discarded. Remove the meat from the claws and tail and cut them into large pieces. Using kitchen scissors, cut the shells into 2- to 4-inch pieces.

2. Melt 1 tablespoon of the butter in a large, heavy saucepan over medium heat. Add the carrot and shallot and cook until softened and just beginning to brown, about 7 minutes. Add the lobster shells and cook, stirring occasionally, until sizzling. Add the tomato paste and cook, stirring a few times, until the tomato paste is evenly distributed and lightly caramelized, about 5 minutes. Add the brandy and, standing back slightly and being careful of dangling hair and long sleeves, carefully light the brandy on fire with a long match. Let the flames die down on their own. Add the vermouth and cook until evaporated. Add the stock and bring to a boil. Add the bouquet garni and simmer over low heat, covered partially, until reduced by half, about 30 minutes.

3. Strain the stock into a heatproof bowl, pressing hard on the solids to extract as much of the liquid as possible. Rinse out the saucepan and melt 2 tablespoons of the butter. Whisk in the flour and cook over medium heat, whisking constantly, until lightly browned, 4 to 5 minutes. While whisking, add the reduced stock and bring to a boil, whisking occasionally. Position the saucepan so that it is sitting half on the burner. Simmer over low heat until thickened and slightly reduced, about 10 minutes, skimming the scum that rises to the surface from time to time. Over low heat, whisk in the tomalley butter or the remaining 2 tablespoons butter. Return the lobster meat to the sauce, season with salt and pepper, and simmer just until heated through before serving. Will keep, tightly covered, in the refrigerator for up to 3 days, or in the freezer for 1 month.

BRINES, MARINADES, AND SPICE PASTES

This chapter was really an outgrowth of the barbecue sauce chapter. I thought it was important to include it as a separate chapter because marinades act as a sort of "pre-sauce" for meat. They flavor the meat before it cooks, so oftentimes it doesn't even require a sauce. Spice pastes, rubbed into the surface of the food before it's grilled, are just a natural extension of marinades.

Foods can marinate anywhere from 30 minutes to a few days, depending on the meat and the marinade. Usually, red meat in a red wine marinade can sit for up to 3 days, whereas fish may need as little as 30 minutes; each recipe carries specific recommendations.

With spice pastes, flavors permeate the meat more slowly because they don't usually contain acid, like wine, vinegar, or citrus juice. For that reason they can stay on meat and fish overnight, but no longer than that for fish because the flesh is so delicate and prone to spoiling quickly. In some cases, it's recommended to make small gashes in the meat on which the paste gets rubbed to let it permeate even deeper.

Also in this chapter are a few recipes for brining. Salt, sugar, and fragrant seasonings are combined with a lot of water to make a sweet, salty solution. Meat or poultry is added and refrigerated for as little as

4 hours or as long as 2 days, depending on the type and size of the meat. The result is succulent, flavorful meat, with a slightly firmer texture. Ham is a perfect example of brining. A pork shoulder, if left in a brine solution long enough, will become ham (minus the excessive pink color, which is due to the addition of saltpeter). Turkey, chicken, pork, and brisket are all well suited for brining.

TIPS FOR GETTING THE MOST FROM YOUR MARINADES AND BRINES

- Zipper-lock plastic freezer bags are great to use with nonoily marinades. Before sealing, press out any excess air so that all the meat is submerged.

- After marinating, be sure to pat the meat dry before browning it in a pot. If grilling, brush with a little oil so that it stays moist.

- Red and white wine marinades can be used as a braising liquid if making a stew. Discard it if you're grilling the meat.

- Don't scrape too much of the spice paste off before grilling; just enough to prevent it from scorching.

- Brining for too long will result in very salty, tight meat. Generally, an overnight stay in the brine solution is plenty, unless the roast is more than 10 pounds, like a large turkey, fresh ham, or bone-in pork loin roast, in which case it can stay in the brine solution longer.

- Only use a marinade for basting for the first half of the cooking to avoid cross contamination. Otherwise, bring the marinade to a boil for a minute and baste throughout.

OLD BAY BRINE

MAKES ABOUT 5 QUARTS

OLD BAY SEASONING is a mixture of spices and herbs that has been around forever. It's used in crab or lobster boils and pickling and brine solutions. It's the perfect flavor for brining all sorts of poultry and pork. Poultry should be brined between 4 and 6 hours and pork 8 hours or overnight.

> 5 quarts water
> 1 cup kosher salt
> 2/3 cup sugar
> 1/2 cup Old Bay seasoning
> 6 small dried red chiles, lightly cracked
> 1 teaspoon cracked black peppercorns

1. In a medium-size saucepan, combine 1 quart of the water, salt, sugar, Old Bay, chiles, and peppercorns and cook over medium heat, stirring just until the salt and sugar dissolve.

2. Transfer to a large bowl and add the remaining water.

LEMONY SPICE BRINE

MAKES ABOUT 5 QUARTS

BRINING, SOAKING MEAT in a watery salt-and-sugar bath, is one of the oldest marinating techniques known. It imparts flavor, but more importantly, it makes the meat (or poultry) incredibly juicy and tender. In this brine, lemongrass and lemon zest lend a sweet lemony flavor. Poultry should be brined between 4 and 6 hours and pork 8 hours or overnight.

> 5 quarts water
> 1 cup kosher salt
> 2/3 cup sugar
> 2 plump stalks lemongrass, cut into 2-inch lengths and pounded
> Zest of 4 lemons, removed with vegetable peeler
> 1 tablespoon coriander seeds, lightly cracked
> 1 tablespoon cracked black peppercorns
> 4 imported bay leaves, broken

1. In a medium-size saucepan, combine 4 cups of the water, the salt, sugar, lemongrass, lemon zest, coriander seeds, peppercorns, and bay leaves and simmer, stirring until the salt and sugar are dissolved. Remove from the heat and let cool slightly.

2. Pour into a large bowl, add the remaining 4 quarts of water, and stir to combine.

SPICY SAKE BRINE

MAKES 4 QUARTS

HOT CHILES, GINGER, sake, and soy add a subtle Asian flavor to this simple brine. Poultry should be brined between 4 and 8 hours and pork overnight. Thick, meaty fish such as salmon, swordfish, and tuna can be brined as well, but for no longer than 2 hours.

> 4 quarts water
> 3/4 cup salt
> 1/3 cup granulated sugar
> 1/3 cup firmly packed light brown sugar
> 2 tablespoons molasses
> 1/4 cup small dried red chiles, lightly cracked
> 1/4 cup peeled and thinly sliced fresh ginger
> 2 cups sake
> 1 cup low-sodium soy sauce

1. In a medium-size saucepan, combine 1 quart of the water, the salt, sugars, molasses, chiles, and ginger and simmer, stirring until the sugars and salt dissolve.

2. Transfer to a large bowl, stir in the remaining 3 quarts water, the sake, and soy sauce, and let cool completely before using.

SWEET PAPAYA-GINGER MARINADE

MAKES ABOUT 2 1/2 CUPS

PAPAYAS CONTAIN AN enzyme that acts as a meat tenderizer. They also have a creamy, sweet flavor when perfectly ripe, so look for one that is about as soft as a ripe pear. This recipe partners beautifully with beef ribs, flank steak, and skirt steak. Marinate for no more than 4 to 6 hours. Scrape off the marinade before grilling.

> 1 large ripe papaya (about 1 pound), peeled, seeded, and cut into large chunks
> One 1-inch piece fresh ginger, peeled
> 1/2 medium-size onion, chopped
> 2 tablespoons fresh lemon juice
> 2 tablespoons water
> 2 teaspoons sugar
> 1/2 teaspoon ground cumin
> 1/2 teaspoon cayenne pepper
> 1/2 teaspoon salt

Combine all the ingredients in a blender and process until smooth.

SWEET SOY–STAR ANISE MARINADE

MAKES ABOUT 1½ CUPS

KECAP MANIS IS a slightly thick, sweetened soy sauce from Indonesia. Also from Indonesia is *sambal oelek,* a coarse paste of red chiles, garlic, and vinegar. Both are widely available in Asian markets and some supermarkets. If *kecap manis* is difficult to find, substitute soy sauce but omit the water and double the amount of sugar. I like this marinade on beef (especially short ribs, skirt steak, or flank steak) and pork (chops, ribs, and tenderloins), but it works well on chicken too. Marinate for 4 to 6 hours.

- 1 cup *kecap manis*
- ¼ cup water
- 2 tablespoons firmly packed light brown sugar
- 2 medium-size shallots, thinly sliced
- One 1-inch piece fresh ginger, peeled and thinly sliced
- 1 teaspoon *sambal oelek* or hot pepper sauce
- 2 whole star anise, broken

Combine all the ingredients in a small saucepan and simmer, stirring, just until the sugar is dissolved. Transfer to a bowl and let cool completely before using.

TANDOORI MARINADE

MAKES ABOUT 2 CUPS

TANDOORS, THE CLAY ovens that traditionally bake bread or roast meats, poultry, and seafood, were once found only in Indian restaurants, but now they've made their way into the kitchens of many dedicated home cooks. This yogurt marinade imparts lots of flavor as well as tenderizes the meat, so only leave it on for 4 to 8 hours. Be sure to make several gashes in the meat to allow the marinade to penetrate.

- 2 teaspoons cumin seeds
- 2 teaspoons coriander seeds
- ¼ teaspoon cardamom seeds (from 6 to 8 pods)
- ½ teaspoon fennel seeds
- ½ teaspoon red pepper flakes
- 2 large garlic cloves, finely chopped
- 1½ teaspoons peeled and finely grated fresh ginger
- 1 tablespoon sweet paprika
- 1 teaspoon salt
- 2 tablespoons canola oil
- 2 cups plain yogurt

1. In a small dry skillet, toast the cumin, coriander, cardamom, fennel seeds, and red pepper flakes over medium heat, tossing the pan constantly until fragrant, about 2 minutes. Transfer to a spice grinder to cool, then grind into a powder.

2. Transfer the spice mixture to a bowl, add the garlic, ginger, paprika, salt, oil, and yogurt, and stir until combined.

TURKISH-STYLE YOGURT MARINADE

MAKES ABOUT 2½ CUPS

LESS SPICY AND not nearly as red as Tandoori Marinade (page 177), this delicate marinade combines yogurt with lots of garlic and lemon juice. The result is incredibly succulent, tender, and flavorful meat. Makes enough for 2 cut-up chickens, 2 to 3 pork tenderloins, or 3 pounds boneless lamb, beef, or pork. Use it with chicken, lamb, beef, or pork and marinate for 4 to 8 hours.

    4 garlic cloves, chopped
    1½ teaspoons coarse salt
    1 teaspoon red pepper flakes
    ¼ cup finely chopped fresh Italian parsley
        leaves
    ¼ cup fresh lime juice
    2 tablespoons extra-virgin olive oil
    ½ teaspoon freshly ground black pepper
    2 cups plain yogurt

On a cutting board, using the flat side of a chef's knife, mash the garlic, salt, and red pepper flakes into a paste. Transfer the paste to a large bowl, add the parsley, lime juice, olive oil, and black pepper, and stir into the paste. Add the yogurt and whisk until smooth.

TUSCAN MARINADE

MAKES ABOUT 1 CUP

OLIVE OIL, ROSEMARY, sage, garlic, and lemon come together in a rustic marinade that typifies Tuscan home cooking. It is suitable for chicken, veal, pork loin, rabbit, and other game. Marinate for 4 hours or overnight.

    4 large garlic cloves, coarsely chopped
    1 teaspoon coarse salt
    4 fresh rosemary sprigs, broken into 1-inch
        lengths
    16 large fresh sage leaves
    Zest of 1 lemon, cut into thin matchsticks
    Freshly ground black pepper
    ¾ cup olive oil

On a cutting board, using the flat side of a chef's knife, mash the garlic with the salt into a paste. Transfer the paste to a large bowl, add the rosemary, sage, and lemon zest and season with pepper. Using a wooden spoon, gently mash the herbs to bruise them lightly. Stir in the olive oil.

VIETNAMESE GARLIC–FISH SAUCE MARINADE

MAKES ABOUT 1½ CUPS

LIKE *NUOC CHAM* (page 258), Vietnam's most widely used dipping sauce, this marinade uses lots of garlic, fresh chiles, ginger, and fish sauce. Try it with chicken, skirt steak, beef short ribs, pork tenderloin or chops, shrimp, or scallops. Let the meats marinate for up to 4 hours and don't scrape off any of the solids.

    4 large garlic cloves, coarsely chopped
    4 Thai bird chiles or 1 large finger chile,
        finely chopped, with seeds
    ½ cup sugar
    ½ cup hot water
    6 tablespoons fresh lime juice
    6 tablespoons Asian fish sauce
    1 large shallot, thinly sliced

In a mortar using a pestle, pound the garlic, chiles, and sugar into a syrupy paste. Add the water and stir until the sugar is dissolved, and let cool. Alternatively, puree the garlic, chile, sugar, and water in a blender. Stir in the lime juice, fish sauce, and shallot.

LIME-CHILE MARINADE

MAKES 1¼ CUPS

I LOVE HOW this versatile, tangy marinade flavors pork, beef (try it with skirt or flank steak), poultry, fish, shrimp—just about anything. Since the lime juice is so acidic, don't let the meat sit in it for more than 2 to 3 hours, and fish 1 to 1½ hours.

    2 large dried chiles, such as ancho, pasilla, or
        guajillo, stemmed
    1 cup boiling water
    4 garlic cloves, peeled
    2 large scallions, cut into 1-inch pieces
    ½ cup loosely packed fresh cilantro leaves
    2 tablespoons sugar
    1 teaspoon salt
    ½ cup fresh lime juice

1. Put the chiles in a heatproof bowl, cover with the boiling water, and let soak until softened, about 20 minutes. Drain the chiles, reserving ½ cup of the soaking liquid. Remove the seeds.

2. Transfer the chiles to a blender, add the garlic, scallions, cilantro, sugar, salt, and reserved soaking liquid and process until smooth. Stir in the lime juice.

MADRAS CURRY MARINADE

MAKES ABOUT ²/₃ CUP

THIS IS GREAT on chicken, meaty fish, lamb, beef, or pork, marinated for as little as 2 hours or overnight. I also like to brush it over sliced zucchini, eggplant, and bell peppers before grilling or roasting them.

¼ cup store-bought curry paste or
   Madras Curry Paste (page 221)
2 large garlic cloves, peeled
2 scallions (white and tender green parts),
   cut into 1-inch pieces
1 jalapeño, seeded
2 tablespoons water
½ cup canola oil
Salt

In a mini–food processor, process the curry paste, garlic, scallions, jalapeño, and water into a coarse paste. Add the oil and puree until smooth. Season with salt.

MAPLE-CHIPOTLE MARINADE

MAKES ABOUT 1¼ CUPS

THIS IS A tasty way to use up any leftover Maple-Chipotle BBQ Sauce; its sweet-and-sour tang works wonderfully with chicken, beef short ribs, and pork. Marinate for 4 hours or overnight.

½ cup Maple-Chipotle BBQ Sauce (page 202)
2 tablespoons cider vinegar
2 tablespoons fresh lemon juice
1 tablespoon salt
½ cup water

Combine all the ingredients in a small bowl.

MARGARITA MARINADE

MAKES ABOUT 2 CUPS

LIME JUICE, TRIPLE SEC, and tequila, the primary ingredients in margaritas, come together here as a marinade for pork, seafood, and chicken. Marinate for up to 4 hours for pork and chicken and 1 to 2 hours for fish and seafood. Though the proportions of ingredients here wouldn't make a suitable drink, feel free to squeeze a few extra limes for a cocktail for while you and your dinner marinate.

    1/2 cup fresh lime juice
    Finely grated zest of 1 orange
    1/4 cup fresh orange juice
    1/4 cup tequila
    2 tablespoons Triple Sec or other orange
        liqueur
    2 garlic cloves, minced
    1/4 cup olive oil
    Salt and freshly ground black pepper

In a medium-size, nonreactive bowl, combine the lime juice, orange zest and juice, tequila, Triple Sec, garlic, and olive oil and season with salt and pepper.

MOROCCAN-SPICED MARINADE

MAKES ABOUT 1/2 CUP

THIS MARINADE COMBINES the sweet spices—cinnamon, nutmeg, cloves, cumin, and coriander—with garlic and oil to create a versatile, flavorful rub suitable for poultry, beef, pork, lamb, or fish. Marinate meats and chicken for up to 4 hours and fish for 1 to 2 hours.

    1/2 cup canola oil
    1 tablespoon ground cumin
    1 1/2 teaspoons ground coriander
    1/2 teaspoon ground cinnamon
    1/4 teaspoon ground nutmeg
    1/8 teaspoon ground cloves
    2 large garlic cloves, minced
    1 teaspoon salt

In a small skillet, heat the oil with the cumin, coriander, cinnamon, nutmeg, and cloves and cook over low heat just until fragrant, stirring constantly, about 1 minute. Stir in the garlic and salt and remove from the heat. Let cool completely before using.

BLOODY MARY MARINADE

MAKES ABOUT 2 CUPS

TOMATO JUICE, HORSERADISH, celery seeds, Worcestershire, and hot sauce come together again, this time as a marinade for beef, pork, chicken, and seafood. Meat and poultry can marinate for up to 3 hours and seafood for up to an hour.

1½ cups tomato juice or V-8, preferably low sodium

2 tablespoons vegetable oil

2 tablespoons prepared horseradish

1 tablespoon Worcestershire sauce

1 teaspoon hot pepper sauce

¼ teaspoon celery seeds

½ cup dry white wine

Salt and freshly ground black pepper

Combine the tomato juice, oil, horseradish, Worcestershire, hot sauce, celery seeds, and wine in a blender and process until smooth. Season with salt and pepper and transfer to a large, nonreactive bowl.

BULGOGI MARINADE

MAKES ABOUT 1½ CUPS

SIMILAR TO THE Korean BBQ Sauce (page 208), this marinade is lighter and designed to allow the meat to sit for several hours or overnight. In Korean cooking, it is used primarily for beef short ribs or thinly sliced pork or beef, but I find it works well with all cuts of pork, beef, and poultry, as well as meaty fish.

6 large garlic cloves, peeled

2 Thai bird chiles or 1 finger chile, seeded and minced

3 tablespoons firmly packed dark brown sugar

1½ tablespoons peeled and finely grated fresh ginger

1 cup low-sodium soy sauce

¼ cup water

½ teaspoon toasted sesame oil

1. In a mortar using a pestle, pound the garlic, chiles, brown sugar, and ginger into a syrupy paste.

2. Transfer the paste to a bowl and stir in the remaining ingredients.

CITRUS-FENNEL MARINADE

MAKES ABOUT 1³/4 CUPS

ORANGE AND FENNEL is a classic Provençal flavor combination. Fresh fennel and fennel seed add lots of flavor to this sweet-tart marinade suitable for salmon, swordfish, whole snapper, and chicken. Marinate up to 4 hours.

1 tablespoon fennel seeds

Zest of 2 oranges, cut into thin matchsticks

1 cup fresh orange juice

2 shallots, thinly sliced

1/2 fennel bulb, very thinly sliced, and fronds finely chopped

1/4 cup olive oil

Freshly ground black pepper

1. In a small skillet, toast the fennel seeds over medium heat until lightly golden, about 1 minute. Let cool, then coarsely chop.

2. Transfer the fennel seeds to a nonreactive bowl, add the orange zest and juice, shallots, fennel bulb and fronds, and olive oil, and season with pepper.

CUBAN MOJO

MAKES ABOUT 2¹/4 CUPS

PRONOUNCED *MO*-HO, THIS Cuban mixture makes a great all-purpose marinade for all sorts of meat, fish, and poultry. Since it's very acidic, don't let foods sit in it for more than a few hours; fish especially should be left to marinate in it for no more than 1 hour.

1/4 cup vegetable oil

1 medium-size onion, sliced paper thin

4 large garlic cloves, thinly sliced

2 scallions, thinly sliced

1 large jalapeño, thinly sliced (leave the seeds in)

1 cup orange juice

1/2 cup fresh lime juice

Salt

In a medium-size saucepan, heat the oil over medium-low heat until shimmering. Add the onion, garlic, scallions, and jalapeño and cook until barely softened, stirring a few times, about 4 minutes. Add the orange juice and lime juice, season with salt, and simmer for 1 minute. Let cool completely before using.

FRAGRANT RIESLING MARINADE

MAKES ABOUT 3 CUPS

RIESLING IS A fruity, crisp white wine that makes a great base for marinating all sorts of lighter meats, like pork, veal, or chicken. Marinate for up to 4 to 6 hours.

> One 750-ml bottle semidry Riesling
> 4 large garlic cloves, thinly sliced
> 2 large shallots, thinly sliced
> 2 imported bay leaves, broken
> 10 fresh thyme sprigs
> 10 fresh Italian parsley sprigs
> 1/4 cup celery leaves
> 1/2 tablespoon cracked black peppercorns

Combine all the ingredients in a large, nonreactive bowl.

HOISIN FIVE-SPICE MARINADE

MAKES ABOUT 1 3/4 CUPS

HOISIN IS A sweet Chinese barbecue sauce, widely available in Asian grocery stores and many supermarkets. When shopping for a sauce of good quality, be sure that the first thing listed in the ingredients is beans and not corn syrup, cornstarch, or glucose, which would indicate a slightly inferior product. Five-spice powder is a blend of several spices: star anise, fennel, Szechuan peppercorn, clove, and cinnamon. It sometimes contains cardamom and ginger. Five-spice powder can be found in Asian grocery stores, but most supermarket spice sections also now carry it. This marinade has a wonderful affinity for pork (try it with spareribs, chops, and tenderloin) and chicken. Let marinate for at least an hour and up to 12 hours.

> 1/2 cup hoisin sauce
> 1/2 cup low-sodium soy sauce
> 1/2 cup water
> 2 tablespoons sugar
> One 1-inch piece fresh ginger, peeled and thinly sliced
> 1 large shallot, thinly sliced
> 1 teaspoon Chinese 5-spice powder
> 1/2 teaspoon ground white pepper
> 1/4 teaspoon toasted sesame oil

Combine all the ingredients, stirring until the sugar is dissolved.

LEMON-GARLIC MARINADE

MAKES ABOUT 1½ CUPS

THE COMBINATION OF lemon and garlic is one of my earliest taste memories. We had roasted lemon chicken pretty often growing up and it never failed to impress and satisfy. Poultry is a natural partner, but pork and veal chops also benefit from a dip in this marinade. Since the lemon is so acidic, keep the marination time to no more than 2 hours.

4 large garlic cloves, thinly sliced
1½ teaspoons coarse salt
2 lemons, halved
½ cup olive oil
6 fresh thyme sprigs
Freshly ground black pepper

On a cutting board, using the flat side of a chef's knife, mash the garlic with the salt into a paste. Scrape the mixture to a medium-size, nonreactive bowl and squeeze in the lemon juice. Cut each lemon half into quarters, add it to the bowl along with the olive oil and thyme, and season generously with pepper. Stir until combined.

ORANGE-SHERRY MARINADE

MAKES 1¾ CUPS

PIMENTON DULCE IS smoked sweet Spanish paprika; you can find it in most gourmet shops. Bitter oranges from Seville in Spain are sometimes difficult to find, so here I've substituted a mixture of fresh orange and lime juices to approximate the taste. If you are lucky enough to find them, use the equivalent of the orange and lime juices combined, 1½ cups. Use this to marinate fish and shellfish up to 2 hours and poultry, beef, pork, and game for up to 4 hours.

1¼ cups fresh orange juice
¼ cup fresh lime juice
¼ cup dry sherry
1 large shallot, thinly sliced
10 fresh Italian parsley sprigs
1 teaspoon *pimenton dulce* or sweet paprika
Small pinch of saffron threads, crushed

Combine all the ingredients in a large, nonreactive bowl.

PINEAPPLE-CHILE MARINADE

MAKES 2 CUPS

PINEAPPLE, LIKE PAPAYA, because of particular enzymes it contains, is a great meat tenderizer. With a little garlic and hot pepper, it makes a fruity, light marinade. Flank steak is a great choice for this marinade because the pineapple will make the meat especially tender. Marinate pork, beef, venison, and poultry for up to 4 hours and fish and shellfish for about 2 hours.

    4 large garlic cloves, thinly sliced
    4 Thai bird chiles or 1 large finger chile,
        thinly sliced, with seeds
    Finely grated zest of 1 lime
    ¼ cup fresh lime juice
    1½ cups pineapple juice
    ¼ cup olive oil
    Salt and freshly ground black pepper

In a large, nonreactive bowl, pound the garlic, chiles, and lime zest together, using a wooden spoon, until lightly mashed. Add the lime and pineapple juices and olive oil and season with salt and pepper.

RED WINE HERB MARINADE

MAKES ABOUT 3 CUPS

I LOVE TO marinate pieces of beef, lamb, or venison in this aromatic red wine marinade before braising. A dry, full-bodied red wine, such as a spicy California zinfandel or a tannic cabernet sauvignon, adds lots of flavor while tenderizing the meat. Marinate up to 6 hours. Be sure to drain the meat and pat it dry before browning.

    One 750-ml bottle dry red wine
    1 medium-size onion, thinly sliced
    1 large carrot, thinly sliced
    2 large garlic cloves, thinly sliced
    12 fresh thyme sprigs
    2 fresh rosemary sprigs
    2 imported bay leaves
    1½ teaspoons cracked black peppercorns

Combine all the ingredients in a large, nonreactive bowl.

ROSEMARY-BALSAMIC MARINADE

MAKES 1¼ CUPS

I LOVE THE sweet-tart flavor that balsamic vinegar gives to foods, especially lamb or beef, which is what I like to use here. Don't waste your expensive balsamic vinegar in this recipe—it would be completely lost. The balsamic from supermarkets is more suitable. A few hours in this aromatic marinade are enough for meat. Make sure you drain and pat the meat dry before grilling it.

    2 tablespoons coarsely chopped fresh
       rosemary leaves
    4 large garlic cloves, thinly sliced
    1 cup balsamic vinegar
    3 tablespoons low-sodium soy sauce
    1 teaspoon freshly ground black pepper

Combine all the ingredients in a small bowl.

SALMORIGLIO (LEMON MARINADE)

MAKES ABOUT 1 CUP

SICILIANS LOVE SWORDFISH, tuna, octopus, shrimp—just about any seafood. This fragrant, lemony marinade, traditionally made with oregano, is perfect for seafood, as well as veal, chicken, rabbit, or pork. Let the meat marinate for several hours; fish and shellfish about an hour. I recommend you make a double batch and use the second as a dressing after the meat is grilled or roasted.

    ⅔ cup extra-virgin olive oil
    Zest of 2 lemons, removed in strips with
       a vegetable peeler
    4 bay leaves, preferably imported
    4 large fresh rosemary sprigs, broken
       into 1-inch pieces
    1 teaspoon cracked black peppercorns
    Generous pinch of salt
    ⅓ cup fresh lemon juice
    ⅓ cup water

In a small saucepan, combine the oil, lemon zest, bay leaves, and rosemary and cook over medium heat until sizzling and the bay leaves brown lightly, about 3 minutes. Add the peppercorns and salt and let cool. Stir in the lemon juice and water.

SPICY BUTTERMILK MARINADE

MAKES ABOUT 4 CUPS

I LOVE TO soak chicken pieces in this marinade before coating them with a spiced flour mixture and frying (see Juicy Southern-Style Fried Chicken, right). I find the buttermilk imparts a slightly tangy flavor as well as tenderizes the meat. If you can't find chipotle powder, increase the cayenne to 1½ teaspoons. Marinate for 4 to 6 hours. Be sure to drain the chicken well, but don't pat it dry; the coating needs some moisture in order to adhere properly.

1 quart buttermilk
1 tablespoon kosher salt
1 tablespoon onion powder
1 teaspoon garlic powder
1 teaspoon cayenne pepper
1 teaspoon pure chipotle chile powder (optional)
1 teaspoon ground cumin
1 teaspoon ground coriander
1 teaspoon celery salt
½ teaspoon dried thyme
½ teaspoon dried sage, crumbled

In a large bowl, combine all the ingredients.

CHARMOULA

MAKES ABOUT ¾ CUP

THIS HIGHLY AROMATIC herbal marinade and condiment comes from Morocco and is used on fish, chicken, beef, and lamb, but I like it on pork and shrimp as well. Make a double batch and serve one as a condiment. Meat and poultry can marinate for up to 8 hours, but don't exceed 2 hours with fish and shellfish. This amount is enough to marinate about 2 pounds of boneless chicken, fish fillets or steaks, shrimp, or meat.

1 cup packed fresh cilantro leaves
½ cup packed fresh Italian parsley leaves
2 large garlic cloves, chopped
1 teaspoon store-bought or homemade harissa (page 352)
1 teaspoon sweet paprika
¼ cup olive oil
3 tablespoons fresh lemon juice
Salt

1. In a food processor, combine the cilantro, parsley, garlic, harissa, and paprika and pulse until finely chopped. Add the oil and pulse to a coarse paste.

2. Transfer to a bowl, stir in the lemon juice, and season with salt.

JUICY SOUTHERN-STYLE
FRIED CHICKEN

MAKES 6 SERVINGS

NOTHING MAKES FRIED chicken more succulent and tender than a few hours marinating in buttermilk. For supreme golden crispy skin, fry gently over medium heat so that it doesn't burn before the chicken is cooked through. And don't drain on a paper towel-lined plate—it will get soggy. Instead, lay paper towels on a wire rack so that air can circulate, or use brown paper bags.

Two 3½-pound chickens, cut into serving pieces
   (cut each breast half in 2 pieces)
1 recipe Spicy Buttermilk Marinade (page 188)
3 cups all-purpose flour
2 tablespoons salt
1½ teaspoons celery salt
1 teaspoon freshly ground black pepper
½ teaspoon cayenne pepper
Vegetable oil for frying

1. In a large, nonreactive bowl, cover the chicken with the marinade, cover, and refrigerate, turning the chicken a couple of times, for 4 hours.

2. In a large zipper-lock plastic bag, combine the flour, the salts, and black and cayenne peppers. Remove the chicken from the marinade, letting any excess drip back into the bowl. Transfer a few pieces to the bag, seal, and shake to coat. Press and gently squeeze the flour onto the chicken to adhere. Transfer to a large baking sheet and continue with the remaining chicken.

3. Heat ½ inch of oil in 2 large, heavy skillets over medium heat. Add the chicken to each and fry gently, turning occasionally, until golden and crisp and cooked through, about 25 minutes. If the oil gets too hot, reduce the heat and cook over medium-low heat until cooked through. Drain on a wire rack and serve right away.

If you're worried that your chicken isn't fully cooked, use an instant-read meat thermometer to test it. Carefully remove the chicken from the oil and insert the thermometer in a thick part, nearest the bone; 165°F is just right.

ANCHO-CUMIN SPICE PASTE

MAKES ABOUT 1/3 CUP

THIS RECIPE MAKES enough to coat one cut-up chicken or a 6-pound bone-in pork shoulder. Make a few slashes in the chicken and pork so you can rub the paste into the meat. Or try it on 2 pounds peeled shrimp or 4 sirloin, shell, or rib-eye steaks or pork chops. After applying the paste, wrap the meat or fish up in plastic and let marinate for at least 4 hours or overnight.

2 large garlic cloves, sliced

1 teaspoon coarse salt

1/4 cup extra-virgin olive oil

2 tablespoons pure ancho chile powder

1/2 tablespoon ground cumin

1/2 teaspoon freshly ground black pepper

1/4 teaspoon dried oregano, crumbled

1. On a cutting board, using the flat side of a chef's knife, mash the garlic with the salt into a paste.

2. Heat the oil in a small skillet over medium heat until shimmering. Add the chile powder, cumin, pepper, and oregano and cook, stirring constantly, until fragrant, about 30 seconds. Add the garlic paste and cook just until fragrant, 10 to 15 seconds longer. Transfer to a bowl and let cool completely before applying.

CREOLE SPICE PASTE

MAKES ABOUT 1/2 CUP

CREOLE REFERS TO the fusion of African, Caribbean, and French cuisine and customs. Louisiana and parts of the West Indies have become synonymous with Creole. The use of spices and aromatic vegetables creates the basis for most savory dishes in Creole cooking. Use this spice paste on shrimp; chicken; pork; goat; lamb; meaty fish like grouper, swordfish, and snapper; and shellfish and let marinate for several hours or overnight. This makes enough to coat 1½ to 2 pounds of meat or fish.

1 small onion, coarsely chopped

1 celery stalk, coarsely chopped

4 large garlic cloves, coarsely chopped

1 small green or red bell pepper, seeded and coarsely chopped

1 large jalapeño, seeded and coarsely chopped

2 teaspoons pure chile powder of your choice

1/2 teaspoon dried thyme

1/2 teaspoon freshly ground black pepper

1/2 teaspoon freshly ground white pepper

1/4 teaspoon cayenne pepper

2 tablespoons canola oil

Salt

1. In a food processor, combine the onion, celery, garlic, bell pepper, jalapeño, chile powder, and thyme, and black, white, and cayenne peppers and pulse until finely chopped.

2. Heat the oil in a medium-size skillet over medium-high heat until shimmering. Add the onion mixture and cook, stirring, until softened and just beginning to brown, 5 to 6 minutes. Season with salt and let cool before using.

SCALLION-GINGER PASTE

MAKES ABOUT 1/2 CUP

USE THIS LIGHT paste to flavor chicken breast or shrimp, scallops, or white-fleshed fish, such as sea bass, snapper, orange roughy, or porgy. If using whole fish, make a few shallow gashes on either side and rub in some of the paste; no matter what you apply it to, limit the marination time to no more than 2 hours because of its powerful flavor. This recipe makes enough for 2 pounds shrimp, scallops, or fish fillets or 4 whole 2-pound fish.

- 4 scallions, thinly sliced
- 1 tablespoon peeled and finely grated fresh ginger
- 1½ teaspoons salt
- 1½ teaspoons sugar
- 1/4 teaspoon red pepper flakes
- 1/4 cup peanut or canola oil

In a mortar using a pestle, pound the scallions, ginger, salt, sugar, and pepper flakes together into a paste. Add the oil and stir until combined.

GINGER-LEMONGRASS PASTE

MAKES ABOUT 1/3 CUP

USE THIS AROMATIC seasoning paste to flavor chicken, shrimp, scallops, or white-fleshed fish, such as sea bass, snapper, orange roughy, or porgy. I like to grill whole fish; if you do too, be sure to make a few shallow gashes on either side and rub in some of the paste. This recipe makes enough to coat 2 pounds shrimp, scallops, fish fillets or steaks, or boneless chicken breasts or 4 whole 2-pound fish. The flavors are so bold, the food needs only about 30 minutes to marinate.

- 1 stalk lemongrass, tough outer leaves and top two-thirds discarded, inner bulb finely chopped
- 1½ teaspoons peeled and finely grated fresh ginger
- 2 Thai bird chiles or 1 finger chile, seeded and minced
- 1 teaspoon salt
- 1 teaspoon light brown sugar
- 1/4 teaspoon finely grated lime zest
- 2 tablespoons vegetable oil

In a mortar using a pestle, pound the lemongrass, ginger, chiles, salt, brown sugar, and lime zest into a paste. Add the oil and stir until combined.

SMOKY PAPRIKA-GARLIC PASTE

MAKES ABOUT 1/4 CUP

PIMENTON DULCE, SMOKED sweet paprika from Spain, lends a slightly bitter, smoky flavor to foods. Regular sweet paprika can be substituted, though the taste won't quite be the same. This recipe makes enough to rub on 1 cut-up chicken; a 6-pound bone-in pork shoulder; 2 pounds shrimp; 4 sirloin, shell, or rib-eye steaks; or pork chops. Make a few slashes in the chicken or pork to rub the paste into and marinate for up to 4 hours.

- 4 large garlic cloves, thinly sliced
- 1½ teaspoons coarse salt
- 1 tablespoon *pimenton dulce*
- Pinch of cayenne pepper
- Pinch of dried oregano
- ¼ cup extra-virgin olive oil

On a cutting board, using the flat side of a chef's knife, mash the garlic with the salt into a paste. Scrape the mixture into a small bowl and stir in the *pimenton,* cayenne, oregano, and olive oil to make a paste.

SATAY PASTE

MAKES ABOUT 1 CUP

WITH SO MANY versions of this Indonesian barbecue marinade, it's hard to say which is the best. I like this one a lot because it is so versatile—try it on chicken, beef, pork, goat, or even shrimp. Rub the paste onto cubes or slices of meat or poultry or seafood and let sit for 3 to 4 hours before grilling. Serve the finished grilled dish with a peanut sauce such as Indonesian Peanut Dressing (page 286), Indonesian Peanut-Shrimp Dipping Sauce (page 250), or Vietnamese Peanut Dipping Sauce (page 259).

- 4 large garlic cloves, coarsely chopped
- 4 small shallots, thinly sliced
- 2 Thai bird chiles or 1 finger chile, seeded and coarsely chopped
- One 1-inch piece fresh ginger, peeled and coarsely chopped
- 1 teaspoon ground coriander
- 1 teaspoon freshly ground black pepper
- ¼ teaspoon turmeric
- 1 tablespoon low-sodium soy sauce
- 1 tablespoon Asian fish sauce
- 2 tablespoons firmly packed light brown sugar

1. Combine all the ingredients in a blender or food processor and pulse to a fairly smooth paste.

2. Scrape the mixture into a medium-size skillet and cook, stirring, over medium heat for about 2 minutes, just until sizzling. Let cool completely before using.

JAMAICAN JERK SEASONING PASTE

MAKES 2/3 CUP

THERE ARE LOTS of variations on this classic, all-purpose seasoning paste from Jamaica. Everyone will agree, though, that allspice, garlic, thyme, and lots of Scotch bonnet or habanero chiles are absolute must-haves for a good jerk paste. A little bit really goes a long, long way. Just a few tablespoons will season a large chicken, 2 pounds large shrimp, 2 pork tenderloins, a 6-pound pork shoulder (bone-in), a large flank steak or 2 pounds skirt steak, or 2 to 3 whole 2-pound fish. Chicken and meat can marinate in it overnight, but fish and shellfish are fine with just a few hours.

4 large garlic cloves, peeled

4 scallions (white and tender green parts), cut into 1-inch pieces

1 tablespoon fresh thyme leaves

1 Scotch bonnet chile, seeded

One 1-inch piece fresh ginger, peeled and coarsely chopped

2 tablespoons distilled white vinegar

1 tablespoon water

1 tablespoon firmly packed dark brown sugar

1/2 teaspoon ground allspice

1/4 teaspoon freshly grated nutmeg

Salt

Combine the garlic, scallions, thyme, chile, ginger, vinegar, water, brown sugar, allspice, and nutmeg in a blender or food processor and pulse into a fine paste. Season with salt.

BARBECUE SAUCES, MOPS, BASTES, AND GLAZES

America is a big country and nearly every region, large and small, has its own idea of what barbecue represents. Kansas City invariably means sweet, oniony tomato barbecue sauce brushed on virtually any kind of grilled meat. This is the most popular commercial-style sauce. Variations of the Kansas City–style sauces are Memphis style, which includes a hit of yellow mustard and is customarily served on the side with pork, and Texas style, which is smoky, much less sweet, and served with beef brisket. The Carolinas also have their own distinct styles. South Carolina's (and parts of Georgia's) is sweet honey-mustard, served on the side, specifically with pork, while the eastern part of North Carolina favors a more sweet-and-sour combination of tomato, vinegar, and yellow mustard—also served on the side with pork.

Mops and bastes are highly seasoned liquids that are liberally brushed on throughout the cooking, which is usually long and slow over a bed of coals. The flavors permeate the meats gradually. Usually the meats are larger, in the form of roasts, so that the long, slow cooking and frequent basting have great benefits. Baste every 20 to 30 minutes for very large roasts. Since they don't contain much sugar, the

sauces will not caramelize or burn. They also can be used as marinades. Retain the marinade. Bring to a boil, and baste frequently.

Glazes can be applied to meats that are cooked in the oven as well as on the grill. Glazes, which have a high sugar content, should be applied very near the end of cooking. In fact, fully cook the meat or poultry before brushing with the sauce, then cook a few minutes longer to set the glaze. This will ensure just the right amount of caramelization, without it burning and turning bitter.

HICKORY-SMOKED BBQ SAUCE

MAKES ABOUT 1½ CUPS

THIS TOMATO-BASED barbecue sauce is a variation on the Kansas City–Style BBQ Sauce (page 206). Great on ribs, burgers, steaks, chicken, and chops, it uses liquid hickory smoke flavoring and is full of flavor. Use this as both a glaze and a sauce.

1 tablespoon unsalted butter

½ small onion, minced

1 large garlic clove, minced

1 tablespoon pure chile powder, preferably ancho or New Mexico

1 cup ketchup

¼ cup firmly packed dark brown sugar

2 tablespoons cider vinegar

2 tablespoons prepared yellow mustard

1 tablespoon Worcestershire sauce

1½ teaspoons liquid hickory smoke flavoring

Pinch of cayenne pepper

Salt

Melt the butter in a medium-size saucepan over medium heat. When the foam subsides, add the onion, garlic, and chile powder and cook, stirring, until softened, about 5 minutes. Add the ketchup, brown sugar, vinegar, mustard, Worcestershire, liquid smoke, and cayenne, season lightly with salt, and simmer over low heat, stirring frequently, until thick and glossy, 15 to 20 minutes. Will keep, tightly covered, in the refrigerator for up to 1 month.

HONEY-MUSTARD BBQ SAUCE

MAKES ABOUT 1½ CUPS

HOW CAN A combination as simple as honey and mustard be so delicious? The answer, though not complicated, lies somewhere in South Carolina, where they've been making barbecue this way forever. It goes especially well with pork, but I also love it on chicken, beef, you name it—it's all good. It's usually served on the side, after the grilling is complete.

1 cup prepared yellow mustard

¼ cup plus 2 tablespoons honey

2 tablespoons firmly packed light brown sugar

2 tablespoons distilled white vinegar

2 tablespoons fresh lemon juice

½ teaspoon ground ginger

¼ teaspoon cayenne pepper

Salt

In a small saucepan, combine the mustard, honey, brown sugar, vinegar, lemon juice, ginger, and cayenne. Season with salt and simmer over medium-low heat until slightly thickened, about 10 minutes. Will keep, tightly covered, in the refrigerator for up to 1 week.

COFFEE BBQ SAUCE

MAKES ABOUT 1¾ CUPS

BREWED COFFEE ALONG with pure ancho chile powder, Worcestershire sauce, and brown sugar combine to make a great, rich, all-purpose barbecue sauce. Smoked sweet paprika, called *pimenton dulce,* comes from Spain and lends a smoky, slightly bitter flavor; you can find it at gourmet shops and good-quality Latin markets. I love this dark, flavorful sauce on all grilled meats and poultry, especially pork spareribs and chicken. But it also makes a terrific addition to baked beans, chilis, and stews. Use this as both a glaze and a sauce.

1 tablespoon unsalted butter

1 tablespoon vegetable oil

1 small Vidalia onion, finely chopped

2 large garlic cloves, peeled

2 tablespoons pure ancho chile powder

1 tablespoon ground cumin

1 teaspoon ground coriander

1 teaspoon smoked sweet paprika (*pimenton dulce)* or regular sweet paprika

½ cup ketchup

½ cup firmly packed dark brown sugar

1 cup brewed coffee, preferably dark roast

½ cup low-sodium chicken broth

½ cup cider vinegar

2 tablespoons Worcestershire sauce

Salt and freshly ground black pepper

1. In a medium-size saucepan, melt the butter in the oil over medium heat. When the foam sub-

sides, add the onion and garlic and cook, stirring frequently, until softened, about 8 minutes. Add the ancho powder, cumin, coriander, and paprika and cook, stirring, until fragrant, about 1 minute. Add the ketchup and brown sugar and cook, stirring, just until the sugar is dissolved, about 2 minutes. Stir in the coffee, broth, vinegar, and Worcestershire, season with salt and pepper, and simmer over medium-low heat until the onions are very soft and the liquid is reduced by half, about 25 minutes.

2. Transfer the sauce to a blender and process until smooth. Will keep, tightly covered, in the refrigerator for up to 1 month.

EVERYTHING'S BETTER WITH BARBECUE SAUCE

Any leftover barbecue sauce or glaze can be stirred into a stew, pan sauce, tomato sauce, or chili to boost the flavor.

SWEET TOMATO-BOURBON BBQ SAUCE

MAKES ABOUT 2 CUPS

I LOVE THE sweet, boozy flavor bourbon imparts. When combined with ketchup and spices, it makes a terrific glaze for all types of roasted or grilled meats and poultry.

2 tablespoons unsalted butter

1/2 cup minced onion

1 large garlic clove, minced

1 tablespoon pure chile powder, preferably ancho or New Mexico

1 1/2 teaspoons ground cumin

2 tablespoons tomato paste

1/4 cup bourbon

1 1/2 cups ketchup

1/2 cup firmly packed dark brown sugar

1/4 cup cider vinegar

1 tablespoon fresh lemon juice

Salt

Hot pepper sauce

Melt the butter in a medium-size saucepan over medium heat. When the foam subsides, add the onion and garlic and cook, stirring, until softened, about 7 minutes. Add the chile powder and cumin and cook, stirring, until fragrant, about 30 seconds. Add the tomato paste and cook, stirring constantly, until lightly caramelized, about 2 minutes. Stir in the bourbon and let simmer until nearly evaporated. Add the ketchup, brown sugar, vinegar, and lemon juice and simmer until thickened and glossy, about 30 minutes. Season with salt and hot sauce. Will keep, tightly covered, in the refrigerator for up to 1 month.

TAMARIND-MOLASSES BBQ SAUCE

MAKES ABOUT 1 1/4 CUPS

TAMARIND'S SWEET-TART flavor is a perfect foil for grilled meats and chicken. It is a key ingredient in Worcestershire sauce, a very popular barbecue sauce ingredient. Chili garlic sauce is available in most supermarkets in the Asian section or Asian markets. This is terrific as a glaze or a sauce.

4 ounces pressed tamarind (see Sweet-and-Sour Tamarind Sauce, page 256)

3/4 cup boiling water

1 tablespoon vegetable oil

1 large shallot, minced

1/4 cup granulated sugar

3 tablespoons unsulfured molasses

1/4 cup firmly packed dark brown sugar

2 tablespoons low-sodium soy sauce

1 tablespoon Worcestershire sauce

1 teaspoon peeled and finely grated fresh ginger

1 teaspoon chili garlic sauce or hot pepper sauce

1. In a heatproof bowl, cover the tamarind with the boiling water and let sit for 15 minutes. Mash the tamarind with the back of a spoon. Strain the pulp through a fine-mesh sieve set over a bowl, pressing hard on the seeds and tough fibers. Discard the seeds and fibers.

2. Heat the oil in a medium-size saucepan over medium heat. Add the shallot and cook, stirring, until softened, about 3 minutes. Add the strained tamarind, granulated sugar, molasses, and brown sugar and cook, stirring, until dissolved. Add the remaining ingredients and simmer over low heat until thickened and glossy, about 15 minutes. Will keep, tightly covered, in the refrigerator for up to 1 month.

MOLE BBQ SAUCE

MAKES ABOUT 2 CUPS

MOLE IS A traditional Mexican sauce that uses chiles, ground seeds, and chocolate. The chocolate isn't strong enough to detect, but it surely adds richness. Here, chiles, tomato, garlic, and just a hint of chocolate make this barbecue sauce a great foil for steaks, ribs, chicken, and meaty fish. Use this as both a glaze and a sauce.

 3 dried ancho chiles, stemmed and seeded
 1 small dried chipotle chile, stemmed and seeded
 Boiling water as needed
 One 15-ounce can peeled whole tomatoes
 1 cup low-sodium chicken broth
 1/2 cup cider vinegar
 1/4 cup plus 2 tablespoons firmly packed dark brown sugar
 1 tablespoon vegetable oil
 1 medium-size onion, minced
 2 large garlic cloves, minced
 1 teaspoon ground cumin
 1 teaspoon ground coriander
 1/2 teaspoon dried oregano
 1/8 teaspoon ground cinnamon

 1/8 teaspoon toasted sesame oil
 1/4 ounce unsweetened chocolate
   (1/4 of a 1-ounce square), coarsely chopped
 Salt

1. Put the anchos and chipotle in a heatproof bowl, cover with boiling water, and let sit until softened, about 20 minutes.

2. Drain and transfer the chiles to a blender, add the tomatoes, broth, vinegar, and brown sugar and process until smooth. Strain the mixture through a fine-mesh sieve, pressing hard on the solids to remove any seeds and tough skins.

3. Heat the oil in a large saucepan over medium heat until shimmering. Add the onion and garlic and cook, stirring, until softened, about 5 minutes. Add the cumin, coriander, oregano, and cinnamon and cook, stirring, until fragrant, about 1 minute. Add the puree and simmer over low heat until thickened and glossy, about 40 minutes.

4. Stir in the sesame oil and chocolate, season with salt, and simmer until the chocolate is melted. Will keep, tightly covered, in the refrigerator for up to 1 month.

CHIPOTLE ADOBO BBQ SAUCE

MAKES ABOUT 1½ CUPS

CHIPOTLES, SMOKED DRIED jalapeños, have become increasingly popular in American cooking over the past few years. They impart an intense smoky flavor and can be quite hot. Use this vinegary tomato-chile barbecue sauce as both a glaze and a sauce on roasted pork, beef, chicken, or meaty fish like salmon or swordfish.

2 to 3 dried chipotle chiles, stemmed
½ cup boiling water
4 large garlic cloves, peeled
1 small onion, coarsely chopped
½ cup ketchup
⅓ cup cider vinegar
¼ cup sugar
1 teaspoon ground cumin
1 teaspoon sweet paprika
½ teaspoon dried oregano
½ cup low-sodium chicken broth
Salt and freshly ground black pepper

1. In a small heatproof boil, soak the chipotles in the boiling water until softened, about 20 minutes. Drain, reserving ¼ cup of the soaking liquid.

2. Transfer the chipotles to a blender along with the reserved soaking liquid and process until smooth. Pass the puree through a fine-mesh sieve, pressing hard on the solids to remove any seeds and tough skins. Return the puree to the blender along with the garlic, onion, ketchup, vinegar, sugar, cumin, paprika, and oregano and process until fairly smooth. Add the broth, season with salt and pepper, and process until completely smooth.

3. Transfer the sauce to a medium-size saucepan and simmer over low heat until thickened and slightly reduced, about 20 minutes. Will keep, tightly covered, in the refrigerator for up to 1 month.

BARBECUE SAUCE— IT'S NOT JUST FOR THE GRILL

- When making chili, substitute any of the following barbecue sauces for the same amount of tomatoes: Chipotle Adobo BBQ Sauce (above), Coffee BBQ Sauce (page 198), Hickory Smoked BBQ Sauce (page 197), Kansas City–Style BBQ Sauce (page 206), Maple-Chipotle BBQ Sauce (page 202), Mole BBQ Sauce (left), Pasilla Chile BBQ Sauce (page 204), Smoky Texas-Style BBQ Sauce (page 204), Tennessee-Style BBQ Sauce (page 206).

- Braise spicy bite-size meatballs in any of the tomato-based barbecue sauces for a simple hot hors d'oeuvre.

- Use as a dip for mini-kebabs.

- Use in place of salsa when making chile-cheese dip.

YELLOW MUSTARD BBQ SAUCE

MAKES ABOUT 1 CUP

DOWN IN PARTS of the Carolinas, they like their barbecue sauce with lots of mustard—and not the Dijon or grainy deli types either. It is served on the side after the meat is slow cooked, not brushed on during grilling. The less expensive and more yellow it is, the better. This sauce goes well with pork, especially pulled pork, ribs, or chops, but I enjoy it on dark-meat chicken as well.

> 3/4 cup prepared yellow mustard
> 2 tablespoons firmly packed light brown sugar
> 2 tablespoons cider vinegar
> 2 tablespoons fresh lemon juice
> 1/2 teaspoon onion powder
> 1/2 teaspoon garlic powder
> 1/2 teaspoon cayenne pepper
> 1/2 teaspoon salt
> 1/4 teaspoon red pepper flakes

Combine all the ingredients in a small bowl and let sit at least 2 hours before using to let the flavors develop. Will keep, tightly covered, in the refrigerator for up to 3 days.

MAPLE-CHIPOTLE BBQ SAUCE

MAKES ABOUT 1 CUP

SWEET MAPLE AND smoky fiery chipotle chiles complement each other in this simple glaze. For a super-spicy sauce, don't strain the chipotles after pureeing them. Brush it on chicken, beef, lamb, pork, or ham during the last few minutes of cooking and serve any extra at the table.

> 1 tablespoon vegetable oil
> 1 medium-size onion, minced
> 2 large garlic cloves, minced
> 3 large canned chipotles packed in adobo, pureed and pushed through a fine-mesh sieve
> 1/4 cup ketchup
> 1/4 cup pure maple syrup
> 1 cup low-sodium chicken broth
> 1/8 teaspoon ground allspice
> Salt and freshly ground black pepper
> 1 tablespoon fresh lemon juice

1. Heat the vegetable oil in a medium-size saucepan over medium-high heat until shimmering. Add the onion and garlic and cook, stirring, until lightly browned, about 5 minutes. Stir in the chipotles, ketchup, maple syrup, broth, and allspice, season with salt and black pepper, and simmer over low heat until thickened and glossy, about 20 minutes.

2. Stir in the lemon juice. Will keep, tightly covered, in the refrigerator for up to 1 month.

RASPBERRY-CHILE BBQ SAUCE

MAKES ABOUT 1¼ CUPS

I LOVE FRUIT-BASED barbecue sauces, especially ones that balance sweetness with tartness. Raspberries are the perfect combination of sweet and tart and make a sauce that complements duck as well as chicken, beef, and pork. Brush it on during the last few minutes of cooking.

    One 10- to 12-ounce package frozen
      sweetened raspberries, thawed
    1 tablespoon tomato paste
    1 shallot, minced
    1 garlic clove, minced
    ¼ cup sugar
    2 tablespoons raspberry vinegar
    2 tablespoons fresh lemon juice
    1 teaspoon dry mustard
    1 teaspoon pure chile powder, such as ancho
      or New Mexico
    ½ teaspoon ground ginger
    ¼ teaspoon cayenne pepper
    Salt

1. In a blender, combine the raspberries, tomato paste, shallot, garlic, sugar, vinegar, lemon juice, mustard, chile powder, ginger, and cayenne and puree until smooth. Strain the puree through a fine-mesh sieve, pressing hard on the solids to remove the seeds.

2. Transfer the puree to a small saucepan and simmer until slightly thickened, about 15 minutes. Season with salt. Will keep, tightly covered, in the refrigerator for up to 1 week.

TANGY VINEGAR-CHILE BBQ SAUCE

MAKES ABOUT 1½ CUPS

VINEGAR-BASED BARBECUE sauces are popular in parts of North Carolina and Georgia and are used only on slow-roasted pork. It is usually served on the side after grilling, but I also like to use it as a baste on other rich meats such as leg of lamb and goat. I think it balances some of the fat as well as the strong flavors.

    1 cup cider vinegar
    3 tablespoons firmly packed light brown
      sugar
    1 tablespoon unsulfured molasses
    1 shallot, minced
    1 teaspoon red pepper flakes
    1 teaspoon pure chile powder, preferably
      ancho or New Mexico
    ½ teaspoon cayenne pepper
    1 tablespoon kosher salt

Combine all the ingredients in a small bowl and stir until the brown sugar and salt are dissolved. Refrigerate the sauce for several hours or overnight so that the flavors can develop before using. Will keep, tightly covered, in the refrigerator for up to 3 days.

PASILLA CHILE BBQ SAUCE

MAKES ABOUT 1¾ CUPS

DRIED PASILLA CHILES have a deep reddish-brown flesh and medium-hot raisin-like flavor. It makes for a rich, dark, vinegary barbecue sauce that goes well with beef, pork, lamb, goat, and chicken. Use it as both a glaze and a sauce. I also love it stirred into baked beans, stews, and chilis.

> 4 dried pasilla chiles, stemmed and seeded
> 1 cup boiling water
> ½ cup ketchup
> ½ cup cider vinegar
> ¼ cup tomato paste
> 2 tablespoons firmly packed light brown sugar
> 1 small onion, chopped
> 2 large garlic cloves, smashed
> 1 cup low-sodium chicken broth
> Salt and freshly ground black pepper

1. In a small heatproof bowl, soak the chiles in the boiling water until softened, about 20 minutes. Drain, reserving ¼ cup of the soaking water.

2. Put the chiles, reserved soaking liquid, ketchup, vinegar, tomato paste, and brown sugar in a blender and pulse until pureed. Add the onion and garlic and process until smooth, adding some of the broth, if necessary.

3. Set a fine-mesh sieve over a medium-size saucepan. Strain the puree, pressing hard on the solids to remove any tough skins. Whisk in the remaining broth and bring to a boil. Simmer over low heat until the sauce is thickened, about 25 minutes. Season with salt and pepper. Will keep, tightly covered, in the refrigerator for up to 1 month.

SMOKY TEXAS-STYLE BBQ SAUCE

MAKES ABOUT 2 CUPS

TEXAS IS A biiiig place and there are as many barbecue sauces as there are square miles, but unlike Kansas City–style sauces, these tend to be much less sweet. This one is seasoned with smoky chipotle chiles, vinegar, Worcestershire sauce, and ketchup and is slowly simmered to bring out lots of flavor. Brisket is the classic meat for this sauce, but I also like it on other cuts of beef, as well as pork, chicken, and lamb. Try it stirred into baked beans, stews, and chilis.

> 1 small onion, finely chopped
> 1 large garlic clove, minced
> ½ teaspoon pure chipotle chile powder or 1 dried chipotle chile, stemmed, seeded and ground in a spice grinder
> 1 teaspoon ground ginger
> 1 teaspoon dry mustard
> 1 tablespoon firmly packed dark brown sugar
> 1 cup ketchup
> ½ cup water
> ¼ cup cider vinegar
> 2 tablespoons Worcestershire sauce

BEST-EVER 20-MINUTE
BBQ "BAKED" BEANS

MAKES 6 SERVINGS

TAILOR THIS RECIPE to your taste by using any of the following sauces: Coffee BBQ Sauce (page 198), Chipotle Adobo BBQ Sauce (page 201), Hickory-Smoked BBQ Sauce (page 197), Kansas City–Style BBQ Sauce (page 206), Mole BBQ Sauce (page 200), Pasilla Chile BBQ Sauce (left), Smoky Texas-Style BBQ Sauce (left), or Tennessee-Style BBQ Sauce (page 206).

2 strips smoky bacon

1 small onion, minced

1 large garlic clove, minced

1 jalapeño chile (optional), seeded and minced

1 cup barbecue sauce of your choice (see the suggestions above)

2 tablespoons cider vinegar

2 tablespoons light brown sugar

Two 15-ounce cans pink or small white beans, drained

1/4 cup water

Salt

In a large saucepan, cook the bacon over medium-high heat until crisp. Remove the bacon and discard, set aside for another purpose, or enjoy yourself. Add the onion, garlic, and jalapeño, if using, to the pan and cook, stirring, until softened, 5 to 6 minutes. Add the sauce, vinegar, and brown sugar and bring to a simmer. Add the beans and water, season with salt, and simmer over medium heat until the sauce is reduced and beans nicely coated, about 15 minutes.

1 tablespoon fresh lemon juice

1 1/2 teaspoons liquid smoke flavoring

Salt and freshly ground black pepper

Combine the onion, garlic, chipotle, ginger, mustard, and brown sugar in a medium-size saucepan.

Add the ketchup and stir until it forms a paste. Whisk in the water, vinegar, Worcestershire, lemon juice, and liquid smoke and simmer over low heat until thick and flavorful, about 30 minutes. Season with salt and pepper. Will keep, tightly covered, in the refrigerator for up to 1 month.

KANSAS CITY–STYLE BBQ SAUCE

MAKES ABOUT 3 CUPS

KANSAS CITY QUITE possibly has the most popular style of barbecue sauces in the country. Tomato ketchup, onions, brown sugar, and spices are among the standard ingredients in this classic style of barbecue sauce. There are many permutations on this sauce—Texas style and Memphis style are all based on Kansas City–style barbecue sauces. Brush it on just about any grilled meat or poultry 5 minutes before the grilling is complete and serve any extra at the table.

3 tablespoons unsalted butter

1 small onion, minced

1 large garlic clove, minced

1 tablespoon pure chile powder, preferably ancho or New Mexico

1/2 teaspoon ground coriander

1/4 teaspoon ground ginger

1/4 teaspoon cayenne pepper

1/8 teaspoon ground cloves

1 1/2 cups ketchup

1/4 cup firmly packed dark brown sugar

2 tablespoons unsulfured molasses

2 tablespoons cider vinegar

2 tablespoons tomato paste mixed with 1 cup water

2 tablespoons Worcestershire sauce

Salt and freshly ground black pepper

Melt the butter in a medium-size saucepan over medium heat. When the foam subsides, add the onion and garlic and cook, stirring, until softened, about 5 minutes. Add the chile powder, coriander, ginger, cayenne, and cloves and cook, stirring, until fragrant, about 30 seconds. Add the ketchup and brown sugar, stirring to dissolve the sugar. Stir in the molasses, vinegar, diluted tomato paste, and Worcestershire and bring to a boil. Season with salt and pepper and simmer over low heat until thickened and flavorful, about 30 minutes. Will keep, tightly covered, in the refrigerator for up to 1 month.

TENNESSEE-STYLE BBQ SAUCE

MAKES ABOUT 2 CUPS

THOUGH SIMILAR TO barbecue sauces from Kansas City, Memphis boasts its own style of barbecue sauce—made with tomato, yellow mustard, vinegar, brown sugar, and spices. It's always served on the side with pork—ribs, pulled pork, chops, etc.—but I like it on chicken as well.

2 tablespoons unsalted butter

1 small onion, minced

1 large garlic clove, minced

1 1/2 tablespoons pure chile powder, preferably ancho or New Mexico

1/2 teaspoon ground ginger

1/4 teaspoon cayenne pepper

1/4 teaspoon ground allspice

Pinch of ground cinnamon

1 cup ketchup

1/4 cup prepared yellow mustard

1/4 cup distilled white vinegar

1/2 cup firmly packed light brown sugar

2 tablespoons unsulfured molasses

1 bay leaf

1 teaspoon liquid smoke flavoring

Salt

Melt the butter in a medium-size saucepan over medium heat. When the foam subsides, add the onion and garlic and cook, stirring, until softened, about 5 minutes. Stir in the spices and cook just until fragrant, about 30 seconds. Stir in the ketchup, mustard, vinegar, brown sugar, molasses, bay leaf, and liquid smoke and simmer until thick and flavorful, about 30 minutes. Season with salt. Will keep, tightly covered, in the refrigerator up to 1 month.

GRILL, DON'T BURN

Always brush sweet barbecue sauces and glazes on at the very end of grilling or roasting, usually the last 5 to 10 minutes. Any earlier and the sugars in the sauce will burn.

JAMAICAN JERK BBQ SAUCE

MAKES 1 CUP

FLAVORED WITH ALLSPICE, garlic, and super-hot Scotch bonnet chiles, Jamaican jerk seasoning provides this light barbecue sauce with a spicy spark. Make your own jerk seasoning or add a good-quality store-bought brand, to taste. Use this as a glaze and a sauce on all grilled meats and poultry as well as fish and shellfish.

3 scallions (white and tender green parts), coarsely chopped

2 garlic cloves, chopped

One 1/2-inch piece fresh ginger, peeled and coarsely chopped

2 tablespoons jerk seasoning, homemade (page 193) or store-bought

3 tablespoons tomato paste

2 tablespoons firmly packed dark brown sugar

2 tablespoons vegetable oil

1/4 cup distilled white vinegar

1 cup low-sodium chicken broth

Salt and freshly ground black pepper

1. Put the scallions, garlic, ginger, jerk seasoning, tomato paste, brown sugar, vegetable oil, and vinegar in a blender and process until finely chopped. Add the broth and process until smooth. Season with salt and pepper.

2. Transfer the sauce to a medium-size saucepan and simmer over medium heat until reduced by half, about 15 minutes. Will keep, tightly covered, in the refrigerator for up to 2 weeks.

KOREAN BBQ SAUCE (BULGOGI)

MAKES ABOUT 1 CUP

THIS SIMPLE SAUCE balances very few ingredients to make a flavorful marinade and barbecue sauce. Traditionally used as a marinade for boneless beef short ribs or pork, I like to use it as a baste for beef, pork, chicken, and salmon, as well as shrimp and scallops.

    ½ cup low-sodium soy sauce
    ¼ cup firmly packed dark brown sugar
    1 tablespoon peeled and finely grated fresh
        ginger
    2 large garlic cloves, minced
    1 Thai bird chile or ½ finger chile, stemmed,
        seeded, and minced
    ¼ cup water
    ½ teaspoon cornstarch dissolved in
        1 teaspoon water
    ¼ teaspoon toasted sesame oil

Combine the soy sauce, brown sugar, ginger, garlic, chile, and water in a small saucepan and simmer, stirring, until the sugar is dissolved. Stir the cornstarch mixture, add it to the sauce, and simmer until glossy and slightly thickened, about 2 minutes. Stir in the sesame oil. Will keep, tightly covered, in the refrigerator for up to 2 days.

GARLICKY SOY BBQ BASTE

MAKES ABOUT 1 CUP

USE THIS THIN but assertively flavored sauce as a baste all throughout the cooking. You can also use it to first marinate the meat, then baste with it as the meat cooks. Just be sure to cook the meat fully after basting it (to avoid any cross-contamination). I like it with pork, beef brisket, lamb, or butterflied whole chickens.

    4 large garlic cloves, minced
    ½ cup low-sodium soy sauce
    ¼ cup rice vinegar
    1 tablespoon unsulfured molasses
    1 teaspoon liquid smoke flavoring
    ¼ teaspoon cayenne pepper

Combine all the ingredients in a small bowl and let sit several hours before using to allow the flavors to develop. Will keep, tightly covered, in the refrigerator for up to 2 days.

CITRUS BBQ MOP

MAKES ABOUT 1 1/2 CUPS

A MOP, LIKE a baste, is a liquidy sauce that is liberally brushed on all throughout the cooking, which is generally slow and over low heat. A mix of fresh citrus juices and zests makes up the base for this tart sauce. Use a vegetable peeler to remove the zest in 1 x 3-inch strips before juicing the fruits. Use this on all meats and poultry.

4 strips orange zest

4 strips lemon zest

4 strips lime zest

4 garlic cloves, thinly sliced

2 tablespoons sugar

1/4 cup water

1 tablespoon salt

1/2 teaspoon red pepper flakes

1/2 cup fresh orange juice

1/4 cup fresh lemon juice

1/4 cup fresh lime juice

1. In a medium-size saucepan, combine the citrus zests, garlic, sugar, water, salt, and red pepper flakes and simmer over medium heat, stirring, until the sugar dissolves.

2. Let cool, then stir in the citrus juices. Will keep, tightly covered, in the refrigerator for up to 3 days.

LEMON, GARLIC, AND ROSEMARY GRILL SPLASH

MAKES ABOUT 3/4 CUP

CLASSIC TUSCAN FLAVORS are combined in this light, thin sauce. Brush it on chicken, lamb, pork, or fish while grilling or roasting or use it as a marinade; either way, use it the day you make it.

4 large garlic cloves, coarsely chopped

1 1/2 tablespoons finely chopped fresh rosemary leaves

1 1/2 teaspoons coarse salt

1 teaspoon finely grated lemon zest

1/3 cup fresh lemon juice

2 tablespoons water

2 tablespoons extra-virgin olive oil

Freshly ground black pepper

In a mortar using a pestle, pound the garlic, rosemary, salt, and lemon zest into a coarse paste. Stir in the lemon juice, water, and olive oil and season with pepper.

SPLASH IT ON!

For extra flavor, use large fresh rosemary sprigs as a brush when applying the splash.

TERIYAKI GRILLING SAUCE

MAKES 3/4 CUP

THE SIMPLE CONFLUENCE of just a few ingredients makes this sauce so versatile. It can be brushed on all meats, poultry, fish, and shellfish, as well as on vegetables, during the last few minutes of grilling, or served over rice.

1/3 cup low-sodium soy sauce

1/4 cup mirin

1/4 cup sake or dry white vermouth

2 tablespoons firmly packed dark brown sugar

1 tablespoon honey

1/4 teaspoon red pepper flakes

1 1/2 teaspoons cornstarch dissolved in 1 tablespoon water

1. Combine all the ingredients in a small saucepan over medium heat and simmer, stirring, until the brown sugar and honey are dissolved.

2. Add the cornstarch and boil until glossy and slightly thickened, about 1 minute. Will keep, tightly covered, in the refrigerator for up to 3 days.

BALSAMIC-PRUNE GLAZE

MAKES ABOUT 1 1/2 CUPS

BALSAMIC VINEGAR, A natural brew of sweet and tart, is paired with prunes and a touch of molasses in this rich, syrupy glaze. It's perfectly suited for duck as well as pork, beef, and dark-meat chicken. I also like to stir a tablespoon or so into a pan sauce or tomato sauce that I'm going to use for braising meats.

1/2 cup pitted prunes

1 1/4 cups boiling water

1 large shallot, coarsely chopped

2 tablespoons unsulfured molasses

2 tablespoons firmly packed light brown sugar

1/2 cup balsamic vinegar

1 tablespoon Worcestershire sauce

1/4 teaspoon red pepper flakes

Salt

1. In a small heatproof bowl, soak the prunes in the boiling water until softened and plump, about 20 minutes.

2. Transfer the prunes and any water remaining to a blender along with the shallot, molasses, and brown sugar and pulse until finely chopped. Add the vinegar and Worcestershire and process until smooth. Pulse in the red pepper flakes.

3. Transfer the mixture to a small saucepan. Season with salt and simmer over low heat, stirring occasionally, until thick and glossy, about 20 minutes. Will keep, tightly covered, in the refrigerator for up to 2 weeks.

HONEY-GINGER GLAZE

MAKES ABOUT 1/2 CUP

THE COMBINATION OF honey and ginger is so versatile, it can be used in sweet or savory dishes. As a glaze for roasted meats, poultry, fish, or shellfish, it is sublime.

- 1/2 tablespoon peeled and finely grated fresh ginger
- 1 garlic clove, minced
- 1/2 teaspoon red pepper flakes
- 1 tablespoon Asian fish sauce or low-sodium soy sauce
- 1 tablespoon fresh lime juice
- 1/4 cup honey
- Salt

In a small bowl, combine the ginger, garlic, red pepper flakes, fish sauce, and lime juice. Stir in the honey and season with salt. Will keep, tightly covered, in the refrigerator for up to 2 days.

LIME-HONEY GLAZE

MAKES ABOUT 1/2 CUP

KAFFIR LIME LEAVES, which impart a lovely lime fragrance, are available in most Asian markets and some supermarkets. If you have trouble finding them, use 1 x 2-inch strips of lime zest removed with a vegetable peeler for each lime leaf. Use this sweet, tangy glaze with chicken, fish, and shellfish.

- 1/3 cup honey
- 3 tablespoons fresh lime juice
- 1 tablespoon seasoned rice vinegar
- 2 lime leaves or strips lime zest (see headnote above), finely shredded
- Pinch of cayenne pepper
- Salt

In a small saucepan over medium-low heat, combine the honey, lime juice, vinegar, lime leaves, and cayenne and cook, stirring, until the honey melts. Season with salt. Will keep, tightly covered, in the refrigerator for up to 2 days.

DRIED CHERRY
PORT GLAZE

MAKES ABOUT ¾ CUP

THE SWEETNESS OF dried cherries and port is a perfect foil for roasted duck. Star anise, very popular in Chinese cooking, imparts an intense licorice flavor. You can find it at Asian markets or gourmet shops. This glaze goes well with pork, chicken, and beef as well. Brush it on during the last minute of cooking and let it caramelize.

> ⅓ cup packed dried sour cherries
> ½ cup ruby port
> 1 tablespoon unsalted butter
> 1 small shallot, minced
> ½ cup low-sodium chicken broth
> 2 tablespoons sugar
> ½ teaspoon dry mustard
> 1 small star anise
> Salt and freshly ground black pepper

1. In a small bowl, soak the dried cherries in the port until softened and plump, about 20 minutes.

2. Melt the butter in a small saucepan over medium heat. Add the shallot and cook, stirring, until softened, about 3 minutes. Add the cherries and any unabsorbed port, the broth, sugar, mustard, and star anise and season with salt and pepper. Simmer until the liquid is reduced by half, about 20 minutes.

3. Discard the star anise, transfer the mixture to a blender, and process until smooth. Will keep, tightly covered, in the refrigerator for up to 1 week.

DRIED CHERRY PORT PAN SAUCE: Stir 1 tablespoon of the glaze into some chicken stock before adding it to a skillet to make a pan sauce.

JALAPEÑO PEPPER
JELLY GLAZE

MAKES ABOUT ¾ CUP

USE A GOOD-QUALITY hot pepper jelly for this simple glaze. Brush it on chicken, pork chops, ribs, and pork tenderloin during the last few minutes of cooking.

> 1 scallion (white and tender green parts), minced
> 1 garlic clove, minced
> ½ teaspoon peeled and finely grated fresh ginger
> 1 tablespoon sugar
> ½ teaspoon salt
> ½ cup jalapeño pepper jelly, melted
> 1½ tablespoons distilled white vinegar

1. On a cutting board, using the flat side of a chef's knife, mash the scallion, garlic, and ginger together with the sugar and salt into a coarse paste.

2. Scrape the mixture into a small skillet, stir in the jelly and vinegar, and bring to a boil. Remove from the heat. Will keep, tightly covered, in the refrigerator for up to 2 days.

MADEIRA-RAISIN GLAZE

MAKES 1 CUP

I LOVE THE sweet, molasses-y flavor of raisins, especially when used with savory dishes. Madeira is a sweet wine similar to Marsala or port. Use this elegant sauce to glaze beef, pork, duck, or chicken, or stir a tablespoon into a pan sauce to add extra flavor.

   1/2 cup dark raisins

   1/2 cup Madeira

   2 tablespoons unsalted butter

   1 large shallot, minced

   2 tablespoons honey

   2 tablespoons firmly packed light brown
      sugar

   1/4 cup red wine vinegar

   1/2 teaspoon minced fresh rosemary leaves

   Salt and freshly ground black pepper

1. In a small bowl, soak the raisins in the Madeira until plump, about 20 minutes.

2. Melt the butter in a medium-size saucepan over medium-high heat. When the foam subsides, add the shallot and cook, stirring, until softened, about 3 minutes. Add the soaked raisins and any unabsorbed Madeira, the honey, brown sugar, vinegar, and rosemary and bring to a boil. Simmer until reduced by about a third, about 5 minutes.

3. Transfer the mixture to a blender and process until smooth. Season with salt and pepper. Will keep, tightly covered, in the refrigerator for up to 2 weeks.

MAPLE-CIDER GLAZE

MAKES ABOUT 1 CUP

SWEET MAPLE SYRUP and apple cider combine to make an outstanding barbecue sauce. Brush it on pork, chicken, beef, or ham steaks 5 minutes before the cooking is finished.

   1 cup fresh apple cider

   1/2 cup pure maple syrup

   2 tablespoons lemon juice

   2 teaspoons dry mustard

   1/2 teaspoon ground ginger

   1/4 teaspoon cayenne pepper

   1/2 teaspoon cornstarch dissolved in
      1 teaspoon water

   Salt

1. Combine the cider, maple syrup, lemon juice, mustard, ginger, and cayenne in a medium-size saucepan over medium heat and simmer until reduced to 1 cup, about 20 minutes.

2. Stir the cornstarch mixture, add it to the saucepan, and boil until thickened slightly and glossy, about 2 minutes. Season with salt. Will keep, tightly covered, in the refrigerator for up to 1 month.

ORANGE-CRANBERRY GLAZE

MAKES ABOUT 1¼ CUPS

THE CLASSIC FLAVORS of Thanksgiving in this simple glaze make turkey an obvious choice, but it goes really well with pork and ham, as well as all other types of poultry. Brush it on near the end of cooking.

1 teaspoon pure chile powder, preferably ancho or New Mexico

1 teaspoon ground coriander

¾ cup canned jellied cranberry sauce

2 tablespoons fresh lemon juice

2 tablespoons firmly packed light brown sugar

2 tablespoons bourbon

1 teaspoon Dijon mustard

1 teaspoon finely grated orange zest

Two 3-inch strips lemon zest

½ cup fresh orange juice

2 tablespoons unsalted butter

1. Toast the chile powder and coriander together in a small saucepan over medium heat until fragrant, about 1 minute.

2. Add the cranberry sauce, lemon juice, brown sugar, bourbon, mustard, and zests and cook, stirring, until melted. Add the orange juice and cook, stirring, for 1 minute. Add the butter and stir until melted. Will keep, tightly covered, in the refrigerator for up to 1 week.

PIÑA COLADA GLAZE

MAKES 1½ CUPS

NOTHING MORE EXOTIC than fresh pineapple, canned coconut cream, and a bit of rum, this glaze pairs well with grilled seafood, meaty fish, such as swordfish, salmon, and halibut, as well as pork, chicken, or ham. Brush it on as a last-minute glaze.

1 teaspoon vegetable oil

1 small yellow onion, minced

½ tablespoon peeled and finely grated fresh ginger

1 jalapeño, seeded and minced

1 cup finely diced fresh pineapple

½ cup canned cream of coconut (like Coco Lopez)

¼ cup white rum

2 tablespoons fresh lime juice

Salt

1. Heat the oil in a medium-size saucepan over medium heat. Add the onion, ginger, and jalapeño and cook, stirring, until softened, about 5 minutes. Add the pineapple, cream of coconut, and rum, and simmer until thickened and glossy, about 20 minutes.

2. Transfer the sauce to a blender and process to a coarse puree. Pulse in the lime juice just to combine and season with salt. Will keep, tightly covered, in the refrigerator for up to 1 week.

PINEAPPLE-HABANERO GLAZE

MAKES ABOUT 1½ CUPS

PINEAPPLE, FRESH, OF COURSE, makes a great base for all types of sauces. When mixed with super-hot habaneros, garlic, and a hint of acid, it makes a great barbecue sauce. The heat of these chiles can vary widely, so add a little bit at a time. Brush it on all grilled or roasted meats, especially pork or chicken, as well as meaty fish, like swordfish, tilapia, halibut, or salmon, and shellfish.

1 tablespoon vegetable oil

1 small onion, minced

1 garlic clove, minced

1 small carrot, shredded

½ medium-size yellow bell pepper, seeded and finely chopped

About ½ habanero chile, seeded and finely chopped

1 cup peeled, cored, and finely diced fresh pineapple

¼ cup plus 2 tablespoons distilled white vinegar

½ cup sugar

1½ teaspoons dry mustard

Salt

1. Heat the vegetable oil in a medium-size saucepan over medium heat. Add the onion, garlic, carrot, bell pepper, and habanero and cook, stirring frequently, until softened, about 8 minutes. Add the pineapple, vinegar, sugar, and mustard and simmer over low heat until glossy and jam-like, about 20 minutes.

2. Transfer the sauce to a blender and process until fairly smooth. Add a few tablespoons of water if the sauce is too thick. Season with salt. Will keep, tightly covered, in the refrigerator for up to 1 week.

PIQUANT ORANGE MARMALADE GLAZE

MAKES ABOUT 1 CUP

ORANGE MARMALADE MAKES a great, and unexpected, base for glazing all sorts of roasted meats and poultry. Brush it on in the last few minutes of cooking ham, pork chops, chicken, flank steak, or hamburgers.

½ cup orange marmalade

2 tablespoons ketchup

2 tablespoons orange or lemon vodka (optional)

2 tablespoons fresh lemon juice

1 teaspoon Dijon mustard

½ teaspoon red pepper flakes

½ teaspoon ground ginger

Pinch of ground allspice or cloves

Pinch of freshly grated nutmeg

Combine all the ingredients in a small saucepan and whisk until combined. Simmer over low heat until melted, about 5 minutes. Will keep, tightly covered, in the refrigerator for up to 1 week.

CURRY SAUCES AND RAITAS

Curry's worldwide popularity is pretty astonishing. It is practically the national dish of Great Britain, brought back from India during the days of the Empire. India, Pakistan, Southeast Asia, the Caribbean, North Africa, West Africa, and the Middle East all have their own variations. My favorite curries are from the Caribbean and India, but especially India, because they are multi-layered with herbs and spices, profoundly rich and flavorful, and varied from region to region.

The curries in this chapter represent basic styles from different world regions. Thailand has red and green coconut curries, made with curry pastes of fresh chiles, lemongrass, garlic, ginger, and cilantro. Vietnam's curry is like a hybrid of India and Thailand in that it uses fresh chiles, ginger, and lemongrass as well as spices such as coriander, fenugreek, mustard, and fennel. Like India with its many densely populated states, the Caribbean is huge and has many different styles of curry. West Indian curry is most like the curries of India, largely because of Great Britain's influence there, and, consequently, India's. Trinidad has a very large Indian population.

An integral sauce is one that is ordinarily not made separately from the dish as a whole. In India and the Caribbean the word *curry* refers to a saucy dish, not the sauce itself. The Thai curries, Spicy Coconut Curry Tomato Sauce, West African Spiced Curry Tomato

Sauce, Curry Yogurt Sauce, and Western-Style Curry Sauce really lend themselves nicely to separate preparations. That is, you can make the sauce before you make the dish. West Indian Curry for Lamb or Goat (page 232) is the only one here that needs to be made as the meat is prepared. Of course, with the others, once you braise the meat in the sauce, the dish will have a richer and more well-developed flavor.

Raitas are lightly seasoned yogurt sauces that have a cooling effect when served with hot and spicy foods, especially curries. At Indian meals, they're also served with mild foods because they're believed to help in digestion. That's due to the presence of acidophilus, a naturally occurring bacterial culture found in yogurt.

Cucumber raita is probably what everyone thinks of when raita is mentioned. The combination—crunchy cucumbers, creamy yogurt, and a little garlic—is classic because it's perfect. However, this style of sauce lends itself to so many permutations. For crunchy texture, you can add pomegranate seeds, grated apple, radish, or Asian pear. Or for a soft, mellow texture, try banana, mango or oven-roasted butternut squash or eggplant.

Some of these raitas function as small salads as well as sauces, especially Curry-Roasted Pumpkin Raita, Spinach Raita with Toasted Spices, and Smoky Eggplant Raita. All are best served within a few hours of making them, since the vegetables—cucumber and apple particularly—can make the sauce watery if it sits too long.

THAI RED CURRY PASTE

MAKES 3/4 CUP

IT'S MOST AUTHENTIC to prepare curry pastes with a mortar and pestle. Don't be deterred. This pungent, aromatic curry paste can also be prepared in a mini–food processor. The result will be a smoother paste, but the flavors won't suffer in the least. Use as a seasoning for any Thai curry using beef, pork, dark-meat chicken, or lamb.

20 small dried red hot chiles, seeded and chopped

2 stalks lemongrass, tender inner bulb from the bottom 5 inches, finely chopped

2 tablespoons finely chopped cilantro (leaves, stems, and roots, if attached)

One 2-inch piece fresh galangal or ginger, peeled and finely chopped

6 garlic cloves, smashed

1 tablespoon shrimp paste

2 kaffir lime leaves, finely chopped

Zest of 1 lime, removed in strips with a vegetable peeler

1 tablespoon ground coriander

1 tablespoon sweet paprika

2 teaspoons salt

1 1/2 teaspoons ground cumin

1 teaspoon freshly ground white pepper

2 tablespoons peanut or other mild-flavored vegetable oil

2 tablespoons water

In a mortar using a pestle or in a food processor, combine all the ingredients except the oil and water and pound or process until coarsely pureed. Add the oil and pound or process until a fairly smooth paste forms. Add the water 1 tablespoon at a time if the paste is too dry to process. Will keep, tightly covered, in the refrigerator for up to 2 weeks.

TIPS FOR USING CURRY SAUCES

- Sauté meats (like cut-up chicken parts, beef, lamb, goat, or pork cut into 1-inch pieces) in a light-flavored oil over medium-high heat until well browned, then reduce the heat to medium-low and add the curry sauce. Simmer until the meat is tender.

- Pork, dark-meat chicken, lamb or goat shoulder, or shin meat works best for Caribbean-style curries, as well as Spicy Coconut Curry Tomato Sauce (page 226) and West African Spiced Curry Tomato Sauce (page 230), because the longer it takes to cook, the more flavorful the stew.

- Light-meat chicken, seafood, or pork tenderloin works best in Thai curries, because the sauce is already flavorful and doesn't need to cook for very long.

- Lean meats, such as boneless chicken breast, pork tenderloin, pork loin, or beef sirloin (which I don't recommend) require little simmering; remove the meat after browning, then add the sauce. Simmer the sauce for a few minutes, then add the meat and cook briefly to avoid overcooking.

DRY CURRY NOODLES

MAKES 4 SERVINGS

THIS DISH GETS even simpler, if that's possible, when I can find fresh udon (thick, round noodles) at my Japanese grocery store. They require very little boiling, maybe a minute, before stir-frying. Dry wide rice noodles, sometimes called medium rice sticks, are a terrific alternative. Add a cup of shredded chicken or pork and this really becomes a substantial meal.

> 1/2 pound dry wide rice noodles
>
> 2 tablespoons peanut oil
>
> 1 medium-size onion, sliced into 1/2-inch-thick wedges
>
> 1/2 large red bell pepper, seeded and cut into thin strips
>
> 1 jalapeño, seeded and thinly sliced lengthwise
>
> 1 1/2 tablespoons Madras Curry Paste (right)
>
> 1 cup snow peas, ends trimmed, and cut in half lengthwise
>
> Salt
>
> 2 tablespoons finely chopped fresh cilantro leaves
>
> Lime wedges for serving

1. Bring a large saucepan of water to a boil. Add the noodles and cook until just tender, 2 to 3 minutes. Drain and cool under cold running water. Let the noodles sit in the colander, tossing them from time to time, until somewhat dry, about 15 minutes.

2. Heat the oil in a large skillet over high heat until almost smoking. Add the onion, bell pepper, and jalapeño and stir-fry until crisp-tender, about 3 minutes. Add the curry paste and cook, stirring constantly, until fragrant and the vegetables are coated, about 2 minutes. Add the noodles and snow peas, season with salt, and cook until the noodles are well coated and the snow peas are crisp-tender, 3 to 4 minutes longer. Stir in the cilantro and serve right away, passing lime wedges at the table.

MADRAS CURRY PASTE

MAKES ABOUT 1/2 CUP

DRIED CURRY LEAVES have an earthy, pungent aroma and add a slightly herbal, bitter flavor; they can be found in gourmet stores or Indian markets or you can order them from Adriana's Caravan, Kalustyan's, or Penzeys Spices. To use, rub the paste into cubes of meat and marinate in the refrigerator for several hours, then brown the meat and add to other curry ingredients.

1/4 cup ground coriander

2 tablespoons ground cumin

1 teaspoon freshly ground black pepper

1 teaspoon turmeric

1 teaspoon dry mustard

1 teaspoon pure chile powder of your choice

10 dried curry leaves, crumbled finely

1 1/2 teaspoons coarse salt

2 teaspoons minced garlic

2 teaspoons peeled and finely grated fresh ginger

1 small Thai bird or serrano chile, seeded and minced

1/4 cup cider vinegar

1/4 teaspoon vegetable oil

1. In a medium-size bowl, combine the powdered spices, curry leaves, and salt. Add the garlic, ginger, and chile and stir to combine. Add the vinegar and stir until a thick paste forms.

2. Heat the oil in a medium-size skillet over high heat until almost smoking. Add the curry paste and cook over low heat until fragrant and lightly browned, about 5 minutes, stirring constantly to prevent scorching. Let cool, then transfer the paste to a jar with tight-fitting lid. Will keep, tightly covered, in the refrigerator for up to 3 months.

CURRY YOGURT SAUCE

MAKES ABOUT 1 1/2 CUPS

SERVE THIS CLASSIC all-purpose curry sauce with grilled or roasted poultry or lamb, rice, and steamed vegetables. Use this sauce as an accompaniment or as a medium for braising small pieces of meat, poultry, or seafood.

2 tablespoons peanut oil

1 medium-size onion, diced

1 1/2 teaspoons peeled and minced fresh ginger

1 1/2 tablespoons Madras curry powder

1 1/2 cups low-sodium chicken broth

1 cup plain whole-milk or lowfat yogurt

2 tablespoons heavy cream

8 cardamom pods, lightly crushed

Pinch of sugar

Salt

1. Heat the oil in a medium-size saucepan over medium-high heat until shimmering. Add the onion and cook, stirring, until softened and just beginning to brown, about 5 minutes. Add the ginger and curry powder and cook, stirring, until fragrant, about 2 minutes. Add the broth and bring to a boil. Reduce the heat to medium and simmer until reduced by about one third, about 10 minutes.

2. Scrape the sauce into a blender, add the yogurt and cream, and process until smooth. Return the sauce to the pan, add the cardamom pods and sugar, and simmer over medium-low heat, stirring occasionally, until slightly thickened, about 20 minutes. Season with salt. The sauce may curdle, but will come together again as it cooks.

THAI GREEN CURRY PASTE

MAKES 3/4 CUP

LIKE THAI RED curry paste (page 219), this one is traditionally made in a mortar and pestle. It's a bit easier to pound than the red, since the chiles called for are fresh. If you don't want a super-spicy curry paste, remove all the seeds from the chiles. Freeze any leftover curry paste in 2-tablespoon lumps. Lemongrass, galangal, lime leaves, and shrimp paste can be found in Asian markets. Use as a seasoning for any of the coconut milk Thai curries with chicken, seafood, or fish.

8 small Thai bird chiles, finely chopped

Three 6-inch-long, mild green chiles, seeded and finely chopped

3 large garlic cloves, crushed

1 large shallot, finely chopped

2 stalks lemongrass, tender inner bulb from the bottom 4 inches, finely chopped

One 1½-inch piece fresh galangal or ginger, peeled and finely chopped

2 kaffir lime leaves, finely chopped, or zest of 1 lime, removed in strips with a vegetable peeler

2 tablespoons finely chopped cilantro (leaves, stems, and roots, if attached)

1½ teaspoons shrimp paste

1 teaspoon ground coriander

1 teaspoon salt

½ teaspoon ground cumin

½ teaspoon freshly ground white pepper

1 tablespoons peanut or other mild-flavored vegetable oil

In a mortar using a pestle, or in a food processor, combine all the ingredients except the oil and pound or process into a coarse puree. Add the oil and pound or process until a fairly smooth paste forms. Will keep, tightly covered, in the refrigerator for up to 2 weeks.

COCONUT CURRY WITH LEEKS AND BASIL

MAKES ABOUT 1½ CUPS

LEEKS AND BASIL add a lovely, sweet flavor to this classic Thai curry sauce. I love using holy basil, which is a Thai variety that adds a distinct perfume. It's often hard to find, so regular basil is a perfectly acceptable substitute. Kaffir lime leaves also add a floral, limey aroma, but are sometimes difficult to find outside of an Asian market. I find lime zest, removed in strips using a vegetable

CURRY YOGURT BRAISED LAMB
(KORMA)

MAKES ABOUT 4 SERVINGS

TENDER, SUCCULENT PIECES of lamb are braised in yogurt, curry, and tomatoes. Serve this fragrant, deeply flavored stew with rice or noodles or as a pita sandwich filling.

2 tablespoons peanut oil

1½ pounds boneless lamb shoulder, trimmed of fat and cut into
    1½-inch pieces

Salt and freshly ground black pepper

1 medium-size onion, diced

¾ cup drained canned peeled whole Italian tomatoes,
    cut into large pieces

1 recipe Curry Yogurt Sauce (page 221)

1 cup low-sodium chicken broth

Pinch of sugar

Steamed basmati rice

2 tablespoons chopped fresh cilantro leaves

1. Heat the oil in a large, heavy casserole or Dutch oven over medium-high heat until shimmering. Season the lamb with salt and pepper, add half of it to the casserole, and cook until browned all over, about 10 minutes. Using a slotted spoon, transfer the lamb to a plate. Brown the remaining lamb and add it to the plate.

2. Add the onion to the casserole and cook, stirring, over medium-high heat until lightly browned, 3 to 4 minutes. Add the tomatoes and cook, stirring occasionally, until the liquid is evaporated and the tomatoes begin to sizzle, about 5 minutes. Return the lamb to the casserole and stir until combined. Add the yogurt sauce, broth, and sugar and bring to a boil. Reduce the heat to low, cover, and simmer until the meat is meltingly tender, about 1½ hours, stirring frequently to prevent sticking.

3. Serve the lamb over the rice, garnished with the cilantro.

FAST VEGETABLE STEW

MAKES 4 SERVINGS

I LIKE USING hearty vegetables like squash and carrots in this, but feel free to use any vegetables you like. This stew is great with couscous.

> 2 tablespoons vegetable oil
>
> 1 large onion, cut into 1/2-inch dice
>
> 2 large carrots, cut into 1-inch-thick rounds
>
> 1 large Yukon Gold potato, peeled and cut into 2-inch chunks
>
> 1/2 small butternut squash, peeled, seeded, and cut into 1-inch cubes
>
> 1 recipe West African Spiced Curry Tomato Sauce (page 230), Spicy Coconut Curry Tomato Sauce (page 226), or Curry Yogurt Sauce (page 221)
>
> Salt and freshly ground black pepper

Heat the oil in a large deep skillet over medium-high heat until shimmering. Add the vegetables and cook, tossing occasionally, until crisp-tender, about 8 minutes. Add the sauce, season with salt and pepper, and simmer over medium-low heat, stirring occasionally, until tender, about 25 minutes. Add water as needed to prevent sticking.

peeler, works great in a pinch. Use a 1/2 x 2-inch strip for each leaf substituted. I like to poach thin slices of chicken, shrimp, scallops, and fish in this sauce at the end. It's also great with sautéed broccoli and string beans.

> 2 tablespoons peanut oil
>
> 3 medium-size leeks (white and tender green parts only), halved lengthwise, washed well, and thickly sliced
>
> 1 garlic clove, minced
>
> 1 teaspoon peeled and minced fresh ginger
>
> 1 teaspoon store-bought or homemade Thai Green Curry Paste (page 222)
>
> 1 1/2 cups low-sodium chicken broth
>
> One 14-ounce can unsweetened coconut milk
>
> 2 kaffir lime leaves (see headnote for substitute)
>
> 1 stalk lemongrass, cut into 3-inch pieces and lightly bruised
>
> 2 tablespoons Asian fish sauce
>
> 1/2 teaspoon light brown sugar
>
> 1/2 cup loosely packed torn fresh basil leaves
>
> 1 tablespoon fresh lime juice

CHICKEN MUGHLAI CURRY

MAKES 4 SERVINGS

CHICKEN THIGHS ARE wonderful for stews and curries because they stay very moist and tender. Pork shoulder, lamb shoulder, or beef chuck are great, too. For a slightly leaner version, use boneless, skinless chicken breasts, but be sure to simmer them for about 20 minutes.

2 tablespoon vegetable oil

6 boneless, skinless chicken thighs, cut into 2-inch pieces

Salt and freshly ground black pepper

1 small onion, minced

1 garlic clove, minced

1 tablespoon peeled and minced fresh ginger

1 recipe Spicy Coconut Curry Tomato Sauce (page 226)

1. Heat the oil in a large deep skillet over medium-high heat until shimmering. Season the chicken with salt and pepper and brown in the hot oil. Transfer to a plate.

2. Add the onion, garlic, and ginger to the pan and cook, stirring a few times, until fragrant. Return the chicken to the pan, add the curry sauce, and scrape all the browned bits from the bottom of the pan. Simmer over medium-low heat until the chicken is tender, about 35 minutes.

1. Heat the peanut oil in a large deep skillet over medium-high heat. Add the leeks and stir-fry until softened and just beginning to brown, about 3 minutes. Transfer the leeks to a medium-size bowl.

2. Add the garlic and ginger to the skillet and cook, stirring, until fragrant, about 1 minute. Stir in the curry paste, broth, coconut milk, lime leaves, lemongrass, 1 tablespoon of the fish sauce, brown sugar, and leeks, and simmer over medium-low heat until thickened and reduced by about half, about 20 minutes. Add the remaining 1 tablespoon fish sauce, the basil, and the lime juice and stir to combine. This is best used right away.

SPICY COCONUT
CURRY TOMATO SAUCE

MAKES ABOUT 3½ TO 4 CUPS

I LIKE TO add cut-up vegetables and chicken breast or shrimp to this sauce for a quick meal, or braise chicken thighs in it for a rich chicken curry. It also makes a great soup—just add some chicken stock, vegetables, chicken or seafood, and rice.

    2 tablespoons mild-flavored oil, such as
        canola or peanut
    1 medium-size yellow onion, thinly sliced
    1 garlic clove, minced
    1 jalapeño, seeded and minced
    ½ teaspoon peeled and minced fresh ginger
    1½ tablespoons Madras curry powder
    One 28-ounce can peeled whole tomatoes,
        with their juices, cut into 1-inch pieces
    One 14-ounce can unsweetened coconut milk
    1 teaspoon sugar
    Salt and freshly ground black pepper
    2 tablespoons chopped fresh cilantro leaves

Heat the oil in a large saucepan over medium-high heat until shimmering. Add the onion, garlic, jalapeño, and ginger and cook, stirring, until softened, about 5 minutes. Add the curry powder and cook until fragrant and lightly golden, about 1 minute. Add the tomatoes, coconut milk, and sugar and bring to a boil. Reduce the heat to medium, season with salt and pepper, and simmer, stirring occasionally, until thickened slightly, about 20 minutes. Stir in the cilantro. Will keep, tightly covered, in the refrigerator for up to 3 days.

SOUTH VIETNAMESE–STYLE
COCONUT CURRY SAUCE

MAKES ABOUT 1½ CUPS

IN PARTS OF Vietnam, the curry is closer to Indian curry than it is to the curry of Thailand. Serve this with rice or noodles, or stirred into a chicken or seafood stir-fry.

    2 tablespoons peanut or other mild-flavored
        oil
    2 large garlic cloves, minced
    1 large shallot, thinly sliced
    1 tablespoon peeled and minced fresh ginger
    2 tablespoons Madras curry powder
    1 stalk lemongrass, cut into 2-inch pieces
        and lightly crushed
    4 small dried red chiles
    1 cup well-stirred canned unsweetened
        coconut milk
    1½ cups low-sodium chicken broth
    2 tablespoons Asian fish sauce
    2 kaffir lime leaves or two ½ x 2-inch strips
        lime zest

Heat the oil in a heavy medium-size saucepan over medium heat until it shimmers. Add the garlic, shallot, and ginger and cook, stirring a few times, until lightly golden. Add the curry powder, lemongrass, and chiles and cook until fragrant, about 2 minutes, stirring to prevent the curry powder from scorching. Add the coconut milk, broth, fish sauce, and lime leaves and simmer over medium heat until flavorful and slightly reduced, about 20 minutes. Will keep in the refrigerator for up to 4 days.

VIETNAMESE SEAFOOD CURRY

MAKES 4 TO 6 SERVINGS

ONCE THE CURRY sauce is assembled, this dish is done in minutes.

> 1 tablespoon vegetable oil
>
> 1 large shallot, thinly sliced
>
> 1 teaspoon Madras curry powder
>
> 12 mussels, scrubbed and debearded
>
> 1/2 pound medium-size shrimp, peeled and deveined
>
> 1/2 pound cleaned small squid, bodies cut into 1/2-inch-wide rings and tentacles halved
>
> 1 recipe South Vietnamese–Style Coconut Curry Sauce (left), warmed

Heat the oil in a large saucepan over high heat. Add the shallot and curry powder and cook, stirring, until fragrant. Add the mussels, shrimp, and squid and stir-fry until lightly coated with the curry powder. Add the curry sauce, cover, and cook just until the mussels begin to open and the shrimp and squid are opaque, 2 to 3 minutes longer. Discard any mussels that will not open. Serve with steamed rice.

THAI RED CURRY COCONUT SAUCE

MAKES ABOUT 1 1/2 CUPS

THIS IS ANOTHER staple of Southeast Asian diets, especially in Thailand and Laos. I like to use this sauce as a base for stewing chicken, beef, or veggies, or even for poaching shrimp or firm-fleshed fish.

2 tablespoons peanut oil

1 garlic clove, minced

1 teaspoon peeled and minced fresh ginger

2 teaspoons store-bought or homemade Thai red curry paste (page 219)

One 14-ounce can unsweetened coconut milk

1/2 cup low-sodium chicken broth

2 tablespoons Asian fish sauce

1 tablespoon firmly packed brown sugar

2 kaffir lime leaves or two 1/2 x 2-inch strips lime zest

Salt

Heat the oil in a medium-size deep skillet over medium heat until it shimmers. Add the garlic and ginger and cook until golden, about 2 minutes. Add the curry paste and cook for 30 seconds. Whisk in the coconut milk, broth, fish sauce, brown sugar, and lime leaves. Bring to a simmer and cook, stirring occasionally, until thickened and slightly reduced, 10 to 15 minutes. Season with salt. This is best used right away.

THAI GREEN CURRY COCONUT SAUCE

MAKES ABOUT 2 CUPS

KAFFIR LIME LEAVES are highly fragrant and are a mainstay of many Southeast Asian curries and stews. Galangal is a rhizome that tastes and looks very similar to ginger. You can find both of them at Asian markets. I like to use this as a sauce in which to poach shrimp or strips of white chicken meat. It's also tasty over rice or rice noodles.

One 14-ounce can unsweetened coconut milk

1 1/2 teaspoons store-bought or homemade Thai green curry paste (page 222)

1 cup low-sodium chicken broth

1 stalk lemongrass, bottom 4 inches, crushed

One 1-inch piece fresh galangal or ginger, peeled and thinly sliced and lightly crushed

4 kaffir lime leaves, lightly crushed, or four 1/2 x 2-inch strips lime zest

3 tablespoons Asian fish sauce

1 1/2 tablespoons firmly packed light brown sugar

2 tablespoons fresh lime juice

1/4 cup coarsely chopped fresh cilantro leaves

2 tablespoons finely chopped fresh basil leaves

1. In a medium-size saucepan, combine 1/4 cup of the coconut milk and the curry paste and whisk until smooth. Add the chicken broth, the remaining coconut milk, the lemongrass, galangal, lime leaves, 2 tablespoons of the fish sauce, and the brown sugar, bring to a simmer, and cook over medium heat until slightly thickened and reduced, about 15 minutes.

2. Using a slotted spoon, remove the lemongrass, ginger, and lime leaves. Stir in the remaining 1 tablespoon fish sauce, the lime juice, cilantro, and basil. This is best used right away.

WESTERN-STYLE CURRY SAUCE

MAKES ABOUT 1 1/4 CUPS

THIS FRENCH-STYLE CURRY sauce is absolutely yummy with grilled and roasted chicken; fish such as skate, flounder, snapper, and grouper; all types of rice pilaf dishes; and rice noodles. It's not intended for braising.

2 tablespoons canola oil or other mild-flavored vegetable oil

1 large shallot, finely chopped

THAI GREEN SEAFOOD CURRY

MAKES 4 TO 6 SERVINGS

THAI CUISINE TO me means two things: hot, spicy green curry and seafood. And this recipe combines them in a quick and super-simple entrée. You'll need to prepare the Thai Green Curry Coconut Sauce, but don't add the cilantro and basil until after the seafood is cooked.

> 1 recipe Thai Green Curry Coconut Sauce (left)
> 1/2 pound medium-size shrimp, peeled and deveined
> 1/2 pound medium-size sea scallops
> 1 dozen mussels, scrubbed and debearded
> 1/2 cup frozen baby peas, thawed
> 1 scallion, thinly sliced

Prepare the recipe for Thai Green Curry Coconut Sauce, reserving the cilantro and basil to add at the end, and bring to a simmer. Add the shrimp, scallops, and mussels, cover, and simmer until the shrimp and scallops are opaque and the mussels are open, about 7 minutes. Add the peas and scallion and cook, uncovered, until heated through. Discard any mussels that will not open. Serve over steamed jasmine rice.

1/2 teaspoon peeled and finely grated fresh ginger

1 tablespoon Madras curry powder

1/3 cup finely diced banana

1 1/2 teaspoons firmly packed light brown sugar

1 1/2 cups low-sodium chicken broth

1/2 cup heavy cream

1 1/2 teaspoons fresh lime juice

Salt

Cayenne pepper

1. Heat the oil in a medium-size saucepan over medium heat. Add the shallot and ginger and cook, stirring, until softened and just beginning to brown, about 3 minutes. Add the curry powder and cook until fragrant and lightly toasted, about 1 minute, stirring constantly. Add the banana and brown sugar and cook until the banana begins to break down, stirring constantly to prevent scorching, 2 to 3 minutes. Add the broth and heavy cream and simmer until thickened and reduced to about 1¼ cups, about 10 minutes.

2. Transfer the sauce to a blender along with the lime juice and process until smooth. Return to the saucepan, bring to a gentle simmer over low heat, and season with salt and cayenne. Will keep, tightly covered, in the refrigerator for up to 2 days. Reheat before serving.

WEST AFRICAN SPICED CURRY TOMATO SAUCE

MAKES 3½ CUPS

MILD, SWEET CURRY flavors many of the dishes of western Africa. Peanuts, known as groundnuts, also figure prominently in African cooking, which tends to be very rustic, predominantly vegetarian, and much milder than you'd expect. Serve this with roasted root vegetables, meats, poultry, or fish, or with rice, couscous, or beans. Or use it as a sauce for braising meats, poultry, or vegetables.

- 2 pounds vine-ripened tomatoes or one 28-ounce can peeled whole plum tomatoes, pureed
- 2 tablespoons peanut or other mild-flavored vegetable oil
- 1 large onion, finely chopped
- 2 medium-size carrots, finely chopped
- 1 tablespoon mild curry powder
- 1 teaspoon sweet paprika
- ¼ teaspoon ground cinnamon
- Pinch of ground cloves or allspice
- ½ cup unsalted dry-roasted peanuts, finely ground

1 bay leaf, preferably imported
Salt and freshly ground black pepper

1. If using fresh tomatoes, bring a medium-size saucepan of water to a boil and fill a large bowl with ice water. Using a sharp paring knife, make a shallow X in the bottom of each tomato. Blanch the tomatoes in the boiling water for 15 to 20 seconds, remove with a slotted spoon, and plunge them immediately into the ice water to cool. Peel, core, and seed the tomatoes, then puree them in a blender.

2. Heat the oil in a large saucepan over medium-high heat until shimmering. Add the onion and carrots and cook, stirring occasionally, until softened and just beginning to brown, 6 to 7 minutes. Add the curry powder, paprika, cinnamon, and cloves and cook, stirring, for 2 minutes. Add the tomatoes and bring to a boil. Reduce the heat to low, stir in the peanuts and bay leaf, and simmer until thickened, 20 to 25 minutes. Season with salt and pepper. Will keep, tightly covered, in the refrigerator for up to 5 days or in the freezer for 1 month.

CLASSIC CUCUMBER RAITA

MAKES ABOUT 1½ CUPS

THIS TRADITIONAL YOGURT condiment is served with roast lamb, grilled meats, and poultry. I also like it with grain salads, bean salads, or curries to cool the palate.

SENEGALESE CHICKEN CURRY

MAKES 4 TO 6 SERVINGS

THIS CURRY FROM Senegal is not terribly spicy. It only uses about half of the West African Spiced Curry Tomato Sauce recipe. Feel free to double the ingredients to serve 8 or have plenty of leftovers. I think curries taste better the second day anyway.

2 tablespoons vegetable oil

1½ pounds boneless, skinless chicken thighs, any fat removed, and cut into 2-inch pieces

1 large onion, thinly sliced

1½ teaspoons Madras curry powder

1½ cups West African Spiced Curry Tomato Sauce (left)

1 large red-skinned potato, cut into ¾-inch cubes

Steamed rice or crusty baguettes for serving

Fresh cilantro leaves for garnish

1. Heat the oil in a large heavy casserole over medium-high heat until shimmering. Add the chicken and cook until browned all over, about 8 minutes. Add the onion and curry powder and cook, stirring, until softened, about 2 minutes. Add the curry sauce, scraping up any bits stuck to the bottom of the pan, and bring to a simmer. Add the potato, reduce the heat to medium-low, and cook until the chicken is tender and the vegetables are cooked through, 15 to 20 minutes. If desired, skim off any excess fat.

2. Serve the curry over steamed rice or with baguettes and garnish with cilantro leaves.

1 hothouse cucumber, peeled and finely diced

1½ teaspoons kosher salt

1 cup plain whole-milk or lowfat yogurt, drained, or ⅔ cup Greek-style yogurt (see The Right Yogurt, page 236)

1 garlic clove, minced

Cayenne pepper

1. Sprinkle the cucumber with the salt and place in a colander to drain for 30 minutes. Rinse briefly under cold running water, drain, and transfer to paper towels. Pat dry.

2. Combine the cucumber, yogurt, and garlic in a medium-size bowl and season with cayenne. This is best enjoyed soon after being made.

WEST INDIAN CURRY
FOR LAMB OR GOAT (COLUMBO)
MAKES ABOUT 6 SERVINGS

LIVING IN A predominantly West Indian section of Brooklyn, I'm flanked on three sides by women from Trinidad, Barbados, and St. Kitts. Sunday afternoon in our neighborhood always means curry. All three neighbors have different recipes, but one thing is the same—the fragrant smells wafting through my windows always make my mouth water. Columbo is a West Indian–style curry powder.

1/2 small green bell pepper, peeled and coarsely chopped

4 garlic cloves, peeled

One 1/2-inch-thick slice peeled fresh ginger

1 teaspoon finely chopped fresh thyme leaves

1/4 habanero or Scotch bonnet chile, seeded and coarsely chopped

3 tablespoons mild curry powder or Columbo curry powder

1/8 teaspoon ground allspice (optional)

1/4 cup vegetable oil

2 tablespoons water

11/2 pounds boneless lamb or goat shoulder, trimmed of fat and cut into 11/2-inch pieces

Salt and freshly ground black pepper

1 large onion, coarsely chopped

11/2 cups low-sodium chicken broth or water

2 medium-size russet potatoes, peeled and cut into 2-inch pieces

11/2 pounds winter squash or pumpkin, such as butternut, calabaza, or buttercup, peeled, seeded, and cut into 1-inch pieces

Fresh lime juice

1. In a food processor, combine the bell pepper, garlic, ginger, thyme, and habanero and pulse until finely chopped. Add the curry powder, allspice, if using, 2 tablespoons of the oil, and the water and process into a paste.

2. Heat the remaining 2 tablespoons oil in a large heavy casserole or Dutch oven over medium-high heat. Season the lamb with salt and pepper, add half of it to the casserole, and cook until brown all over, about 8 minutes. Using a slotted spoon, transfer the meat to a plate. Brown the remaining meat and add it to the meat on the plate. Add the onions to the casserole and cook, stirring occasionally, until lightly browned. Add the curry paste and cook over low heat, stirring constantly, until toasted, about 2 minutes.

3. Return the meat to the casserole and stir until each piece is coated with the curry. Add the broth, potatoes, and squash and bring to a boil. Reduce the heat to medium-low and simmer, partially covered, until very tender, about 1½ hours. Season with salt and pepper and lime juice before serving. Will keep, tightly covered, in the refrigerator for up to 4 days.

RADISH-CUCUMBER RAITA

MAKES ABOUT 1½ CUPS

I LOVE THE peppery kick that the radishes add to this variation on classic cucumber raita. Serve it with all types of grilled meats and poultry, beans, and grains.

1 small hothouse or 3 large Kirby cucumbers, peeled, seeded, if necessary, and finely diced

1½ teaspoons coarse salt

1 cup plain whole-milk or lowfat yogurt, drained, or ⅔ cup Greek-style yogurt (see The Right Yogurt, page 236)

6 large radishes, ends trimmed and finely diced

1 garlic clove, minced

1 tablespoon extra-virgin olive oil

½ teaspoon yellow or brown mustard seeds

½ teaspoon cumin seeds

Cayenne pepper

1. Sprinkle the cucumber with the salt and place in a colander to drain for 30 minutes. Rinse briefly under cold running water, drain, and transfer to paper towels. Pat dry. Combine the drained yogurt, cucumber, radishes, and garlic in a small bowl.

2. Heat the oil in a small skillet over medium heat. Add the mustard and cumin seeds and cook until the mustard seeds begin to pop. Add the spice mixture to the raita, taste for salt, and season with cayenne. This is best used right away.

CUMIN-SCENTED
CARROT RAITA

MAKES ABOUT 2/3 CUP

SERVE THIS BRIGHT orange raita with any type of grilled or roasted meat, as well as lentils, beans, or grains.

2 tablespoons extra-virgin olive oil

1 garlic clove, minced

1/2 teaspoon cumin seeds

2 medium-size carrots, coarsely shredded

2 scallions (white and tender green parts), finely chopped

2/3 cup plain whole-milk or lowfat yogurt, drained, or 1/2 cup Greek-style yogurt (see The Right Yogurt, page 236)

1 tablespoon finely chopped fresh cilantro leaves

Salt

Cayenne pepper

1. Heat the oil in a small skillet over medium heat until shimmering. Add the garlic and cumin seeds and cook until fragrant, about 1 minute, stirring frequently. Add the carrots and scallions and cook, stirring, just until heated through, about 1 minute. Scrape the mixture into a small bowl and let cool.

2. Fold in the yogurt and cilantro and season with salt and cayenne. This is best used right away.

CURRY-ROASTED
PUMPKIN RAITA

MAKES ABOUT 1 1/2 CUPS

THE SWEETNESS OF the pumpkin is enhanced by oven roasting. I love to serve this hearty, creamy raita as an accompaniment to lamb, beef, grains, and beans, or with toasted pita.

2 cups peeled, seeded, and diced (1/2-inch) winter squash, such as butternut, butter-cup, kabocha, or sweet dumpling

2 tablespoons vegetable oil

1 teaspoon Madras curry powder

Pinch of sugar

Salt

1/2 cup plain whole-milk or lowfat yogurt, drained, or 1/3 cup Greek-style yogurt (see The Right Yogurt, page 236)

1 scallion, finely chopped

1 tablespoon finely chopped fresh cilantro leaves

1 tablespoon fresh lemon juice

2 tablespoons shelled sunflower seeds, toasted (see page 364)

1. Preheat the oven to 425°F. In a medium-size bowl, toss the squash, oil, curry powder, and sugar together until the squash is coated, then season with salt. Spread the squash out in a single layer on a baking sheet and roast until lightly browned and tender, about 20 minutes. Let cool slightly.

2. In a medium-size bowl, combine the yogurt, scallion, cilantro, and lemon juice. Gently fold in the squash and sunflower seeds. This is best used right away.

THAI MASSAMAN CURRY

MAKES 4 TO 6 SERVINGS

THIS RECIPE REFERS to the cuisine of the northern region of Thailand, specifically where the population is heavily influenced by Muslim culture.

2 tablespoons peanut oil

1 pound boneless, skinless chicken thighs, any fat removed and cut into 2-inch pieces

1 medium-size onion, coarsely chopped

1 large red-skinned potato, cut into 1-inch pieces

1 recipe Thai Red Curry Coconut Sauce (page 227)

1/4 cup unsalted dry-roasted peanuts

Low-sodium chicken broth as needed

1. Heat the oil in a large heavy casserole over medium-high heat until shimmering. Add the chicken and cook until lightly browned all over, about 8 minutes. Using a slotted spoon, transfer the chicken to a plate. Add the onion and cook, stirring, until translucent, about 3 minutes.

2. Return the chicken to the pot, add the potato and curry sauce, and simmer over medium-low heat until the chicken and potato are tender and the sauce is thickened, about 20 minutes. Add the peanuts and simmer for 5 minutes. Thin the curry with broth if it gets too thick. Serve over steamed jasmine rice.

SMOKY EGGPLANT RAITA

MAKES ABOUT 1½ CUPS

THIS RAITA DOES double duty as part condiment and part salad. It's great with lentils, lamb, steak, poultry, grains, and vegetables, but I like it especially with warm pita bread or toasted sliced baguettes.

1 medium-size eggplant (about 1 pound)

Vegetable oil

1 cup plain whole-milk or lowfat yogurt, drained, or ⅔ cup Greek-style yogurt (see The Right Yogurt, below)

1 tablespoon fresh lemon juice

¼ cup finely chopped onion

1 garlic clove, mashed into a paste

2 tablespoons finely chopped fresh cilantro leaves

1 tablespoon finely chopped fresh mint leaves

1 tablespoon extra-virgin olive oil

½ teaspoon pure chile powder of your choice

Salt and freshly ground black pepper

1. Preheat the oven to 450°F. Lightly rub the eggplant all over with vegetable oil and place on a sturdy baking sheet. Roast the eggplant until blackened, very tender, and collapsed, about 45 minutes. Let cool. Peel the eggplant and cut lengthwise into strips. Scrape away as many seeds as possible without losing too much of the eggplant pulp. Chop the eggplant and transfer to a colander to drain for 10 minutes.

2. Transfer the eggplant to a medium-size bowl, add the drained yogurt and lemon juice, and stir until creamy. Stir in the onion, garlic, cilantro, and mint.

3. Heat the olive oil in a small skillet over medium heat. Add the chile powder and cook just until fragrant, about 30 seconds. Scrape the chile oil into the raita, stir, and season with salt and pepper. This is best used right away.

THE RIGHT YOGURT

Greek-style yogurt is rich, thick, and creamy and is far superior to commercial American-style yogurt. Kalustyan's (see Internet and Mail-Order Suppliers, page 387) in New York makes a delicious one. A wonderful brand of Greek-style yogurt is Total. Even their fat-free yogurt is outstanding—rich, thick, and not in the least "dietetic." If you can't find one, another way to achieve that thick and luscious consistency is to drain regular yogurt (full fat or lowfat only—don't try this with nonfat yogurt) in a strainer lined with a coffee filter, paper towel, or two layers of cheesecloth for about an hour in the refrigerator before adding the other ingredients. One cup of regular yogurt will end up yielding about ⅔ cup thick yogurt.

FRIED SCALLION–CUCUMBER RAITA

MAKES ABOUT 1½ CUPS

FRIED SCALLIONS ADD a sweet oniony flavor to this all-purpose raita. Serve it with grilled steak, chicken, burgers, and all types of bean or grain salads, as well as toasted pita bread.

> ½ large European or 3 Kirby cucumbers, peeled, seeded, if necessary, and finely diced
> 1½ teaspoons kosher salt
> ¾ cup plain whole-milk or lowfat yogurt, drained, or ½ cup Greek-style yogurt (see The Right Yogurt, left)
> 2 tablespoons extra-virgin olive oil
> 4 scallions, thinly sliced
> 1 small garlic clove, minced
> ½ teaspoon pure chile powder, preferably ancho
> 1 tablepoon fresh lemon juice
> Freshly ground black pepper

1. Sprinkle the cucumber with the salt and place in a colander to drain for 30 minutes. Rinse briefly under cold running water, drain well, and transfer to paper towels. Pat dry. Combine the drained yogurt with the cucumber in a medium-size bowl.

2. Heat the oil in a small skillet over high heat until shimmering. Add the scallions and garlic and cook, stirring frequently, until lightly browned, 3 to 4 minutes. Add the chile powder and toast for 1 minute. Scrape the mixture into the raita, add the lemon juice, and season with pepper and stir well to combine. Serve warm or chilled. Will keep in the refrigerator for up to 2 days.

SHREDDED BEET RAITA

MAKES ABOUT 2/3 CUP

VIVIDLY PINK, THIS raita combines caramelized shredded beets with yogurt. It's delicious with salmon, swordfish, and other meaty fish, as well as with steaks, burgers, and chicken.

> 1 tablespoon canola or other mild-flavored vegetable oil
> ¼ cup finely chopped red onion
> 1 garlic clove, minced
> 1 medium-size red beet (about 3 inches in diameter), peeled and coarsely shredded
> ½ teaspoon sugar
> 2/3 cup plain whole-milk or lowfat yogurt, drained, or ½ cup Greek-style yogurt (see The Right Yogurt, left)
> Salt and freshly ground black pepper

1. Heat the oil in a small skillet over medium heat until shimmering. Add the onion and garlic and cook, stirring, until softened, about 5 minutes. Add the shredded beet and sugar and cook, stirring frequently, until tender and lightly caramelized, about 8 minutes. Transfer to a bowl and let cool.

2. Fold in the yogurt and season with salt and pepper. This is best enjoyed right away.

SPINACH RAITA WITH TOASTED SPICES

MAKES ABOUT 1¼ CUPS

THIS WAS INSPIRED by a wonderful Turkish home cook, Irena. It's more like a spinach yogurt salad. Serve it with all grilled meats and poultry, as well as with grains and warm pita bread.

One 10-ounce bag spinach, tough stems removed and washed well

¼ cup finely diced sweet onion, such as Vidalia or Walla Walla

2 tablespoons finely chopped fresh mint leaves

1 cup plain whole-milk or lowfat yogurt, drained, or ⅔ cup Greek-style yogurt (see The Right Yogurt, page 236)

2 teaspoons fresh lemon juice

2 tablespoons extra-virgin olive oil

½ teaspoon ground cumin

½ teaspoon pure chile powder of your choice

½ teaspoon ground coriander

Pinch of cayenne pepper

Salt

1. Heat a large saucepan over medium-high heat. Add the spinach in handfuls and cook, tossing,

---

CURRY SAUCE AND RAITA PAIRINGS

Mix and match any of the curries below to any of the raitas below.

CURRIES:
Curry Yogurt Sauce (page 221)
Spicy Coconut Curry Tomato Sauce (page 226)
West African Spiced Curry Tomato Sauce (page 230)
West Indian Curry for Lamb or Goat (Columbo) (page 232)
Western-Style Curry Sauce (page 228)

RAITAS:
Apple-Ginger Raita (right)
Asian Pear Raita with Lime and Chiles (page 240)
Banana-Kiwi Raita (right)

Classic Cucumber Raita (page 230)
Cumin-Scented Carrot Raita (page 234)
Curry-Roasted Pumpkin Raita (page 234)
Fried Scallion–Cucumber Raita (page 237)
Mango Raita with Mint and Chiles (page 240)
Pistachio Yogurt Sauce (page 243)
Pomegranate-Mint Raita (page 241)
Radish-Cucumber Raita (page 233)
Shredded Beet Raita (page 237)
Smoky Eggplant Raita (page 236)
Spinach Raita with Toasted Spices (page 238)
Tamarind Yogurt Sauce (page 242)
Tart Cherry Raita with Scallions and Sunflower Seeds (page 241)

until wilted and the liquid is exuded, 3 to 4 minutes. Transfer the spinach to a colander and let cool. Squeeze out any excess moisture. Chop the spinach and transfer it to a bowl. Add the onion and mint, then fold in the yogurt and lemon juice.

2. Heat the oil in a small skillet over medium heat. Add the cumin, chile powder, coriander, and cayenne and cook just until fragrant, about 30 seconds. Scrape the spice mixture into the raita, stir, and season with salt. This is best enjoyed right away.

APPLE-GINGER RAITA

MAKES ABOUT 2 CUPS

THIS TART, REFRESHING raita is great with all types of grilled meats and poultry, especially if it's spicy.

- 1 cup plain whole-milk or lowfat yogurt, drained, or 2/3 cup Greek-style yogurt (see The Right Yogurt, page 236)
- 2 tart green apples, such as Granny Smith, peeled, cored, and finely diced
- 1 teaspoon peeled and finely grated fresh ginger
- 1 tablespoon finely chopped fresh mint leaves
- 2 teaspoons fresh lime juice
- Pinch of cayenne pepper

Combine all the ingredients in a medium-size bowl. Serve chilled or at room temperature. This is best served soon after being made.

BANANA-KIWI RAITA

MAKES ABOUT 1 CUP

GOLDEN KIWI IS a new variety from New Zealand. In cross section, it looks like a yellow starburst. If you can't find them, the green ones will do just fine. Serve this sweet-tart raita with all types of grilled meats, poultry, and fish.

- 1/2 cup plain whole-milk or lowfat yogurt, drained, or 1/3 cup Greek-style yogurt (see The Right Yogurt, page 236)
- 3 tablespoons finely chopped sweet onion, such as Vidalia or Walla Walla
- 1 tablespoon finely chopped fresh cilantro leaves
- 1 large slightly under-ripe banana, peeled and finely diced
- 1 golden kiwi, peeled and finely diced
- Salt
- Cayenne pepper

In a medium-size bowl, combine the yogurt, onion, and cilantro. Gently fold in the banana and kiwi and season with salt and cayenne. This is best served soon after it is made.

MANGO RAITA
WITH MINT AND CHILES

MAKES ABOUT 1½ CUPS

THE SWEETNESS OF the mango makes this raita a perfect accompaniment to grilled or roasted fish, especially swordfish, grouper, halibut, and snapper.

> 1 cup plain whole-milk or lowfat yogurt, drained, or ⅔ cup Greek-style yogurt (see The Right Yogurt, page 236)
>
> 2 tablespoons minced red onion
>
> 2 tablespoons finely chopped fresh mint leaves
>
> 1 serrano or jalapeño chile, seeded and minced
>
> Pinch of Madras curry powder
>
> 1 large ripe mango, peeled, pitted, and finely diced
>
> Salt

Combine the yogurt, onion, mint, chile, and curry powder in a small bowl. Fold in the mango and season with salt. This is best served right away.

ASIAN PEAR RAITA
WITH LIME AND CHILES

MAKES ABOUT 1½ CUPS

ASIAN PEARS ARE relatively new to this country, though there are several orchards in California that have been growing many varieties for decades. Tasting like a cross between an apple and a pear, its skin is pale golden and sort of papery-rough, while the flesh is very sweet, crisp, and crunchy. Serve this with spicy curries, grains, or beans, and warm pita bread.

> 1 cup plain whole-milk or lowfat yogurt, drained, or ⅔ cup Greek-style yogurt (see The Right Yogurt, page 236)
>
> 1 large Asian pear or 2 Bosc pears, peeled, cored, and finely diced
>
> 1 small jalapeño, seeded and finely diced
>
> 2 tablespoons fresh lime juice
>
> ½ teaspoon finely grated lime zest
>
> Salt and freshly ground black pepper

Combine the drained yogurt, pear, jalapeño, lime juice, and lime zest in a small bowl. Season with salt and pepper. This is best enjoyed right away.

POMEGRANATE-MINT RAITA

MAKES ABOUT 1 CUP

THE POMEGRANATE IS a staple of Middle Eastern cooking. A beautiful red skin encloses tiny, juicy seeds. The juice is very tart and tannic—it has a slight drying effect on your tongue. They're available early autumn through winter. This raita is especially good with lamb—roasted, grilled, or braised.

1 medium-size pomegranate
1 cup plain whole-milk yogurt, drained, or 2/3 cup Greek-style yogurt (see The Right Yogurt, page 236)
1/4 cup finely chopped fresh mint leaves
Salt
Cayenne pepper

Cut the pomegranate into quarters. Pull off the outer skin and carefully remove the seeds from the white inner membranes. Transfer the seeds to a bowl, add the drained yogurt and mint, stir to combine well, and season with salt and cayenne. This is best enjoyed right away.

TART CHERRY RAITA WITH SCALLIONS AND SUNFLOWER SEEDS

MAKES ABOUT 2/3 CUP

DRIED SOUR CHERRIES add an interesting sweet-tart flavor and chewy texture to this otherwise aromatic raita. I love the contrast of the cherries with the crunch of the sunflower seeds. Serve it with poultry, steaks, pork, and lamb.

1/3 cup dried tart cherries
1/2 cup boiling water
3/4 cup plain whole-milk or lowfat yogurt, drained, or 1/2 cup Greek-style (see The Right Yogurt, page 236)
2 scallions, thinly sliced
1 1/2 teaspoons fresh lime juice
3 tablespoons salted shelled sunflower seeds, toasted (see page 364) and chopped
Salt and freshly ground black pepper

1. Soak the cherries in the boiling water until plumped, about 15 minutes. Drain and coarsely chop the cherries.

2. In a medium-size bowl, combine the cherries, drained yogurt, scallions, lime juice, and sunflower seeds. Season with salt and pepper. This is best served right away.

TAMARIND YOGURT SAUCE

MAKES ABOUT ½ CUP

TAMARIND CONCENTRATE IS the pulp of the tamarind pod that has been mixed with a small amount of water, then strained of all its seeds and strings. You can find it at any Asian grocer. This tart-sweet sauce is great alongside grilled seafood or poultry, or vegetable curries.

1 tablespoon peanut oil

1½ teaspoons peeled and minced fresh ginger

1 small garlic clove, minced

¼ teaspoon ground coriander

⅛ teaspoon ground cardamom

⅛ teaspoon cayenne pepper

1 tablespoon tamarind concentrate mixed with ¼ cup water

½ cup plain whole-milk or lowfat yogurt, drained, or ⅓ cup Greek-style yogurt (see The Right Yogurt, page 236)

Salt

1. Heat the oil in a medium-size saucepan over medium heat. Add the ginger and garlic and cook, stirring, until softened and lightly browned, about 1 minute. Add the coriander, cardamom, and cayenne and cook just until fragrant, about 30 seconds. Add the tamarind mixture, bring to a simmer, and cook until slightly reduced, about 5 minutes.

2. Remove from the heat, whisk in the yogurt, and season with salt. Serve warm or chilled. Will keep in the refrigerator for up to 2 days.

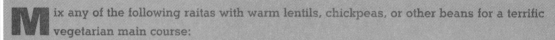

OTHER USES FOR RAITA

Mix any of the following raitas with warm lentils, chickpeas, or other beans for a terrific vegetarian main course:

- Classic Cucumber Raita (page 230)
- Cumin-Scented Carrot Raita (page 234)
- Curry-Roasted Pumpkin Raita (page 234)
- Fried Scallion–Cucumber Raita (page 237)
- Shredded Beet Raita (page 237)
- Smoky Eggplant Raita (page 236)
- Spinach Raita with Toasted Spices (page 238)
- Tart Cherry Raita with Scallions and Sunflower Seeds (page 241)

PISTACHIO YOGURT SAUCE

MAKES ABOUT 1 CUP

PISTACHIOS HAVE THE sweetest nutty flavor—
I love them! Please don't use the scary red ones
for this sauce, or it may look more like tandoori
than intended. Sumac, available in Middle Eastern
markets, imparts a tart, citrusy flavor, but feel
free to use lemon juice. Serve this delicious raita-
like sauce with grilled, roasted, or poached meats
and poultry, cooked lentils, or grilled breads. I
sometimes thin this sauce with a few tablespoons
of milk to use it as a dressing.

2 tablespoons extra-virgin olive oil

1/2 cup shelled pistachio nuts, coarsely chopped

1 large garlic clove, minced

1/2 teaspoon pure ancho chile powder

1/2 teaspoon ground cumin

1/4 teaspoon ground coriander

1 cup plain whole-milk or lowfat yogurt,
    drained, or 3/4 cup Greek-style yogurt
    (see The Right Yogurt, page 236)

2 tablespoons finely chopped fresh cilantro
    leaves

1/2 teaspoon ground sumac or 1 tablespoon
    fresh lemon juice

Salt and freshly ground black pepper

1. Heat the oil in a medium-size skillet over
medium heat until shimmering. Add the pistachios and cook, stirring, until lightly golden,
about 2 minutes. Add the garlic, chile powder,
cumin, and coriander and cook, stirring, until
fragrant, about 30 seconds longer.

2. Scrape the mixture into a food processor and
let cool, then grind until finely chopped. Add the
yogurt, cilantro, and sumac and pulse until combined. Season with salt and pepper. This is best
used right away, but you can cover tightly and
refrigerate for up to 2 days. Serve warm, chilled,
or at room temperature.

DIPPING SAUCES

Southeast Asia, a large and culturally diverse area, boasts more dipping sauces than anywhere else in the world. The cuisines of Vietnam, Laos, Thailand, India, Malaysia, China, Korea, Philippines, and Indonesia have subtle nuances and differences, but also much in common. Probably the best known dipping sauce, common to many of those cuisines, is the peanut sauce. Sometimes called satay (or saté) sauce, sambal kacang, nuoc leo, gado gado, etc., it is nearly always used with grilled marinated meats of some sort on a stick.

Many of the following sauces can be served at the same meal and with a variety of foods of these ethnicities. Unlike the dipping sauces found in other chapters, these are intended to go with dumplings, pork buns, and grilled meat, chicken, and seafood skewers and kebabs.

CILANTRO-MINT DIPPING SAUCE

MAKES ABOUT 3/4 CUP

THIS FRESH-TASTING DIPPING sauce is standard fare in Indian cooking. It is served as a condiment, along with Tamarind Yogurt Sauce (page 242) and Fresh Onion-Chile Relish (page 346), to accompany curries, grilled meats, breads, rice, you name it. Thai bird chiles, called *nam prik,* are tiny, fiery chiles used in Southeast Asian cooking. Serrano or jalapeño peppers are good alternatives. I've included it in this chapter because it's really delicious as a dip for fresh vegetables, grilled chicken, and pork or beef kebabs, as well as chilled shrimp.

    1 cup packed fresh cilantro leaves
    1/4 cup packed fresh mint leaves
    1 garlic clove, coarsely chopped
    1 small Thai bird chile, seeded and finely
       chopped
    1 tablespoon sugar
    3 tablespoons fresh lime juice
    1/4 cup water
    Salt

In a large mortar using a pestle, pound the cilantro, mint, garlic, chile, and sugar together into a fairly smooth paste. Add the lime juice and water and pound until smooth. Season with salt. Alternatively, combine all the ingredients in a blender and process until you have a fine puree. Will keep, tightly covered, in the refrigerator overnight.

CHINESE GINGER-SOY DIPPING SAUCE

MAKES 1/2 CUP

I LOVE THIS sauce with dumplings, pork meatballs, and grilled or poached fish or chicken, but it also makes a terrific marinade for pork tenderloin, chicken breasts, or salmon fillets. The brands of chili garlic sauces I like to use are Lee Kum Kee or Tuong Ot Toi Vietnam, both of which are available in supermarkets.

    1/2 cup soy sauce
    1 1/2 teaspoons peeled and minced
       fresh ginger
    1 large garlic, minced
    1/4 teaspoon chili garlic sauce
    1/4 teaspoon toasted sesame oil
    Pinch of sugar

Combine all the ingredients in a small bowl and let sit for 15 minutes before serving to let the flavors develop. Will keep, tightly covered, in the refrigerator for up to 3 days.

A QUICK PRIMER OF ASIAN INGREDIENTS

Asian fish sauce: This pungent, fragrant extract of fermented salted anchovies is ubiquitous in the cooking of Southeast Asia. It's called *nam pla* in Thailand, *nuoc mam* in Vietnam, and *patis* in the Philippines.

Black bean sauce: A commercial sauce sold in jars, its texture and flavor greatly varies, sometimes very smooth, sometimes very chunky. I like the Lee Kum Kee brand.

Chiles: Dried red chiles are usually about 2 inches long and can be very hot. Fresh bird's eye or Thai chiles (also called *prik*) are tiny and extremely hot. Serrano or jalapeño chiles can be substituted in a pinch.

Chili garlic sauce: A pungent and spicy jarred paste from China that combines chiles, garlic, and often soybeans.

Chinese black vinegar: This very dark, rich rice vinegar is much like balsamic, without the sweetness. Unseasoned rice vinegar with a few drops of Worcestershire sauce added is the best substitute.

Chinese cooking wine (Shao xing, Shao-Hsing): A rice wine used in Chinese cooking. Dry sherry can be substituted.

Chinese 5-spice powder: A combination of equal parts star anise, Szechuan peppercorn, fennel seed, clove, and cinnamon. Licorice root, cardamom, and ginger are sometimes added.

Cilantro: Also known as fresh coriander, the leaves of the coriander plant are used in the cooking of Southeast Asia, Latin America, the Caribbean, and the Middle East.

Coconut milk: Canned unsweetened coconut milk is used in the cooking of Southeast Asia, India, the Caribbean, and Latin America. The best brand is Chaokoh from Thailand, but other decent ones are Thai Kitchen and Taste of Thai. Some need to be stirred before using since the coconut cream tends to separate and rise to the top.

Curry leaves: These extremely pungent leaves are used in Indian cooking and can be found fresh, frozen, or dried in Indian markets. Fresh leaves can be frozen.

Dried shrimp or shrimp paste: These tiny dried fermented shrimp are commonly found in Southeast Asian cooking and are used in curry pastes

Fermented (salted) black beans: Soybeans that have been salted and fermented, they are sold in plastic bags in Asian markets. Rinse thoroughly before using.

Hoisin sauce: This sweet, garlicky sauce is used in Chinese cooking. Lee Kum Kee is a very decent brand widely available in most supermarkets.

Kaffir lime leaves: Used in the cooking of Southeast Asia, these fragrant leaves can be found frozen in Asian markets. One-inch-wide strips of lime zest can be substituted.

Lemongrass: This long stalk-like grass with a tender inner bulb is used most commonly in Southeast Asian cooking. It imparts a sweet, fragrant lemon flavor without any of the tartness of lemon juice. Avoid using dried lemongrass.

Mirin: A sweetened sake used in Japanese cooking.

Miso: A soybean paste used in Japanese cooking, most commonly to make soups. White or yellow miso is the least aged and very mild. Red miso is slightly more aged and has a more pronounced pungent flavor. Brown miso is aged the most and has a deep fermented flavor.

Oyster sauce: A commercial Chinese sauce, it is sold in bottles. Salty, sweet, thick, and deep brown, it is used in many stir-fries. Look for oyster sauce that contains real oyster essence, not flavoring and avoid brands with caramel coloring.

Rice vinegar, seasoned and unseasoned: A light, low-acid vinegar made from rice. Seasoned rice vinegar is sweetened.

Sake: This Japanese rice wine is used in cooking and for drinking.

Soy sauce: A thin, salty soybean sauce.

Star anise: This beautiful flower-shaped pod imparts a licorice flavor. A pinch of Chinese 5-spice powder can sometimes be substituted, though it will contain other flavors.

Tamarind: A pod-shaped fruit found in Latin American, Southeast Asian, and Caribbean cooking, it imparts a tart, slightly raisin-y flavor. It is sold in 16-ounce bricks that need to be reconstituted and strained, in deeply concentrated jarred pastes that need thinning, or as more watery liquids which are sometimes labeled "tamarind concentrate."

Thai green curry paste: A paste of green chiles, shallots, garlic, lemongrass, shrimp paste, cilantro, lime leaves, and spices, it is used in Thai curries, especially those made with coconut milk.

Thai red curry paste: A paste of dried red chiles, lemongrass, ginger, lime leaves, shrimp paste, and spices, it is used in Thai curries. Both curry pastes can be found in Asian markets and large supermarkets or you can make them yourself (pages 219, 222).

Toasted sesame oil: Sometimes referred to as Asian sesame oil, this is very fragrant and dark in color. It is used for seasoning and flavoring, but generally not for frying since it can burn very easily.

GINGER DIPPING SAUCE (NUOC MAM GUNG)

MAKES 1/3 CUP

THIS SPICY AND pungent Vietnamese dipping sauce is traditionally served with steamed or poached chicken, but I also like it with fish, shrimp, or steamed rice. Pounding the ingredients together in a mortar and pestle releases the essential oils in the ginger and chiles and lends a more intense flavor.

1½ tablespoons peeled and coarsely chopped fresh ginger

2 Thai bird or serrano chiles, thinly sliced (don't remove the seeds)

1 scallion (white part only), thinly sliced

1 garlic clove, coarsely chopped

1½ tablespoons sugar

2 tablespoons fresh lime juice

2½ tablespoons Asian fish sauce

In a mortar using a pestle, pound the ginger, chiles, scallion, garlic, and sugar together into a paste. Stir in the lime juice and fish sauce. Let sit for at least 15 minutes before using to let the flavors develop. Will keep, tightly covered, in the refrigerator overnight.

CHUNKY PEANUT-CHIPOTLE SAUCE

MAKES ABOUT 2 CUPS

I PREFER NATURAL chunky peanut butter here because it has great flavor and texture with no added sugar or partially hydrogenated vegetable oils. Serve this intense peanut sauce with grilled or roasted meats or poultry and rice, or use it as a sauce to braise chicken.

1 tablespoon canola oil

1 small onion, minced

1 large garlic clove, minced

1 teaspoon sweet paprika

½ teaspoon dried oregano, preferably Mexican, crumbled

1 tablespoon tomato paste

2 canned chipotle chiles in adobo sauce, seeded and finely chopped, plus 1 tablespoon adobo sauce

3/4 cup low-sodium chicken broth

3/4 cup water

½ cup chunky natural peanut butter

1 small bay leaf, preferably imported

Pinch of sugar

Salt and freshly ground black pepper

In a medium-size saucepan, heat the oil over medium heat until shimmering. Add the onion and garlic and cook, stirring occasionally, until softened, about 5 minutes. Add the paprika and oregano and cook for 1 minute. Add the tomato paste and chipotle and adobo sauce and cook, stirring, just until the onion is evenly coated. Using a whisk, add the broth and water, then the peanut butter, whisking until smooth. Add the bay leaf and sugar, season with salt and pepper, and simmer over low heat until thickened, about 10 minutes. Use warm or at room temperature. Will keep, tightly covered, in the refrigerator for up to a week.

INDONESIAN PEANUT-SHRIMP DIPPING SAUCE

MAKES ABOUT 1 CUP

THICKER AND A bit sweeter than the Vietnamese peanut sauce *nuoc leo* (page 259), this peanut sauce is traditionally served with grilled meats or chicken skewers, called satay. Tamarind pulp is pressed with its seeds into 1-pound blocks and can be found in Asian, Indian, and Caribbean markets. To use it, break it into pieces, cover with equal parts boiling water, and let sit until hydrated. Press the pulp through a fine-mesh sieve to remove the seeds and strings before using. Both red curry paste and shrimp paste are available in Asian markets and some larger supermarkets.

- 1 tablespoon vegetable oil
- 1 large shallot, minced
- 1 teaspoon store-bought or homemade Thai red curry paste (page 219)
- 1/4 teaspoon shrimp paste or 2 dried shrimp, pounded into a paste
- 2 tablespoons hydrated tamarind pulp (see headnote)

1/2 cup water

1 1/2 tablespoons sugar

1/2 cup smooth peanut butter, preferably natural

Salt

Fresh lime juice

Heat the oil in a large saucepan over high heat until shimmering. Add the shallot and cook, stirring, until browned, 2 to 3 minutes. Add the curry, shrimp paste, and tamarind and cook, stirring, until sizzling, about 2 minutes. Add the water and sugar and bring to a boil. Add the peanut butter, whisking until smooth, and simmer over low heat until the flavors are melded and the sauce is thick, about 5 minutes. Add a few tablespoons of water if the sauce thickens too quickly. Season with salt and lime juice. Will keep, tightly covered, in the refrigerator for up to 5 days. Reheat gently before using.

MANGO DIPPING SAUCE

MAKES ABOUT 1 1/2 CUPS

SWEET, FRAGRANT MANGOES and fresh, peppery ginger make up the base for this ketchup-like dipping sauce. I like to serve it with grilled or roasted meats, especially chicken kebabs and roasted pork, but it's also delicious as a barbecue sauce, brushed on at the last second. Cardamom pods are available at gourmet markets, Indian grocers, and some supermarkets.

FAST STEAMED PORK BUNS

MAKES ABOUT 10 BUNS

PAIR THIS WITH any of the 8 Best Dumpling Dipping Sauces listed on page 259.

1/2 cup bulk pork breakfast sausage

1/4 cup finely chopped kimchee (look in the Asian section
of your supermarket), or 1/4 cup drained sauerkraut
mixed with 1 teaspoon chili garlic sauce

1 scallion, chopped

2 canned water chestnuts, minced

2 packages store-bought buttermilk biscuit dough

1. In a small bowl, mix together the sausage, kimchee, scallion, and water chestnuts.

2. Flatten each biscuit slightly and place some of the mixture in the center. Pinch the tops closed.
Place in a steamer for 12 to 15 minutes.

3. Serve steaming hot with the dipping sauce of your choice on the side.

1 garlic clove, minced

1 large ripe mango, peeled, pitted, and cut
into 1-inch pieces

1 tablespoon peeled and finely chopped
fresh ginger

1/2 cup water

1/4 cup sugar

1/4 cup rice vinegar

6 cardamom pods

1/2 cinnamon stick

1 dried red chile

Salt

1. In a medium-size saucepan, combine all the ingredients, except the salt, and bring to a boil. Reduce the heat to medium-low and simmer until the mango is softened and just beginning to break down, about 15 minutes. Remove and discard the cardamom pods, cinnamon stick, and chile.

2. Transfer the mango mixture to a blender and process until smooth. Return the sauce to the saucepan and simmer over low heat until thickened, about 5 minutes. Season with salt and let cool before serving. Will keep, tightly covered, in the refrigerator for up to 3 days.

EASY PORK MEATBALLS

MAKES 4 SERVINGS

HERE'S A GREAT recipe to enjoy with any of the dipping sauces in this chapter.

1 pound ground pork
1 plump lemongrass stalk, bottom third only, minced
2 tablespoons finely chopped fresh cilantro
1 tablespoon soy sauce
1 1/2 teaspoons peeled and minced fresh ginger
1 garlic clove, minced
1/2 teaspoon salt
1/2 teaspoon ground white pepper

1. In a medium-size bowl, combine the pork, lemongrass, cilantro, soy sauce, ginger, garlic, salt, and pepper. Using lightly moistened hands, form 2 tablespoons of the mixture at a time into balls. Transfer in a single layer to a large heatproof plate.

2. Fill a large pot (large enough that the plate will fit in it) with a tight-fitting lid with 1 inch of water. Form 3 golf ball–size balls of aluminum foil, place them in the water, and bring to a boil. Add the plate, cover, and steam until the meatballs are cooked through, about 8 minutes. Alternatively, fry the meatballs over medium-high heat in 1/4 inch hot vegetable oil until browned on all sides and cooked through, 5 to 6 minutes.

PLUM DUCK SAUCE

MAKES 1½ CUPS

THE DUCK SAUCE in those little packets you get from Chinese take-out restaurants is pretty awful. The sweet, cornstarch-y, flavorless glop does more to obliterate your food than enhance it. But a really good duck sauce is hard to beat. I like to use the small oval-shaped Italian, or prune, plums, but any type will do. Serve this sauce with fried chicken, grilled meats, or poultry.

1½ teaspoons vegetable oil

1 garlic clove, minced

½ small onion, minced

¾ pound plums, pitted and coarsely chopped

¼ cup sugar

¼ cup water

1 teaspoon cornstarch dissolved in 1 tablespoon water

½ teaspoon chili garlic sauce

1½ teaspoons soy sauce

1. Heat the oil in a medium-size saucepan over low heat. Add the garlic and onion and cook, stirring occasionally, until softened, about 6 minutes. Add the plums, sugar, and water and bring to a boil. Reduce the heat to low and simmer until the plums are very soft and have released their liquid, about 10 minutes.

2. Transfer the sauce to a blender and process to a coarse puree. Return the sauce to the saucepan. Stir the cornstarch mixture, add it to the sauce, and simmer over medium-low heat until thickened, about 3 minutes. Stir in the chili garlic sauce and soy sauce, remove from the heat, and let cool to room temperature before serving. Will keep, tightly covered, in the refrigerator for up to 4 days.

SPICY PINEAPPLE AND ANCHOVY DIPPING SAUCE (MAM NEM)

MAKES ¾ CUP

THIS IS ONE of my favorite Vietnamese sauces. *Mam nem* combines sweet and juicy pineapple with salty anchovies and fiery chiles to make a pungent but lovely sauce, though my seven-year-old daughter, Pia, would tell you otherwise. It is traditionally served with beef dishes, but I find it complements roasted pork or lamb as well.

2 garlic cloves, coarsely chopped

2 red Thai bird or serrano chiles, seeded and finely chopped

6 anchovy fillets, rinsed

1 tablespoon sugar

½ cup peeled and finely chopped ripe fresh pineapple

2 tablespoons fresh lime juice

In a large mortar using a pestle, pound the garlic, chiles, anchovies, and sugar together into a paste. Add the pineapple and pound until lightly crushed. Stir in the lime juice. Will keep in the refrigerator overnight.

SESAME-LIME DIPPING SAUCE

MAKES ABOUT 1/3 CUP

GREAT WITH ALL types of dumplings, gyoza, and shu mai, I also like to serve this sauce with grilled salmon or tuna and steamed rice. Mirin is sweetened sake used in Japanese cooking. You can substitute 1 teaspoon sake and 1 teaspoon superfine sugar if you can't find mirin.

1½ teaspoons sesame seeds
3 tablespoons soy sauce
2 tablespoons fresh lime juice
1 teaspoon mirin (optional)
¼ teaspoon toasted sesame oil
¼ teaspoon hot chile oil

1. Toast the sesame seeds in a small dry skillet over medium-high heat, stirring or shaking constantly, until golden, about 2 minutes.

2. Transfer the seeds to a small bowl, add the remaining ingredients, and mix well. Will keep, tightly covered, in the refrigerator up to 2 days.

SPICY LEMONGRASS-CILANTRO DIPPING SAUCE

MAKES ABOUT 1 CUP

I LOVE THE bright flavors of Southeast Asia, especially cilantro and lemongrass. This sauce goes extremely well with all types of grilled meats and poultry as well as rice noodles or steamed or pan-fried fish. Dried shrimp and shrimp paste can be found in an Asian market.

1 stalk lemongrass, tough outer leaves and top two thirds discarded and inner bulb finely chopped
2 Thai bird chiles or 1 finger chile, finely chopped (don't remove the seeds)
1 scallion (white and tender green parts), thinly sliced
1 large garlic clove, chopped
2 dried shrimp or ¼ teaspoon shrimp paste (optional)
2 tablespoons sugar
¼ cup chopped fresh cilantro leaves
3 tablespoons Asian fish sauce
2 tablespoons fresh lime juice
2 tablespoons water

In a mortar using a pestle, pound the lemongrass, chiles, scallion, garlic, shrimp, and sugar together into a paste. Add the cilantro and pound until fine. Stir in the fish sauce, lime juice, and water and let the sauce sit for 10 minutes before using, to let the flavors develop. Will keep, tightly covered, in the refrigerator for up to 2 days.

SWEET SAKE-SOY DUMPLING SAUCE

MAKES ABOUT 3/4 CUP

THIS DIPPING SAUCE is slightly reminiscent of Teriyaki Grilling Sauce (page 210). It's great with seafood dumplings or grilled shrimp but also works well as a marinade or barbecue sauce, brushed on at the last minute. Sake is becoming more widely available in most liquor stores, but if you should have trouble finding it, I find vodka or dry white vermouth work very well instead.

1/4 cup soy sauce

1/4 cup sake

2 tablespoons firmly packed light brown sugar

2 tablespoons water

1 tablespoon rice vinegar

1 teaspoon peeled and finely grated fresh ginger

Combine all the ingredients in a small saucepan and simmer over medium heat, stirring, just until the sugar is dissolved. Let cool before serving. Will keep in the refrigerator for 4 days.

SWEET THAI CHILE DIPPING SAUCE

MAKES 2/3 CUP

I LOVE THIS sauce on all things fried crispy! The sweet, spicy flavors complement spring rolls, fried calamari, dumplings, or whole fried fish. It's also great used as a dressing for cucumbers, bean sprouts, and chopped peanuts.

5 tablespoons sugar

1/4 cup rice vinegar

2 tablespoons water

1 Thai bird or serrano chile, thinly sliced (don't remove the seeds)

1/4 cup seeded and finely chopped red bell pepper

1/2 teaspoon cornstarch dissolved in 1 tablespoon water

In a small saucepan, combine the sugar, vinegar, and water and cook over medium heat, stirring, just until the sugar dissolves. Add the chile and bell pepper and simmer for 2 minutes. Stir the cornstarch mixture, add it to the sauce, and cook until thickened, about 2 minutes. Let cool before serving. Will keep, tightly covered, in the refrigerator for up to 4 days.

SWEET-AND-SOUR TAMARIND SAUCE

MAKES ABOUT 1½ CUPS

THE FRUIT OF the tamarind tree grows in long, hard, brownish pods. The flesh inside is sweet-tart, sticky, and surrounds large bean-like seeds. Sitting in the central park in Antigua, Guatemala, every afternoon, I would watch little kids gather the pods and nibble on the fruit, skillfully avoiding the seeds and tough fibers. Tamarind grows in warm tropical climates and is prominent in the cooking of Latin America and Southeast Asia. It's sold in a number of ways: pressed into blocks, complete with seeds, fibers, and bits of hard shell, as well as in thick, syrupy concentrate or thin pulpy juice. I prefer the pressed blocks. In Indian restaurants, this sauce is usually served alongside Cilantro-Mint Dipping Sauce (page 246) and Fresh Onion-Chile Relish (page 346) to accompany rice dishes, grilled breads, curries, and roasted meats, fish, and poultry.

> 8 ounces (½ of a 1-pound block) pressed tamarind flesh, broken into 2-inch pieces
>
> 1¼ cups boiling water
>
> 1 tablespoon vegetable oil
>
> ¼ teaspoon ground ginger
>
> ¼ teaspoon ground cardamom
>
> ¼ teaspoon ground cinnamon
>
> ¼ teaspoon cayenne pepper
>
> ½ cup firmly packed light brown sugar
>
> Salt

1. In a heatproof bowl, cover the tamarind with the boiling water and let sit for 15 minutes. Mash the tamarind with the back of a spoon. Strain the pulp through a fine-mesh sieve set over a bowl, pressing hard on the seeds and tough fibers. Discard the seeds and fibers.

2. In a small saucepan, heat the oil over medium heat until shimmering. Add the ginger, cardamom, cinnamon, and cayenne and cook, stirring, for 1 minute. Add the tamarind pulp and brown sugar and simmer just until the sugar is dissolved. Season with salt and let cool before serving. Will keep in the refrigerator for up to 1 week.

TANGY CHINESE DUMPLING SAUCE

MAKES ¼ CUP

THIS TOTALLY SIMPLE dipping sauce is one of my favorites. It balances the salty with the tart and aromatic with just three ingredients. I like to use unseasoned rice vinegar here because it is unsweetened. Use this on any type of dumpling or meatball as well as on grilled chicken or steamed fish.

> 1 tablespoon paper-thin fresh ginger slices
> 2 tablespoons soy sauce
> 2 tablespoons rice vinegar

In a mortar or small bowl, lightly pound the ginger until bruised. Add the soy sauce and vinegar and let sit for 10 minutes before serving to let the flavors develop. Will keep in the refrigerator for up to 1 week.

ASIAN RICE NOODLE SALAD

MAKES 6 SERVINGS

FOR ME, THIS is one of the most refreshing, flavorful, and versatile salads going. You can use pretty much any type of grilled or roasted meat, poultry, or seafood as well as all sorts of vegetables. Rotisserie chickens or Cuban roast pork, both relatively easy to find, work extremely well. Depending on the meat, this salad is also pretty low in fat and calories. Rice sticks, ¼-inch-wide dried rice noodles, can be found in most supermarkets nowadays.

8 ounces dried rice sticks

1½ cups coarsely shredded roasted chicken, pork, or beef, or cooked medium-size shrimp

2 large carrots, shredded

¼ pound mung bean sprouts, bean end discarded

1 small Kirby cucumber, peeled, seeded, and cut into 2-inch-long matchsticks

2 radishes, thinly sliced

1 scallion, thinly sliced

1 recipe Vietnamese Fish Dipping Sauce (page 258), Ginger Dipping Sauce (page 249), or Spicy Lemongrass-Cilantro Dipping Sauce (page 254)

⅓ cup torn fresh cilantro leaves

⅓ cup torn fresh mint leaves

Salt

½ cup chopped unsalted dry-roasted peanuts

1. Bring a large pot of salted water to a boil. Add the rice noodles and cook, stirring occasionally, until *al dente*, 6 to 8 minutes. Drain and rinse under cold running water until thoroughly cooled. Drain again, shaking out any excess water, and let the noodles sit until dry, about 20 minutes, shaking the colander occasionally.

2. Transfer the noodles to a large bowl, add the meat, carrots, bean sprouts, cucumber, radishes, and scallion, and toss to combine. Add ¼ cup of the sauce and toss well. Add the cilantro and mint, season with salt, and toss until combined, adding more sauce if the noodles seem dry. Sprinkle with the peanuts and serve.

THAI NAM PLA PRIK (SPICY FISH SAUCE WITH LIME)

MAKES ABOUT 1/3 CUP

THE SALTY, TART, and spicy flavors of this sauce make it a perfect match with grilled meats or fried dumplings, spring rolls, or savory fritters like scallion pancakes. When I want a milder sauce, I use 2 tablespoons each soy sauce and fish sauce.

  2 tablespoons fresh lime juice

  1/4 cup Asian fish sauce

  4 Thai bird chiles or 2 finger chiles, very thinly sliced (don't remove the seeds)

Combine all the ingredients in a small bowl and let sit 15 minutes before using to let the flavors develop. Will keep, tightly covered, in the refrigerator for up to 3 days.

VIETNAMESE FISH DIPPING SAUCE (NUOC CHAM)

MAKES 1 CUP

THE MOST VERSATILE and widely served sauce in Vietnamese cuisine is *nuoc cham*. It uses the ubiquitous *nuoc mam*, also called *nam pla* in Thailand, which is a sauce made from the pressings of fermented salted anchovies. It is quite a bit saltier than soy sauce, but has a lighter consistency and imparts a unique rich flavor that is characteristic of Southeast Asia. Watching my friend and coworker Marcia Kiesel, a Vietnamese cooking maven, make this sauce for many years, I think this one will do her proud. Serve this with all types of grilled meats, spring rolls, dumplings, rice, rice noodles, or steamed or pan-fried fish.

  2 large garlic cloves, coarsely chopped

  2 Thai bird chiles or 1 finger chile, finely chopped (don't remove the seeds)

  1/4 cup sugar

  3 tablespoons boiling water

  5 tablespoons fresh lime juice

  1/4 cup Asian fish sauce

  1 shallot, sliced paper thin

1. In a mortar, pound the garlic, chiles, and sugar together into a syrupy paste. Add the boiling water and stir until the sugar is dissolved and let cool.

2. Stir in the lime juice, fish sauce, and shallot. Will keep, tightly covered, in the refrigerator for up to 3 days.

VIETNAMESE PEANUT DIPPING SAUCE (NUOC LEO)

MAKES 1 1/2 CUPS

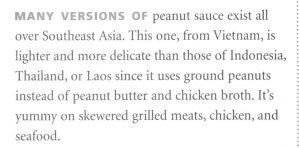

MANY VERSIONS OF peanut sauce exist all over Southeast Asia. This one, from Vietnam, is lighter and more delicate than those of Indonesia, Thailand, or Laos since it uses ground peanuts instead of peanut butter and chicken broth. It's yummy on skewered grilled meats, chicken, and seafood.

1 tablespoon peanut oil or other mild-flavored oil

1/2 small onion, minced

2 garlic cloves, minced

2 Thai bird or serrano chiles, minced (don't remove the seeds)

1/2 cup unsalted dry-roasted peanuts, finely ground

3/4 cup low-sodium chicken broth

1/2 cup well-stirred canned unsweetened coconut milk

1 tablespoon Asian fish sauce

1 tablespoon hoisin sauce or ketchup

1 tablespoon sugar

Heat the oil in a medium-size saucepan over medium heat until shimmering. Add the onion, garlic, and chiles and cook, stirring, until softened, about 3 minutes. Add the peanuts and cook, stirring, until lightly golden, about 3 minutes longer. Add the remaining ingredients and simmer over very low heat until thickened, about 10 minutes. Will keep, tightly covered, in the refrigerator for up to 3 days. Reheat gently or bring to room temperature before serving.

8 BEST DUMPLING DIPPING SAUCES

1. Chinese Ginger-Soy Dipping Sauce (page 246)

2. Ginger Dipping Sauce (page 249)

3. Sesame-Lime Dipping Sauce (page 254)

4. Sweet Sake-Soy Dumpling Sauce (page 255)

5. Sweet Thai Chile Dipping Sauce (page 255)

6. Tangy Chinese Dumpling Sauce (page 256)

7. Thai Nam Pla Prik (left)

8. Vietnamese Fish Dipping Sauce (left)

VINAIGRETTES AND DRESSINGS

I can honestly say that my mother never served bottled or packaged salad dressing when I was growing up. Which isn't to say that I grew up loving salads (although I do now). Most often it was vegetable oil and cider vinegar, salt and pepper, though occasionally it was red wine vinegar and olive oil. Only when we went out did we get something different—blue cheese, creamy Italian, Thousand Island. These were exotic! Little did I know that America was having more interesting salads than I (unlike absolutely everything else my fabulous cook of a mother made). What it took me years to realize was that the oil and vinegar of my childhood was actually far superior to the bottled dressings I came to want.

Prepared without all those additives, preservatives, and what have you, those popular American classics can be outstanding. Blue Cheese Dressing (page 276), still a favorite of mine, combines relatively few ingredients—mayonnaise, crème fraîche, shallots, and blue cheese. And Ranch Dressing (page 289), quite possibly the most popular commercially bottled dressing and easiest to make, adds a little tangy buttermilk and lots of black pepper for a kick.

Aside from dressing salad greens, vegetables, beans, and more, vinaigrettes can make terrific marinades for meats, fish, and poultry before roasting or grilling. With the high acidity from the vinegar or lemon juice, you should keep the marinating time fairly short—one to two hours is plenty for meat and poultry, and about 30 minutes for fish and shellfish.

BASIC VINAIGRETTE

MAKES ABOUT ½ CUP

THIS ALL-PURPOSE DRESSING, following the 1 to 3 ration of acid to oil, is suitable for all greens, steamed vegetables, bean salads, potato salads, and chilled seafood salads.

2 tablespoons white wine vinegar
1 teaspoon Dijon mustard
Pinch of sea salt
6 tablespoons extra-virgin olive oil
Freshly ground black pepper

In a small bowl, whisk together the vinegar, mustard, and salt. Slowly add the oil in a thin, steady stream, whisking until the dressing thickens. Season with pepper. Will keep, tightly covered, in the refrigerator for up to 5 days.

BALSAMIC VINAIGRETTE I

MAKES ABOUT 1 CUP

USE THIS SIMPLE vinaigrette with all types of salad greens, as a dressing for warm potatoes, chicken or potato salads, or as a marinade for beef, poultry, pork, or lamb.

⅔ cup extra-virgin olive oil
⅓ cup balsamic vinegar
1½ teaspoons finely chopped fresh basil
    leaves
Pinch each of salt and freshly ground black
    pepper

Combine all the ingredients in a jar and shake until blended. Will keep, tightly covered, in the refrigerator for up to 5 days.

VINAIGRETTE 101

Vinaigrettes are dead simple. These are little more than vinegar, oil, and seasonings. The proportions of ingredients vary; some cooks prefer 3 parts oil to 1 part vinegar, while others use 2 to 1. It really is a matter of taste. As for the seasonings, mustard, shallots, garlic, ginger, herbs, and chiles are all perfectly acceptable. The most important seasonings, however, are enough salt and pepper to spark all the other flavors.

BALSAMIC VINAIGRETTE II

MAKES ABOUT 3/4 CUP

MUSTARD AND SHALLOT make this dressing a perfect match for all types of salad greens or as a dressing for potatoes, cold pasta salads, lentils or other beans, and steamed vegetables.

3 tablespoons balsamic vinegar

1 teaspoon Dijon mustard

1 teaspoon minced shallot

1/2 cup extra-virgin olive oil

Salt and freshly ground black pepper

In a small bowl, whisk together the vinegar, mustard, and shallot. In a thin, steady stream, whisk in the oil until the dressing thickens. Season with salt and pepper. Will keep, tightly covered, in the refrigerator for up to 5 days.

BEET VINAIGRETTE

MAKES ABOUT 3/4 CUP

I LOVE THE shreds of beets in this beautiful rosy dressing. Golden beets obviously will yield a peachy-colored vinaigrette, but the flavor won't change. Try it over the watercress salad on page 275 or use on roasted vegetables, grilled meats, chilled tofu, steamed vegetables, potatoes, or sliced ripe melon.

1 small beet, about 11/2 inches in diameter, peeled and coarsely grated

1/4 cup water

2 tablespoons orange juice

2 tablespoons red wine vinegar

1 teaspoon sugar

1 teaspoon whole-grain mustard

1 tablespoon chopped fresh chives

6 tablespoons pure olive oil

Salt and freshly ground black pepper

1. Combine the grated beet, water, orange juice, vinegar, and sugar in a small skillet and simmer over medium-low heat until tender and the liquid is reduced to a few tablespoons, about 10 minutes.

2. Scrape the mixture into a heatproof bowl and let cool. Whisk in the mustard, chives, and oil and season with salt and pepper. Will keep, tightly covered, in the refrigerator for up to 5 days.

BLACK TRUFFLE VINAIGRETTE

MAKES ABOUT 1/2 CUP

BLACK SUMMER TRUFFLES have a sweet, earthy flavor and subtle musty aroma. They're much less expensive than white truffles, which can fetch hundreds of dollars per ounce. I like to add a few drops of white truffle oil, which is a mild-flavored oil scented with white truffles, to this dressing to punch up the flavor. If fresh truffles aren't available, canned ones will do quite nicely. Serve this as a dressing for warm sliced potatoes or on poached fish.

- 1 1/2 teaspoons minced black truffle, preferably fresh
- 2 tablespoons champagne vinegar
- 1 teaspoon minced shallot
- 1/2 teaspoon Dijon mustard
- Pinch of sea salt
- 6 tablespoons grapeseed or other mild-flavored vegetable oil
- 1/4 teaspoon good-quality white truffle oil, or more to taste
- Freshly ground black pepper

1. In a small skillet, combine the truffle and vinegar and cook over medium heat just until heated through. Transfer to a bowl and let cool.

2. Whisk in the shallot, mustard, and salt. Add the grapeseed oil in a thin, steady stream, whisking constantly, until the dressing thickens. Whisk in the truffle oil and season with pepper. Will keep, tightly covered, in the refrigerator for up to 5 days.

CHOPPED OLIVE VINAIGRETTE

MAKES ABOUT 2/3 CUP

THIS CHUNKY, SALTY, briny-flavored dressing is great on spinach salad with oranges and red onion, as well as on sliced tomatoes, warm potato or chicken salad, roasted vegetables or roasted meats, avocados, or halved hard-cooked eggs.

- 1 garlic clove, minced
- 1 anchovy fillet, rinsed and chopped
- 1 teaspoon Dijon mustard
- 2 tablespoons red wine vinegar
- 1/4 cup extra-virgin olive oil
- 1/4 cup mixed green and black brine-cured olives, such as Picholine, Sicilian, Kalamata, niçoise, or gaeta, pitted and coarsely chopped
- 1 tablespoon chopped capers
- 1 tablespoon finely chopped fresh Italian parsley leaves
- Salt
- Red pepper flakes

In a small bowl, mash together the garlic and anchovy with the back of a spoon into a paste. Whisk in the mustard and vinegar. Add the olive oil and whisk until blended. Stir in the olives and capers and season with parsley, salt, and red pepper flakes. Will keep, tightly covered, in the refrigerator for up to 5 days.

CHERRY BALSAMIC VINAIGRETTE

MAKES ABOUT ¼ CUP

FRUIT-FLAVORED BALSAMIC vinegars have become quite popular. They are infused with fruit juices or essences; in some cases, the juices are fermented in the balsamic-vinegar style. They're available at gourmet markets and some high-end supermarkets. Use this with any type of green, or grilled chicken, duck, or beef.

1 tablespoon cherry balsamic vinegar
1 teaspoon fresh lemon juice
1 teaspoon minced shallot
3 tablespoons extra-virgin olive oil
Salt and freshly ground black pepper

Combine the vinegar, lemon juice, and shallot and whisk in the oil. Season with salt and pepper. Will keep, tightly covered, in the refrigerator for up to 5 days.

CITRUS VINAIGRETTE

MAKES ¼ CUP

I MAKE THIS tart, crisp dressing more than any other one because it's so easy and so satisfying. My favorite salad is romaine with toasted pecans, thinly sliced apple, goat cheese or manchego, and this dressing. Also try it with roasted potatoes, steamed vegetables, or grilled chicken.

1 tablespoon fresh lemon juice
½ teaspoon minced garlic
3 tablespoons extra-virgin olive oil
Salt and freshly ground black pepper

Combine the lemon juice, garlic, and oil in a small bowl and whisk until blended. Season with salt and pepper. Will keep, tightly covered, in the refrigerator for up to 5 days.

5 VINEGARS YOU WANT TO KEEP IN YOUR PANTRY

- **Balsamic vinegar:** sweet, heavy, distinctive flavor
- **Red wine vinegar:** great all-purpose vinegar with a bold flavor
- **Rice vinegar:** lighter, less acidic flavor, slightly neutral
- **Sherry vinegar:** flavorful and rich
- **White wine vinegar:** great all-purpose vinegar when looking for a lighter flavor

MIXED CITRUS VINAIGRETTE

MAKES 2/3 CUP

SERVE THIS FRESH-FLAVORED citrus dressing with all types of greens, poached or grilled salmon or other fish, steamed or roasted vegetables, or sliced avocados or tomatoes.

2 tablespoons fresh orange juice

1 tablespoon fresh lemon juice

1 1/2 teaspoons fresh lime juice

1 1/2 teaspoons minced shallot

1 teaspoon Dijon mustard

1/4 teaspoon finely grated lemon or orange zest

6 tablespoons extra-virgin olive oil

Salt and freshly ground black pepper

In a small bowl, combine the citrus juices, shallot, mustard, and zest. In a thin, steady stream, whisk in the oil until the dressing thickens, and season with salt and pepper. Will keep, tightly covered, in the refrigerator for up to 5 days.

CREAMY ORANGE-FENNEL VINAIGRETTE

MAKES ABOUT 1/2 CUP

FENNEL AND ORANGE make a super match—a classic dressing for poached salmon. I'd serve this creamy vinaigrette with all types of grilled or poached fish, spinach or any other leafy green salad, chicken, steamed vegetables, or ripe melon.

1/2 teaspoon fennel seeds

2/3 cup fresh orange juice

1/2 cup minced fresh fennel bulb, plus 2 tablespoons finely chopped fennel fronds

1 tablespoon fresh lemon juice

1 tablespoon sour cream

1/4 cup extra-virgin olive oil

Salt and freshly ground black pepper

1. Toast the fennel seeds in a small dry skillet over medium heat until fragrant and lightly browned, about 2 minutes. Transfer the fennel seeds to a cutting board and coarsely crush with the side of a knife.

2. Add the orange juice, minced fennel bulb, and chopped fennel seeds to the skillet and simmer over medium-low heat until reduced by about three-quarters. Strain the mixture through a fine-mesh sieve set over a small bowl, pressing hard on the solids, and let cool.

3. Add the lemon juice and sour cream to the bowl and stir. In a thin, steady stream, whisk in the oil until the dressing thickens, and season with salt and pepper. Stir in the fennel fronds. Will keep, tightly covered, in the refrigerator for up to 5 days.

DIJON VINAIGRETTE

MAKES ABOUT 1/2 CUP

THE SHARP, BRIGHT flavors of mustard really come through in this simple vinaigrette. It's perfect with all greens, as well as with warm lentils, chickpeas, or other beans; potatoes; roasted or steamed vegetables; and chicken salad. It's also great as a marinade for chicken, beef, lamb, and pork.

  2 tablespoons sherry vinegar
  1 1/2 teaspoons Dijon mustard
  1 1/2 teaspoons whole-grain mustard
  1 small garlic clove, crushed
  1/2 teaspoon finely chopped fresh thyme
     leaves
  6 tablespoons extra-virgin olive oil
  Salt and freshly ground black pepper

In a small bowl, whisk together the vinegar, mustards, garlic, and thyme. In a thin, steady stream, whisk in the oil until the dressing thickens. Season with salt and pepper. Will keep, tightly covered, in the refrigerator for up to 5 days.

HONEY-MUSTARD VINAIGRETTE

MAKES ABOUT 2/3 CUP

SWEET AND TART, this vinaigrette is great with all greens, sliced tomatoes and melon, and chicken salad.

  2 tablespoons balsamic vinegar
  2 tablespoons honey mustard
  1 1/2 teaspoons minced shallot
  Pinch of salt
  1/2 cup grapeseed or other mild-flavored
     vegetable oil
  Freshly ground black pepper

In a small bowl, whisk together the vinegar, mustard, shallot, and salt. While whisking, add the oil in a thin, steady stream, until the dressing thickens. Season with pepper. Will keep, tightly covered, in the refrigerator for up to 5 days.

LEMON-MINT VINAIGRETTE

MAKES ABOUT ¼ CUP

SERVE THIS SIMPLE lemony dressing with salad greens, sliced melon or tomatoes, and poached or grilled fish.

1 tablespoon fresh lemon juice
1 tablespoon finely chopped mint leaves
Pinch of salt
3 tablespoons extra-virgin olive oil
Freshly ground black pepper

1. In a small bowl, combine the lemon juice, mint, and salt and let sit for 5 minutes.

2. Add the olive oil and whisk until the dressing thickens. Season with pepper. Will keep, tightly covered, in the refrigerator for up to 5 days.

LEMONGRASS-CHILE VINAIGRETTE

MAKES ABOUT ½ CUP

THE BRIGHT FLAVORS of lemongrass, lime juice, fish sauce, and chile make this Thai-inspired dressing perfectly suited for shredded cabbage slaws, greens, avocados, cold rice noodle salads, and chilled seafood salads.

1 stalk lemongrass, bottom 4 inches
1 garlic clove, smashed
1 small Thai bird or serrano chile, seeded and chopped
1 teaspoon sugar
2 tablespoons fresh lime juice
2 teaspoons Asian fish sauce
¼ cup peanut oil
1 tablespoon finely chopped fresh cilantro leaves

Peel the outer leaves of the lemongrass stalk, revealing the tender inner white bulb. Finely chop the lemongrass and transfer it to a mini–food processor. Add the garlic, chile, and sugar and pulse until finely chopped. Add the lime juice and fish sauce and process until the sugar is dissolved. With the machine running, add the oil in a thin, steady stream and process until the dressing thickens. Add the cilantro and pulse until combined. Will keep, tightly covered, in the refrigerator for up to 5 days.

PASSION FRUIT VINAIGRETTE

MAKES ABOUT 1/2 CUP

I LOVE THE flowery, perfumey quality of passion fruit, especially when paired with savory dishes. Crème fraîche, which can be added at the end, makes this dressing very rich. I like it with or without. Serve it with tender greens or a salad of melon, avocado, or papaya, sliced onions, and chicken.

- 3 ripe passion fruit or 1½ tablespoons passion-fruit concentrate
- 1 teaspoon minced shallot
- ½ teaspoon Dijon mustard
- Pinch of sugar
- ¼ cup grapeseed or other mild-flavored vegetable oil
- Salt and freshly ground white pepper
- 2 tablespoons crème fraîche, heavy cream, or sour cream (optional)

Working over a small bowl, cut the passion fruit in half and scoop out the pulp and seeds. If desired, press the pulp and juice through a fine-mesh sieve to remove the seeds. Whisk in the shallot, mustard, and sugar. Whisk in the oil in a thin, steady stream until the dressing thickens. Season with salt and white pepper. Whisk in the crème fraîche, if desired. Will keep, tightly covered, in the refrigerator for up to 5 days.

PESTO VINAIGRETTE

MAKES ABOUT 1/2 CUP

SERVE THIS WITH warm or cold potatoes, sturdy greens, or sliced hard-cooked eggs, avocados, or tomatoes.

- 2 tablespoons Classic Pesto Genovese (page 94)
- 2 tablespoons red wine vinegar
- ¼ cup extra-virgin olive oil
- Salt and freshly ground black pepper

Combine the pesto and vinegar in a small bowl. In a thin, steady stream, whisk in the oil until the dressing thickens. Season lightly with salt and pepper. Will keep, tightly covered, in the refrigerator for up to 5 days.

SIMPLE POTATO SALAD

In a large saucepan with water to cover, boil 2 pounds red-skinned potatoes until fork tender. Drain, let cool, and cut into chunks. Toss with about ½ cup dressing or vinaigrette of your choice (see page 272), adding more if the potatoes seem dry, chopped celery, minced red onion, chopped cornichons or dill pickles, capers, and the chopped fresh herbs of your choice.

POMEGRANATE VINAIGRETTE I

MAKES ABOUT ½ CUP

THE CHOICE OF fruit-flavored vinegars at gourmet markets is no longer limited to raspberry. Now there are fig, cherry, and pear balsamic, and, my favorite, pomegranate. It's tart, slightly tannic flavor is stilled with the vinegar and is a perfect foil for any salad green, warm lentils, sliced avocados, and grilled lamb and pork chops, steaks, or duck.

2 tablespoons pomegranate–red wine vinegar
1 teaspoon Dijon mustard
1 tablespoon minced onion
½ teaspoon sugar
6 tablespoons extra-virgin olive oil
Salt and freshly ground black pepper

In a small bowl, combine the vinegar, mustard, onion, and sugar and whisk until the sugar is dissolved. In a thin, steady stream, whisk in the oil until the dressing thickens and season with salt and pepper. Will keep, tightly covered, in the refrigerator for up to 5 days.

POMEGRANATE VINAIGRETTE II

MAKES ABOUT ¼ CUP

POMEGRANATE MOLASSES IS the syrupy reduction of the juice and figures prominently in Middle Eastern cuisines; you'll find it in gourmet markets and ethnic grocers. I love this dressing stirred into cooked lentils, bulgur for tabbouleh, or faro—an ancient grain from Italy that resembles wheat berries.

1 tablespoon pomegranate molasses
1 tablespoon red wine vinegar
1 teaspoon minced shallot
½ teaspoon sugar
2 tablespoons extra-virgin olive oil
Salt
Tabasco sauce
2 tablespoons crème fraîche or plain yogurt

In a small bowl, combine the pomegranate molasses, vinegar, shallot, and sugar and whisk until the sugar is dissolved. Whisk in the olive oil until the dressing thickens, and season with salt and Tabasco. Whisk in the crème fraîche. Will keep, tightly covered, in the refrigerator for up to 5 days.

ROASTED PEAR-BALSAMIC VINAIGRETTE

MAKES ABOUT 1 CUP

THIS FRAGRANT, SILKY dressing is a great match for any salad green, chicken, poached or grilled fish, and sliced melon.

> 1 firm but ripe Bartlett or Anjou pear, peeled, cored, and quartered lengthwise
> 4 small garlic cloves, left unpeeled
> 4 small fresh sage leaves, torn
> 1/2 teaspoon fresh thyme leaves
> 3 tablespoons balsamic vinegar
> 6 tablespoons extra-virgin olive oil
> Salt and freshly ground black pepper

1. Preheat the oven to 425°F. In a medium-size bowl, toss the pear with the garlic, sage, thyme, 1 tablespoon of the vinegar, and 2 tablespoons of the olive oil. Spread the mixture in a small baking dish and roast until the pears are softened and lightly browned and the garlic is softened, about 30 minutes. Let cool, then peel the garlic.

2. Transfer the pear and garlic along with any caramelized pan juices and herbs to a blender or mini–food processor and process until smooth. Add the remaining 2 tablespoons vinegar and process until combined. With the machine running, add the remaining 1/4 cup oil in a thin, steady stream and process until the dressing thickens. Season with salt and pepper. Will keep, tightly covered, in the refrigerator for up to 5 days.

ROASTED GARLIC VINAIGRETTE

MAKES ABOUT 3/4 CUP

THE MELLOW FLAVOR of roasted garlic makes this vinaigrette a terrific match for cooked lentils and other beans, avocados, tomatoes, warm potatoes, chicken salad, and sturdy salad greens.

> 8 garlic cloves, peeled
> 1/2 cup pure olive oil
> 1 tablespoon fresh thyme leaves
> 3 tablespoons sherry vinegar
> 1 teaspoon Dijon mustard
> Pinch of sugar
> Salt and freshly ground black pepper

1. Combine the garlic, olive oil, and thyme in a small saucepan and simmer over low heat until the garlic is golden and soft, about 15 minutes. Let the garlic and oil cool together.

2. Transfer the garlic and thyme to a blender, add the vinegar, mustard, and sugar, and process until fairly smooth. With the machine running, add the cooled garlic oil in a thin, steady stream and process until the dressing thickens. Season with salt and pepper. Will keep, tightly covered, in the refrigerator for up to 5 days.

ROASTED LEMON VINAIGRETTE

MAKES ABOUT 3/4 CUP

THE CARAMELIZED BITS of lemon rind, along with the roasted garlic cloves, makes this rich, flavorful dressing a perfect foil for warm potatoes, poached salmon, grilled chicken, warm lentils and other beans, and sliced avocados.

1/2 lemon, seeded and thinly sliced

4 large garlic cloves, left unpeeled

1 teaspoon fresh rosemary leaves

1 teaspoon fresh thyme leaves

1/2 cup plus 3 tablespoons water

1/3 cup plus 2 tablespoons extra-virgin olive oil

Salt and freshly ground black pepper

1 tablespoon finely chopped fresh Italian parsley leaves

1. Preheat the oven to 350°F. In a small bowl, toss together the lemon slices, garlic, rosemary, thyme, 3 tablespoons of the water, and 2 tablespoons of the olive oil. Season with salt and pepper and transfer to a medium-size baking dish. Cover loosely with a sheet of aluminum foil and roast until tender and the juices are slightly caramelized, about 35 minutes. Let cool, then peel the garlic.

2. Scrape the mixture and any oil or juices into a blender. Add the remaining 1/2 cup water to the baking dish, scraping up any caramelized juices. Add the liquid to the blender and process until fairly smooth. With the machine running, add the remaining 1/3 cup olive oil in a thin, steady stream and process until the dressing thickens. Stir in the parsley and season with salt and pepper. Will keep, tightly covered, in the refrigerator for up to 5 days.

17 GREAT DRESSINGS FOR POTATO SALAD

ROASTED RED PEPPER VINAIGRETTE

MAKES ABOUT 1¼ CUPS

CANNED OR JARRED peppers (⅓ cup) can be used in a pinch if you're pressed for time. The tart, bright flavor of the peppers is a great match for roasted potatoes, sturdy greens, or grilled chicken or steak.

    1 small red bell pepper
    1 large garlic clove, smashed
    1 large or 2 small anchovy fillets, rinsed
    1½ tablespoons balsamic vinegar
    1½ tablespoons sherry vinegar
    2 tablespoons mayonnaise
    ½ cup extra-virgin olive oil
    Salt and freshly ground black pepper

1. Roast the pepper over a gas flame or under a broiler, turning, until softened and blackened all over. Transfer the pepper to a bowl, cover with plastic wrap, and let sit until collapsed and cool to the touch, about 15 minutes. Peel, core, and seed the pepper, removing any inner ribs. Pat completely dry. Coarsely chop the pepper.

2. Combine the bell pepper, garlic, and anchovy in a blender and pulse until finely chopped. Add the vinegars and mayonnaise and process until fairly smooth. With the machine running, add the oil in a thin, steady stream, processing until the dressing thickens. Season with salt and pepper. Will keep, tightly covered, in the refrigerator for up to 5 days.

CREAMY SESAME VINAIGRETTE

MAKES ABOUT ¾ CUP

TOASTED SESAME OIL adds a distinctive richness to this creamy East/West-inspired dressing. Serve it with greens, avocado, tofu, shredded cabbage, roasted chicken or pork, sliced tomatoes, or warm potatoes.

    3 tablespoons rice vinegar
    1½ tablespoons mayonnaise
    1 tablespoon soy sauce
    1 teaspoon Dijon mustard
    1 small garlic clove, finely chopped
    ½ cup peanut or other mild-flavored vegetable oil
    ½ teaspoon toasted sesame oil
    Salt
    Cayenne pepper

In a blender or mini–food processor, combine the vinegar, mayonnaise, soy sauce, mustard, and garlic and process until smooth. With the machine running, add the peanut oil in a thin, steady stream and process until the dressing thickens. Add the sesame oil and season with salt and cayenne. Will keep, tightly covered, in the refrigerator for up to 5 days.

SHALLOT-SOY VINAIGRETTE

MAKES ABOUT 1/3 CUP

CHINESE BLACK VINEGAR is a very dark, rich vinegar, much like balsamic without the sweetness. Unseasoned rice vinegar (1½ table-spoons) and a few drops of Worcestershire sauce would be the best substitute if you can't find it. Serve this dressing with all types of greens, sliced tomatoes or avocados, steamed vegetables, or chilled tofu.

> 3 tablespoons peanut oil
> 1 tablespoon minced shallot
> 1½ tablespoons Chinese black vinegar
> 1 tablespoon soy sauce
> Cayenne pepper

1. Heat the oil in a small skillet over medium heat. Add the shallot and cook, stirring, until softened but not browned, about 2 minutes.

2. Transfer to a bowl and let cool. Whisk in the vinegar and soy sauce and season with cayenne. Will keep, tightly covered, in the refrigerator for up to 5 days.

VERJUS VINAIGRETTE

MAKES ABOUT 1/2 CUP

VERJUS IS UNFERMENTED grape juice, which tastes like tart, tannic grape juice, and is available in gourmet markets and some liquor stores. Seedless white or green grapes can be substituted for it. Serve this dressing over tender greens or with melon, mangoes, or grapes for a sweet-savory fruit salad.

> 2 tablespoons verjus or 1/3 cup seedless green grapes
> 1 teaspoon fresh lemon juice
> 2 tablespoons crème fraîche or sour cream
> 1/4 cup extra-virgin olive oil
> Salt and freshly ground black pepper

In a small bowl, combine the verjus, lemon juice, and crème fraîche. (If using grapes, puree them in a blender with the lemon juice and crème fraîche.) In a thin, steady stream, whisk in the olive oil until the dressing thickens. Season with salt and pepper. Will keep, tightly covered, in the refrigerator for up to 5 days.

WATERCRESS AND ENDIVE SALAD
WITH GOAT CHEESE AND WALNUTS
MAKES 6 TO 8 SERVINGS

PEPPERY WATERCRESS AND juicy, crunchy endive make great foils for the beet vinaigrette. The goat cheese adds a lovely richness.

1/2 cup walnut halves

2 large bunches watercress, tough, thick stems discarded

2 heads Belgian endive, cut into 1-inch pieces

1 recipe Beet Vinaigrette (page 263), Dijon Vinaigrette (page 267),
    Verjus Vinaigrette (left), or Tarragon-Shallot Dressing (page 290)

Salt and freshly ground black pepper

1 cup packed fresh mild goat cheese

1. Preheat the oven to 350°F. Spread the walnuts on a baking sheet and toast until golden and fragrant, 8 to 10 minutes. Let cool, then coarsely chop the nuts.

2. In a large bowl, toss together the watercress, endive, and about three quarters of the vinaigrette. Season with salt and pepper. Crumble in half of the goat cheese and half of the walnuts, toss gently, and transfer to a large platter. Scatter the remaining goat cheese and walnuts on top and drizzle with the remaining vinaigrette. Serve immediately.

SWEET WINE VINAIGRETTE

MAKES ABOUT 1/2 CUP

I ALWAYS SEEM to have a cup or so of dessert wine in my fridge—a whole bottle is usually more than we can drink in one sitting—so aside from sabayon, this is my next favorite way to use it up. Serve it on tender greens, melon slices, or a salad of baby greens with pears and gorgonzola. It's low in fat as well!

1 cup sweet white wine, such as late-harvest Riesling, Muscato, or Beaumes de Venise

1 tablespoon minced shallot

1 teaspoon Dijon mustard

1 tablespoon fresh lemon juice

2 tablespoons grapeseed or other mild-flavored oil

Salt and freshly ground black pepper

1. Combine the wine and shallot in a small saucepan and bring to a boil. Simmer over medium heat until reduced to 1/3 cup, about 10 minutes. Transfer to a small bowl and let cool.

2. Whisk in the mustard and lemon juice. In a thin, steady stream, whisk in the oil until the dressing thickens. Season with salt and pepper. Will keep, tightly covered, in the refrigerator for up to 5 days.

BLUE CHEESE DRESSING

MAKES ABOUT 1 1/4 CUPS

BLUE CHEESE DRESSING was the height of sophistication for me as a kid—I felt so grown up ordering it in restaurants. This version is truly sophisticated, with crème fraîche, shallot, and pungent blue cheese. Use it on all sturdy greens, with potatoes, or as a dip for crudités or sliced ripe tomatoes.

1 1/2 tablespoons white wine vinegar or champagne vinegar

2 tablespoons mayonnaise

2 tablespoons crème fraîche or sour cream

1 teaspoon Dijon mustard

1 teaspoon minced shallot

1/2 cup grapeseed or other mild-flavored vegetable oil

1/2 cup finely crumbled blue cheese, such as Maytag or Roquefort

Salt and freshly ground black pepper

In a small bowl, combine the vinegar, mayonnaise, crème fraîche, mustard, and shallot and whisk until smooth. In a thin, steady stream, whisk in the oil until the dressing thickens. Whisk in the blue cheese and season with salt and a generous pinch of black pepper. Will keep, tightly covered, in the refrigerator for up to 5 days.

CAESAR DRESSING

MAKES ABOUT 3/4 CUP

FOR A SERIOUS anchovy lover like me, most Caesar dressings are seriously lacking in that department. I say, why bother calling it Caesar then? This one has a definite anchovy presence, but it is well balanced with the other ingredients. Uncooked egg yolks do carry a slight risk of salmonella, but it is getting safer all the time. Use very fresh eggs from a reliable source and exercise caution in whom you serve it to.

2 large anchovy fillets, rinsed and chopped
1 garlic clove, mashed
Pinch of salt
1 large egg yolk
2 tablespoons fresh lemon juice
2 tablespoons freshly grated parmesan cheese
1/2 cup pure olive oil
Freshly ground black pepper

In a medium-size bowl, mash the anchovies, garlic, and salt together into a paste. Whisk in the egg yolk, lemon juice, and parmesan until smooth. Add the oil in a thin, steady stream, whisking until the dressing thickens. Season with pepper. Use immediately.

EGGLESS CAESAR DRESSING

MAKES ABOUT 2/3 CUP

THE ABSENCE OF an egg yolk makes this Caesar dressing totally safe, that is, unless anchovies send you into fits of apoplexy.

1 large garlic clove, smashed
2 large anchovy fillets, rinsed and chopped
1/4 cup mayonnaise
2 tablespoons fresh lemon juice
2 tablespoons freshly grated parmesan cheese
1 tablespoon water
1/4 cup extra-virgin olive oil
Freshly ground black pepper

In a mini–food processor or blender, combine the garlic, anchovies, mayonnaise, lemon juice, parmesan, and water and process until smooth. With the machine running, add the oil in a thin, steady stream and process until the dressing thickens. Season with pepper. Will keep, tightly covered, in the refrigerator for up to 5 days.

CAESAR SALAD

MAKES ABOUT 6 LARGE SERVINGS

THERE IS NO salad that consistently calls to me like Caesar salad. The subtle lemon and not-so-subtle anchovy flavor mixed with crunchy salad greens and crisp romaine is satisfying beyond belief.

½ loaf Italian bread, crusts removed

2 tablespoons extra-virgin olive oil

1 large garlic clove, mashed into a paste

Salt and freshly ground black pepper

2 tablespoons freshly grated parmesan cheese

1 large head or 2 small heads romaine lettuce, trimmed and torn
    into bite-size pieces

1 recipe Caesar Dressing or Eggless Caesar Dressing (page 277)

1. Preheat the oven to 325°F. Cut the bread into ½-inch cubes and toss them in a large bowl with the oil and garlic. Season with salt and pepper and spread them in a single layer on a baking sheet. Toast the bread cubes, tossing occasionally, until golden and crisp, about 15 minutes. Return the croutons to the bowl and toss with the parmesan until evenly coated. Spread the croutons on the baking sheet and bake again, just until the cheese is melted and nutty, 8 to 10 minutes longer. Let cool.

2. In a large serving bowl, toss the lettuce with half of the dressing. Add the croutons and the remaining dressing and toss until everything is well coated. Season with salt and pepper and serve right away.

CARROT-GINGER DRESSING

MAKES ABOUT 1 CUP

THE FIRST THING I look forward to at a Japanese restaurant is the (usually lame) green salad that's coated with a delicious carrot-ginger dressing. Tart, sweet, fragrant, and very refreshing, this dressing is perfect for all types of greens, cold rice noodle salad, chilled tofu, chicken salad, steamed veggies, chilled seafood salad, or slices of ripe melon or avocado.

1/2 cup fresh carrot juice

2 tablespoons fresh lime juice

1 tablespoon soy sauce

1 medium-size carrot, coarsely chopped

One 3/4-inch-thick slice peeled fresh ginger, thinly sliced

1/2 cup peanut oil

Cayenne pepper

1. In a small saucepan, boil the carrot juice until reduced to 3 tablespoons. Let cool.

2. In a blender or mini–food processor, combine the reduced carrot juice, lime juice, soy sauce, carrot, and ginger and process until finely chopped. While the machine is running, add the oil in a thin, steady stream and process until blended. Season with cayenne. Will keep, tightly covered, in the refrigerator for up to 5 days.

CLASSIC FRENCH DRESSING

MAKES ABOUT 3/4 CUP

THOSE BOTTLES OF gloppy orange-colored French dressing are so frightening, it's a wonder more people don't run screaming down that aisle in the supermarket. This is a classic American-style French dressing because it has ketchup, Worcestershire, and onion. Use it on all greens, roasted vegetables, potatoes, and steamed veggies.

2 tablespoons grated sweet onion, such as Vidalia or Walla Walla

2 tablespoons red wine vinegar

2 tablespoons ketchup

1 teaspoon Dijon mustard

1 teaspoon Worcestershire sauce

1/2 teaspoon Tabasco sauce

1/4 cup grapeseed or other mild-flavored oil

Salt

1. Put the grated onion in a fine-mesh sieve, set over a bowl, and, using the back of a spoon, press to extract as much of the juice as possible. Discard the onion bits.

2. Add the vinegar, ketchup, mustard, Worcestershire, and Tabasco to the bowl and whisk until smooth. In a thin, steady stream, whisk in the oil until the dressing thickens, and season with salt. Will keep, tightly covered, in the refrigerator for up to 5 days.

CLASSIC COLESLAW DRESSING

MAKES ABOUT 1¼ CUPS

WHEN MOST PEOPLE think of coleslaw, this mayonnaise-based dressing comes to mind. Creamy, tangy, and slightly spicy, this one won't disappoint. It's also good on potatoes, sturdy salad greens, and steamed vegetables.

3 tablespoons cider vinegar

1 tablespoon sugar

Pinch of salt

2 tablespoons minced sweet onion, such as Vidalia or Walla Walla

1 cup mayonnaise

Tabasco sauce

Freshly ground black pepper

Combine the vinegar, sugar, and salt in a small bowl and whisk until dissolved. Add the onion and mayonnaise and whisk until smooth. Season with Tabasco and pepper. Will keep, tightly covered, in the refrigerator for up to 5 days.

CREAMY ITALIAN DRESSING

MAKES ABOUT ¾ CUP

USE THIS CREAMY, tangy dressing on all types of greens, potatoes, tomatoes, steamed or roasted veggies, chicken salad, and sliced avocado and hard-cooked eggs.

1 large garlic clove, minced

Large pinch of salt

1 teaspoon Dijon mustard

2 tablespoons white wine vinegar

3 tablespoons mayonnaise

3 tablespoons heavy cream or crème fraîche

6 tablespoons pure olive oil

1 tablespoon finely chopped fresh Italian parsley leaves

1 teaspoon finely chopped fresh oregano leaves

Salt and freshly ground black pepper

In a small bowl, mash the garlic and salt together into a paste, using the back of a spoon. Whisk in the mustard, vinegar, mayonnaise, and heavy cream. In a slow, steady stream, whisk in the olive oil until the dressing thickens. Stir in the parsley and oregano and season with salt and pepper. Will keep, tightly covered, in the refrigerator for up to 5 days.

BASIC COLESLAW

MAKES 6 TO 8 SERVINGS

BASIC? YES. SIMPLE? For sure. Delicious? Totally! Add what you like to embellish it. Just eat it pretty quickly so it stays crisp.

4 cups packed cored and shredded green cabbage

4 cups packed cored and shredded red cabbage

2 large carrots, shredded

2 scallions, thinly sliced

1 red or yellow bell pepper, seeded and very thinly sliced into strips

4 radishes, thinly sliced

1 recipe Classic Coleslaw Dressing (left)

Salt and freshly ground black pepper

In a large bowl, combine the cabbages, carrots, scallions, bell pepper, and radishes. Add the dressing, season with salt and pepper, and toss. Serve fairly soon thereafter.

CREAMY LEMON DRESSING

MAKES ABOUT 3/4 CUP

I LOVE THIS tart, rich dressing on all types of greens, especially arugula with its peppery kick, but try it on steamed or roasted vegetables, grilled chicken, and sliced avocados, tomatoes, or ripe melon.

3 tablespoons fresh lemon juice

1/2 teaspoon finely grated lemon zest

3 tablespoons crème fraîche or heavy cream (though the dressing will be a bit thinner)

6 tablespoons extra-virgin olive oil

1 tablespoon finely chopped fresh Italian parsley leaves

Salt

Cayenne pepper

In a small bowl, whisk together the lemon juice, lemon zest, and crème fraîche until smooth. In a thin, steady stream, whisk in the oil until the dressing thickens. Stir in the parsley and season with salt and cayenne. Will keep, tightly covered, in the refrigerator for up to 5 days.

10 GREAT SALAD COMBINATIONS

1. Romaine lettuce, croutons, shaved parmesan cheese, and Caesar Dressing (page 277), Basic Vinaigrette (page 262), Ranch Dressing (page 289), Dijon Vinaigrette (page 267), or Citrus Vinaigrette (page 265)

2. Watercress, crumbled blue cheese, apple or pear slices, toasted walnuts, and Basic Vinaigrette (page 262), Balsamic Vinaigrette I (page 262), Dijon Vinaigrette (page 267), Creamy Sherry Vinegar Dressing (page 284), or Ranch Dressing (page 289)

3. Baby greens, toasted sliced almonds, shaved parmesan or manchego cheese, olives, and Balsamic Vinaigrette II (page 263) or Basic Vinaigrette (page 262)

4. Arugula, shaved parmesan cheese, toasted pecans, and Creamy Lemon Dressing (page 281), Basic Vinaigrette (page 262), Dijon Vinaigrette (page 267), or Ranch Dressing (page 289)

5. Chopped romaine lettuce, chopped olives, chopped cucumbers, chopped celery, and Creamy Pesto Dressing (right), Creamy Italian Dressing (page 280), Chopped Olive Vinaigrette (page 264), Basic Vinaigrette (page 262), or Ranch Dressing (page 289)

6. Classic Cobb: chopped iceberg lettuce, crumbled bacon, avocado chunks, chopped chicken breast, crumbled blue cheese, chopped hard-boiled eggs, and Basic Vinaigrette (page 262), Dijon Vinaigrette (page 267), or Ranch Dressing (page 289)

7. Watercress, shredded carrots, sliced cucumbers, and Beet Vinaigrette (page 263), Carrot-Ginger Dressing (page 279), Ginger-Soy Dressing (page 284), or Miso-Ginger Dressing (page 288)

8. Tomato chunks, sliced cucumbers, sliced scallions, crumbled feta cheese, olives, and Tahini Dressing (page 290), Creamy Lemon Dressing (page 281), Basic Vinaigrette (page 262), Dijon Vinaigrette (page 267), or Pomegranate Vinaigrette (page 270)

9. Sliced oranges, shaved fennel bulb, tangerine segments, sliced red onion, and Creamy Lemon Dressing (page 281), Carrot-Ginger Dressing (page 279), Basic Vinaigrette (page 262), Citrus Vinaigrette (page 265), or Cherry Balsamic Vinaigrette (page 265)

10. Radicchio, endive, arugula, and Creamy Italian Dressing (page 280), Caesar Dressing (page 277), Ranch Dressing (page 289), Basic Vinaigrette (page 262), Dijon Vinaigrette (page 267), or Citrus Vinaigrette (page 265)

CREAMY PESTO DRESSING

MAKES ABOUT 2/3 CUP

FOLD THIS DRESSING into warm potatoes or warm chickpeas or lentils for a fabulous side dish, or use it with poached or grilled salmon, chicken, potatoes, tomatoes, steamed vegetables, or any salad greens.

2 tablespoons Classic Pesto Genovese (page 94)

3 tablespoons mayonnaise, preferably homemade

1 tablespoon white wine vinegar

2 tablespoons water

2 tablespoons extra-virgin olive oil

Salt and freshly ground black pepper

In a small bowl, whisk together the pesto, mayonnaise, vinegar, and water until smooth. Add the oil and whisk until the dressing thickens. Season with salt and pepper. Will keep, tightly covered, in the refrigerator for up to 5 days.

OTHER PESTOS FOR CREAMY PESTO DRESSING

There are a number of other pesto recipes that work well with this dressing recipe. Try any one of the following instead of the Classic Pesto Genovese:

- Anchovy-Parsley Pesto (page 105)
- Charred Garlic-Jalapeño Pesto with Queso Fresco (page 119)
- Chèvre and Piquillo Pepper Pesto (page 119)
- Green Chile and Scallion Pesto (page 117)
- Mint, Parsley, and Scallion Pesto (page 99)
- Olive, Caper, and Mint Pesto (page 102)
- Parsley Pesto Enriched with Egg Yolks (page 103)
- Parsley Sauce (Salsa Verde) (page 104)
- Pignoli-Herb Sauce (page 98)
- Pistou (page 95)
- Roasted Red Pepper Pesto with Pecorino Pepato (page 109)
- Salsina Verde (page 104)
- Scallion-Macadamia Pesto (page 116)
- Summer Herb Pesto (page 97)
- Sun-Dried Tomato Pesto (page 113)

CREAMY SHERRY VINEGAR DRESSING

MAKES ABOUT 2/3 CUP

USE THIS WITH warm lentils, potatoes, or chicken, steamed vegetables, and any type of green salad, as well as sliced avocados and tomatoes.

2 tablespoons sherry vinegar

2 tablespoons crème fraîche, heavy cream, or sour cream

1 teaspoon minced shallot

6 tablespoons extra-virgin olive oil

Sea salt and freshly ground pepper

In a small bowl, whisk together the vinegar, crème fraîche, and shallot until smooth. In a thin, steady stream, slowly whisk in the oil until the dressing thickens, then season with salt and pepper. Will keep, tightly covered, in the refrigerator for up to 5 days.

GINGER-SOY DRESSING

MAKES ABOUT 2/3 CUP

THE LOVELY PEPPERY-SWEET flavor of fresh ginger really stands out in this creamy East-West dressing. The little bit of mayonnaise mellows any sharpness and lends just the right body to make this dressing perfect for greens, sliced avocado, tofu, steamed veggies, and poached or grilled fish or chicken.

1 tablespoon peeled and finely chopped fresh ginger

1 small garlic clove, smashed

4 teaspoons soy sauce

1/2 teaspoon Dijon mustard

Pinch of sugar

2 tablespoons rice vinegar

2 tablespoons mayonnaise

1/3 cup grapeseed or other mild-flavored vegetable oil

In a mini–food processor or blender, combine the ginger, garlic, soy sauce, mustard, and sugar and process until finely chopped. Scrape down the sides of the bowl as needed. Add the vinegar and mayonnaise and process until fairly smooth. While the machine is running, add the oil in a thin, steady stream and process until the dressing thickens. Will keep, tightly covered, in the refrigerator for up to 5 days.

GREEN GODDESS DRESSING

MAKES ABOUT 1 CUP

THE FLAVORS OF this classic American dressing are very similar to those of tartar sauce and gribiche. Serve it with salad greens, steamed vegetables, sliced hard-cooked eggs, potatoes, or tomatoes, or chilled seafood.

1/2 cup mayonnaise

2 tablespoons finely chopped cornichons or gherkins

1 tablespoon Dijon mustard

1 tablespoon finely chopped fresh Italian parsley leaves

1 1/2 teaspoons finely chopped fresh tarragon leaves

1 teaspoon capers, drained

1 small garlic clove, mashed

1 1/2 tablespoons white wine vinegar

1/4 cup mild-flavored vegetable oil

Salt

Cayenne pepper

Combine the mayonnaise, cornichons, mustard, parsley, tarragon, capers, garlic, and vinegar in a blender or mini–food processor and process just until combined. While the machine is running, add the oil in a thin, steady stream, and process until the dressing thickens and is fairly smooth. Season with salt and cayenne. Will keep, tightly covered, in the refrigerator for up to 5 days.

TIPS FOR FRESH-TASTING SALADS AND SALAD DRESSINGS

- Choose the right greens to pair with a particular salad dressing. Sturdy greens are best with heavier, creamy dressings like Blue Cheese, Green Goddess, and Thousand Island as well as lighter dressings and vinaigrettes. Tender greens are best with vinaigrettes.

- Vinegars can vary in acidity. I find that anything over 6 percent is way too acidic and throws the balance off a little.

- Rice vinegar that is labeled as seasoned contains sugar and is quite sweet. Avoid it unless a recipe specifically calls for it.

- In most cases, vinaigrettes can be assembled in a jar and shaken just before serving. It may not always create an emulsion, but is perfectly fine.

- Generally, 5 to 6 tablespoons of dressing is plenty for 10 to 12 cups of greens (4 to 6 servings).

- For potato, chicken, bean, and grain salads, use 2 to 3 tablespoons of dressing per cup of potatoes, meat, etc.

INDONESIAN PEANUT DRESSING (GADO GADO)

MAKES ABOUT 1½ CUPS

THIS IS ONE of my all-time favorite dressings. Rich with the flavor of coconut, peanuts, and spicy chiles, when tossed with greens, vegetables, or meats, it's substantial enough to make a great main dish. *Sambal oelek* is a fresh red chile sauce from Indonesia and is available in Asian markets and most supermarkets.

1 tablespoon peanut oil

1 large shallot, finely chopped

1 large garlic clove, finely chopped

½ cup chunky peanut butter, preferably natural

¼ cup well-stirred unsweetened coconut milk

1 tablespoon firmly packed dark brown sugar

1 teaspoon *sambal oelek,* chili garlic sauce, or hot pepper sauce

½ teaspoon peeled and finely grated fresh ginger

1 cup water

2 tablespoons fresh lime juice

2 tablespoons finely chopped unsalted dry-roasted peanuts

Salt

1. In a medium-size saucepan, heat the oil over medium heat until shimmering. Add the shallot and garlic and cook, stirring, until golden, about 3 minutes.

2. Off the heat, add the peanut butter, coconut milk, brown sugar, *sambal oelek,* and ginger and whisk until pasty. Gradually whisk in the water and simmer over medium-low heat until slightly thickened, about 10 minutes.

3. Let cool, then whisk in the lime juice and peanuts and season with salt. Serve warm, at room temperature, or chilled. Will keep, tightly covered, in the refrigerator for up to 5 days.

POBLANO-LIME DRESSING

MAKES ABOUT ¾ CUP

POBLANO CHILES, THE fresh version of the dried ancho, have a bright, refreshing, slightly bitter flavor and can vary in heat from completely mild to pretty spicy—two large jalapeños being a close approximation. Serve this dressing with warm or cold potatoes, chicken, greens, sliced hard-cooked eggs, honeydew melon, tomatoes, or avocados.

1 large poblano chile

¼ cup plus 2 tablespoons grapeseed or other mild-flavored vegetable oil

¼ cup fresh lime juice

2 tablespoons chopped fresh cilantro leaves

1 garlic clove, peeled

3 tablespoons sour cream

Salt

1. Lightly rub the poblano chile with 1 teaspoon of the oil and roast over a gas flame or under a broiler until blackened all over. Transfer to a bowl; cover with plastic and let steam until collapsed and cool. Peel, core, and seed the chile and remove any inner ribs. Pat completely dry. Be careful when working with chiles not to touch your eyes. Coarsely chop the chile.

2. In a blender or mini–food processor, combine the poblano, lime juice, cilantro, garlic, and sour cream and process until finely chopped. While the machine is running, add the remaining oil in a thin, steady stream and process until smooth and the dressing thickens. Season with salt. Will keep, tightly covered, in the refrigerator for up to 5 days.

23 VINAIGRETTES AND DRESSINGS THAT MAKE TASTY DIPS FOR CRUDITÉS

LOWFAT GOAT CHEESE–BUTTERMILK DRESSING

MAKES ABOUT 1 CUP

GOAT CHEESE MAKES this light, creamy dressing taste more indulgent than it is. Use it with sturdy greens, sliced melon, tomatoes, hard-cooked eggs, warm potatoes, or chicken.

4 ounces mild fresh goat cheese, such as chèvre, softened

6 tablespoons buttermilk

2 tablespoons sherry vinegar

1 tablespoon water

1 tablespoon extra-virgin olive oil

1 teaspoon finely chopped shallot

Salt and freshly ground black pepper

Cayenne pepper

1 tablespoon minced fresh chives

In a blender or mini–food processor, combine the goat cheese, buttermilk, vinegar, water, and olive oil and process until smooth. Season with salt and a generous pinch of black pepper and cayenne. Add the chives and process just until combined. Will keep, tightly covered, in the refrigerator for up to 5 days.

MISO-GINGER DRESSING

MAKES ABOUT 1 CUP

IF YOU'RE LUCKY enough to have an Asian market nearby, the endless choices of miso can be a bit intimidating, especially if the labels are only in Japanese. White miso, with its pale mustard color, is very mild and well suited for this dressing. Red and brown misos are darker and more flavorful, but they are just fine too. All health food stores and many supermarkets now carry miso. Serve this silky dressing with any type of salad green, avocados, melon, tomatoes, tofu, chilled seafood, and poached or grilled fish or chicken.

3 tablespoons white (shiro) miso

1 teaspoon peeled and finely grated fresh ginger

1/4 cup seasoned rice vinegar

1 tablespoon fresh lemon juice

1 tablespoon mayonnaise

1/2 cup grapeseed or other mild-flavored vegetable oil

Salt and freshly ground black pepper to taste

In a food processor, combine the miso, ginger, vinegar, lemon juice, and mayonnaise and process until smooth. While the machine is running, add the oil in a thin, steady stream and process until creamy and smooth. Season with salt and pepper. Will keep, tightly covered, in the refrigerator for up to a week.

RANCH DRESSING

MAKES ABOUT 1 CUP

THIS IS DEFINITELY one of my all-time favorite dressings. Sharp, creamy, and peppery, it's great with greens, steamed vegetables, potatoes, crudités, grilled tomatoes, and sliced tomatoes, avocados, melon, and hard-cooked eggs—just about anything.

> 1 large garlic clove, crushed
>
> Large pinch of salt
>
> 1/4 cup buttermilk
>
> 1/4 cup mayonnaise
>
> 2 tablespoons plain whole-milk yogurt
>
> 4 teaspoons cider vinegar
>
> 1/4 cup grapeseed or other mild-flavored vegetable oil
>
> 1 scallion, minced
>
> Generous pinch of freshly ground black pepper
>
> Generous pinch of cayenne pepper

In a small bowl, mash the garlic and salt together into a paste using the back of a spoon. Add the buttermilk, mayonnaise, yogurt, and vinegar and whisk until smooth. In a thin, steady stream, whisk in the oil until the dressing thickens. Stir in the scallion and season with salt, black pepper, and the cayenne. Will keep, tightly covered, in the refrigerator for up to 5 days.

RUSSIAN DRESSING

MAKES ABOUT 1 CUP

"RUSSIAN" DRESSING WAS one of my first culinary feats as a kid. I stirred together equal parts ketchup and mayonnaise and was totally good to go. Unfortunately, iceberg was the only lettuce available then. Now I enjoy it with all sturdy greens, shredded carrots and cabbage, and crudités.

> 2 tablespoons grated sweet onion, such as Vidalia or Walla Walla
>
> 2 tablespoons cider vinegar
>
> 1/2 teaspoon sugar
>
> 1/4 cup ketchup
>
> 1/4 cup mayonnaise
>
> 1/4 cup grapeseed or other mild-flavored oil
>
> Salt
>
> Tabasco sauce

1. Put the grated onion in a fine-mesh sieve, set over a small mixing bowl, and press to extract as much of the juice as possible. Discard the onion bits.

2. Add the vinegar and sugar to the bowl and whisk until the sugar is dissolved. Add the ketchup and mayonnaise and whisk until smooth. In a thin, steady stream, whisk in the oil. Season with salt and Tabasco. Will keep, tightly covered, in the refrigerator for up to 4 days.

TAHINI DRESSING

MAKES ABOUT 1 CUP

THIS IS ONE of the classic dressings of Middle Eastern cooking and served with falafel, kibbe (meat and bulgur patties), green salads, kebabs— just to name a few. I love it with salads and feta cheese in pita bread. Tahini, sesame seed paste, is almost universally available in supermarkets; if not, try a health food store.

    1 large garlic clove, crushed
    Pinch of salt
    1/2 cup tahini
    1/2 cup lukewarm water
    2 tablespoons fresh lemon juice
    Cayenne pepper

In a mini–food processor, combine the garlic and salt and pulse several times. Add the tahini and about 1/4 cup of the water and process until combined. Add the remaining water 1 tablespoon at a time, processing after each addition to incorporate it, and process until creamy and barely pourable. Add the lemon juice, process to combine, and season with salt and cayenne. Will keep, tightly covered, in the refrigerator for up to 5 days.

TARRAGON-SHALLOT DRESSING

MAKES ABOUT 1/2 CUP

USE WITH ALL types of salad greens, warm potatoes, or sliced hard-cooked eggs or tomatoes.

    2 tablespoons white wine vinegar
    1 tablespoon minced shallot
    1 tablespoon finely chopped fresh tarragon
       leaves
    1 teaspoon whole-grain mustard
    6 tablespoons extra-virgin olive oil
    Salt and freshly ground black pepper

1. In a small bowl, combine the vinegar, shallot, and tarragon and let sit for 5 minutes.

2. Stir in the mustard. In a thin, steady stream, add the oil, whisking constantly, until the dressing thickens. Season with salt and pepper. Will keep, tightly covered, in the refrigerator for up to 5 days.

TART LEMON-HERB DRESSING

MAKES ABOUT 1 CUP

HARISSA IS A slow-cooked fiery chile paste very prominent in Moroccan cooking. It's sold in tubes or cans in Middle Eastern markets. Chinese chili garlic sauce can be substituted. Serve this dressing with greens, vegetables, and poached chicken.

⅓ cup fresh lemon juice

3 tablespoons finely chopped fresh Italian parsley leaves

3 tablespoons finely chopped fresh mint leaves

1½ teaspoons finely chopped fresh oregano leaves

1 teaspoons harissa, homemade (page 352) or store-bought

½ cup extra-virgin olive oil

Salt

In a small bowl, combine the lemon juice, parsley, mint, oregano, and harissa. In a slow, steady stream, whisk in the oil until the dressing thickens and season with salt. Will keep, tightly covered, in the refrigerator for up to 5 days.

21 GREAT MARINADES FOR LAMB, CHICKEN, PORK, AND FLANK STEAK

THAI HERB-LIME DRESSING

MAKES 2/3 CUP

THE THREE PROMINENT herbs in Thai cuisine are mint, cilantro, and basil. Thai or holy basil has a small leaf and a perfumey, intense licorice-y flavor. Serve this dressing with greens, vegetables, pork, and chicken.

- 1 teaspoon minced garlic
- 1 Thai bird or serrano chile, finely chopped (don't remove the seeds)
- 1 tablespoon firmly packed light brown sugar
- 1/4 cup fresh lime juice
- 2 tablespoons Asian fish sauce
- 2 tablespoons finely chopped fresh basil leaves, preferably Thai
- 2 tablespoons finely chopped fresh cilantro leaves
- 2 tablespoons finely chopped fresh mint leaves

In a mortar using a pestle, mash the garlic, chile, and brown sugar together into a coarse paste. Stir in the lime juice, fish sauce, and the herbs. Will keep, tightly covered, in the refrigerator for up to 5 days.

THOUSAND ISLAND DRESSING

MAKES ABOUT 1 CUP

THIS CLASSIC AMERICAN dressing couldn't be easier. With just a few simple ingredients, it's amazing to me that people still settle for the bottled stuff. Vinegar and Tabasco balance out the sweetness of the ketchup and pickles.

- 1/2 cup mayonnaise
- 1/4 cup ketchup
- 4 teaspoons cider vinegar
- 1 tablespoon water
- 2 tablespoons finely chopped sweet gherkins
- 1 tablespoon finely chopped fresh Italian parsley leaves
- Salt
- Tabasco sauce

In a small bowl, whisk together the mayonnaise, ketchup, vinegar, and water until smooth and creamy. Stir in the gherkins and parsley and season with salt and Tabasco. Will keep, tightly covered, in the refrigerator for up to 5 days.

THAI-STYLE CABBAGE SLAW

MAKES ABOUT 4 TO 6 SERVINGS

A LIGHT, REFRESHING salad that is equally good when paired with roast pork, chicken, beef, or duck. It's best to dress the slaw just before serving since it tends to get soggy after about 30 minutes.

1/2 small head green cabbage
2 large carrots, coarsely shredded
2 scallions, cut into 2-inch-long matchsticks
2 tablespoons each packed mint, basil, and cilantro leaves
1 recipe Thai Herb-Lime Dressing (left)
Salt and freshly ground black pepper
2 tablespoons chopped unsalted dry-roasted peanuts

1. Core the cabbage and slice it as thinly as possible. A mandoline or slicing disc on a food processor works very well.

2. In a large bowl, combine the cabbage, carrots, scallions, and herbs. Add the dressing, season with salt and pepper, and toss to combine well.

3. Just before serving, sprinkle with the peanuts.

WARM FRIZZLED CAPER DRESSING

MAKES ABOUT 2/3 CUP

BECAUSE THIS DRESSING is eaten hot, it's best served with warm potatoes, lentils or other beans, or roasted or steamed vegetables, as well as with greens that you intend to wilt.

1/2 cup extra-virgin olive oil
2 tablespoons capers, rinsed and patted dry

1 tablespoon minced shallot
1 tablespoon finely chopped fresh Italian parsley leaves
2 tablespoons white wine vinegar
2 tablespoons dry white wine
Salt and freshly ground black pepper

Heat the oil in a medium-size skillet over high heat until it shimmers. Add the capers, shallot, and parsley and cook, stirring a few times, until the capers and shallot are golden and crisp, about 2 to 3 minutes. Add the vinegar and wine and season with salt and pepper. Use right away.

WARM LENTIL SALAD

MAKES 6 SERVINGS

I LOVE *lentilles du puy*, the green French lentils, but they are sometimes hard to find. Brown lentils, easy to find at any supermarket, are good also. Just don't use red or pink lentils because they fall apart too quickly.

1/2 pound dried green or brown lentils (about 11/4 cups), picked over and rinsed

4 cups water

1 large carrot, cut in half

1 garlic clove, thickly sliced

1 small onion, halved

1 bay leaf

2 sprigs fresh thyme

Salt and freshly ground black pepper

1 teaspoon cumin seeds

1/2 cup Yogurt-Lime Dressing (right), Radish-Cucumber Raita (page 233), Pistachio Yogurt Sauce (page 243), or Curry-Roasted Pumpkin Raita (page 234), warm or at room temperature

1. In a medium-size saucepan, combine the lentils, water, carrot, garlic, onion, bay leaf, and thyme and bring to a boil. Reduce the heat to medium-low and cook, partially covered, until the lentils are tender but not mushy, 35 to 40 minutes. About 10 minutes before the lentils are done, season with salt and pepper.

2. Drain the lentils, reserving 1/2 cup of the cooking liquid, and transfer them to a bowl. Discard the bay leaf and thyme sprigs. Cut the carrot and onion into 1/2-inch pieces and return them to the lentils along with the reserved cooking liquid.

3. Toast the cumin seeds in a small dry skillet over high heat until golden and fragrant, about 2 minutes, shaking the pan constantly. Add the cumin to the lentils and toss with the dressing. Serve warm or at room temperature, passing any extra dressing on the side.

WARM BACON DRESSING

MAKES ABOUT 1/2 CUP

(ENOUGH FOR 8 OUNCES BABY SPINACH)

I LOVE SPINACH salad with warm bacon dressing. I also love *frisée aux lardons,* which is a classic French bistro salad using frisée (curly endive), lots of bacon, and sometimes blue cheese. Both are usually so over-the-top rich that I don't order anything else but a glass of wine. This version is a bit tamer, but still pretty decadent.

4 ounces smoked bacon, coarsely chopped
1/3 cup finely chopped shallots
1 1/2 teaspoons light brown sugar
3 tablespoons red wine vinegar
1/3 cup extra-virgin olive oil
Salt and freshly ground black pepper

1. In a medium-size skillet, cook the bacon over medium heat until browned and crispy, about 6 minutes. Using a slotted spoon, transfer the bacon to a paper towel–lined plate.

2. Pour off all but 1 tablespoon of the fat in the skillet. Add the shallots and cook, stirring, over medium heat until softened, about 5 minutes. Add the brown sugar and cook, stirring, just until melted. Add the vinegar and oil and whisk until combined. Season with salt and pepper and use right away. Garnish the salad with the cooked bacon.

YOGURT-LIME DRESSING

MAKES ABOUT 3/4 CUP

SERVE THIS HIGHLY seasoned yogurt dressing with sturdy greens, sliced avocados or tomatoes, warm potatoes, thinly sliced grilled lamb, chicken, or sausage in a pita sandwich, or with warm lentils.

1/2 cup plain whole-milk yogurt
2 1/2 tablespoons fresh lime juice
2 tablespoons extra-virgin olive oil
1 teaspoon minced garlic
1/4 teaspoon red pepper flakes
2 tablespoons finely chopped fresh Italian parsley leaves
1 tablespoon snipped fresh chives
Salt

1. In a small bowl, whisk together the yogurt and lime juice until smooth.

2. Heat the oil in a small skillet over medium heat. Add the garlic and pepper flakes and cook, stirring, until the garlic is fragrant and lightly golden, about 2 minutes. Scrape the garlic-and-oil mixture into the yogurt, add the parsley and chives, and whisk until smooth. Season with salt. Will keep, tightly covered, in the refrigerator for up to 5 days.

MAYONNAISE, AIOLI, AND ROUILLE

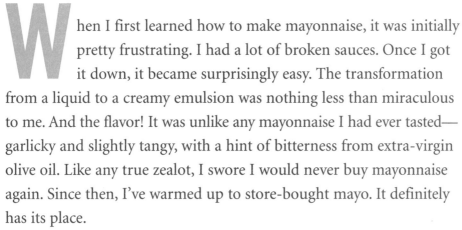

When I first learned how to make mayonnaise, it was initially pretty frustrating. I had a lot of broken sauces. Once I got it down, it became surprisingly easy. The transformation from a liquid to a creamy emulsion was nothing less than miraculous to me. And the flavor! It was unlike any mayonnaise I had ever tasted—garlicky and slightly tangy, with a hint of bitterness from extra-virgin olive oil. Like any true zealot, I swore I would never buy mayonnaise again. Since then, I've warmed up to store-bought mayo. It definitely has its place.

Be aware, though, as you make your own mayonnaise, that raw egg yolks can carry salmonella, a food-borne bacteria that may cause severe gastric upset. To minimize the risk of salmonella, use the freshest eggs possible, purchased from a reliable source where the turnover of eggs is rapid. Always keep your eggs and mayonnaise refrigerated. Pasteurized eggs are also available, though they tend to be more expensive. If you are concerned and want to avoid raw egg yolks altogether, starting with commercial mayonnaise and adding some wonderful seasonings, such as curry, garlic, pesto, olive tapenade, and canned chipotle chiles in adobo sauce is a great "cheat." One last thing I like to do with these "almost homemade" mayonnaises is to whisk in a few tablespoons of extra-virgin olive oil for a creamier texture and a little of that olive oil flavor commercial mayonnaise is missing.

CLASSIC HANDMADE
MAYONNAISE

MAKES ABOUT 1 CUP

THIS CREAMY, EGG-Y mayonnaise is really so delicious and so unlike store-bought—it's definitely worth overcoming your possible initial trepidation about making mayonnaise from scratch.

- ½ cup grapeseed or other mild-flavored vegetable oil
- ½ cup pure olive oil
- 2 large egg yolks, at room temperature
- 1 teaspoon Dijon mustard
- 1 tablespoon fresh lemon juice
- Pinch of sea salt
- 1½ teaspoons boiling water

1. Combine the oils in a pitcher or glass measuring cup with a spout.

2. In a small bowl, whisk together the egg yolks, mustard, lemon juice, and salt. Add a few drops of the oil and whisk until incorporated. Continue to add the oil a few drops at a time, whisking constantly, until slightly thickened and pale yellow. When about half of the oil has been added and the mayonnaise is creamy and pale, whisk in the remaining oil, adding it in a thin, steady stream.

3. Thin the mayonnaise with the boiling water. This helps stabilize the mayonnaise. Taste for salt and lemon juice and refrigerate until ready to use.

ELECTRIC MAYONNAISE

MAKES ABOUT 1 CUP

THIS IS THE easiest way to get mayonnaise, short of buying it from the market. It surely is the fastest way to get the best mayonnaise. I've found this method foolproof. If it should break, start with another egg yolk and use the broken mayonnaise in place of the oil.

- ½ cup grapeseed or other mild-flavored vegetable oil
- ½ cup pure olive oil
- 2 large egg yolks, at room temperature
- 1 teaspoon Dijon mustard
- 1 tablespoon fresh lemon juice
- Sea salt
- 1 tablespoon boiling water

1. Combine the oils in a pitcher or glass measuring cup with a spout.

2. In a blender or mini–food processor, combine the egg yolks, mustard, lemon juice, and salt to taste. While the machine is running, add a few drops of the oil and blend until combined. Continue to add the oil, a few drops at a time, until the mixture is slightly thickened and pale yellow. Slowly add the remaining oil in a thin, steady stream, blending constantly, until pale and creamy. Add the boiling water slowly and taste for salt. Refrigerate until chilled before serving.

TART LIME-GINGER MAYONNAISE

MAKES ABOUT 1 CUP

THIS IS GREAT with all sorts of steamed green vegetables, and poached, grilled, or roasted chicken, fish, and shellfish.

1 garlic clove, smashed

1½ teaspoons peeled and grated fresh ginger

3 tablespoons fresh lime juice

2 large egg yolks, at room temperature

Pinch of sea salt

1 cup grapeseed or other mild-flavored vegetable oil

Cayenne pepper

Put the garlic, ginger, and 1 tablespoon of the lime juice in a mini–food processor and process until finely chopped. Add the egg yolks and salt and process until smooth. While the machine is running, add a few drops of the oil at a time and process until a thick emulsion begins to form. Add the remaining oil in a thin, steady stream and process until thick and creamy. Add the remaining 2 tablespoons lime juice and process until combined. Taste for salt and season with cayenne. Refrigerate until chilled before serving.

TIPS FOR SUCCESSFUL MAYONNAISE

- If the mayonnaise separates or breaks, start with a new egg yolk plus 1 teaspoon fresh lemon juice in a clean bowl. Add the broken mayonnaise a drop at a time, whisking until a thick emulsion forms. After about half is added, you can increase the drops to a very thin stream, whisking constantly.

- A combination of olive oil and vegetable oil will make a great all-purpose mayonnaise. All olive oil will make an intense mayonnaise, and all vegetable oil a mild mayonnaise.

- Mayonnaise can be served on cold or warm foods.

- For potato or chicken salads, use 2 to 3 tablespoons mayonnaise per cup of potatoes or chicken.

- Food-processor or blender mayonnaise is not cheating!

GINGER-CURRY MAYONNAISE

MAKES ABOUT 1 CUP

THIS CURRY MAYONNAISE makes a terrific chicken salad. I like to add crunchy cashews, currants, and alfalfa sprouts for a fabulous lunch.

- 1 cup grapeseed or other mild-flavored vegetable oil
- 2 teaspoons peeled and finely grated fresh ginger
- 1½ teaspoons Madras curry powder
- 2 large egg yolks, at room temperature
- 1 tablespoon fresh lime juice
- Pinch of sugar
- Pinch of sea salt
- 1 tablespoon boiling water

1. Heat 2 tablespoons of the oil in a small skillet over medium heat. Add the ginger and curry powder and cook, stirring, until fragrant and lightly golden, about 1 minute. Scrape the mixture into a small bowl and let cool.

2. Whisk in the egg yolks, lime juice, sugar, and salt. Whisking constantly, add the oil, a few drops at a time until a thick emulsion forms. Slowly add the remaining oil in a thin, steady stream, whisking constantly, until thick and creamy. Whisk in the boiling water and taste for salt. Refrigerate until chilled before serving.

LEMON MAYONNAISE

MAKES ABOUT 1¼ CUPS

TART AND LEMONY, this mayonnaise is great on all sorts of poached, sautéed, and fried fish, as well as on potatoes, beans, broccoli, asparagus, chicken, and pork.

- 2 large egg yolks, at room temperature
- 2 teaspoons Dijon mustard
- 3 tablespoons fresh lemon juice
- Pinch of sea salt
- 1 cup pure olive oil
- Cayenne pepper

Combine the egg yolks, mustard, 2 tablespoons of the lemon juice, and the salt in a small bowl. Drizzle in the oil, a few drops at a time, whisking constantly until a thick emulsion forms. Add the remaining oil in a thin, steady stream, whisking until thick and creamy. Whisk in the remaining 1 tablespoon lemon juice. Taste for salt, season with cayenne, and refrigerate until chilled before serving.

LIME-ANCHO MAYONNAISE

MAKES ABOUT 1 CUP

ANCHO CHILES, WHICH are dried poblano peppers, add a smoky, subtle heat to this tart mayonnaise. Serve it with roast turkey, chicken or pork, steaks, or a meaty fish such as salmon, tuna, or swordfish.

1 small ancho chile

2 garlic cloves, unpeeled

1 cup boiling water

Pinch of sea salt

3/4 cup mayonnaise, homemade (page 298) or store-bought

1/4 cup grapeseed or other mild-flavored vegetable oil

2 tablespoons fresh lime juice

Cayenne pepper

1. Remove the stem from the ancho and, using scissors, cut the chile in half lengthwise. Scrape out the seeds and flatten the chile. Heat a cast-iron skillet or griddle over medium heat until hot to the touch. Add the unpeeled garlic cloves and toast until blackened in spots and softened, about 10 minutes. Let cool, then peel.

2. Meanwhile, add the flattened ancho to the griddle, pressing with a metal spatula until just pliable, about 30 seconds per side. Remove from the heat, cut the ancho into 2-inch pieces, transfer to a heatproof bowl, and cover with the boiling water. Let soak until completely softened, about 15 minutes. Drain and pat dry.

3. Put the rehydrated ancho, peeled garlic, and salt in a mini–food processor or blender and process until finely chopped, scraping down the sides of the bowl as necessary. Add the mayonnaise and process until smooth.

4. Pass the mixture through a fine-mesh sieve, pressing to remove any skins from the chile for a creamier mayonnaise. Return the mixture to the processor. While the machine is running, add the

9 BEST MAYOS FOR CHICKEN SALAD

1. Black Olive Tapenade Aioli (page 311)

2. Chipotle Mayonnaise (page 303)

3. Garlic Confit Aioli (page 313)

4. Ginger-Curry Mayonnaise (left)

5. Green Onion Mayonnaise (page 302)

6. Pesto Mayonnaise (page 302)

7. Quick Curry Mayonnaise (page 305)

8. Quick Herb Mayonnaise (page 307)

9. Sun-Dried Tomato Aioli (page 313)

oil in a thin, steady stream and process until creamy. Add the lime juice and process to combine. Taste for salt and season with cayenne. Refrigerate until chilled.

PESTO MAYONNAISE

MAKES ABOUT 1 CUP

SERVE THIS SIMPLE, yummy mayonnaise on sandwiches, roasted or poached poultry or meat, and all types of veggies.

- 2 tablespoons Classic Pesto Genovese (page 94)
- 3/4 cup mayonnaise, homemade (page 298) or store-bought
- 1 teaspoon fresh lemon juice

In a small bowl, whisk together the pesto, mayonnaise, and lemon juice until smooth. Refrigerate until chilled before serving.

GREEN ONION MAYONNAISE

MAKES 1 CUP

SCALLIONS ADD A bright oniony, fresh flavor to this lovely pale green mayonnaise. It's totally yummy on potatoes, tuna steaks, chicken, pork, and all sorts of steamed vegetables.

- 1/2 cup grapeseed or other mild-flavored vegetable oil
- 1/2 cup extra-virgin olive oil
- 2 scallions, finely chopped
- 1 large garlic clove, coarsely chopped
- Generous pinch of sea salt
- 1 tablespoon fresh lemon juice
- 2 large egg yolks, at room temperature
- 1 tablespoon boiling water (optional)
- Cayenne pepper

1. Combine the oils in a pitcher or glass measuring cup with a spout.

2. In a mortar using a pestle, pound the scallions, garlic, and sea salt together into a paste. Add the lemon juice and egg yolks, one at a time, stirring and pounding until smooth. Add a few drops of the oil and pound until incorporated. Continue to add the oil, a few drops at a time, pounding and stirring until a thick, pale emulsion forms. When about half of the oil has been used, it may be necessary to thin the mixture with the boiling water. Continue to add the oil in a very thin stream, stirring constantly, until thick and creamy. Taste for salt and season with cayenne. Refrigerate until chilled before serving.

CHIPOTLE MAYONNAISE

MAKES ABOUT 1 CUP

SERVE THIS SMOKY, spicy mayonnaise on turkey or roast pork sandwiches, in chicken salads and potato salads, and especially on burgers.

2 canned chipotle chiles in adobo sauce, seeded and finely chopped, plus 1 teaspoon of the sauce

1 garlic clove, finely chopped

Generous pinch of sea salt

1 cup mayonnaise, homemade (page 298) or store-bought

1 tablespoon fresh lime juice

2 tablespoons finely chopped fresh cilantro leaves

1. In a mortar using a pestle, or on a cutting board and using the side of a chef's knife, mash the chipotles, garlic, and salt together into a paste.

2. Transfer to a small bowl and whisk in the mayonnaise, lime juice, and adobo sauce. Taste for salt and stir in the cilantro. Refrigerate until chilled before serving.

EASY ANCHOVY MAYONNAISE

MAKES ABOUT 1 CUP

THIS SUPER-FAST anchovy mayo uses prepared mayonnaise, garlic, and anchovies. Use it on all sorts of boiled, steamed, or roasted vegetables, roast chicken and turkey, steaks, and meaty fish like swordfish or tuna.

4 large anchovy fillets, rinsed and patted dry

1 large garlic clove, coarsely chopped

2 tablespoons fresh lemon juice

Pinch of sea salt

3/4 cup store-bought mayonnaise

1/4 cup extra-virgin olive oil

Freshly ground black pepper

1. Place the anchovies, garlic, 1 tablespoon of the lemon juice, and the salt in a mini–food processor or blender and process until finely chopped. Scrape down the sides of the bowl, if necessary.

2. Add the mayonnaise and process until fairly smooth. While the machine is running, add the oil in a thin, steady stream and process until creamy and smooth. Add the remaining 1 tablespoon lemon juice and season with pepper. Refrigerate until chilled before serving.

ROASTED RED PEPPER MAYONNAISE

MAKES ABOUT 1 CUP

TO MAKE THIS mayonnaise even faster and easier, buy good-quality roasted peppers from an Italian deli. Serve it on all vegetables, potatoes, sandwiches, meats, fish, and poultry.

1 small red bell pepper
1 garlic clove, smashed
1/2 cup store-bought mayonnaise
1/4 cup extra-virgin olive oil
Sea salt
Cayenne pepper

1. Roast the bell pepper over a gas flame or under a broiler until softened and blackened all over. Transfer the pepper to a bowl, cover with plastic wrap, and let steam for 15 minutes. Scrape the skins from the pepper, and remove the core, seeds, and inner ribs. Pat dry with paper towels and coarsely chop.

2. Put the pepper and garlic in a mini–food processor and process until finely chopped. Add the mayonnaise and process until smooth. While the machine is running, add the oil in a thin, steady stream and process until smooth and creamy. Season with salt and cayenne and refrigerate until chilled before serving.

14 BEST AIOLIS AND MAYONNAISES TO SERVE FOR DIPPING CRUDITÉS

Any of the mayonnaises can be used for crudités, but these are my absolute favorites. You may need to whisk a few tablespoons of water, sour cream, or buttermilk into the mayonnaise or aioli to thin it out slightly.

ROQUEFORT MAYONNAISE

MAKES ABOUT 1 CUP

THIS BLUE-CHEESE mayonnaise is great on roast beef sandwiches. Add some peppery arugula or watercress and thin-sliced onions and you're set.

1/4 cup crumbled Roquefort cheese

1 hard-boiled egg yolk

1 teaspoon Dijon mustard

1 tablespoon white wine vinegar

1/2 cup mayonnaise, homemade (page 298) or store-bought

1/4 cup grapeseed or other mild-flavored vegetable oil

1 tablespoon boiling water

Sea salt and freshly ground black pepper

1. In a mini–food processor, combine the Roquefort, egg yolk, mustard, and vinegar and process until fairly smooth. Add half of the mayonnaise and pulse until creamy.

2. Scrape the mixture into a small bowl and whisk in the remaining mayonnaise. Add the oil in a thin, steady stream, whisking constantly. Whisk in the boiling water and season with salt and pepper. Refrigerate until chilled before serving.

QUICK CURRY MAYONNAISE

MAKES ABOUT 1 CUP

THIS ULTRA-FAST mayonnaise makes for a yummy, full-flavored chicken salad. Madras curry powder can range from mild to quite spicy. Let your tolerance for heat dictate how much you use.

2 tablespoons grapeseed or other mild-flavored oil

1 1/2 teaspoons Madras curry powder

1 teaspoon honey

1 cup mayonnaise, homemade (page 298) or store-bought

2 tablespoons mango chutney, homemade (page 343) or store-bought

Sea salt

Pinch of cayenne pepper

1. Heat the oil in a small skillet over medium heat. Add the curry powder and cook, stirring, until fragrant and slightly darkened, about 2 minutes. Stir in the honey and transfer the mixture to a small bowl. Let cool.

2. Whisk the mayonnaise and chutney into the curry mixture and season with salt and cayenne. Refrigerate until chilled before serving.

QUICK HAZELNUT MAYONNAISE

MAKES ABOUT 1 CUP

THE COMBINATION OF hazelnuts and rich, creamy mayonnaise is a perfect foil for cold poached or roasted chicken or fish, as well as potatoes and pasta salads. Blanched hazelnuts are not always easy to find, but don't let that deter you. Unblanched nuts are perfectly fine.

2 tablespoons extra-virgin olive oil

1/3 cup hazelnuts, preferably blanched, coarsely chopped

1 medium-size garlic clove, coarsely chopped

1/2 cup mayonnaise, preferably homemade (page 298)

1 tablespoon hazelnut oil

1 tablespoon fresh lemon juice

1 tablespoon snipped fresh chives

1 tablespoon finely chopped fresh Italian parsley leaves

Sea salt and freshly ground black pepper

1. Heat the oil over medium heat in a small skillet until shimmering. Add the hazelnuts and cook, stirring occasionally, until golden and fragrant, about 6 minutes. Using a slotted spoon, transfer the hazelnuts to a plate to cool. Reserve the oil and let cool.

2. Combine the garlic and hazelnuts in a mini–food processor and pulse until finely chopped. Add the mayonnaise and pulse just until combined. While the machine is running, add the reserved oil and the hazelnut oil through the feed tube in a thin stream and process until the mixture thickens. Add the lemon juice, chives, and parsley and season with salt and pepper. Transfer the mayonnaise to a bowl and refrigerate until chilled before using.

10 BEST MAYOS FOR POTATO SALAD

1. Black Olive Tapenade Aioli (page 311)

2. Classic Aioli (page 309)

3. Classic Handmade Mayonnaise (page 298)

4. Easy Tapenade Aioli (page 312)

5. Garlic Confit Aioli (page 313)

6. Green Onion Mayonnaise (page 302)

7. Pesto Mayonnaise (page 302)

8. Quick Herb Mayonnaise (right)

9. Remoulade Sauce (right)

10. Sun-Dried Tomato Aioli (page 313)

QUICK HERB MAYONNAISE

MAKES ABOUT 1 CUP

BASIL, PARSLEY, CHIVES, and thyme are my herbs of choice here, but I also love cilantro or tarragon. Use this on all poached fish, steamed or roasted vegetables, burgers, or sandwiches.

2 tightly packed tablespoons fresh basil leaves

2 tightly packed tablespoons fresh Italian parsley leaves

2 tablespoons snipped fresh chives

1 teaspoon fresh thyme leaves

1 large garlic clove, coarsely chopped

1 tablespoon fresh lemon juice

3/4 cup mayonnaise, preferably homemade (page 298) or store-bought

1/4 cup extra-virgin olive oil

Sea salt and freshly ground black pepper

1. Put the basil, parsley, chives, thyme, garlic, and lemon juice in a mini–food processor and process until finely chopped. Scrape down the sides of the bowl as necessary.

2. Add the mayonnaise and process until smooth. While the machine is running, add the oil in a thin, steady stream and process until thick and creamy. Season with salt and pepper and refrigerate until chilled before serving.

REMOULADE SAUCE

MAKES ABOUT 1 CUP

CREOLE MUSTARD, A slightly spicy brown mustard, can be found in most supermarkets. Dijon or whole-grain Dijon is a fine substitute.

1 cup mayonnaise, preferably homemade (page 298) or store-bought

2 tablespoons finely chopped cornichons or gherkins

1 1/2 tablespoons Creole mustard

1 tablespoon finely chopped fresh tarragon leaves

1 1/2 teaspoons finely chopped capers

1 small garlic clove, smashed into a paste

1 tablespoon white wine vinegar

Sea salt

Tabasco sauce

Combine the mayonnaise, cornichons, mustard, tarragon, capers, garlic, and vinegar in a small bowl. Season with salt and Tabasco and refrigerate until chilled before serving.

TARTAR SAUCE

MAKES ABOUT 1 CUP

IT'S NOT JUST an expletive on *Spongebob Squarepants!* Fried, poached, broiled, grilled, or sautéed fish and shellfish are all yummy with this great, easy sauce.

> 1 cup mayonnaise, preferably homemade (page 298)
> 2 tablespoons finely chopped sweet gherkins
> 1 tablespoon finely chopped capers
> 1 1/2 teaspoons finely chopped fresh tarragon leaves
> 1 1/2 teaspoons fresh lemon juice
> Fine sea salt
> Tabasco sauce

Combine the mayonnaise, gherkins, capers, tarragon, and lemon juice in a small bowl. Season to taste with salt and Tabasco. Refrigerate until chilled before serving.

GRIBICHE SAUCE

MAKES ABOUT 1 CUP

THIS CLASSIC SAUCE is very similar to tartar sauce in that it contains chopped pickles, capers, and tarragon. What sets it apart is the shallot, chopped egg, and mustard. Serve it with boiled or steamed vegetables and poached, steamed, or fried seafood.

> 1 large hard-boiled egg, halved
> 1 tablespoon Dijon mustard
> 1 tablespoon white wine vinegar
> 1 cup mayonnaise, preferably homemade (page 298)
> 2 tablespoons finely chopped cornichons or gherkins
> 1 tablespoon finely chopped fresh tarragon leaves
> 2 teaspoons minced shallot
> 1 1/2 teaspoons finely chopped capers
> Sea salt
> Cayenne pepper

1. Press the cooked egg yolk through a fine-mesh sieve or mash it with a spoon in a small bowl. Add the mustard and vinegar and mash into a smooth paste. Add the mayonnaise and stir until smooth.

2. Finely chop the egg white and add it to the sauce along with the cornichons, tarragon, shallot, and capers. Season with salt and cayenne and refrigerate until chilled before serving.

CLASSIC AIOLI

MAKES ABOUT 1 CUP

AIOLI IS AN intensely garlicky mayonnaise that accompanies a traditional Provençal meal—the Grand Aioli. The ingredients are rather mild—poached artichokes, hard-cooked eggs, steamed vegetables, chickpeas, beets, and boiled potatoes—so the sauce really takes center stage. It is ordinarily made with olive oil, but I like to use equal parts grapeseed oil and olive oil for a slightly milder flavor. Use this aioli as you would any mayonnaise. It's especially good with artichoke hearts, but steamed asparagus is a whole lot easier to prepare.

½ cup grapeseed or other mild-flavored vegetable oil

½ cup extra-virgin olive oil

4 large garlic cloves, coarsely chopped

Pinch of sea salt

1 tablespoon fresh lemon juice

2 large egg yolks

1 to 2 tablespoons boiling water, as needed

Cayenne pepper

1. Combine the oils in a pitcher or glass measuring cup with a spout.

2. In a mortar using a pestle, pound the garlic and sea salt together into a paste. Add the lemon juice and egg yolks, stirring and pounding until smooth. Add a few drops of the oil and pound until incorporated. Continue to add the oil, a few drops at a time, pounding and stirring until the emulsion is thickened and pale. When about half of the oil has been used, it may be necessary to thin the aioli with 1 tablespoon of the boiling water. Continue to add the oil in a very thin stream, stirring constantly, until thick and creamy. Taste for salt and season with cayenne. Refrigerate until chilled before serving.

UNUSUAL USES FOR MAYONNAISE

• Stir a few tablespoons of any of the garlicky mayonnaises into fish soups or vegetable soups for a creamier texture.

• Brush firm-fleshed white fish (such as seabass, snapper, halibut, or cod) with mayonnaise then sprinkle with breadcrumbs and bake.

• Use plain, unflavored mayonnaise to replace the oil in cake or muffin batter.

• Spread any of the flavored mayonnaises on toasted baguette slices and float them in soups or stews.

QUICK EGGLESS AIOLI

MAKES ABOUT 1 CUP

I'M ALWAYS ASKED to come up with an "eggless" aioli or mayonnaise because of the fear of salmonella. Though I've never had any experience with salmonella, it's not unheard of. If you're pregnant or just plain cautious, this is the mayo for you.

2 large garlic cloves, coarsely chopped
Generous pinch of sea salt
3/4 cup store-bought mayonnaise
1/4 cup extra-virgin olive oil
1 tablespoon fresh lemon juice
Cayenne pepper

1. In a large mortar using a pestle or on a cutting board using the side of a chef's knife, crush the garlic with the salt into a smooth paste.

2. Add the mayonnaise and stir until smooth. Add the oil in a thin, steady stream, stirring and pounding until thick and creamy. Stir in the lemon juice. Taste for salt and season with cayenne. Refrigerate until chilled before serving.

FIVE-SPICE SESAME AIOLI

MAKES ABOUT 1 CUP

THIS ASIAN-INFLUENCED aioli has a slightly retro feel about it. I love it with cold roast beef or pork.

2 large egg yolks, at room temperature
1 tablespoon rice vinegar
1/8 teaspoon Chinese 5-spice powder
Pinch of sea salt
1 cup grapeseed or other mild-flavored vegetable oil
1 teaspoon toasted sesame oil
1 tablespoon boiling water

In a mini–food processor or blender, combine the egg yolks, vinegar, 5-spice powder, and salt. While the machine is running, add the oil a few drops at a time and process until a thick emulsion begins to form. Add the remaining grapeseed oil along with the sesame oil in a thin, steady stream, processing until thick and creamy. Add the boiling water slowly and process until combined. Taste for salt. Refrigerate until chilled before serving.

ANCHOVY AIOLI

MAKES ABOUT 1 CUP

SERVE THIS LUSCIOUS aioli on hard-cooked eggs, boiled potatoes, beets, green beans, or any other classic salad niçoise-type ingredient.

- 1/2 cup grapeseed or other mild-flavored vegetable oil
- 1/2 cup extra-virgin olive oil
- 4 large anchovy fillets, rinsed and patted dry
- 1 large garlic clove, coarsely chopped
- 1 teaspoon Dijon mustard
- 2 tablespoons fresh lemon juice, plus more to taste
- 2 large egg yolks, at room temperature
- 1 tablespoon boiling water
- Sea salt and freshly ground black pepper

1. Combine the oils in a small pitcher or glass measuring cup with a spout.

2. In a large mortar using a pestle, pound the anchovies, garlic, and mustard together into a paste. Add the lemon juice and egg yolks and pound until smooth and creamy. Add the oil, a few drops at a time, pounding and stirring until a thick emulsion forms. Continue adding the remaining oil in a thin, steady stream, stirring and pounding until the aioli is thick and creamy. Add the boiling water and season with salt and pepper. Refrigerate until chilled before serving.

BLACK OLIVE TAPENADE AIOLI

MAKES ABOUT 1¼ CUPS

THIS AIOLI IS yummy with tuna and sword-fish steaks, boiled potatoes, beans, asparagus, and broccoli, as well as roast chicken or lamb.

- 1/2 cup grapeseed or other mild-flavored vegetable oil
- 1/2 cup extra-virgin olive oil
- 2 tablespoons finely chopped pitted black olives, such as Kalamata, niçoise, or Gaeta
- 1 teaspoon chopped capers
- 1 large garlic clove, coarsely chopped
- 1 large anchovy fillet, rinsed and patted dry
- 1½ tablespoons red or white wine vinegar
- 2 large egg yolks, at room temperature
- Sea salt and freshly ground black pepper

1. Combine the oils in a pitcher or glass measuring cup with a spout.

2. Put the olives, capers, garlic, anchovy, and vinegar in a mini–food processor and process until finely chopped. Add the egg yolks and process until fairly smooth. With the machine running, add the oil a few drops at a time and process until a thick emulsion begins to form. Slowly add the remaining oil in a thin, steady stream and process until thick and creamy. Season with salt and pepper. Chill before serving.

EASY TAPENADE AIOLI

MAKES ABOUT 1 CUP

THE ONLY WAY this aioli could get easier is if you just stirred tapenade into store-bought mayonnaise. Simply by adding minced garlic and vinegar and whisking in a little extra-virgin olive oil, this quick aioli is elevated from simple to sublime. Use it with grilled fish, especially tuna, swordfish, or halibut; potatoes; steamed vegetables; and grilled chicken and pork.

3 tablespoons store-bought black olive
    tapenade

1 garlic clove, crushed

1 tablespoon white wine vinegar

3/4 cup mayonnaise, homemade (page 298)
    or store-bought

2 tablespoons extra-virgin olive oil

Sea salt and freshly ground black pepper
    to taste

Combine the tapenade, garlic, and vinegar in a small bowl. Add the mayonnaise and whisk until smooth. Slowly add the oil in a thin, steady stream, whisking constantly until thick and creamy. Season with salt and pepper and refrigerate until chilled before serving.

MOROCCAN PRESERVED LEMON AIOLI

MAKES ABOUT 1 CUP

PRESERVED LEMONS ARE a staple in Moroccan cuisine. Lemons are pickled in a salty, sweet liquid for several weeks. Traditionally, they are added to stews or tagines, marinades, and salads. Use this bright aioli on all roasted meats or poultry, steamed or roasted veggies, and fish.

1/4 preserved lemon

1 large garlic clove, coarsely chopped

2 tablespoons fresh lemon juice

2 large egg yolks, at room temperature

1 cup pure olive oil

1 tablespoon boiling water

Sea salt and freshly ground black pepper

Rinse the preserved lemon quarter under running water and pat dry. Coarsely chop, then place in a mini–food processor along with the garlic and lemon juice until finely chopped. Add the egg yolks and process until fairly smooth. While the machine is running, add the oil a few drops at a time until a thick emulsion begins to form. Add the remaining oil in a thin, steady stream until the mayonnaise is thick and creamy. Add the boiling water, process until combined, and season with salt and pepper. Refrigerate until chilled before serving.

GARLIC CONFIT AIOLI

MAKES ABOUT 1 CUP

SLOWLY COOKING GARLIC in oil mellows the garlic while infusing the oil with lots of flavor. This aioli is great on potatoes and other roasted, steamed, or blanched veggies; chicken, pork, or steaks; and grilled, poached, or sautéed fish or shellfish.

6 large cloves garlic, peeled
1/2 cup pure olive oil
1 tablespoon fresh lemon juice
Pinch of sea salt
1/2 cup mayonnaise, homemade (page 298) or store-bought
Cayenne pepper

1. Combine the garlic and olive oil in a small saucepan and cook over low heat until the garlic is golden and soft, about 15 minutes. Remove from the heat and let the garlic cool in the oil.

2. Transfer the garlic to a mortar, add the lemon juice and salt and pound into a paste. Add the mayonnaise, pounding and stirring until smooth. Add the cooled garlic oil, a few drops at a time, stirring and pounding until thick and creamy. Taste for salt and season with cayenne. Refrigerate until chilled before serving.

Alternatively, you can puree the sautéed garlic with the lemon juice and salt in a mini–food processor and add the oil in a thin, steady stream.

SUN-DRIED TOMATO AIOLI

MAKES ABOUT 1 CUP

SERVE THIS WITH all types of sandwiches, especially cheese, roasted veggies, and grilled chicken.

1/4 tightly packed cup drained oil-packed sun-dried tomatoes
1 large garlic clove, smashed
1 1/2 tablespoons red wine vinegar
Pinch of sea salt
3/4 cup mayonnaise, homemade (page 298) or store-bought
1/4 cup extra-virgin olive oil
Freshly ground black pepper

Put the sun-dried tomatoes, garlic, vinegar, and salt in a mini–food processor and process until finely chopped. Scrape down the sides of the bowl as necessary. Add the mayonnaise and process until fairly smooth. While the machine is running, add the oil in a thin, steady stream and process until thick and creamy. Taste for salt, season with pepper, and refrigerate until chilled before serving.

ROUILLE I

MAKES ABOUT 1 CUP

ROUILLE IS A classic French garnish for bouillabaisse, the Provençal fish and shellfish stew. There are so many versions that I've included three. This one uses stale bread as an emulsifier in place of egg yolks.

- ½ cup grapeseed or other mild-flavored vegetable oil
- ½ cup extra-virgin olive oil
- One 2-inch-thick slice Italian bread, crusts removed
- 1 large garlic clove, mashed
- 1 teaspoon sweet paprika
- Large pinch of sea salt
- Large pinch of cayenne pepper
- 1 tablespoon boiling water (optional)
- 1 to 2 tablespoons fresh lemon juice, to your taste

1. Combine the oils in a pitcher or glass measuring cup with a spout.

2. Soak the bread in a small bowl of water until moistened. Drain and squeeze out any excess water. Transfer the bread to a mini–food processor, add the garlic, paprika, salt, and cayenne and process until fairly smooth. While the machine is running, add the oil in a thin, steady stream and process until thick and smooth. Thin the rouille with the boiling water, if necessary, and add the lemon juice to taste. Refrigerate until chilled before serving.

ROUILLE II

MAKES ABOUT 1 CUP

THIS VERSION IS so easy. It also uses stale bread, but includes piquillo peppers, which are roasted, slightly spicy red peppers from Spain. You can find them at gourmet shops and some supermarkets. If you can't find them, use pimentos (canned) and 1 teaspoon sweet paprika.

- One 2-inch-thick slice Italian bread, crusts removed
- 4 canned or jarred piquillo peppers
- 2 garlic cloves, smashed
- 2 tablespoons fresh lemon juice
- ½ cup extra-virgin olive oil
- Sea salt
- Cayenne pepper

Soak the bread in water until softened. Squeeze out any moisture and put the bread in a mini–food processor or blender. Add the peppers, garlic, and lemon juice and process until fairly smooth. While the machine is running, add the oil in a thin, steady stream and process until thick and creamy. Season with salt and cayenne and refrigerate until chilled before serving.

ROUILLE III

MAKES ABOUT 1 CUP

TO ME, THIS rouille, with the addition of saffron, is classic. I love stirring a few tablespoons of this into seafood stews, vegetable soups, and minestrones.

- ½ cup grapeseed or other mild-flavored vegetable oil
- ½ cup extra-virgin olive oil
- Small pinch of saffron threads, crushed to a powder
- 2 tablespoons red or white wine vinegar
- 2 garlic cloves, smashed
- 1 teaspoon Dijon mustard
- ½ teaspoon cayenne pepper
- 2 large egg yolks, at room temperature
- Sea salt

1. Combine the oils in a small pitcher or glass measuring cup with a spout.

2. In a mini–food processor or blender, combine the saffron and vinegar and let sit for 5 minutes. Add the garlic, mustard, and cayenne and process until finely chopped. Add the egg yolks and process until fairly smooth. While the machine is running, add the oil a few drops at a time and process until a thick emulsion begins to form. Add the remaining oil in a thin, steady stream until thick and creamy. Season with salt and refrigerate until chilled before serving.

SALSAS

Every year I visit the Fancy Food Show in New York City to see what's hot and new. I'm always amazed at the number of salsas available. Some are pretty good, while others are downright horrid! One thing is for sure: salsa is, and will continue to be, very popular. It has replaced ketchup as the number-one-selling condiment in America.

The flavor of homemade salsa, using perfectly fresh, ripe ingredients with no additives, is unsurpassed. It tastes like what it comes from—vegetables!—which is partly what defines a salsa, as opposed to any other type of sauce or condiment. Salsa combines fresh vegetables, which can be charred or grilled, but once combined are not cooked again. The result is a fresh, clean-tasting sauce. As a condiment for meats, fish, and poultry, it balances out the richness of the meat. It is also great as a topping for bruschetta, as a filling for tortillas, as an addition to soups and stews, and, of course, as a dip for chips.

For many of the tomato-based salsa recipes in this chapter, it pays to make them in the summer—when vegetables are at their peak—but even in winter, when tomatoes are generally pretty awful, you can use cherry tomatoes. Or make Smoky Roasted Tomato and Chipotle Salsa (page 319), where the tomatoes are roasted to bring out extra flavor. Or try Quick Classic Tomato Salsa (page 319) which uses good-quality canned tomatoes—it's like a commercial-style jarred salsa, only good! Then, of course, there are the salsas that can be made all year long—those that use peppers, onions, tomatillos, avocados, pineapple, olives, and more.

PICO DE GALLO

MAKES ABOUT 3 CUPS

A CLASSIC RED salsa from Mexico, this combines tomatoes, cilantro, garlic, and lime. It's mild, so it complements spicy foods but is great with chips as well.

2 ripe beefsteak tomatoes (about ¾ pound each), cored and chopped

¼ cup finely chopped fresh cilantro leaves

2 scallions, finely chopped

1 large garlic clove, minced

2 tablespoons fresh lime juice

2 tablespoons pure olive oil

Salt and freshly ground black pepper

In a medium-size bowl, combine the tomatoes, cilantro, scallions, garlic, lime juice, and olive oil until well mixed. Season with salt and pepper and let sit 10 minutes before serving to let the flavors develop. Will keep, covered, in the refrigerator for up to 2 days.

TIPS FOR MAKING THE BEST POSSIBLE SALSA

- Jalapeños, serranos, Thai bird chiles, habaneros, and Scotch bonnets are all pretty hot and contain volatile oils that can be quite painful if they come into contact with your eyes and sensitive skin. I'd advise using latex gloves when handling them.

- When buying limes, look for plump fruit that yields a bit when you squeeze it. This means it's juicy and not dried out.

- When buying lemons, look for fruit with smooth skin and no large knobs at the ends. These tend to have thinner skins and more juice.

- Cilantro, unlike parsley, has tender stems. Don't waste time pulling off the leaves. Simply trim the stems after the leaves stop.

- When roasting small chiles like jalapeños, thread them onto skewers so they don't fall through the grates.

- Don't bother to peel or seed tomatoes for salsa—just make sure they're very ripe and flavorful. That is unless, of course, you're making Green Tomato Salsa (page 320), in which case, the harder the better.

QUICK CLASSIC TOMATO SALSA

MAKES ABOUT 1½ CUPS

CANNED DICED TOMATOES are a relatively new addition to supermarket shelves. They are absolutely great in this super-quick salsa.

1 jalapeño, seeded and coarsely chopped

1 large garlic clove, coarsely chopped

½ small red onion, coarsely chopped

¼ cup packed fresh cilantro leaves

1½ teaspoons distilled white vinegar

Pinch of sugar

One 14-ounce can diced tomatoes, drained, reserving 2 tablespoons of the juice

Salt

Cayenne pepper

In a food processor, combine the jalapeño, garlic, onion, cilantro, vinegar, and sugar and process until finely chopped. Add the tomatoes and reserved juice and pulse just until combined. Season with salt and cayenne. Will keep, tightly covered, in the refrigerator for up to 2 days.

SMOKY ROASTED TOMATO AND CHIPOTLE SALSA

MAKES ABOUT 2 CUPS

THE TOMATOES PICK up a smoky flavor from grilling, and the chipotles are smoky and spicy. Serve this with chips, grilled meats, poultry, and fish.

6 ripe plum tomatoes (about ¾ pound)

2 garlic cloves, peeled

Vegetable oil

1 canned chipotle chile in adobo sauce, seeded and minced, plus 1 teaspoon of the sauce

¼ cup minced sweet onion, such as Vidalia or Walla Walla

1 tablespoon finely chopped fresh cilantro leaves

1 teaspoon fresh lime juice

Salt

1. Preheat a cast-iron griddle or grill pan. Rub the tomatoes and garlic lightly with oil and roast over medium heat, turning occasionally until blackened all over, 7 to 8 minutes. Transfer the tomatoes and garlic to a medium-size bowl, cover with plastic wrap, and let sit for 20 minutes.

2. Coarsely chop the tomatoes and finely chop the garlic. Return them to the bowl, add the chipotle and reserved adobo sauce, onion, cilantro, and lime juice, and toss to combine well. Season with salt and let cool before serving. Will keep, covered, in the refrigerator for up to 4 days.

GREEN TOMATO SALSA

MAKES ABOUT 1 CUP

THIS IS ONE of my favorite salsas. I actually look forward to the end of summer when the last stragglers on my tomato plants refuse to turn red just so I can make this salsa. Serve it with chips and all grilled or roasted meats, poultry, or a meaty fish like swordfish, halibut, or salmon.

    3 medium-size green tomatoes, cored and
      finely chopped
    1 scallion, finely chopped
    1/2 habanero chile, seeded and minced
    2 tablespoons extra-virgin olive oil
    1/2 teaspoon pure chile powder of your
      choice (but don't use chipotle in this one)
    1/2 teaspoon ground cumin
    1 1/2 teaspoons fresh lime juice
    Pinch of sugar
    Salt

1. In a heatproof bowl, combine the tomatoes, scallion, and habanero.

2. Heat the olive oil in a small skillet over medium heat. Add the chile powder and cumin and cook, stirring, until fragrant, about 30 seconds. Pour the hot oil over the tomato mixture. Add the lime juice and sugar, season with salt, and toss well to combine. Will keep, tightly covered, in the refrigerator for up to 2 days.

FRESH TOMATILLO SALSA VERDE

MAKES ABOUT 1 1/2 CUPS

I LOVE THE tart, mouth-puckering quality of tomatillos. With the addition of cilantro, lime juice, and scallions, this is a great chip salsa. Serve it with grilled or roasted meats, poultry, eggs, or fish. *Hoja santa* is a large-leaved herb found in Mexico, available at Latin markets, but you can use good-quality dried oregano in its place.

    8 large tomatillos, husks removed and
      coarsely chopped
    2 scallions, coarsely chopped
    1 large jalapeño, seeded and coarsely
      chopped
    1 garlic clove, chopped
    1/4 cup finely chopped fresh cilantro leaves
    1 small leaf dried *hoja santa* or 1/4 teaspoon
      dried oregano, crumbled
    2 tablespoons extra-virgin olive oil
    1 tablespoon fresh lime juice
    Pinch of sugar
    Salt and freshly ground black pepper

Place the tomatillos, scallions, jalapeño, and garlic in a blender or food processor and pulse until finely chopped. Scrape down the sides of the bowl as necessary. Add the cilantro, *hoja santa*, oil, lime juice, and sugar and process until fairly smooth. Season with salt and pepper. Will keep, tightly covered, in the refrigerator for up to 2 days.

CHARRED GARLIC–TOMATILLO SALSA

MAKES ABOUT 1½ CUPS

COOKING THE GARLIC and tomatillo in a cast-iron skillet imparts a mellow, smoky flavor to this tart green salsa. Serve it with chips, fish, poultry, eggs, or meat.

  ½ teaspoon cumin seeds

  6 garlic cloves, left unpeeled

  1 large jalapeño

  8 medium-size tomatillos (about ½ pound), husks removed

  2 tablespoons finely chopped fresh cilantro leaves

  2 tablespoons fresh lime juice

  1 tablespoon peanut or other mild-flavored oil

  Salt and freshly ground black pepper

1. Heat a small cast-iron skillet or griddle until very hot to the touch. Add the cumin seeds and toast until fragrant, about 1 minute. Coarsely grind the cumin in a spice or coffee grinder.

2. Add the garlic and jalapeño to the skillet and cook over medium-low heat, turning occasionally, until charred all over, about 15 minutes for the garlic and 10 minutes for the jalapeño. Transfer to a plate. Let cool, then peel the garlic and stem and seed the jalapeño. Meanwhile, add the tomatillos to the skillet and cook over high heat until blackened in spots, about 5 minutes.

3. Place the garlic, jalapeño, cumin, and cilantro in a blender or food processor and pulse until finely chopped. Add the tomatillos, lime juice, and oil and pulse to a chunky puree. Season with salt and pepper.

BLACK BEAN AND CHAYOTE SALSA

MAKES ABOUT 2½ CUPS

CHAYOTE IS A squat, roundish zucchini-like squash, which is sometimes called christophine in the French Caribbean, chocho in African Caribbean, and mirliton in Louisiana. You can use a cucumber instead, peeled, seeded, and diced. This salsa is great with chips as well as with all grilled meats, poultry, and meaty fish like swordfish, snapper, and grouper.

  One 15-ounce can black beans, drained and rinsed

  2 large garlic cloves, minced

  2 tablespoons fresh lime juice

  2 tablespoons extra-virgin olive oil

  1 small chayote, cut in half, peeled, and finely diced

  ½ cup seeded and finely diced red bell pepper

  ¼ cup finely diced red onion

  ¼ cup finely chopped fresh cilantro leaves

  Salt and freshly ground black pepper

1. In a food processor, combine half of the black beans with the garlic, lime juice, and olive oil and process to a chunky puree.

2. Scrape the mixture into a bowl and add the remaining beans along with the chayote, bell pepper, onion, and cilantro. Season with salt and pepper. Will keep, tightly covered, in the refrigerator overnight.

CORN AND BLACK BEAN SALSA

MAKES ABOUT 3½ CUPS

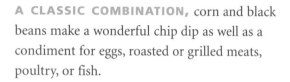

A CLASSIC COMBINATION, corn and black beans make a wonderful chip dip as well as a condiment for eggs, roasted or grilled meats, poultry, or fish.

  3 ears fresh corn
  One 15-ounce can black beans, drained and rinsed
  ¼ cup minced onion
  1 small ripe tomato, finely chopped
  1 scallion, finely chopped
  2 tablespoons finely chopped fresh cilantro leaves
  1 jalapeño, seeded and finely chopped
  3 tablespoons fresh lime juice
  ¼ cup pure olive oil
  ½ teaspoon ground cumin
  Salt
  Cayenne pepper

1. Bring a pot of salted water to a boil. Add the corn and cook until tender but not mushy, about 3 minutes. Drain and cool under cold running water. Cut the kernels from the cob. Place the corn in a medium-size bowl and add the black beans, onion, tomato, scallion, cilantro, jalapeño, and lime juice.

2. Heat the oil in a small skillet over high heat. Add the cumin and cook, stirring, until fragrant, about 30 seconds. Scrape the cumin and oil into the salsa. Season with salt and cayenne, toss well to combine, and let cool before serving.

14 SUPER SALSAS FOR CHIP DIPPING

1. Black Bean and Chayote Salsa (page 321)

2. Charred Garlic–Tomatillo Salsa (page 321)

3. Corn and Black Bean Salsa (above)

4. Fresh Tomatillo Salsa Verde (page 320)

5. Green Tomato Salsa (page 320)

6. Guacamole (page 330)

7. Pico de Gallo (page 318)

8. Quick Classic Tomato Salsa (page 319)

9. Roasted Corn Salsa (right)

10. Roasted Pepper, Avocado, and Corn Salsa (page 325)

11. Roasted Poblano with Mango and Corn Salsa (page 326)

12. Roasted Sweet Pepper Salsa (page 328)

13. Salsa of Fire-Roasted Chiles (page 328)

14. Smoky Roasted Tomato and Chipotle Salsa (page 319)

ROASTED CORN SALSA

MAKES ABOUT 3 CUPS

SERVE THIS YUMMY roasted salsa with chips, tortillas, grilled meats, poultry, or fish. The little bit of sour cream really enlivens this salsa and mellows the lime juice.

- 4 ears fresh corn, husked
- 1 poblano or jalapeño chile
- Vegetable oil
- 1 large garlic clove, minced
- 2 tablespoons finely chopped fresh cilantro leaves
- 1/4 cup sour cream
- 2 tablespoons fresh lime juice
- Pinch of ground cumin
- Salt and freshly ground black pepper

1. Light a charcoal grill or preheat a broiler. Lightly rub the corn and poblano with oil and grill or broil, turning occasionally, until browned in spots. Transfer the pepper to a bowl, cover with plastic wrap, and let steam until collapsed and cool to the touch. Set the ears of corn aside.

2. Peel, seed, and chop the chile and transfer it to a medium-size bowl. Cut the kernels from the corn and add it to the bowl, as well as the garlic and cilantro, and toss to combine well. Add the sour cream, lime juice, and cumin and stir to combine well. Season with salt and pepper. Will keep, covered, in the refrigerator for up to 2 days.

THAI CUCUMBER SALSA

MAKES ABOUT 1 1/4 CUPS

CRUNCHY AND REFRESHING, this salsa is a great accompaniment to grilled pork chops, barbecued chicken or ribs, or anything spicy.

- 2 tablespoons rice vinegar
- 1 tablespoon sugar
- 1/4 teaspoon red pepper flakes
- Pinch of salt
- 1 cup peeled and finely diced hothouse (seedless) cucumber
- 1/4 cup seeded and finely diced red bell pepper

1. In a small saucepan, combine the vinegar, sugar, red pepper flakes, and salt and cook over medium heat, stirring, just until the sugar dissolves. Transfer to a small bowl and let cool.

2. Add the cucumber and bell pepper and refrigerate at least 15 minutes before using to let the flavors develop. This is best eaten the day it is made.

FIRE-ROASTED ONION SALSA

MAKES ABOUT 2 CUPS

THE SWEETNESS OF the onions is really brought out by grilling. This salsa is a great condiment for grilled steaks, burgers, meaty fish, and pork chops.

1 large sweet onion (about 1¼ pounds), such as Vidalia or Walla Walla, peeled

1 large red onion, peeled

Pure olive oil

Salt and freshly ground black pepper

1½ teaspoons balsamic vinegar

1½ teaspoons fresh lemon juice

2 tablespoons finely chopped fresh Italian parsley leaves

½ teaspoon fresh thyme leaves

Pinch of dried oregano, preferably Mexican, crumbled

Cayenne pepper

1. Light a charcoal grill or preheat a cast-iron grill pan. Cut the onions crosswise, into ½-inch-thick slices, keeping the slices intact. Carefully skewer each slice with a toothpick or bamboo skewer to keep the rings together. Brush the onion slices with oil and season with salt and pepper. Grill the onions over a medium flame until softened and charred in spots, about 15 minutes, turning occasionally. Transfer the onions to a plate, cover with plastic wrap, and let cool. Coarsely chop the onions.

2. In a medium-size bowl, combine the onions and any accumulated juices, vinegar, lemon juice, parsley, thyme, oregano, and 1 tablespoon olive oil until well mixed. Season with salt and cayenne. Will keep, tightly covered, in the refrigerator for up to 3 days.

BEST SALSAS FOR QUESADILLAS AND GRILLED CHEESE SANDWICHES

Adding 1 or 2 tablespoons of salsa to your quesadilla or grilled cheese sandwich can make an old standby a new favorite. Just spread the salsa on the cheese before cooking. These are my picks for the best flavor:

Black Bean and Chayote Salsa (page 321)

Corn and Black Bean Salsa (page 322)

Fire-Roasted Onion Salsa (above)

Fresh Three-Pepper Salsa (page 327)

Green Tomato Salsa (page 320)

Olive Salsa (page 330)

Pico de Gallo (page 318)

Piquillo Pepper Salsa (page 326)

Quick Classic Tomato Salsa (page 319)

Roasted Corn Salsa (page 323)

Roasted Pepper, Avocado, and Corn Salsa (right)

Roasted Sweet Pepper Salsa (page 328)

Salsa of Fire-Roasted Chiles (page 328)

Smoky Roasted Tomato and Chipotle Salsa (page 319)

JICAMA AND CUCUMBER SALSA WITH LIME

MAKES ABOUT 2½ CUPS

THIS SALSA IS very crunchy and refreshing especially when served with steaks, pork chops, or chicken.

    1 cup peeled and finely diced jicama
    1 cup peeled and finely diced hothouse
        (seedless) cucumber
    ¼ cup thinly sliced scallions
    ¼ cup finely chopped sweet onion, such as
        Vidalia or Walla Walla
    ¼ cup finely chopped fresh cilantro leaves
    2½ tablespoons fresh lime juice
    2 tablespoons extra-virgin olive oil
    Salt and freshly ground black pepper

In a medium-size bowl, combine the jicama, cucumber, scallions, onion, cilantro, lime juice, and oil until well mixed. Season with salt and pepper and let sit 15 minutes before serving to let the flavors develop. Will keep, tightly covered, in the refrigerator for up to 2 days.

ROASTED PEPPER, AVOCADO, AND CORN SALSA

MAKES 2½ CUPS

I LOVE THIS salsa with grilled or roasted meats, chicken, or fish, but especially with chips.

    1 large red bell pepper
    1 tablespoon fresh lime juice
    1 tablespoon extra-virgin olive oil
    Pinch of ground cumin
    Salt
    Cayenne pepper
    1 ear fresh young corn, kernels cut from
        the cob
    2 tablespoons finely chopped fresh cilantro
        leaves
    1 scallion, finely chopped
    1 ripe but firm Hass avocado, peeled, pitted,
        and finely diced

1. Roast the pepper over a gas flame or under a broiler, turning, until charred all over. Transfer the pepper to a bowl, cover with plastic wrap, and let steam until collapsed and cool to the touch. Peel and seed the pepper and finely dice.

2. In a medium-size bowl, whisk together the lime juice, oil, and cumin and season with salt and cayenne. Stir in the roasted pepper, corn, cilantro, and scallion until well combined. Gently fold in the avocado and season again with salt and cayenne. Will keep, tightly covered, in the refrigerator for up to 2 days.

ROASTED POBLANO WITH MANGO AND CORN SALSA

MAKES ABOUT 3 CUPS

SLIGHTLY BITTER, SLIGHTLY sweet, slightly spicy, poblano chiles add deep flavor to foods. Jalapeños are a fine substitute, especially the larger ones, which tend to be a bit milder. Serve this with meats, poultry, or chips.

1 poblano or 2 large jalapeño chiles

Vegetable oil

1 large ripe mango, peeled, pitted, and cut into 1/4-inch dice

1 ear fresh young corn, kernels cut from cob

1/2 cup finely diced sweet onion, such as Vidalia or Walla Walla

2 to 3 tablespoons fresh lime juice, to your taste

2 tablespoons finely chopped fresh cilantro leaves

2 tablespoons snipped fresh chives

Salt and freshly ground black pepper

1. Lightly rub the poblano with oil and roast over a gas flame or under a broiler until blackened all over, turning occasionally. Transfer the chile to a bowl, cover with plastic wrap, and let steam until collapsed and cool. Peel, seed, and finely chop the chile.

2. In a medium-size bowl, combine the poblano, mango, corn, onion, lime juice, cilantro, and chives. Season with salt and pepper. Will keep, tightly covered, in the refrigerator for up to 2 days.

PIQUILLO PEPPER SALSA

MAKES ABOUT 1 CUP

ROASTED PIQUILLO PEPPERS from Spain are slightly spicy and very flavorful. If you can't find them, substitute 2 roasted bell peppers and 1 teaspoon paprika. Serve this with grilled meats as well as with chips and croutons.

1/4 cup blanched or natural whole almonds

1 large garlic clove, smashed

1 tablespoon extra-virgin olive oil

1 teaspoon fresh lemon juice

One 7-ounce jar or can piquillo peppers

1/2 teaspoon finely chopped fresh thyme leaves

Pinch of sugar

Salt

Cayenne pepper

1. Preheat the oven to 350°F. Spread the almonds on a small baking sheet and toast until fragrant and lightly golden, about 10 minutes. Remove from the oven and let cool.

2. Place the nuts, garlic, oil, and lemon juice in a blender or mini–food processor and pulse until finely chopped. Add the piquillo peppers and their juices, thyme, and sugar and pulse just until chopped. Season with salt and cayenne. Will keep, tightly covered, in the refrigerator for up to 2 days.

ANCHO, ORANGE, AND SWEET ONION SALSA

MAKES ABOUT 4 CUPS

THIS JUICY SALSA is terrific with grilled or roast beef, chicken, or pork, as well as with shellfish and meaty fish like halibut, swordfish, snapper, and grouper.

- 1 small ancho chile, seeded
- 4 large navel oranges
- 1 large sweet onion, such as Vidalia or Walla Walla, quartered lengthwise and thinly sliced
- 2 tablespoons fresh lemon juice
- 2 tablespoons pure olive oil
- 2 tablespoons snipped fresh chives
- Salt and freshly ground black pepper

1. Heat a cast-iron skillet or griddle. Using kitchen scissors, cut the ancho into large pieces. Place it on the hot griddle and press with a metal spatula until pliable, about 15 seconds per side. Remove from the pan and, when cool enough to handle, using scissors, cut the ancho into very thin strips.

2. Set a sieve over a medium-size bowl. Using a sharp knife, peel the oranges, removing all the bitter white pith. Working over the bowl, cut between the membranes and release the segments into the sieve. Squeeze the membranes to extract the juice. Cut the segments into ½-inch pieces and add them to the bowl along with the onion, ancho, lemon juice, olive oil, and chives. Toss well to combine. Season with salt and pepper

and let sit at least 15 minutes before serving to let the flavors develop. Will keep, tightly covered, in the refrigerator for up to 2 days.

FRESH THREE-PEPPER SALSA

MAKES ABOUT 2½ CUPS

IF YOU CAN'T find banana chiles, substitute cubanelles or Italian frying peppers. Jalapeños can be substituted for the poblanos. Use this with steaks, grilled pork, chicken, or swordfish.

- 1 medium-size red bell pepper, seeded and finely diced
- 1 poblano chile, seeded and finely diced
- 2 banana or cubanelle chiles, seeded and finely diced
- ½ cup finely diced red onion
- 1 small garlic clove, minced
- 2 tablespoons fresh lime juice
- 2 tablespoons orange juice
- 2 tablespoons peanut or other mild-flavored oil
- Salt and freshly ground black pepper

Combine the peppers, onion, garlic, lime juice, orange juice, and oil in a medium-size bowl. Season with salt and pepper. Will keep, tightly covered, in the refrigerator for up to 2 days.

ROASTED SWEET PEPPER SALSA

MAKES ABOUT 2½ CUPS

NOT ONLY TASTY but also beautiful, this salsa combines different-colored bell peppers and jalapeños. Serve this with chips or grilled steaks and chops.

> 3 medium-size red bell peppers, or 1 each red, yellow, and orange bell pepper
>
> 2 jalapeños
>
> 2 large garlic cloves, mashed into a paste
>
> 2 large anchovies, rinsed, patted dry, and chopped
>
> Pinch of salt
>
> 2 tablespoons balsamic vinegar
>
> 1 tablespoon fresh lemon juice
>
> ¼ cup extra-virgin olive oil
>
> 2 tablespoons finely chopped fresh Italian parsley leaves
>
> Freshly ground black pepper

1. Roast the bell peppers and the jalapeños over a gas flame or under a broiler until blackened all over, turning occasionally. Transfer the peppers to a bowl, cover with plastic wrap, and let steam until collapsed and cool to the touch. Peel, seed, and chop the peppers and transfer to a medium-size bowl, along with any accumulated juices.

2. In a small bowl, mash together the garlic, anchovies, and salt into a paste. Stir in the vinegar, lemon juice, and oil, then pour the mixture over the peppers. Stir in the parsley and season with salt and pepper.

SALSA OF FIRE-ROASTED CHILES

MAKES ABOUT 1½ CUPS

THE FOUR DIFFERENT types of peppers each add a distinct flavor. Anaheims are mellow and slightly bitter, poblanos are slightly spicy, banana chiles are sweet and mild, and yellow bell peppers are pure sweetness. Feel free to experiment with other fresh chiles, though be careful—some are exquisitely potent and volatile. This is great with chips, meats, poultry, and fish.

> 2 Anaheim chiles
>
> 1 poblano chile
>
> 1 banana chile
>
> 1 medium-size yellow bell pepper
>
> Vegetable oil
>
> 2 large garlic cloves, left unpeeled
>
> ½ teaspoon ground cumin
>
> ½ teaspoon pure chile powder of your choice
>
> ½ teaspoon dried oregano, preferably Mexican, crumbled
>
> 2 scallions, minced
>
> 1 tablespoon fresh lime juice
>
> Salt and freshly ground black pepper

1. Light a grill or preheat a broiler. Lightly rub the peppers with vegetable oil and grill or broil, turning occasionally, until blackened all over. Transfer the peppers to a bowl, cover with plastic wrap, and let steam until cool to the touch. Peel, seed, and finely dice the peppers and transfer to a medium-size bowl, along with any accumulated juices.

SOME LIKE IT HOTTER

Many of the salsas in this book are a bit on the mild side and not intended to clear your sinuses, as salsa is often served as an accompaniment to very spicy foods to have a cooling effect. In addition, quite a few of them are meant to be served with more delicate flavors such as fish, chicken, or seafood, and intense heat may be inappropriate for them. However, if you prefer it that way, by all means punch up any of the salsa recipes with more chiles and cayenne.

On the other hand, these recipes will make your eyes water.

- Charred Garlic–Tomatillo Salsa (page 321)
- Corn and Black Bean Salsa (page 322)
- Fresh Tomatillo Salsa Verde (page 320)
- Green Tomato Salsa (page 320)
- Honeydew Salsa with Lime and Hot Chiles (page 332)
- Island Pineapple Salsa with Habanero and Lime (page 331)
- Olive Salsa (page 330)
- Pico De Gallo (page 318)
- Quick Classic Tomato Salsa (page 319)
- Roasted Corn Salsa (page 323)
- Roasted Pepper, Avocado, and Corn Salsa (page 325)
- Roasted Poblano with Mango and Corn Salsa (page 326)
- Salsa of Fire-Roasted Chiles (left)
- Smoky Roasted Tomato and Chipotle Salsa (page 319)

2. Skewer the garlic cloves on a bamboo or metal skewer and grill until blackened in spots. Remove from the heat, let cool enough to handle, then peel and mash the garlic.

3. Heat 2 tablespoons of vegetable oil in a small skillet over medium heat. Add the cumin, chile powder, and oregano and cook, stirring, until fragrant, about 30 seconds. Add the mixture to the peppers, along with the mashed garlic, scallions, and lime juice and toss well to combine. Season with salt and pepper. Will keep, tightly covered, in the refrigerator for up to 3 days.

GUACAMOLE

MAKES ABOUT 1½ CUPS

THERE ARE MORE variations on guacamole than almost any other salsa I know. The characteristics seem entirely personal and highly subjective, depending upon the maker. Some add tomatoes, while others would never dream of it! Because I love the rich and creamy flavor of avocado, I tend to lean toward a simpler guacamole.

4 ripe Hass avocados, cut in half lengthwise and pitted

2 tablespoons fresh lime juice

2 tablespoon extra-virgin olive oil

1 large scallion, thinly sliced

1 jalapeño, seeded and finely chopped

2 tablespoons finely chopped fresh cilantro leaves

Salt

Cayenne pepper

Scoop the flesh from the avocado skins and transfer them to a medium-size bowl. Coarsely mash the avocados, then add the lime juice, oil, scallion, jalapeño, and cilantro and mix well. Season with salt and cayenne. Will keep, tightly covered, in a refrigerator for up to 2 days. If not using right away, press a piece of plastic wrap directly onto the surface of the guacamole to keep it from discoloring.

OLIVE SALSA

MAKES ABOUT 1½ CUP

A BIT TOO juicy and chunky to be a tapenade or relish, this salsa is great with croutons and chips as well as with grilled lamb, chicken, or a meaty fish like swordfish, halibut, or snapper.

2 large anchovies, rinsed, patted dry, and chopped

1 large garlic clove, minced

Pinch of salt

2 tablespoons fresh lemon juice

2 tablespoons extra-virgin olive oil

¼ teaspoon red pepper flakes

2 cups mixed brine-cured olives, such as Kalamata, gaeta, Cerignola, and/or Sicilian, pitted and coarsely chopped

1 tablespoon capers, drained and chopped

2 tablespoons finely chopped fresh Italian parsley leaves

½ teaspoon finely chopped fresh thyme leaves

In a medium-size bowl, mash the anchovies, garlic, and salt into a paste. Stir in the lemon juice, olive oil, and red pepper flakes. Add the remaining ingredients and toss well to combine. Will keep, tightly covered, in the refrigerator for up to 2 days.

ISLAND PINEAPPLE SALSA WITH HABANERO AND LIME

MAKES ABOUT 2½ CUPS

IT MAY SEEM kind of '80s, but I still love pineapple salsa with swordfish, tuna, or shellfish.

2 cups peeled, cored, and finely diced fresh ripe pineapple

½ cup finely diced sweet onion, such as Vidalia or Walla Walla

¼ to ½ habanero chile, seeded and finely chopped

2 tablespoons fresh lime juice

2 tablespoons finely chopped fresh cilantro leaves

½ teaspoon finely grated lime zest

Salt and freshly ground black pepper

In a medium-size bowl, combine the pineapple, onion, habanero, lime juice, cilantro, and lime zest until well mixed. Season with salt and pepper. Will keep, covered, in the refrigerator for up to 2 days.

GOLDEN KIWI AND PINEAPPLE SALSA WITH MINT

MAKES ABOUT 3 CUPS

GOLDEN KIWI FROM New Zealand is brand new to this country. A little sweeter than green kiwi, these golden ones are so pretty and jewel-like when diced and mixed into a salsa. Serve this with fish, shellfish, or grilled meat and poultry.

2 tablespoons fresh lemon juice

2 tablespoons peanut or other mild-flavored oil

2 cups peeled, cored, and finely diced golden pineapple

2 golden kiwis, peeled and cut into ½-inch dice

½ cup finely diced onion

2 tablespoons finely chopped fresh mint leaves

Salt

Cayenne pepper

In a medium-size bowl, whisk together the lemon juice and oil. Add the pineapple, kiwis, onion, and mint and toss well to combine. Season with salt and cayenne. Let sit for 15 minutes before serving to develop the flavors. Will keep, tightly covered, in the refrigerator overnight.

MINTY MANGO SALSA

MAKES ABOUT 1½ CUPS

ANOTHER '80S THROWBACK, but when it works, it works! Serve this with fish, pork, chicken, and as an accompaniment to spicy curries.

1 large ripe mango, peeled, pitted, and cut into ¼-inch dice

¼ cup seeded and finely diced red bell pepper

2 tablespoon finely diced red onion

2 tablespoons finely chopped fresh mint leaves

1 tablespoon snipped fresh chives

1 tablespoon fresh lemon juice

Salt

Cayenne pepper

In a medium-size bowl, combine the mango, bell pepper, onion, mint, chives, and lemon juice until well mixed. Season with salt and cayenne. This is best eaten the day it is made.

HONEYDEW SALSA WITH LIME AND HOT CHILES

MAKES ABOUT 2 CUPS

THIS SALSA, THOUGH great on grilled, pan-fried, or roasted pork, chicken, and fish, is also tasty when simply eaten with a spoon.

2 tablespoons fresh lime juice

½ teaspoon peeled and finely grated fresh ginger

¼ to ½ habanero, to your taste, seeded and minced

½ large jalapeño, seeded and thinly sliced

2 cups seeded and diced (¼-inch) honeydew

2 tablespoons finely chopped fresh mint leaves

Salt

In a medium-size bowl, combine the lime juice, ginger, habanero, and jalapeño. Add the honeydew and mint, combine well, and season with salt. Will keep, tightly covered, in the refrigerator overnight.

GINGERY PINEAPPLE SALSA WITH COCONUT AND PEANUTS

MAKES ABOUT 2½ CUPS

THIS TROPICAL-TASTING salsa is great served alongside spicy jerked chicken or pork, spice-rubbed shrimp, or even a hot curry.

1 tablespoon peeled and minced fresh ginger

1 small garlic clove, minced

1 Thai bird or serrano chile, minced (leave the seeds in for spicy salsa)

2 tablespoons fresh lime juice

1 tablespoon Asian fish sauce or soy sauce

2 cups peeled and finely diced fresh ripe pineapple

¼ cup grated fresh coconut

1 tablespoon finely chopped fresh cilantro leaves

1 tablespoon finely chopped fresh basil leaves

1 tablespoon finely chopped fresh mint leaves

2 tablespoons coarsely chopped unsalted dry-roasted peanuts

1. In a mortar using a pestle, pound the ginger, garlic, and chile together into a coarse paste. Add the lime juice and fish sauce and stir to combine.

2. In a medium-size bowl, combine the pineapple, coconut, and herbs. Add the dressing and toss to combine well. Will keep, tightly covered, in the refrigerator for up to 2 days.

3. Just before serving, toss with the peanuts.

KETCHUPS, CHUTNEYS, RELISHES, SAVORY FRUIT SAUCES, AND HOT SAUCES

Clear definitions of each of these types of sauces may be a little tricky. Really, aren't they all just types of condiments? I think what makes them different is greatly dependent upon several things: the ingredients and how they're put together, the culture from which they emerge, and the foods they accompany.

In a chutney, for example, fruit is most often cooked in larger pieces, whereas in a relish, the pieces of fruit tend to be finer. Relishes, usually highly seasoned, accompany a simply cooked and mildly seasoned meat, while chutneys ordinarily accompany something quite spicy. But in India, chutneys can be cooked or uncooked, chunky or pureed, spicy or mild, and accompany just about anything.

And then there is ketchup, which is decidedly American, though some believe that a thick and sweet soy sauce from Indonesia called *kecap manis* may have some relation, even if only in name. Ketchups are highly seasoned, sweet-tart fruit purees, traditionally tomato, that

are slowly cooked until thick and richly flavored. One fashionable trend of the 1990s was to make just about any fruit into ketchup. Tropical fruits, especially pineapple, mango, and guava, were quite popular because they lent themselves to just such preparation. It seems kind of funny to make your own ketchup—especially tomato ketchup, as there are so many commercial ones available, many of which I love. But as a condiment, fresh, homemade ketchup is unsurpassed for flavor and texture. (Plus, you can control the levels of salt and sugar—commercial ketchup is off the charts for sodium content.) Just don't use it as an ingredient in other sauces; all of the subtlety will be lost and overwhelmed by the other ingredients in the recipe.

COOKING WITH CONDIMENTS

- Stir any of the sweet-tart chutneys or condiments into yogurt, sour cream, or mayonnaise for a simple dip.

- Add a dash of Trinidadian Hot Pepper Sauce (page 353) to mayonnaise for a super spicy sandwich spread.

- Add a few tablespoons of Mango Chutney (page 343), Dried Fruit Chutney (page 344), Fresh Banana Chutney (page 345), Pineapple Chutney with Golden Raisins (page 341), Quince and Cranberry Compote (page 351), Quince and Red Onion Relish (page 347), and Sweet-and-Sour Peach Chutney (page 342) into chicken salad for an unexpected burst of flavor.

- Add a few tablespoons of any of the ketchups to mayonnaise for a delicious sandwich spread.

HOMEMADE TOMATO KETCHUP

MAKES ABOUT 2 CUPS

NEARLY ANY SAUCE with the right balance of vinegar, sugar, spices, onions, and some type of fruit that's cooked long enough can technically qualify as ketchup—which is probably why it became such a popular restaurant trend a few years ago. But simple tomato ketchup, with fresh tomatoes, vinegar, spices, garlic, and onions, is my favorite. Use it with all sorts of grilled, roasted, or sautéed meats, game, and poultry, or with breaded and fried vegetables, chicken cutlets, pork cutlets, and fish fillets, and, of course, French fries. Using a food mill will save you the trouble of peeling, seeding, and chopping the tomatoes in step 1 and yield a smoother ketchup.

- 4 pounds ripe tomatoes
- 1 tablespoon vegetable oil
- 1 small onion, minced
- 1 large garlic clove, minced
- 1/2 teaspoon ground cumin
- 1/2 teaspoon ground coriander
- 1/2 teaspoon ground ginger
- 1/2 teaspoon pure chile powder, preferably ancho or New Mexico
- Pinch of ground cinnamon
- Pinch of freshly grated nutmeg
- 1/2 cup cider vinegar
- 3/4 cup sugar
- Salt
- Cayenne pepper

1. Bring a large saucepan of water to a boil and fill a medium-size bowl with ice water. Using a sharp paring knife, make a shallow X on the bottom of each tomato. Add the tomatoes to the boiling water for 15 to 20 seconds, then immediately transfer them to the ice water until cold, 2 to 3 minutes. Drain the tomatoes, remove the skins, and halve crosswise. Set a strainer over a bowl, and working over the strainer, pry out the tomato seeds. Press on the pulp to extract as much of the juice as possible. Finely chop the tomatoes and add them to the tomato juice.

2. Heat the oil in a large, heavy saucepan over medium-high heat. Add the onion and garlic and cook until softened, about 4 minutes. Add the cumin, coriander, ginger, chile powder, cinnamon, and nutmeg and cook just until fragrant, about 30 seconds. Add the tomatoes and vinegar and cook over medium heat, stirring occasionally, until the liquid is evaporated and the tomatoes are broken down, about 30 minutes.

3. Add the sugar and cook over low heat, stirring frequently, until thickened and glossy, 10 to 15 minutes longer. Be careful not to let the sauce scorch. Season with salt and cayenne and let cool. Will keep, tightly covered, in the refrigerator for up to 2 weeks.

APPLE-TAMARIND KETCHUP

MAKES ABOUT 1½ CUPS

TAMARIND ADDS AN unexpected tartness and richness to this velvety smooth sauce. Part apple butter, part chutney, this tangy, slow-cooked condiment is wonderful with any roasted meat, game, or poultry. I think it's even pretty great on hot dogs and other sausages.

2 ounces (⅛ of a 1-pound block) pressed tamarind flesh, broken into 2-inch pieces

½ cup boiling water

1 pound tart apples, peeled, cored, and thinly sliced

1 small onion, minced

¼ cup cider vinegar

½ teaspoon ground ginger

¼ teaspoon ground cinnamon

½ cup plus 2 tablespoons firmly packed light brown sugar

Salt

Cayenne pepper

1. In a heatproof bowl, cover the tamarind with the boiling water and let sit for 15 minutes, then mash the tamarind with the back of a spoon. Strain the pulp through a fine-mesh sieve set over a bowl, pressing hard on the seeds and tough fibers. Discard the seeds and fibers.

2. Transfer the tamarind paste to a medium-size, heavy saucepan, add the apples, onion, vinegar, ginger, and cinnamon, and bring to a boil. Cover and cook over medium-low heat until the apples are softened and beginning to break down, about 20 minutes.

3. Remove the lid and cook, mashing the apples with a wooden spoon, until the liquid is completely evaporated, 5 to 10 minutes. Add the brown sugar and cook over low heat, stirring frequently, until the sauce is thickened and glossy, 15 to 20 minutes longer. Season with salt and cayenne and let cool before serving. Will keep, tightly covered, in the refrigerator for up to 2 weeks.

HOMEMADE ISN'T ALWAYS THE BEST CHOICE. . . .

Though homemade ketchup is far superior to commercial brands, I wouldn't use it as an ingredient in, say, barbecue sauce or a marinade. Its flavor would be overwhelmed by those of the other ingredients.

GINGER-CARROT KETCHUP

MAKES ABOUT 1½ CUPS

CARROT AND GINGER are a terrific combination, especially when the overall taste is slightly sweet and sour, as in this ketchup. It makes a great sandwich spread as well as a condiment for roasted, grilled, or sautéed meats, poultry, game, and seafood. I also like to add a tablespoon or so of it to yogurt, sour cream, or mayonnaise for a piquant dip or creamy sandwich spread.

1 tablespoon vegetable oil

½ small yellow onion, minced

1 tablespoon peeled and finely grated fresh ginger

1 Thai bird chile, preferably red, or ½ finger chile, seeded and finely chopped

1 pound carrots, peeled and cut into 1-inch pieces

¼ teaspoon ground cumin

Pinch of turmeric

Pinch of ground cinnamon

Salt

2 cups water

5 tablespoons distilled white vinegar

1 tablespoon tomato paste

¾ cup sugar

1. In a medium-size, heavy saucepan with a tight-fitting lid, heat the oil over medium heat. Add the onion, ginger, and chile and cook just until softened, stirring a few times, about 3 minutes. Add the carrots, cumin, turmeric, and cinnamon and season with salt. Add the water, ¼ cup of the vinegar, and the tomato paste and bring to a boil. Cover and cook over medium-low heat until the carrots are tender and the liquid is nearly evaporated, 25 minutes.

2. Scrape the carrots and any liquid into a blender or food processor and process until smooth. Add the sugar and return the puree to the saucepan. Simmer over medium heat, stirring frequently, until thick and glossy and all of the liquid is absorbed, about 20 minutes longer. Stir in the remaining 1 tablespoon vinegar, season with salt, and let cool. Serve at room temperature or chilled. Will keep, tightly covered, in the refrigerator for up to 2 weeks.

VIDALIA ONION KETCHUP

MAKES ABOUT 1 CUP

VIDALIA ONIONS ARE so sweet and they lend themselves to a silky ketchup like no other vegetable, except maybe tomatoes, but they're technically fruit, so there you have it. Serve this condiment with ribs, beef, chicken, pork, even salmon or shrimp.

1 tablespoon unsalted butter

1 tablespoon vegetable oil

1 large Vidalia or other sweet onion (about 1¼ pounds), coarsely chopped

2 tablespoons tomato paste

¼ cup bourbon

¼ cup cider vinegar

Pinch of freshly grated nutmeg

Pinch of ground allspice or cloves

½ cup low-sodium chicken broth

¼ cup firmly packed light brown sugar

Cayenne pepper

Salt and freshly ground black pepper

1. In a medium-size, heavy saucepan, melt the butter in the oil. Add the onion and cook over medium heat, stirring occasionally, until softened, about 8 minutes. Add the tomato paste and cook, stirring, until the onions are coated and lightly caramelized, about 2 minutes. Add the bourbon and cook until nearly evaporated. Add the vinegar and spices and simmer over low heat until the onion is very soft and the liquid reduced, about 5 minutes.

2. Transfer the mixture to a blender along with the broth and brown sugar and process until smooth.

3. Return the mixture to the saucepan and simmer over low heat until thickened and jam-like, about 20 minutes. Season with cayenne, salt, and black pepper. Can be served warm or cold. Will keep, tightly covered, in the refrigerator for up to 2 weeks.

PINEAPPLE-MANGO KETCHUP

MAKES ABOUT 1 CUP

THE TROPICAL FLAVORS of pineapple and mango make this ketchup a great match for grilled or sautéed shrimp, scallops, or meaty fish like swordfish, sea bass, and halibut, and for grilled, roasted, or sautéed poultry, beef, and pork. This keeps well for several weeks in the fridge.

1 tablespoon vegetable oil

½ small onion, minced

1 large garlic clove, minced

1 Thai bird chile or ½ finger chile, seeded and finely chopped

1 teaspoon peeled and finely grated fresh ginger

½ teaspoon ground coriander

1 cup peeled, cored, and finely chopped fresh pineapple

1 cup peeled and finely chopped fresh mango

3 tablespoons rice vinegar

½ cup sugar

Salt

Cayenne pepper

1. Heat the oil in a medium-size, heavy saucepan over medium-high heat. Add the onion, garlic, chile, ginger, and coriander and cook until softened, stirring a few times, about 3 minutes. Add the pineapple, mango, and vinegar and cook over medium heat, stirring occasionally, until the fruit is just beginning to break down and the liquid is evaporated, about 8 minutes.

2. Transfer the mixture to a blender along with the sugar and process until smooth.

3. Return the mixture to the saucepan and cook over very low heat, stirring frequently, until thickened and glossy, about 15 minutes longer. Be careful of the sputtering. Let cool, then season with salt and cayenne. Serve warm, at room temperature, or cold.

MY FAVORITE HOT DOG CONDIMENTS

Apple-Tamarind Ketchup (page 338)

Fresh Onion-Chile Relish (page 346)

Ginger-Carrot Ketchup (page 339)

Harissa II (page 352)

Homemade Tomato Ketchup (page 337)

Mango Chutney (page 343)

Quince and Red Onion Relish (page 347)

Vidalia Onion Ketchup (left)

PINEAPPLE CHUTNEY WITH GOLDEN RAISINS
MAKES ABOUT 2 CUPS

THIS BEAUTIFUL GOLDEN-COLORED chutney can be served with poultry, pork, and beef, as well as shellfish and fish. It makes a lovely, cooling accompaniment to Indian or Caribbean curries.

> 2 cups peeled, cored, and diced (1/2-inch) golden pineapple
> 1/2 small sweet onion, such as Vidalia or Maui, finely chopped
> 1/2 small green bell pepper, seeded and finely chopped
> 1/4 cup sugar
> 1/4 cup cider vinegar
> 6 cardamom pods
> 1 tablespoon finely chopped crystallized ginger
> 1/2 cup golden raisins
> Salt

1. In a medium-size, heavy saucepan, combine the pineapple, onion, bell pepper, sugar, vinegar, cardamom, ginger, and raisins and let sit until very juicy, about 1 hour, stirring occasionally.

2. Bring to a boil over high heat, stirring occasionally. Reduce the heat to low and simmer until thickened slightly, about 30 minutes. Season with salt and let cool. Serve warm, at room temperature, or cold. Will keep, tightly covered, in the refrigerator for up to 2 weeks.

SWEET-AND-SOUR PEACH CHUTNEY

MAKES ABOUT 2 CUPS

SUMMER IS REALLY the only time to make peach chutney. I make mega-batches when there is an overabundance of sweet, juicy peaches and put them up in 8-ounce jars. It may seem like a lot of work at the time, but you know, when it's 28 degrees outside in mid-February and it feels like there's about 4 hours of sunlight, I'm sitting pretty, basking in my peaches. Serve this with grilled, roasted, or sautéed meats, poultry, and seafood, as well as curries and stews.

2 pounds ripe peaches

2/3 cup firmly packed light brown sugar

1/3 cup cider vinegar

1/2 small yellow bell pepper, seeded and cut into 1/2-inch pieces

1/2 small yellow onion, cut into 1/2-inch pieces

1/4 cup golden raisins or finely diced dried apricots

1 tablespoon fresh lime juice

Salt

1. Bring a large saucepan of water to a boil and fill a large bowl with ice water. Using a sharp paring knife, mark a shallow X in the bottom of each peach. Drop the peaches into the boiling water for about 1 minute, then immediately plunge them into the ice water to cool. Remove the skins and pits and cut the peaches into 1/2-inch pieces.

2. In a medium-size, heavy saucepan, combine the brown sugar and vinegar and bring to a boil, stirring, until the sugar dissolves. Add the bell pepper, onion, raisins, and peaches, cover partially, and simmer over low heat, stirring occasionally, until the fruit is softened and the sauce jam-like, about 30 minutes. Stir in the lime juice and season with salt. Serve warm, at room temperature, or chilled. Will keep, tightly covered, in the refrigerator for up to 2 weeks.

QUICK MANGO CHUTNEY RAITA

Stir a few tablespoons of mango chutney into 1/2 cup drained plain or Greek-style yogurt (see The Right Yogurt, page 236) for a sweet raita.

MANGO CHUTNEY

MAKES ABOUT 1 CUP

LOOK FOR SWEET, ripe mangoes since they have an almost intoxicating perfume. Serve this gingery mango chutney as a cooling accompaniment to any spicy curry and grilled or roasted beef, pork, veal, lamb, poultry, or fish.

1/2 cup firmly packed light brown sugar

1/2 cup water

1/4 cup cider vinegar

11/2 teaspoons peeled and finely grated fresh ginger

6 cardamom pods

1 cinnamon stick

1 large ripe mango, peeled and cut off the seed into 1/2-inch pieces

Salt

In a medium-size, heavy saucepan, combine the brown sugar, water, vinegar, ginger, cardamom, and cinnamon and bring to a boil, stirring, until the sugar dissolves. Add the mango and simmer, partially covered, over low heat until the fruit is translucent and the liquid is thickened and glossy, about 20 minutes longer. Season with salt and let cool. Will keep, tightly covered, in the refrigerator for up to 2 weeks.

GREEN MANGO CHUTNEY

MAKES ABOUT 11/2 CUPS

THIS TART, FRESH chutney comes from India and is a great accompaniment to rich curries and stews and roasted or grilled beef, pork, veal, poultry, or meaty fish. If green (under-ripe) mangoes are hard to find, just use the most under-ripe mango you can find and be sure to season well. Salt really brings out the flavor of the mango.

1 large under-ripe mango, peeled and cut off the seed into large pieces

1 tablespoon packed fresh mint leaves

1 teaspoon sugar

1/4 teaspoon mild Madras curry powder

Pinch of ground cloves

Pinch of ground cumin

Pinch of ground coriander

2 tablespoons fresh lime juice

Salt

Cayenne pepper

In a food processor, combine the mango, mint, sugar, curry powder, cloves, cumin, and coriander and pulse into a chunky puree. Stir in the lime juice, season with salt and cayenne, and refrigerate until chilled. This is best eaten the day it is made.

GREEN PAPAYA CHUTNEY

MAKES ABOUT 1½ CUPS

THIS UNCOOKED CHUTNEY is inspired by a popular salad in Southeast Asia that uses green, unripe papayas. It's a refreshing and cooling complement to grilled or roasted fish, meats, or spicy curries. Green papaya, tart and crunchy, is different than the sweeter orange-fleshed papaya and is usually found in Asian or Latin markets. Unripe green mangoes make a better substitution than ripe orange or red papayas.

½ small green papaya, peeled, seeded, and shredded

Salt

2 tablespoons fresh lime juice

2 tablespoons sugar

2 tablespoons Asian fish sauce

2 Thai bird chiles or 1 finger chile, seeded and finely chopped

2 tablespoons finely chopped fresh cilantro leaves

1 tablespoon finely chopped unsalted dry-roasted peanuts

1. Sprinkle the papaya with salt and let sit in a colander in the sink for 10 minutes. Rinse well, squeeze slightly, and pat dry.

2. In a medium-size bowl, whisk the lime juice with the sugar until dissolved. Add the fish sauce, chiles, cilantro, and papaya and toss to combine. Season with salt.

3. Just before serving, sprinkle with the peanuts. Serve right away.

DRIED FRUIT CHUTNEY

MAKES ABOUT 2 CUPS

SERVE THIS RICHLY flavored, sweet chutney as an elegant accompaniment to Thanksgiving turkey or holiday goose, capon, or pork roast. I also like to use it for stuffing a pork tenderloin. Simply run the handle of a wooden spoon or knife-sharpening steel lengthwise down the center of the tenderloin and work the chutney into the hole. Just don't stuff it too tightly, since it will expand slightly during roasting.

½ cup dried apricots, finely chopped

½ cup dried figs, black Mission or Calmyrna, stemmed and finely chopped

½ cup dried sour cherries or cranberries, coarsely chopped

1 cup ruby port

1 cup apple juice

¼ cup firmly packed light brown sugar

1 cinnamon stick

1 bay leaf

In a medium-size, heavy saucepan, combine all the ingredients and bring to a boil. Reduce the heat to low and simmer until the fruit is softened and most of the liquid is absorbed, about 25 minutes. Discard the cinnamon stick and bay leaf. For a finer texture, transfer the mixture to a food processor and pulse to a coarse puree. Serve warm, cold, or at room temperature. Will keep, tightly covered, in the refrigerator for up to 1 month.

FRESH BANANA CHUTNEY

MAKES ABOUT 1 CUP

RIPE, CREAMY BANANAS make this fresh-tasting uncooked chutney a perfect partner for grilled fish, especially when seasoned with Satay Paste (page 192), Ginger-Lemongrass Spice Paste (page 149), or Scallion-Ginger Spice Paste (page 191). I also like it with spicy grilled steaks, chops, or poultry. Look for bananas that are just ripe—yellow with a hint of green at the stem and no brown spots. Since it tends to oxidize upon sitting, it's best to use this chutney right away.

2 just-ripe bananas, peeled and finely diced

2 tablespoons minced onion

1 scallion, thinly sliced

2 tablespoons fresh lime juice

1/4 teaspoon finely grated lime zest

1 tablespoon finely chopped fresh cilantro leaves

1 tablespoon finely chopped fresh mint leaves

1 tablespoon Asian fish sauce (optional)

Salt

Cayenne pepper

In a medium-size bowl, combine the bananas, onion, scallion, lime juice and zest, cilantro, and mint. Stir in the fish sauce, if using, and season with salt and cayenne.

FRESH INDIAN CHILE-TOMATO RELISH

MAKES ABOUT 2 CUPS

EVEN IN WINTER when tomatoes aren't exactly at their best, you can still make this spicy, fragrant relish with cherry or grape tomatoes or even plum tomatoes that have been left out to ripen slightly. There's no need to peel cherry tomatoes. Serve with grilled or roasted meats, fish, shellfish, or poultry, as well as curries, rice dishes, or breads.

1 pound ripe tomatoes, peeled, seeded, and finely diced

4 scallions, thinly sliced

3 Thai bird chiles or serrano chiles, stemmed and thinly sliced, with seeds

1/4 cup distilled white vinegar

1 1/2 tablespoons sugar

1 teaspoon kosher salt

1/4 cup vegetable oil

2 large garlic cloves, thinly sliced

1 tablespoon peeled and minced fresh ginger

1 teaspoon yellow mustard seeds

1/2 teaspoon ground cumin

1/2 teaspoon ground coriander

1/2 teaspoon freshly ground black pepper

1/2 teaspoon red pepper flakes

1/4 teaspoon turmeric

1 tablespoon finely chopped fresh cilantro leaves

1. In a medium-size bowl, combine the tomatoes, scallions, and chiles.

2. In a small, microwave-safe bowl, combine the vinegar, sugar, and kosher salt and microwave for 30 seconds. Stir until dissolved.

3. In a small skillet, heat the oil until shimmering over high heat. Add the garlic and ginger and cook just until fragrant, but not browned, 30 seconds. Add the mustard seeds, cumin, coriander, black pepper, red pepper flakes, and turmeric, cover, and cook just until the mustard seeds begin to pop, about 30 seconds. Immediately pour the hot mixture over the tomato mixture and toss to combine. Add the dressing, season with salt and black pepper, and stir in the cilantro. Will keep, tightly covered, in the refrigerator for up to 4 days. Bring to room temperature before serving.

FRESH ONION-CHILE RELISH

MAKES ABOUT 1 CUP

ONE OF MY favorite things about New York City's Indian restaurants is the three-condiment caddy that sits on every table—which consists of, without variation, tamarind sauce, cilantro chutney, and onion-chile relish. Serve this refreshing but spicy relish as part of your own "condiment caddy" with Cilantro-Mint Dipping Sauce (page 246) and Sweet-and-Sour Tamarind Sauce (page 256) to accompany all types of grilled, roasted, or sautéed meats, fish, and poultry; curries or stews; and any of the myriad Indian breads, like naan, chapati, or poori.

1 cup finely diced Vidalia or other sweet onion

1 cup cold water

Pinch of salt

1 hot red chile, about 5 inches long, stemmed and thinly sliced, with seeds

1/2 teaspoon sweet paprika

1/4 teaspoon cayenne pepper

1 tablespoon distilled white vinegar

1 tablespoon vegetable oil

Freshly ground black pepper

1. In a small bowl, soak the onion in the cold water and salt for 10 minutes. Drain well and pat dry.

2. Wipe out the bowl and combine the onion, chile, paprika, cayenne, vinegar, and oil in it. Season with salt and black pepper. Will keep, tightly covered, in the refrigerator for up to 2 days.

QUINCE AND RED ONION RELISH

MAKES ABOUT 1 1/2 CUPS

EACH TIME I cook with quinces, I am perennially surprised when they begin to color—anywhere from pale pink to deep crimson. Here, they're paired with sweet red onions to make a sweet-tart relish that goes well with burgers; roasted meats, poultry, or game; sausages; and sandwiches.

> 1 cup water
> 1/2 cup white wine
> 1/2 cup sugar
> 1 cinnamon stick
> 1 quince, peeled, cored, and cut into 1-inch pieces
> 1/2 small red onion, thinly sliced lengthwise
> 1 tablespoon fresh lemon juice
> Salt and freshly ground black pepper

1. In a medium-size, heavy saucepan, combine the water, wine, sugar, cinnamon, and quince and bring to a boil. Reduce the heat to low and simmer, stirring occasionally, until the quince is tender, about 20 minutes.

2. Add the onion and simmer until the sauce is jam-like, about 20 minutes longer, stirring occasionally.

3. Stir in the lemon juice and season with salt and pepper. Serve warm or at room temperature. Will keep, tightly covered, in the refrigerator for up to 2 weeks.

SWEET-AND-SOUR CARROT RELISH

MAKES ABOUT 1 CUP

THIS REFRESHING SHREDDED-CARROT condiment goes well with curries and stews, or as part of an Indian meal. I like to serve it along with several other condiments, such as any of the yogurt-based raitas on pages 230–243. This is best enjoyed the day it is made.

> 2 tablespoons vegetable oil
> 1 1/2 teaspoons Madras curry powder
> Pinch of ground cinnamon
> Pinch of cayenne pepper
> 4 medium-size carrots, coarsely shredded
> 1 teaspoon peeled and grated fresh ginger
> 3 tablespoons distilled white vinegar
> 1 1/2 tablespoons sugar
> 1/4 cup unsweetened finely grated coconut
> Salt

1. Heat the oil in a medium-size skillet over medium heat. Add the curry powder, cinnamon, and cayenne and cook just until fragrant, about 30 seconds. Add the carrots and ginger and cook until crisp-tender, about 2 minutes, stirring constantly. Transfer to a bowl and let cool.

2. In the same skillet, heat the vinegar and sugar and cook, stirring, just until the sugar dissolves. Pour over the carrots. Add the coconut, season with salt, and stir until everything is well coated. Serve warm, at room temperature, or chilled.

CUMBERLAND SAUCE

MAKES ABOUT 1 CUP

SERVE THIS CLASSIC English sauce with roasted ham, venison, lamb, beef, or poultry.

1 large shallot, minced

1 navel orange, scrubbed

1 small lemon, scrubbed

½ cup seedless red currant jelly

⅓ cup ruby port

1 teaspoon cornstarch, dissolved in 1 tablespoon water

¼ teaspoon ground ginger

Salt

Cayenne pepper

1. In a small saucepan, cover the shallot with cold water. Bring to a boil and simmer just until translucent, about 2 minutes. Drain well and return it to the saucepan.

2. Using a vegetable peeler, remove the zest from the orange and lemon in 1-inch-wide strips without taking any of the white pith beneath. Cut the strips into short, thin matchsticks. Squeeze the juice from the orange and lemon and add it to the shallots along with the zest, jelly, port, cornstarch, and ginger and bring to a boil, whisking until smooth and thickened slightly. Season with salt and cayenne. Serve hot. Will keep, tightly covered, in the refrigerator for up to 1 week.

HAROSET

MAKES ABOUT 1½ CUPS

TRADITIONALLY SERVED AS part of an elaborate Passover meal, this dried fruit and nut sauce is symbolic of the mortar used by the enslaved Jews laying bricks for the pharaoh. Serve it with roasted poultry or beef, but I also like it with lamb or even stirred into my morning oatmeal. I prefer the combination of raisins, cherries, and currants, but feel free to use whatever you like, as long as the fruit measures about ⅔ cup. Pineapple juice is a great alternative to the apple juice and lemon juice.

½ cup whole natural almonds

¼ cup golden raisins

¼ cup dried tart cherries

2 tablespoons dried currants

1 cup apple juice

2 tablespoons fresh lemon juice

½ teaspoon ground cinnamon

Pinch of freshly grated nutmeg

Pinch of salt

1 tart, crisp apple, such as Pippin, Granny Smith, or Honey Crisp, peeled, cored, and coarsely grated

1. Preheat the oven to 350°F. Spread the almonds in a pie plate and toast until golden and fragrant, about 10 minutes. Let cool, then transfer to a food processor and pulse until they are about ¼-inch pieces.

2. Meanwhile, in a small saucepan, combine the raisins, cherries, currants, apple juice, and lemon juice and bring to a simmer. Cover, remove from the heat, and let sit until plump, about 20 minutes.

3. Drain the fruit, reserving the liquid separately, and transfer it to a food processor along with the cinnamon, nutmeg, and salt. Pulse several times until coarsely chopped, adding several tablespoons of the liquid if the mixture is too dry. Transfer to a bowl and stir in the apple and almonds. Serve at room temperature. Will keep, tightly covered, in the refrigerator for up to 1 week.

ORANGE-CRANBERRY SAUCE

MAKES ABOUT 2 CUPS

THIS CLASSIC THANKSGIVING cranberry sauce is so easy that opening a can of that jellied stuff will seem like too much effort for the result.

> One 12-ounce bag fresh or thawed frozen cranberries, picked over for stems
> 3/4 cup sugar
> Finely grated zest of 1 orange
> 1/2 cup fresh orange juice

In a medium-size, heavy saucepan, combine all the ingredients and bring to a boil. Reduce the heat to medium-low and simmer until the sauce is jam-like, about 25 minutes. Serve warm, at room temperature, or cold. Will keep, tightly covered, in the refrigerator for up to 1 month.

CLASSIC APPLESAUCE

MAKES ABOUT 2 CUPS

AUTUMN MEANS SEVERAL things to me—comfortable running weather, beautiful fall colors, and apple picking—which in turn means applesauce! My favorite apple for applesauce is Macintosh because it's tart, crisp, and softens just right when cooked, but Macoun, Honey Crisp, Granny Smith, and Pippin are great too. The apples are peeled and cored first, because I prefer chunky applesauce with big hunks of soft, creamy apples suspended in a thick sweet-tart juice. Make a double batch and freeze half.

> 2 pounds apples, peeled, cored, and cut into 2-inch pieces
> 1/4 cup sugar
> 1/2 cup water
> 1 tablespoon fresh lemon juice

1. In a medium-size, heavy saucepan, combine the apples, sugar, and water and bring to a boil. Cover and simmer over medium-low heat until the apples are tender and broken down, about 15 minutes, stirring once or twice.

2. Raise the heat to medium-high and cook, uncovered, until the liquid is slightly reduced, about 5 minutes longer. Stir in the lemon juice. For a smooth applesauce, stir frequently or puree in a food processor or food mill. Serve warm or cold. Will keep, tightly covered, in the refrigerator for up to 1 month or in the freezer for 2 months.

CURRIED APPLESAUCE

MAKES ABOUT 2 CUPS

A LITTLE HIT of curry powder and butter makes this tart applesauce a perfect accompaniment to roasted, grilled, or sautéed meats, game, or poultry. Tart apples, such as Macintosh, Granny Smith, Mutsu, or Pippin, work best for this sauce. Depending on the sweetness of the apples, you may want to use more or less lime juice.

2 tablespoons unsalted butter

1 large shallot, minced

1½ teaspoons mild Madras curry powder

1½ pounds apples, peeled, cored, and thinly sliced

⅓ cup firmly packed light brown sugar

¼ cup water

1 to 2 tablespoons fresh lime juice, to your taste

Salt

Cayenne pepper

1. In a medium-size, heavy saucepan, melt the butter. When the foam subsides, add the shallot and cook over medium heat, stirring a few times, until softened, about 3 minutes. Add the curry powder and cook, stirring, for 1 minute. Add the apples, brown sugar, and water and bring to a boil. Cover and simmer over low heat until softened, about 20 minutes.

2. Increase the heat to medium-high, remove the cover, and cook, stirring a few times, until the liquid is nearly evaporated and the apples completely broken down, about 5 minutes longer. Stir

in the lime juice and season with salt and cayenne. Will keep, covered, in the refrigerator for up to 1 week or the freezer for 1 month.

CRANBERRY-PORT COMPOTE

MAKES ABOUT 2 CUPS

SWEET RUBY PORT adds an elegant touch to this simple cranberry sauce. Serve it at Thanksgiving or any time you serve roasted or grilled beef, pork, or poultry.

½ cup ruby port

Three 1 x 3-inch strips orange zest, cut into thin matchsticks

½ cup fresh orange juice

One 12-ounce bag fresh or thawed frozen cranberries, picked over for stems

¾ cup sugar

In a medium-size, nonreactive, heavy saucepan, combine the port and orange zest and orange juice and bring to a boil. Add the cranberries and sugar and simmer over medium-low heat until the sauce is jam-like, about 25 minutes. Serve warm, at room temperature, or cold. Will keep, tightly covered, in the refrigerator for up to 1 month.

PEAR AND PRUNE COMPOTE

MAKES ABOUT 2 1/2 CUPS

I LOVE THE creamy, velvety texture of cooked pears, especially Bartlett, Anjou, or Comice. When paired with prunes steeped in cognac, lemon zest, and fragrant bay leaf, this luscious compote will complement any roasted meat, poultry, or game.

1/2 cup pitted prunes

1/4 cup cognac, Armagnac, or other brandy

1/4 cup sugar

1 cup apple juice or sparkling apple cider

1 bay leaf, preferably imported

1 cinnamon stick

Four 1 x 3-inch strips lemon zest

4 ripe pears, peeled, cored, and cut into 1/2-inch pieces

2 tablespoons fresh lemon juice

1. In a small bowl, toss the prunes with the cognac and let sit for 20 minutes.

2. In a medium-size, heavy saucepan, combine the sugar, apple juice, bay leaf, cinnamon stick, and lemon zest and bring to a simmer, stirring until the sugar dissolves. Add the pears and prunes along with any unabsorbed cognac and simmer, partially covered, over low heat until the fruit is softened and the liquid is nearly evaporated, about 20 minutes. Stir in the lemon juice. Serve warm, at room temperature, or cold. Will keep, tightly covered, in the refrigerator for up to 2 weeks.

QUINCE AND CRANBERRY COMPOTE

MAKES ABOUT 3 CUPS

QUINCE, THAT KNOBBY, hard yellow fruit that looks like a large apple, is completely inedible raw. But when cooked, it becomes exquisitely creamy and delicious and turns the most beautiful shade of crimson. Quince is a bit tricky to work with, since it is so hard. A sturdy melon baller does a great job removing the core and seeds after the quinces are cut in half. Serve this deep-red cranberry sauce at Thanksgiving or any time you serve roasted meat, poultry, or game.

2 cups apple juice or sparkling apple cider

1/2 cup sugar

1 cinnamon stick

1 pound quinces, peeled, cored, and cut into 3/4-inch pieces

One 12-ounce bag fresh or thawed frozen cranberries, picked over for stems

1. In a medium-size, heavy saucepan, combine the apple juice, sugar, and cinnamon stick and bring to a boil, stirring to dissolve the sugar. Add the quinces and cook, uncovered, over medium heat, stirring occasionally, until tender, about 30 minutes.

2. Add the cranberries, bring to a simmer, and cook, uncovered, over medium-low heat until the compote is thick, about 20 minutes. Discard the cinnamon stick before serving. Serve warm, at room temperature, or chilled. Will keep, tightly covered, in the refrigerator for up to 1 month.

HARISSA
(MOROCCAN CHILE PASTE)

MAKES ABOUT 1 CUP

THIS RED-HOT CHILE paste figures very prominently in Middle Eastern cooking, especially in Morocco. This variation uses fresh chiles. Used as a condiment as well as a seasoning ingredient, it adds a fresh, piquant flavor. Serve it with grilled or roasted meats, fish, and poultry; mixed into ground meat for meatballs and kibbe (ground-meat patties usually made from lamb); as a seasoning paste and marinade for meat, fish, and vegetables; or mix some into tomato sauce for an unexpected kick. I don't ordinarily wear latex gloves when handling 1 or 2 chiles, but strongly recommend it when a recipe calls for more, as this one does.

> 1/2 pound hot red chiles (try cayenne, Hungarian, or hot Korean chiles), about 5 inches long, stemmed
>
> 1 garlic clove, peeled
>
> 1/4 cup water
>
> Salt
>
> 1/4 cup plus 2 tablespoons extra-virgin olive oil

1. Wearing rubber or latex gloves, cut the chiles into large pieces. Transfer the chiles and seeds, garlic, and water to a blender or food processor and process into a fine paste, scraping down the sides occasionally. Season with salt.

2. In a medium-size, heavy saucepan, heat the oil over medium-low heat until shimmering. Add the chile paste and cook, stirring occasionally, until all of the liquid is evaporated and the oil has separated from the chiles, about 20 minutes. Let cool, then transfer to a jar. Will keep, tightly covered, in the refrigerator for up to 2 weeks.

HARISSA II

MAKES ABOUT 2 CUPS

THIS HARISSA WAS inspired by one of my favorite women in the food world, and a great expert on all things Middle Eastern, Paula Wolfert. Harissa is a staple of Moroccan cuisine and is used as a marinade, ingredient, and condiment. I love it as a rub on all types of meat, sausage, and poultry that are to be grilled or roasted, and meaty firm-fleshed fish like swordfish, salmon, halibut, cod, and snapper, though it's also a great condiment and hot sauce on meats, vegetables, breads, stews, and curries.

> 5 dried ancho chiles (2 ounces), stemmed and seeded
>
> 1 to 2 dried chipotle chiles, stemmed and seeded
>
> Boiling water
>
> 3 oil-packed sun-dried tomatoes, coarsely chopped
>
> 1 large clove garlic, peeled
>
> 3/4 cup extra virgin olive oil
>
> 2 1/2 teaspoons kosher salt
>
> 4 teaspoons *pimenton dulce* (smoked sweet paprika; available in gourmet stores)
>
> 1 teaspoon sherry vinegar

1 teaspoon fresh lemon juice

1/2 teaspoon cayenne pepper

1/2 teaspoon ground cumin

1/2 teaspoon caraway seeds, ground in a
   spice grinder

1. In a heatproof bowl, cover the chiles with boiling water and let sit until softened, about 20 minutes.

2. Drain the chiles and transfer to a food processor. Add the tomatoes, garlic, and oil and process until smooth. Add the remaining ingredients and process until smooth. Will keep, tightly covered, in the refrigerator for up to 1 month.

TRINIDADIAN HOT PEPPER SAUCE

MAKES ABOUT 4 CUPS

MY GOOD FRIEND and neighbor Dick Hosten, who splits his time between Trinidad and Brooklyn, generously gave me his prized recipe for hot pepper sauce, this after years of bringing me bottles of his own. I always seem to have some on hand, partly because a little goes a long way, but mostly because his recipe makes so darn much. It lasts for months in the fridge, but I have adapted it to make a bit less. He was glad to make it in my kitchen because, he claims, his wife, Annette, won't let him do it at home—she says the hot pepper fumes are too intense for her (well, if he stopped making Navy Fleet–size batches . . .). Serve it (just a dab will do) with grilled or roasted meats, poultry, fish and shellfish; curries; rice; scrambled eggs; sandwiches; you name it. Please be careful handling the chiles, as they are just about the hottest chile on Earth—and be careful as you remove the cover of the blender, as the fumes can be quite strong.

10 Scotch bonnet or habanero chiles,
   stemmed

2 medium-size carrots, cut into 1/2 -inch
   pieces

1 large head garlic, peeled

1 bunch scallions, coarsely chopped

1 cup packed fresh cilantro leaves

1/2 cup packed fresh Italian parsley leaves

2 tablespoons fresh thyme leaves

3/4 cup distilled white vinegar

1/2 cup prepared yellow mustard

2 tablespoons fresh lime juice

Generous pinch of salt

1. Bring a medium-size saucepan of water to a boil. Add the chiles and blanch for 1 minute. Using a slotted spoon, transfer them to a blender or food processor. Add the carrots and garlic to the boiling water and blanch for 30 seconds. Drain, transfer to the blender, and let cool.

2. Add the scallions, cilantro, parsley, thyme, vinegar, mustard, and lime juice and pulse into a coarse puree. Add the salt and transfer to a large jar. Store, tightly covered, in the refrigerator.

DESSERT SAUCES

Some say putting a sauce on a dessert, however simple, is gilding the lily. And in some cases it may be, but for someone who gets as immense a pleasure out of all things sweet and frilly like me, I say bring it on! Need I mention how much I loved working on this chapter?

The success of any dessert sauce is not entirely about the sauce itself, but the way it is used. A good dessert is one that balances all the constituent elements. It can be as simple and elegant as pound cake and a fruit coulis, vanilla ice cream and hot fudge, or slices of tart apple dipped in warm caramel. Or it can be more complicated, like panna cotta served with tuiles, praline powder, two fruit sauces, and macerated berries. If all the components are in harmony, the dessert works.

Generally, creamy desserts, such as custards, panna cotta, tapioca, and rice puddings are best paired with fruit sauces, whereas fruit desserts, such as poached, roasted, or sautéed fruits, sliced fresh fruit, fresh berries, fruit tarts, etc., most often will benefit from being paired with custard-y sauces. Cakes, bread puddings, and shortcakes are a little more versatile and can go either way. And, of course, ice cream, especially vanilla, is almost a blank canvas, waiting for you to work your creative impulses upon it.

CHOCOLATE SAUCE

MAKES ABOUT 1½ CUPS

CALLED GANACHE, THIS elegant chocolate sauce couldn't be simpler—bittersweet chocolate and heavy cream. The proportion of chocolate to cream can vary a little, depending upon how you plan to use your ganache. For cake frosting or chocolate truffles, for example, the proportion of chocolate to cream would be slightly higher than for a pouring sauce, which is what we have here. Even though it's meant for pouring, it will nonetheless thicken and harden as it cools, so it will need to be warmed before serving. Use it with ice cream, puddings and custards, cakes, tarts, and cream puffs.

1 cup heavy cream
8 ounces bittersweet or semisweet chocolate, coarsely chopped

1. In a medium-size, heavy saucepan, heat the cream over medium heat until small bubbles appear around the rim, about 4 minutes. Off the heat, add the chocolate and let sit without stirring for 5 minutes.

2. Using a whisk, stir the sauce until the chocolate is melted and thoroughly mixed into the cream. You can use immediately, let cool at bit, or chill, then reheat before using. Will keep, tightly covered, in the refrigerator for up to 2 weeks.

CHOCOLATE SYRUP

MAKES ABOUT 2 CUPS

IF YOU LIKE chocolate milk, stir a few tablespoons of this syrup into a tall cold glass of milk. You'll never use the commercial stuff again. Or serve it warm or cold over ice cream or with cakes, pastries, and puddings. It lasts for months in your refrigerator, but I doubt it will be lying around that long. Be sure to use a good-quality cocoa powder—it really makes a difference. Valrhona makes the best cocoa I've ever tasted—it gives everything a deep, rich velvety flavor.

½ cup unsweetened cocoa powder
1½ cups sugar
Pinch of salt
1½ cups boiling water
½ cup light corn syrup
1 tablespoon pure vanilla extract

In a medium-size, heavy saucepan, combine the cocoa, sugar, and salt. In a thin stream, add the boiling water, whisking until smooth. Whisk in the corn syrup and bring to a boil, stirring until the sugar is dissolved. Insert a candy thermometer in the mixture, if you have one. Reduce the heat to low and cook until the thermometer registers 220°F and the liquid is slightly reduced, about 10 minutes. Be careful not to let the liquid boil over. Let cool, then stir in the vanilla. Will keep, tightly covered, in the refrigerator for up to 2 months.

HOT FUDGE SAUCE

MAKES ABOUT 1½ CUPS

I KNOW THERE are a lot of chocolate sauces in this chapter, but what sets this one apart is its irresistible thick, gooey consistency and rich, deep flavor. It lasts in the fridge, but won't be around long enough to stand the test of time. When reheating the sauce, it will be necessary to add a little water, a few teaspoons at a time, and whisk until smooth and silky. Always serve it hot over ice cream.

- ½ cup plus 2 tablespoons water
- ½ cup heavy cream
- ¼ cup light corn syrup
- ½ cup sugar
- 4 ounces bittersweet chocolate, coarsely chopped
- 2 ounces unsweetened chocolate, coarsely chopped
- 2 tablespoons cold unsalted butter, cut into ½-inch cubes
- 1 teaspoon pure vanilla extract

1. In a medium-size, heavy saucepan, combine ½ cup of the water, the heavy cream, corn syrup, and sugar and bring to a boil, stirring until the sugar is dissolved. Using a pastry brush dipped in water, brush the sides of the pan to dissolve and wash down any sugar crystals. Cook over medium heat until reduced by half, about 7 minutes.

2. Off the heat, add the chocolates and butter and let sit until melted, about 2 minutes. Return to low heat and cook, stirring constantly, until

glossy and smooth. If the sauce appears broken, add the remaining 2 tablespoons water and beat until smooth and glossy. Stir in the vanilla. Will keep, tightly covered, in the refrigerator for up to 2 months. Reheat before serving.

MINT-CHOCOLATE SAUCE

MAKES ABOUT 1⅓ CUPS

THERE ARE TWO kinds of people in this world—those who love the combination of chocolate and mint and those who don't. I most emphatically belong to the former group and do not suffer those from the latter population with any great gladness. This sauce is, without apology, for us choco-mint lovers—the rest of you, well, keep reading. Just be sure to use a good-quality peppermint (not spearmint—check the bottle label carefully if it says only "mint" extract) extract. I particularly like to spread it chilled on Oreo cookies—it tastes like my favorite Girl Scout cookie, only better.

- 3/4 cup heavy cream
- 1/4 cup light corn syrup
- 1/4 cup sugar
- 4 ounces bittersweet chocolate, coarsely chopped
- 1 ounce unsweetened chocolate, coarsely chopped
- 2 tablespoons cold unsalted butter, cut into ½-inch cubes
- ½ teaspoon pure peppermint extract

1. In a medium-size, heavy saucepan, combine the cream, corn syrup, and sugar and cook over medium-high heat, stirring, until the sugar dissolves and the liquid is slightly reduced, about 3 minutes.

2. Off the heat, add the chocolates and let sit for 5 minutes without stirring until melted. Whisk until smooth. Add the butter and whisk until smooth. Whisk in the peppermint extract. Use hot or chilled. Will keep, tightly covered, in the refrigerator for up to 2 weeks.

HAZELNUT-CHOCOLATE SAUCE

MAKES ABOUT 1 1/2 CUPS

LEAVE IT TO the Italians to invent something as exquisite as gianduia—a hazelnut-chocolate confection, originally, the story goes, created as a way to extend precious chocolate during wartime. Serve it warm with cakes, tarts, ice creams, roasted or poached pears, or eat it by the spoonful right out of the refrigerator.

1/2 cup hazelnuts

1 cup heavy cream

1/4 cup light corn syrup

1/4 cup sugar

4 ounces bittersweet chocolate, coarsely chopped

1 ounce unsweetened chocolate, coarsely chopped

2 tablespoons cold unsalted butter, cut into 1/2-inch cubes

2 tablespoons hazelnut-chocolate spread (Nutella)

1 tablespoon hazelnut liqueur (optional)

1. Preheat the oven to 350°F. Put the hazelnuts in a pie plate and toast until fragrant and the skins begin to blister, about 12 minutes. Let them cool, then finely grind the nuts in a food processor.

2. Place the nuts in a medium-size, heavy saucepan with the cream and simmer over medium-low heat just until small bubbles appear around the rim, about 5 minutes. Turn the heat off, cover, and let the cream steep for 30 minutes.

3. Set a fine-mesh sieve over a medium-size bowl and strain the cream, pressing hard on the solids to extract as much of the liquid as possible. Discard the hazelnuts. Wipe out the saucepan and return the cream to it along with the corn syrup and sugar and cook over medium-high heat, stirring, until the sugar dissolves and the liquid is slightly reduced, about 3 minutes.

4. Off the heat, add the chocolates and let sit for 5 minutes without stirring until melted. Whisk until smooth. Add the butter and Nutella and whisk until smooth. Whisk in the hazelnut liqueur. Will keep, tightly covered, in the refrigerator for up to 2 weeks.

ORANGE-CHOCOLATE SAUCE

MAKES ABOUT 1 1/3 CUPS

THE COMBINATION OF orange and chocolate always reminds me of Tootsie Rolls, which were one of my favorite childhood candies. This interpretation is smooth, silky, and sophisticated. Serve it with cakes, ice creams, puddings, custards, and cooked fruits.

- 3/4 cup heavy cream
- 1/4 cup light corn syrup
- 1/4 cup sugar
- Zest of 1 orange, removed in strips with a vegetable peeler
- 4 ounces bittersweet chocolate, coarsely chopped
- 1 ounce unsweetened chocolate, coarsely chopped
- 2 tablespoons cold unsalted butter, cut into 1/2-inch cubes
- 2 tablespoons Grand Marnier or other orange liqueur

1. In a medium-size, heavy saucepan, combine the cream, corn syrup, sugar, and orange zest and cook over medium-high heat, stirring, until the sugar dissolves and the liquid is slightly reduced, about 3 minutes. Remove from the heat and let cool.

2. Remove the orange zest and cook over medium heat just until hot.

3. Off the heat, add the chocolates and let sit for 5 minutes without stirring until melted. Whisk until smooth. Add the butter and whisk until smooth. Whisk in the orange liqueur. Serve hot or warm. Will keep, tightly covered, in the refrigerator for up to 2 weeks; reheat before serving.

TIPS FOR SUCCESSFUL DESSERT SAUCES

- For custard sauces, be sure to use a heavy-bottomed saucepan, one that distributes heat evenly so that the eggs don't curdle.

- For custard sauces, before you begin, set a fine-mesh sieve in a heatproof bowl and set the bowl in an ice water bath so that it's ready. I've scrambled plenty of custards in the time it takes to set that up.

- With fruit sauces, look for very ripe fruit and cut away any bruises for the brightest, cleanest flavor.

- When making caramel sauces, be sure to have a skillet or basin filled with an inch or two of cool water nearby before you begin. That way you're not rushing around at the end and your caramel won't burn in the 1 minute it takes to fill the pan.

CARAMEL SAUCE

MAKES ABOUT 1½ CUPS

THIS GREAT ALL-PURPOSE dessert sauce was another staple in my pastry kitchen repertoire at various restaurants and catering kitchens I've worked in over the years. Not only would we use it with ice creams, cakes, bread puddings, or tarts, but we would combine it with chocolate sauces, vanilla custards, fruit sauces, and yogurt to make other desserts like ice cream, flans, puddings, and cake frostings. One of my guilty pleasures is spreading it cold on crisp, tart apple slices—kind of defeats the healthy purpose of eating an apple, but so be it! It can be refrigerated for quite a while, but should be warmed slightly before serving.

> 1½ cups sugar
> ¾ cup water
> Pinch of salt
> ½ cup heavy cream

1. Fill a large skillet with 1 inch of cold water and keep nearby. In a medium-size, heavy saucepan, combine the sugar, ½ cup of the water, and the salt. Cook over medium heat, stirring, just until the sugar dissolves. Using a pastry brush dipped in water, brush the sides of the pan to dissolve and wash down any sugar crystals. Increase the heat to high and cook the sugar syrup without stirring until a deep honey-colored caramel forms, 8 to 10 minutes. Set the saucepan into the cold water to slow the cooking.

2. Off the heat, stand back slightly and add the cream and remaining ¼ cup water. Be careful, the caramel will steam and bubble up and harden. When the bubbling has nearly subsided, stir the caramel, return it to low heat, and cook just until the caramel is melted, about 5 minutes. Serve warm. Will keep, tightly covered, in the refrigerator up to 1 month.

Variation: For a richer caramel sauce, use ¾ cup heavy cream at the end instead of the combination of cream and water.

RASPBERRY CARAMEL SAUCE

MAKES ABOUT 2 CUPS

THIS SAUCE IS inspired by my absolute favorite caramels, which I would get every year at Christmas time. They were buttery, chewy, creamy caramels with a slight rosy color and subtle raspberry flavor. Use this crimson caramel sauce warmed with ice creams, puddings and custards, tarts, bread puddings, cakes, and poached, roasted, or sautéed fruits.

> One 12-ounce package individually frozen raspberries, thawed
> 1 cup water
> 1½ cups sugar
> Pinch of salt
> ¼ cup (½ stick) unsalted butter

1. Puree the raspberries in a blender or food processor with ½ cup of the water. Strain the berries through a fine-mesh sieve, pressing hard

- When making caramel, be sure to have all your ingredients at hand—once you start, you should not leave the stove until it's done.

- A saucepan of proper size and one with straight sides works best.

- Have a clean pastry brush sitting in a glass of water nearby. This is to moisten any undissolved sugar granules sitting above the surface of the syrup on the sides of the pot.

- Once the sugar is dissolved and the sugar crystals have been moistened, do not stir again until the water or cream is added because sometimes stirring will cause the sugar to recrystallize after it has dissolved. If this happens, there is nothing you can do but start over using a clean pan.

- Once the sugar syrup begins to color around the edges, very gently swirl the pan to incorporate the darker parts into the center. Let cook a little longer, until the caramel is a lovely deep amber color—somewhere between honey and maple syrup. The lighter the color, the subtler the flavor will be. Conversely, the darker the color, the more intense (and bitter) the flavor will be.

- After the sugar syrup has reached the desired color, remove it from the heat and slowly add the liquid. Be sure to stand back and do *not* lean over the caramel—it will steam, bubble up, and, in some cases, seize up and harden. Once the liquid has been added, return it to low heat and gently stir until any hardened caramel is melted and the liquid is completely incorporated.

and scraping on the solids to remove the seeds. There should be about 1¼ cups. Fill a large skillet with 1 inch of cold water and keep nearby.

2. In a medium-size, heavy saucepan, combine the sugar, remaining ½ cup water, and the salt. Cook over medium heat, stirring, just until the sugar dissolves. Using a pastry brush dipped in water, brush the sides of the pan to dissolve and wash down any sugar crystals. Cook the sugar syrup over high heat, without stirring, until a deep honey-colored caramel forms, 8 to 10 minutes. Set the saucepan in the cold water to slow the cooking.

3. Off the heat, stand back slightly and add the butter and raspberry puree. Be careful, the caramel will steam and bubble up and harden. When the bubbling has nearly subsided, stir the caramel, return it to low heat, and cook until the caramel is melted, 5 to 6 minutes. Serve warm or let cool, then refrigerate, reheating gently when ready to use. Will keep, tightly covered, in the refrigerator for up to 1 month.

BALSAMIC CARAMEL SAUCE

MAKES ABOUT 2/3 CUP

SWEET-TART BALSAMIC vinegar elevates this simple caramel sauce to quite another level. With all the varieties of flavored balsamic vinegar—cherry, fig, pomegranate—you can really go wild. Serve this beautiful clear amber sauce with vanilla ice cream, pound cake, bread puddings and other custards, as well as with cooked fruit desserts such as poached pears or quinces.

3/4 cup sugar

1/2 cup water

Pinch of salt

1 1/2 tablespoons balsamic vinegar, preferably fruit flavored

1. Fill a large skillet with 1 inch of cold water and keep nearby. In a small, heavy saucepan, combine the sugar, 1/4 cup of the water, and the salt. Cook over medium heat, stirring, just until the sugar dissolves. Using a pastry brush dipped in water, brush the sides of the pan to dissolve and wash down any sugar crystals. Increase the heat to high and cook the sugar syrup, without stirring, until a deep amber caramel forms, about 6 minutes. Set the saucepan into the cold water to slow the cooking.

2. Off the heat, stand back slightly and add the remaining 1/4 cup water and the balsamic vinegar. Be careful: The caramel will steam and bubble up and harden. When the bubbling has nearly subsided, stir the caramel, return it to medium heat, and cook just until the caramel is melted. Serve warm or refrigerate and serve chilled. Will keep, tightly covered, in the refrigerator for up to 1 month.

16 BEST SAUCES TO POUR OVER VANILLA ICE CREAM

BUTTERSCOTCH SAUCE

MAKES ABOUT 2 CUPS

BUTTERSCOTCH SAUCE WAS the epitome of sophistication for me as a kid. Like sipping Shirley Temples while my folks had cocktails, I always felt so grown up when I ordered an ice cream sundae with butterscotch sauce. It's really nothing more than brown sugar, cream, butter, and a bit of whisky and it will make you feel incredibly worldly and sophisticated (but hopefully child-like) when you drizzle it over your favorite sundae.

> 1¼ cups firmly packed dark brown sugar
> ½ cup light corn syrup
> ¼ cup water
> ¼ cup (½ stick) unsalted butter
> Pinch of salt
> ½ cup heavy cream
> 1½ tablespoons whisky
> ½ teaspoon pure vanilla extract

1. In a medium-size, heavy saucepan, combine the brown sugar, corn syrup, water, butter, and salt and bring to a boil. Reduce the heat to medium and cook, stirring a few times, until the sugar is completely dissolved and the syrup is slightly reduced, about 4 minutes. Add the cream, bring to a boil, and let boil for 1 minute.

2. Off the heat, stir in the whisky and vanilla, and serve warm. Will keep, tightly covered, in the refrigerator for up to 2 weeks.

DULCE DE LECHE

MAKES ABOUT 1½ CUPS

DULCE DE LECHE, a golden, gooey caramel made by simmering sugar and milk together very slowly, is made all over Latin America. "The only way to make it," the Puerto Rican mother of an ex-boyfriend assured me, "is to simmer an unopened can of sweetened condensed milk in a large pot of water for about 4 hours." Well, that does in fact work, but it's not always perfect every time. (Depending on how hot the water is, or how old the can is, the resulting sauce can vary in color and consistency from thick and gooey golden brown to runny and pale. It can also be dangerous if the water boils too vigorously or, worse yet, evaporates, resulting in the can exploding.) Here is a much safer and foolproof method. Even if the sauce looks curdled, it can be redeemed by pureeing it in a food processor or blender until creamy and silky. Use it on ice cream, on custards and puddings, on cakes, as a filling for crepes, and with cooked fruits.

> One 14-ounce can sweetened condensed milk
> 2 cups whole milk
> ½ cup sugar
> 1 teaspoon pure vanilla extract

In a medium-size, heavy saucepan, combine the condensed milk, whole milk, and sugar and bring just to a boil. Reduce the heat to very low and cook, stirring occasionally, until thick and deep golden brown, about 1½ hours. Be careful the sauce doesn't boil over. Stir in the vanilla. If the sauce curdles, transfer it to a blender and process until smooth and silky. Serve warm, at room temperature, or chilled. Will keep, tightly covered, in the refrigerator for up to 1 month.

TOASTING NUTS AND SEEDS

Preheat the oven to 350°F. Spread the nuts on a baking sheet or pie plate and toast until golden.

- Almonds
    Sliced—5 minutes
    Whole—10 to 12 minutes

- Hazelnuts
    Unblanched—about 12 minutes

- Pecans and walnuts
    Halves—8 minutes

- Pine nuts
    Whole—3 to 4 minutes

- Pistachios
    Whole—7 to 8 minutes

- Pumpkin and sunflower seeds
    Shelled—5 minutes

MAPLE-CIDER NUT SAUCE

MAKES ABOUT 2/3 CUP

I LIKE TO serve this warm, wintry sauce with French toast, waffles, pancakes, poached fruits, bread puddings, and vanilla ice cream. Pecans and walnuts both work nicely, so use whatever you have on hand; also, I leave out the bourbon, with fine results, when I make this for pancakes for my kids.

    1 cup fresh apple cider
    Pinch of ground cinnamon
    Pinch of ground nutmeg
    Pinch of ground cloves
    1/4 cup pure maple syrup
    1/2 teaspoon cornstarch dissolved in
        1 tablespoon water
    1/2 cup chopped pecans or walnuts, toasted
        (see box at left)
    1 tablespoon bourbon (optional)
    1/2 teaspoon pure vanilla extract

1. In a medium-size, heavy saucepan, combine the cider, cinnamon, nutmeg, and cloves and bring to a boil. Reduce the heat to medium and simmer until reduced to a thin syrup, about 15 minutes. Stir in the maple syrup and bring to a boil. Add the cornstarch and simmer until slightly thickened and glossy, about 2 minutes longer.

2. Let cool slightly, then stir in the nuts, bourbon, if using, and vanilla. Will keep, tightly covered, in the refrigerator for up to 2 weeks.

BOURBON HARD SAUCE

MAKES ABOUT 1 CUP

THIS BOOZY SAUCE is a staple in Southern cooking, especially in New Orleans. Nothing more than butter, confectioners' sugar, and bourbon, this thick, creamy sauce, which has the consistency of buttercream, is always served with warm desserts, such as steamed puddings or bread puddings. The warmth of the dessert melts the sauce to a rich, heady decadence, surely much greater than the sum of its parts.

½ cup (1 stick) unsalted butter, softened
1¼ cups confectioners' sugar
3 tablespoons bourbon
Seeds from ½ vanilla bean, or ½ teaspoon
    pure vanilla extract

1. In a medium-size bowl, using a handheld electric mixer, beat the butter until creamy. Add the confectioners' sugar and beat on medium-low speed until fluffy. Add the bourbon and vanilla seeds and beat just until combined.

2. Transfer to a small bowl and refrigerate until chilled before using. Will keep, tightly covered, in the refrigerator for up to 1 month.

GINGER-PORT DESSERT SAUCE

MAKES ABOUT ⅔ CUP

THERE ALWAYS SEEMS to be a half-full bottle of ruby port lying around, and this is one of my favorite ways to use it up before it's no longer at its peak for drinking. Chewy ginger candies, called Ting Ting, come from Southeast Asia and can be found in Asian markets and specialty candy shops. Crystallized ginger is a perfectly fine substitute, but be sure to strain for a smooth, clear sauce. Serve it with any fresh or cooked fruit dessert, with custards or puddings, or stirred into seltzer for a refreshing nonalcoholic spritzer.

2 cups ruby port, free of any sediment
4 chewy ginger candies, finely diced, or
    2 tablespoons minced crystallized ginger
⅓ cup sugar
½ teaspoon pure vanilla extract

1. In a medium-size, heavy saucepan, combine the port, ginger candies, and sugar and bring to a boil, stirring until the sugar dissolves. Simmer over medium-low heat until the ginger candies are completely melted and the liquid is reduced to a medium-thin syrup, about 15 minutes.

2. If using crystallized ginger, strain the sauce through a fine-mesh sieve to remove any bits. Stir in the vanilla. Serve warm, at room temperature, or chilled. Will keep, tightly covered, for up to 2 weeks.

RUM RAISIN SAUCE

MAKES ABOUT 1 CUP

RUM RAISIN IS one of those grown-up flavors that I couldn't truly appreciate until I was a grown-up. The heady, boozy perfume of dark rum combined with the earthy sweetness of raisins makes a perfect match for ice cream and other creamy desserts, as well as pound cakes or warm, cinnamony bread puddings.

1/2 cup dark raisins

1 cup hot water

1/2 cup firmly packed dark brown sugar

1/4 teaspoon ground nutmeg

1/4 cup dark rum

1 1/2 teaspoons cornstarch dissolved
      in 1 tablespoon water

1. In a medium-size, heavy saucepan, soak the raisins in the water until plump, about 20 minutes.

2. Add the brown sugar and nutmeg and bring to a boil, stirring until the sugar is dissolved. Simmer over medium-low heat until the liquid is reduced by about half, about 7 minutes. Add the rum and cook for 1 minute. Stir the cornstarch mixture into the sauce and boil until slightly thickened and glossy, about 2 minutes. Serve warm or at room temperature. Will keep, tightly covered, in the refrigerator for up to 2 weeks; reheat gently before serving.

SPICED WINE DESSERT SAUCE

MAKES ABOUT 2/3 CUP

ANY FULL-BODIED red wine will do for this warmly spiced dessert sauce, reminiscent of mulled wine. Serve it warm with poached pears or quinces, roasted apples or bananas, or tarte tatin, apple pie, or almost any wintry fruit dessert.

2 cups dry red wine

1 cup sugar

1 cinnamon stick

1 bay leaf

Two 1-inch strips orange zest

4 cloves or allspice berries

2 cardamom pods

1/2 vanilla bean

In a medium-size, heavy saucepan, combine all the ingredients and bring to a boil, stirring occasionally, until the sugar dissolves. Reduce the heat to medium-low and simmer until it is a thin syrup and reduced by about two thirds, about 15 minutes. Strain the sauce through a fine-mesh sieve. Serve warm. Will keep, tightly covered, in the refrigerator for up to 2 weeks; reheat before serving.

ZABAGLIONE

MAKES ABOUT 1 1/2 CUPS

THIS ETHEREAL ITALIAN custard sauce, also known as *sabayon* in French, is traditionally served warm with strawberries and crumbled amaretto cookies. It can also be chilled for up to 4 hours in wineglasses with mixed berries for a more refreshing dessert, or spooned over berries or sliced ripe peaches, pears, or bananas in a shallow baking dish and broiled until golden for a lovely dessert gratin.

3/4 cup superfine sugar

4 large egg yolks, at room temperature

1/2 cup sweet wine, such as Sauternes, Moscato, Marsala, or late-harvest Riesling

1. In a large, stainless-steel bowl, combine the sugar with the egg yolks and whisk until lemon colored, about 2 minutes. Add the wine and whisk until combined.

2. Set the bowl over a saucepan filled with 2 inches of barely simmering water. Do not let the bowl touch the water. Cook the custard over medium heat, whisking constantly, until pale and foamy and doubled in volume, 8 to 10 minutes. Serve right away or refrigerate in glasses until chilled. Will keep, tightly covered, in the refrigerator for up to 8 hours (overnight).

CRÈME ANGLAISE

MAKES ABOUT 2 1/4 CUPS

THIS "ENGLISH" CUSTARD sauce couldn't possibly be more French. Used as a sauce for cakes, tarts, puddings, pastries, and fruit desserts, its applications are nearly endless. But treat it as an ingredient in other preparations and it opens up an entirely new set of possibilities. For example, use it as a base for ice creams and gelatos. Or add caramel, chocolate, or fruit purees to make flavored custard sauces. Whisk a few more whole eggs into it, soak cubes of brioche or other bread in the mixture, then bake for a rich and silky bread pudding.

2 cups half-and-half or whole milk

1 vanilla bean, split, or 1 teaspoon pure vanilla extract

1/2 cup sugar

4 large egg yolks, at room temperature

1. In a medium-size, heavy saucepan, combine the half-and-half and vanilla bean and simmer over medium-low heat just until small bubbles appear around the rim, about 5 minutes. Keep warm.

2. Set a fine-mesh sieve over a medium-size, heatproof bowl and place the bowl into a shallow pan of cold water.

3. Meanwhile, in another medium-size bowl, whisk the sugar with the egg yolks just until combined. Whisking the egg yolks constantly, add half of the hot liquid in a thin stream.

Return the mixture to the saucepan, whisking well. Cook the custard gently over medium heat, stirring with a wooden spoon, without boiling, until thickened slightly, about 5 minutes. The custard should coat the back of the wooden spoon and leave a distinct line when you run your finger across the back of the spoon.

4. Immediately strain the sauce into the bowl in the cold water bath to stop the cooking. Scrape the seeds of the vanilla bean into the sauce (or add the vanilla extract) and refrigerate until chilled before serving. Will keep, tightly covered, in the refrigerator for up to 3 days.

CARAMEL CRÈME ANGLAISE

MAKES ABOUT 2 1/2 CUPS

A GREAT WAY to use up any leftover caramel sauce, this sauce is a lighter version of Dulce de Leche (page 363), but is just as yummy. It makes an incredible sauce for ice cream as well as for cakes, puddings, and fruit desserts such as poached pears, quinces, and figs, or sautéed bananas or pineapple.

> 1/2 cup Caramel Sauce (page 360)
> 1 recipe Crème Anglaise (page 367), warmed

In a small saucepan, warm the caramel sauce over medium heat until pourable. Whisk the caramel sauce into the warm crème anglaise, and refrigerate until chilled before using. Will keep, tightly covered, in the refrigerator for up to 3 days.

CHOCOLATE CUSTARD SAUCE

MAKES ABOUT 2 1/2 CUPS

SOME CHOCOLATE CUSTARD recipes call for cocoa, but I think bittersweet chocolate, with its just-right balance of sweetness and bitterness, adds more richness and depth to crème anglaise. Serve this warm or chilled with cakes, custards, puddings, ice cream, and poached pears. It makes a terrific ice cream, too!

> 4 ounces bittersweet chocolate, finely chopped
> 2 tablespoons water
> 2 cups half-and-half or milk
> 1 vanilla bean, split, or 1 teaspoon pure vanilla extract
> 1/2 cup sugar
> 4 large egg yolks, at room temperature
> Pinch of salt

1. In a small, heavy saucepan, melt the chocolate with the water over low heat, then remove from the heat.

2. In a medium-size, heavy saucepan, combine the half-and-half with the vanilla bean and simmer over medium-low heat just until small bubbles appear around the rim, about 5 minutes. Stir in the melted chocolate and keep warm.

3. Set a fine-mesh sieve over a medium-size, heatproof bowl and set the bowl in a shallow pan of cold water.

4. Meanwhile, in another medium-size bowl, whisk the sugar, egg yolks, and salt together just

until combined. Whisking the egg yolks constantly, add half of the hot liquid in a thin stream. Return the mixture to the saucepan, whisking well. Cook the custard gently over medium heat, stirring with a wooden spoon, without boiling, until thickened slightly, about 5 minutes. The custard should coat the back of the wooden spoon and leave a distinct line when you run your finger across the back of the spoon.

5. Immediately strain the sauce into the bowl set in the cold water bath to stop the cooking. Scrape the seeds of the vanilla bean into the sauce (or stir in the vanilla extract) and refrigerate until chilled before serving. Will keep, tightly covered, in the refrigerator for up to 3 days.

TURNING SAUCE INTO ICE CREAM

Crème anglaise is the base for rich French-style ice creams. All of the crème anglaise sauces in this chapter make terrific ice cream. To do so, let the sauce cool, then freeze it according to the manufacturer's instructions for your particular ice cream maker.

PISTACHIO CRÈME ANGLAISE

MAKES 2 CUPS

AS I WAS searching for a decent pistachio ice cream—not the kind with mushy nuts and alien-scary green color—I sort of stumbled upon this sauce. It's only ever so slightly green, but full of real pistachio flavor. Serve it with poached, roasted, or sautéed fruit; bread puddings; pound cakes; or, of course, turn it into ice cream. You'll need to add some finely chopped toasted pistachios near the end of the freezing cycle.

> 1/2 cup shelled raw, dye-free pistachios
> 2 1/4 cups half-and-half or whole milk
> 1 vanilla bean, split lengthwise, or 1 teaspoon pure vanilla extract
> 1/2 cup sugar
> 4 large egg yolks, at room temperature
> 1 tablespoon amaretto or other nut-flavored liqueur

1. Preheat the oven to 350°F. Put the pistachios in a pie plate and toast until fragrant and lightly browned, about 7 minutes. Let them cool, then coarsely chop the nuts.

2. Place the nuts in a medium-size, heavy saucepan, add the half-and-half and vanilla bean, and simmer over medium-low heat just until small bubbles appear around the rim, about 5 minutes. Turn off the heat, cover, and let steep for 30 minutes. Set a fine-mesh sieve over a medium-size bowl and strain the liquid, pressing hard on the solids to extract as much of the cream as possible. Discard the pistachios.

3. Wipe out the saucepan and return the cream and vanilla bean to it. Keep warm. Rinse the sieve and bowl. Set the sieve over the bowl and place the bowl into a shallow pan of cold water.

4. Meanwhile, in another medium-size bowl, whisk the sugar with the egg yolks just until combined. Whisking the egg yolks constantly, add half of the warm liquid in a thin stream. Return the mixture to the saucepan, whisking well. Cook the custard gently over medium heat, stirring with a wooden spoon, without boiling,

until thickened slightly, about 5 minutes. The custard should coat the back of the wooden spoon and leave a distinct line when you run your finger across the back of the spoon.

5. Immediately strain the sauce into the bowl set in the cold water bath to stop the cooking. Scrape the seeds of the vanilla bean into the sauce (or add the vanilla extract), stir in the liqueur, let cool, and refrigerate until chilled before serving. Will keep, tightly covered, in the refrigerator for up to 3 days.

TIPS FOR MAKING CRÈME ANGLAISE

- Always use a heavy-bottomed saucepan. This will ensure even cooking.

- Before you start, prepare an ice water bath in a large bowl and have a smaller bowl with a strainer set in it nearby. Having this step done in advance will prevent the likelihood of overcooking your sauce (and scrambling the eggs). Once the sauce overcooks and the eggs scramble, there is nothing you can do except start over.

- Don't walk away, answer the phone or the door, etc., while the custard is cooking. It needs constant attention (even if only for the 5 minutes it takes to cook).

- When adding the smallish amount of hot liquid to the egg mixture (called tempering), whisk constantly and add it in a steady stream. (It's not as slowly as you would add oil to mayonnaise, but it's not in one quick pour either.) This step gently heats the eggs and thins them out just enough to add to the remaining hot milk, making it easier to incorporate them without scrambling.

- Switch to a wooden spoon once the tempered eggs have completely been incorporated. A whisk may add too much air, making the sauce foamy. The foam will dissipate once the sauce cooks and thickens, but it's easier to tell it is done without having to push aside the foam.

ESPRESSO CRÈME ANGLAISE

MAKES ABOUT 2½ CUPS

THROW THIS SAUCE in the ice cream maker, following the manufacturer's instructions, for a truly delicious coffee ice cream. Toward the end of the freezing time, add some chopped bittersweet chocolate for coffee–chocolate chip. Of course, it's great as is, especially poured over a molten chocolate cake or cinnamony bread pudding.

2 cups half-and-half or whole milk

1 vanilla bean, split, or 1 teaspoon pure vanilla extract

¼ cup strong brewed espresso

½ cup sugar

4 large egg yolks, at room temperature

1. In a medium-size, heavy saucepan, combine the half-and-half and vanilla bean and simmer over medium-low heat just until small bubbles appear around the rim, about 5 minutes. Keep warm.

2. Set a fine-mesh sieve over a medium-size, heatproof bowl and place the bowl into a shallow pan of cold water.

3. Meanwhile, in another medium-size bowl, whisk the espresso, sugar, and egg yolks together just until combined. Whisking the egg yolks constantly, add half of the hot half-and-half in a thin stream. Return the mixture to the saucepan, whisking well. Cook the custard gently over medium heat, stirring with a wooden spoon, without boiling, until thickened slightly, about 5 minutes. The custard should coat the back of the wooden spoon and leave a distinct line when you run your finger across the back of the spoon.

4. Immediately strain the sauce into the bowl set in the cold water bath to stop the cooking. Scrape the seeds of the vanilla bean into the sauce (or add the vanilla extract) and refrigerate until chilled before serving. Will keep, tightly covered, in the refrigerator for up to 3 days.

COCONUT CRÈME ANGLAISE

MAKES ABOUT 1½ CUPS

USING CREAM OF COCONUT, a key ingredient in piña coladas, makes this an incredibly luscious custard sauce. It is the perfect foil for grilled or roasted pineapple or bananas, sliced fresh mangoes and strawberries, tropical fruit sorbets or custards, tarts, and puddings. Or make a double batch for an incredible ice cream.

1 cup half-and-half or whole milk

½ cup canned cream of coconut (like Coco Lopez)

1 vanilla bean, split lengthwise, or 1 teaspoon pure vanilla extract

¼ cup sugar

2 large egg yolks, at room temperature

1. In a medium-size, heavy saucepan, combine the half-and-half, cream of coconut, and vanilla bean and simmer over medium-low heat just until small bubbles appear around the rim, about 5 minutes. Keep warm.

2. Set a fine-mesh sieve over a medium-size, heatproof bowl and place the bowl into a shallow pan of cold water.

3. Meanwhile, in another medium-size bowl, whisk the sugar with the egg yolks just until combined. Whisking the egg yolks constantly, add half of the hot liquid in a thin stream. Return the mixture to the saucepan, whisking well. Cook the custard gently over medium heat, stirring with a wooden spoon, without boiling, until thickened slightly, about 5 minutes. The custard should coat the back of the wooden spoon and leave a distinct line when you run your finger across the back of the spoon.

4. Immediately strain the sauce into the bowl set in the cold water bath to stop the cooking. Scrape the seeds of the vanilla bean into the sauce (or add the vanilla extract) and refrigerate until chilled before serving. Will keep, tightly covered, in the refrigerator for up to 3 days.

GINGER CRÈME ANGLAISE

MAKES ABOUT 2 1/4 CUPS

WILLIAMS-SONOMA'S CRYSTALLIZED ginger from Australia has a peppery bite and an intense, flowery fragrance—perfect for this custard sauce. It makes an incredible ice cream, especially when you stir in a little extra minced crystallized ginger after it's frozen. Of course, it's great on its own as a sauce for cakes, tarts, fresh and cooked fruit, and warm bread puddings.

2 cups half-and-half

1/4 cup finely chopped crystallized ginger

One 1/2-inch piece peeled fresh ginger, thinly sliced

1 vanilla bean, split lengthwise, or 1 teaspoon pure vanilla extract

1/2 cup sugar

4 large egg yolks, at room temperature

13 BEST SAUCES TO DRIZZLE OVER POUND CAKE

1. In a medium-size, heavy saucepan, combine the half-and-half, crystallized and fresh ginger, and vanilla bean and simmer over medium-low heat just until small bubbles appear around the rim, about 5 minutes. Keep warm.

2. Set a fine-mesh sieve over a medium-size, heatproof bowl and place the bowl into a shallow pan of cold water.

3. Meanwhile, in another medium-size bowl, whisk the sugar with the egg yolks just until combined. Whisking the egg yolks constantly, add half of the hot half-and-half in a thin stream. Return the mixture to the saucepan, whisking well. Cook the custard gently over medium heat, stirring with a wooden spoon, without boiling, until thickened slightly, about 5 minutes. The custard should coat the back of the wooden spoon and leave a distinct line when you run your finger across the back of the spoon.

4. Immediately strain the sauce into the bowl set in the cold water bath, pressing hard on the solids to stop the cooking. Scrape the seeds of the vanilla bean into the sauce (or add the vanilla extract) and refrigerate until chilled before serving. Will keep, tightly covered, in the refrigerator for up to 3 days.

LEMONGRASS CRÈME ANGLAISE

MAKES ABOUT 2 1/4 CUPS

LEMONGRASS, GINGER, AND lime leaves add a subtle, delicate fragrance to this East-West crème anglaise. All are available in Asian markets and some large supermarkets. If you can't find lime leaves, use 1 X 2-inch strips of lime zest that you've removed using a vegetable peeler. This sauce makes an exotic, tropical ice cream as well as a sauce for fresh or cooked fruit, tarts, cakes, and puddings.

2 cups half-and-half or whole milk

2 stalks lemongrass, the bottom 4 inches, crushed

One 1/2-inch piece peeled fresh ginger, thinly sliced and lightly crushed

2 kaffir lime leaves, lightly crushed, or 2 strips lime zest (see headnote)

1 vanilla bean, split lengthwise, or 1 teaspoon pure vanilla extract

1/2 cup sugar

4 large egg yolks, at room temperature

1. In a medium-size, heavy saucepan, combine the half-and-half, lemongrass, ginger, lime leaves, and vanilla bean and simmer over medium-low heat just until small bubbles appear around the rim, about 5 minutes. Turn off the heat, cover, and let steep for 30 minutes. Strain the liquid through a fine-mesh sieve, pressing hard on the solids to extract as much of the liquid as possible. Wipe out the saucepan and return the half-and-half to it. Heat until small bubbles appear around the rim. Keep warm.

2. Rinse out the sieve, set it over a medium-size, heatproof bowl, and place the bowl into a shallow pan of cold water.

3. Meanwhile, in another medium-size bowl, whisk the sugar with the egg yolks just until combined. Whisking the egg yolks constantly, add half of the hot half-and-half in a thin stream. Return the mixture to the saucepan, whisking well. Cook the custard gently over medium heat, stirring with a wooden spoon, without boiling, until thickened slightly, about 5 minutes. The custard should coat the back of the wooden spoon and leave a distinct line when you run your finger across the back of the spoon.

4. Immediately strain the sauce into the bowl set in the cold water bath, pressing hard on the solids to stop the cooking. Scrape the seeds of the vanilla bean into the sauce (or add the vanilla extract) and refrigerate until chilled before serving. Will keep, tightly covered, in the refrigerator for up to 3 days.

HAZELNUT CRÈME ANGLAISE

MAKES ABOUT 2 CUPS

TOASTED HAZELNUTS AND hazelnut liqueur lend a fragrant richness that makes this custard sauce almost too good. I love it with chocolate cake, bread pudding, and especially as an ice cream.

> 1/2 cup hazelnuts
> 2 1/4 cups half-and-half or whole milk
> 1 vanilla bean, split lengthwise, or
>   1 teaspoon pure vanilla extract
> 1/2 cup sugar
> 4 large egg yolks, at room temperature
> 2 tablespoons hazelnut liqueur

1. Preheat the oven to 350°F. Put the hazelnuts in a pie plate and toast until fragrant and the skins begin to blister, about 12 minutes. Remove from the oven, let cool a bit, and finely chop the nuts.

2. Place the nuts in a medium-size, heavy saucepan, add the half-and-half and vanilla bean, and simmer over medium-low heat just until small bubbles appear around the rim, about 5 minutes. Remove from the heat, cover, and let steep for 30 minutes.

3. Set a fine-mesh sieve over a medium-size, heatproof bowl and strain the half-and-half, pressing hard on the solids to extract as much of the liquid as possible. Discard the hazelnuts.

4. Wipe out the saucepan and return the liquid and vanilla bean to it. Keep warm. Rinse the sieve and bowl. Set the sieve over the bowl and place the bowl into a shallow pan of cold water.

5. Meanwhile, in another medium-size bowl, whisk the sugar with the egg yolks just until combined. Whisking the egg yolks constantly, add half of the warm liquid in a thin stream. Return the mixture to the saucepan, whisking well. Cook the custard gently over medium heat, stirring with a wooden spoon, without boiling, until thickened slightly, 4 to 5 minutes. The custard should coat the back of the wooden spoon and leave a distinct line when you run your finger across the back of the spoon.

6. Immediately strain the sauce into the bowl set in the cold water bath to stop the cooking. Scrape the seeds of the vanilla bean into the sauce (or add the vanilla extract), stir in the liqueur, and refrigerate until chilled before serving. Will keep, tightly covered, in the refrigerator for up to 3 days.

CHUNKY BLUEBERRY SAUCE

MAKES 2 CUPS

SERVE THIS LUSCIOUS, slightly tart blueberry sauce warm or cold with ice cream, custards, or puddings; pancakes, waffles, or French toast; and simple cakes like angel food, chiffon, or pound cakes.

1/2 cup sugar
1/2 cup apple juice or white grape juice
1 teaspoon finely grated lemon zest
1/8 teaspoon ground cinnamon
1 pint fresh or individually frozen blueberries (not in syrup)
1/2 teaspoon cornstarch dissolved in 1 teaspoon water
1 tablespoon fresh lemon juice

1. In a medium-size, heavy saucepan, combine the sugar, apple juice, lemon zest, and cinnamon and bring to a boil, stirring until the sugar dissolves. Add the blueberries and cook over medium heat, lightly crushing the berries, until softened, about 10 minutes.

2. Stir the cornstarch into the sauce and cook until thickened slightly and glossy, about 2 minutes longer. Stir in the lemon juice and remove from the heat. Will keep, tightly covered, in the refrigerator for up to 2 weeks.

STRAWBERRY-RHUBARB SAUCE

MAKES ABOUT 1½ CUPS

THE COMBINATION OF strawberries and rhubarb is classically American—and one I like to use in sweet as well as savory preparations. Here it is a dessert sauce, but with a few tablespoons less sugar, it can be used with roasted pork, game, and poultry. Serve it fully sugared with bread puddings, dumplings, tapioca or rice pudding, custards, tarts, and ice cream.

> ½ pound rhubarb, leaves removed and stalks cut into 1-inch pieces
>
> 1 pint strawberries, hulled and thickly sliced
>
> ¾ cup sugar
>
> ¼ cup water
>
> Seeds from ½ vanilla bean, or ½ teaspoon pure vanilla extract

1. Combine all the ingredients in a medium-size, heavy saucepan and let sit for 1 hour, until the fruit is very juicy.

2. Bring to a boil, stirring constantly, and cook over medium heat until the fruit is broken down, about 20 minutes. Discard the vanilla bean.

3. Transfer to a blender or food processor and process until smooth. Strain the sauce through a fine-mesh sieve, pressing hard and scraping the solids to extract as much of the liquid as possible. Serve warm or chilled. Will keep, tightly covered, in the refrigerator for up to 1 week.

LEMON CURD SAUCE

MAKES ABOUT 1 CUP

THIS SAUCE IS more pourable than a standard lemon curd, so it's well suited for serving either warm or chilled on ice creams, custards, fruit desserts, gingerbread, angel food, or plain pound cakes. I also like it with waffles or French toast.

> ½ cup water
>
> ½ cup sugar
>
> Pinch of salt
>
> Finely grated zest of 1 lemon
>
> 1 tablespoon cornstarch dissolved in 2 tablespoons water
>
> ¼ cup fresh lemon juice
>
> 1 large egg yolk
>
> 1 tablespoon unsalted butter

1. In a medium-size, heavy saucepan, combine the water, sugar, salt, and lemon zest. Whisk the cornstarch into the saucepan and bring to a boil over medium heat. Cook, stirring, until thickened and glossy, about 2 minutes.

2. In a small bowl, whisk the lemon juice with the egg yolk. Whisking constantly, add a few tablespoons of the hot mixture to the egg, then return the mixture to the saucepan and, whisking constantly, bring to a simmer and cook for 2 minutes. Add the butter and stir until melted and well incorporated. Strain the sauce through a fine-mesh sieve to remove the lemon zest, if desired. Let cool, then refrigerate until chilled or serve warm. Will keep, tightly covered, in the refrigerator for up to 4 days.

FRESH CHERRY SAUCE

MAKES ABOUT 1 1/2 CUPS

SOUR CHERRIES HAVE such a short season that when they do appear in early June, it's like a feeding frenzy at my house—jams, compotes, pies, and sauces are always working. Use a cherry or olive pitter to remove the stones or the fat end of a chopstick. Frozen sour cherries are available by mail order from Friske Orchards in Michigan (see page 387). Serve this versatile, sweet-tangy sauce with ice cream; custards and puddings; angel food, chiffon, and pound cakes; molten chocolate cake; crepes; and waffles—go wild.

- 1 pound fresh sour cherries, pitted, or one 10-ounce bag individually frozen pitted cherries
- 1 cup sugar
- 2 teaspoons cornstarch dissolved in 1 1/2 tablespoons water
- 1/4 teaspoon pure almond extract (optional)

1. In a medium-size, heavy saucepan, combine the cherries and sugar and let sit until the cherries are very juicy, about 30 minutes.

2. Bring to a boil, stirring until the sugar is dissolved. Reduce the heat to medium and simmer until the cherries are softened and translucent and the liquid is slightly reduced, about 20 minutes. Stir the cornstarch into the cherries and simmer until thickened and glossy, about 3 minutes longer. Stir in the almond extract and remove from the heat. Serve warm, at room temperature, or chilled. Will keep, tightly covered, in the refrigerator for up to 1 week.

SOUR CHERRY– BALSAMIC DESSERT SAUCE

MAKES ABOUT 3/4 CUP

AGED BALSAMIC VINEGAR and dried tart cherries come together to create an elegant and sophisticated sauce that goes well with vanilla ice cream, panna cotta, flan, custards, and other milky desserts, but I also like it with poached pears or roasted bananas or even savory roasted duck or pork. Using a flavored balsamic vinegar, such as cherry, pomegranate, or fig, will add another dimension.

- 1/2 cup dried tart cherries, coarsely chopped
- 1 cup warm water
- 1/4 cup sugar
- 1/4 cup aged balsamic vinegar
- 1/4 teaspoon cornstarch dissolved in 1 teaspoon water
- 1 teaspoon pure vanilla extract

1. In a medium-size, heavy saucepan, soak the cherries in the water until plump, about 20 minutes.

2. Add the sugar and vinegar and simmer over medium-low heat until the liquid is reduced to a thin syrup, about 10 minutes. Add the cornstarch slurry and simmer until slightly thickened and glossy, about 2 minutes longer. Stir in the vanilla and serve warm. Will keep, tightly covered, in the refrigerator for up to 4 days.

COCONUT-MANGO
TAPIOCA SAUCE

MAKES ABOUT 1 1/2 CUPS

TRENDY TAPIOCA PEARL drinks are the inspiration for this coconut dessert sauce. The large balls of tapioca floating in the drink have an intriguing, chewy texture. Serve this cool, tropical sauce with custards and puddings and pineapple, mango, melon, and strawberries. You can substitute pineapple juice, passion-fruit juice, or apricot nectar for the mango, or simply use water for a more intense coconut flavor.

    1/4 cup large pearl tapioca (look for it near
        the Jell-O in the supermarket)
    1 cup cold water
    1/2 cup canned cream of coconut (like Coco
        Lopez)
    1 cup mango juice
    1 1/2 teaspoons fresh lime juice
    Pinch of freshly grated nutmeg

1. In a medium-size bowl, cover the tapioca with the cold water and refrigerate overnight. Drain well.

2. In a medium-size, heavy saucepan, combine the cream of coconut, 3/4 cup of the mango juice, and drained tapioca and bring to a boil. Reduce the heat to medium and simmer until the tapioca is translucent throughout and the liquid is slightly thickened, 10 to 12 minutes.

3. Let cool, then stir in the remaining 1/4 cup mango juice, the lime juice, and the nutmeg and refrigerate until chilled before serving. Will keep, tightly covered, in the refrigerator for up to 4 days.

PINEAPPLE-GINGER
DESSERT SAUCE

MAKES ABOUT 1 3/4 CUPS

I MUCH PREFER the flavor of fresh pineapple and juice here, but canned pineapple juice and slices packed in natural juice are fine in a pinch. Serve this chunky pineapple sauce hot or cold on ice cream—add a banana, some whipped cream, and, of course, a cherry for a real grown-up sundae. It's also very nice warmed, with warm bread puddings, roasted bananas and custards, puddings, or panna cotta.

    1 cup finely chopped pineapple
    1 cup pineapple juice
    1/2 cup sugar
    1 1/2 tablespoons minced crystallized ginger
    1 1/2 teaspoons cornstarch dissolved in
        1 tablespoon water

In a medium-size, heavy saucepan, combine the pineapple and juice, sugar, and ginger and simmer over medium heat until the pineapple is softened and broken down and the juice is reduced by about two thirds, 5 to 6 minutes. Stir in the cornstarch and cook until thickened and glossy. Will keep, tightly covered, in the refrigerator for up to 4 days.

PIÑA COLADA DESSERT SAUCE

MAKES ABOUT 2 CUPS

FRESH PINEAPPLE HAS a more intense fruit flavor and is a bit more tart than canned pineapple. I think both work just fine here. Cream of coconut (like Coco Lopez) is a canned sweetened coconut milk found in the Latin section of the supermarket and is used for making piña coladas. Serve this oh-so-tropical sauce with ice creams, puddings, custards, cakes, tarts, and fruit desserts. Or try freezing it to make sorbet.

1 cup pineapple juice

1 cup canned cream of coconut

2/3 cup finely chopped pineapple

1 1/2 teaspoons cornstarch dissolved in 1 tablespoon water

2 tablespoons light rum

1 tablespoon fresh lime juice

1. In a medium-size, heavy saucepan, combine the pineapple juice, cream of coconut, and pineapple and bring to a boil. Reduce the heat to medium and simmer until reduced by a quarter, about 5 minutes. Transfer the sauce to a blender and process until smooth.

2. Wipe out the saucepan and strain the sauce back into it through a fine-mesh sieve, pressing hard and scraping the solids to remove any tough fibers. Add the cornstarch and simmer over medium heat until thickened and glossy, about 2 minutes longer. Stir in the rum and lime juice, let cool, and refrigerate until chilled. Will keep, covered, in the refrigerator for up to 4 days.

GINGER-BLUEBERRY COULIS

MAKES ABOUT 1 1/4 CUPS

A BEAUTIFUL, DEEP-PURPLE color and with a sweet-tart flavor, this blueberry sauce is perfect with pear tart, pound cake, vanilla ice cream, creamy panna cotta, or any coconut or vanilla custard or pudding. It's also great with fruit sorbets or fruit salads, but for an interesting twist, I sometimes like to serve this sauce with grilled or roasted chicken or pork. Chewy ginger candies, called Ting Ting, come from Southeast Asia and can be found in Asian markets and specialty candy shops.

1 pint fresh or individually frozen blueberries, thawed if necessary

1/2 cup sugar

3 chewy ginger candies, finely diced, or 2 tablespoons minced crystallized ginger

1/2 cup apple juice

Pinch of salt

1 1/2 teaspoons cornstarch dissolved in 1 tablespoon water

1. In a medium-size, heavy saucepan, combine the blueberries, sugar, ginger candies, apple juice, and salt and, using a potato masher or fork, crush the blueberries. Let the mixture sit until the berries are very juicy, about 1 hour.

2. Bring to a boil, then reduce the heat to medium-low and simmer, crushing the berries occasionally, until they are broken down and the ginger candy, if using, is melted, about 5 minutes.

3. Transfer the sauce to a blender and process until smooth. Strain the sauce into a heatproof bowl, pressing hard and scraping the solids to extract as much of the liquid as possible.

4. Wipe out the saucepan and return the strained puree to it. Add the cornstarch and simmer over medium-low heat until thickened and glossy, about 5 minutes. Serve warm or chilled. Will keep, tightly covered, in the refrigerator for up to 1 week.

BEST SAUCES TO TURN INTO ICE CREAM OR SORBET

See Turning Sauce into Ice Cream (page 369) for directions on doing this.

Ice Cream:

- All of the crème anglaise–custard sauces (pages 367–374)
- Piña Colada Dessert Sauce (page 379)

Sorbet:

- Ginger-Blueberry Coulis (page 379)
- Honey-Pear Coulis (page 383)
- Midori Melon Coulis (page 384)

RASPBERRY COULIS

MAKES ABOUT 1 1/2 CUPS

THIS VERSATILE SAUCE is great with fruit desserts, chocolate desserts, custards, sorbets, ice creams, you name it. Frozen raspberries are preferable to (and a lot cheaper than) fresh. Any leftover sauce can be made into smoothies.

> One 10-ounce package frozen raspberries in syrup, thawed
> 1/4 cup sugar
> 1/2 cup water
> 1 1/2 teaspoons cornstarch dissolved in 1 1/2 tablespoons water
> 1 tablespoon Chambord or framboise liqueur (optional)

1. In a large saucepan, combine the raspberries, sugar, and water and bring to a boil. Reduce the heat to medium-low and simmer, crushing the berries, until they are completely broken down, about 15 minutes.

2. Strain the berries through a fine-mesh sieve set over a bowl, scraping and pressing hard on the solids to remove the seeds.

3. Wipe out the saucepan and return the raspberry juice to it. Add the cornstarch and simmer over medium-low heat until slightly thickened, about 5 minutes. Let cool, then stir in the Chambord, if using. Refrigerate until chilled before serving. Will keep, tightly covered, in the refrigerator for up to 3 days.

STRAWBERRY COULIS

MAKES ABOUT 1½ CUPS

I LOVE THIS sauce over strawberry shortcake, but it's also terrific on vanilla ice cream, lemon sorbet, or frozen sliced bananas.

½ cup water

½ cup sugar

1 pint ripe strawberries, hulled and thickly sliced

½ teaspoon cornstarch dissolved in 1 tablespoon water

1 tablespoon fresh lemon juice

1. In a medium-size saucepan, combine the water and sugar and bring to a boil, stirring until the sugar dissolves.

2. Transfer the mixture to a blender, add the strawberries, and process until smooth. Strain the strawberries through a fine-mesh sieve, scraping and pressing hard on the solids to remove the tiny seeds.

3. Return the puree to the saucepan, add the cornstarch, and simmer over medium-low heat just until thickened and glossy, about 2 minutes.

4. Remove from the heat, let cool, then stir in the lemon juice. Skim any foam the rises to the surface. Refrigerate until chilled before serving. Will keep, tightly covered, in the refrigerator for up to 4 days.

AMARETTO-PEACH COULIS

MAKES ABOUT 1½ CUPS

THE FLAVORS OF peach and almond complement each other exceedingly well in this exquisite dessert sauce. Summer is the only time to make it, when peaches are at their absolute best. The good thing, though, is that it freezes really well, so you can serve it in the middle of winter—just when you're craving anything that even remotely hints at summer. This is best enjoyed on ice cream, custards, pound cake, and bread pudding.

1 pound ripe peaches

½ cup water

½ cup sugar

1 tablespoon fresh lemon juice

2 tablespoons amaretto liqueur

1. Bring a large pot of water to a boil and fill a large bowl with ice water. Using a sharp knife, make a shallow X in the bottom of each peach. Put the peaches in the boiling water and cook for 1 minute. Using a slotted spoon, transfer the peaches to the ice water bath to chill until they are cool enough to handle. Peel the peaches and remove the stones.

2. Thickly slice the peaches, put them in a medium-size saucepan along with the water, sugar, and lemon juice, and bring to a boil. Reduce the heat to low, cover, and simmer until the peaches are very soft, 15 to 20 minutes.

3. Transfer the peaches and their liquid to a blender and process until smooth. Strain the sauce through a fine-mesh sieve, stir in the amaretto, and refrigerate until chilled. Stir in a tablespoon or two of water if the puree is very thick. Will keep, tightly covered, in the refrigerator for up to 2 days or in the freezer for several months.

8 SUPER BREAKFAST SAUCES

Forget about maple syrup on your pancakes, French toast, and waffles! Serve each of these great sauces warm, except for Lemon Curd Sauce.

1. Bay-Scented Plum Coulis (right)

2. Chunky Blueberry Sauce (page 375)

3. Fresh Cherry Sauce (page 377)

4. Ginger-Blueberry Coulis (page 379)

5. Lemon Curd Sauce (page 376)

6. Maple-Cider Nut Sauce (page 364)

7. Pineapple-Ginger Dessert Sauce (page 378)

8. Strawberry-Rhubarb Sauce (page 376)

BAY-SCENTED PLUM COULIS

MAKES ABOUT 1½ CUPS

I PREFER RED or purple plums for this sauce because they're juicy and tart and a perfect accompaniment for ice cream. Serve with pound cake, puddings, custards, and panna cotta.

¾ pound plums, pitted and coarsely chopped
¼ cup plus 2 tablespoons sugar
½ cup water
2 bay leaves
Three 1 x 3-inch strips lemon zest
1 tablespoon fresh lemon juice
½ teaspoon cornstarch dissolved in 1 tablespoon water

1. In a medium-size saucepan, combine the plums, sugar, water, bay leaves, and lemon zest and bring to a boil. Reduce the heat to low and simmer until the plums are softened, 15 to 20 minutes.

2. Remove the bay leaves and lemon strips (don't throw away the bay leaves), transfer the mixture to a blender, and process until smooth. Return the sauce to the saucepan along with the lemon juice and cornstarch and simmer over medium heat until thickened and glossy, about 2 minutes.

3. Return the bay leaves to the sauce and refrigerate until chilled. Stir in a tablespoon or two of water if the sauce seems too thick. Discard the bay leaves before serving. Will keep, tightly covered, in the refrigerator for up to 4 days or in the freezer for several months.

COCONUT-MANGO COULIS

MAKES ABOUT 2 CUPS

I LOVE TO serve this sauce over candied ginger scones topped with sliced mangoes and whipped cream for a tropical twist on strawberry short-cake. Coconut juice, the water from fresh coconuts, is available in Asian markets or in the Latin foods section of supermarkets. I like it better than coconut milk for this recipe because it's lighter and fresher tasting. Any leftover coulis makes a great sorbet.

- 1½ cups canned coconut juice (*not* coconut milk)
- 1 large ripe mango, peeled, pitted, and cut into ½-inch pieces
- ¼ cup plus 2 tablespoons sugar
- 2 tablespoons fresh lime juice
- ½ teaspoon peeled and finely grated fresh ginger

1. In a medium-size saucepan, combine 1 cup of the coconut juice with the mango, sugar, lime juice, and ginger and bring to a boil. Reduce the heat to low and simmer until the mango is very tender and the liquid slightly reduced, about 15 minutes.

2. Transfer the mixture to a blender, add the remaining ½ cup coconut juice, and process until smooth. Let cool to room temperature, then refrigerate until chilled. Stir in a tablespoon or two of water if the sauce is very thick. Will keep, tightly covered, in the refrigerator for up to 4 days or in the freezer for several months.

HONEY-PEAR COULIS

MAKES ABOUT 2 CUPS

I USUALLY HAVE a little leftover dessert wine on hand and I'm always on the lookout for ways to use it up. Here it adds a sweetness that echoes the flavor of the ripe pears. When the weather gets cold, I love to serve this aromatic autumn fruit sauce warm with poached dried fruit and creamy mascarpone. But I also like it frozen as a granita, and served with crème fraîche. Bartlett, Comice, or Anjou is my pear choice here, since each of them has a silky texture and heady perfume. Just be sure that the pears are ripe.

- 3 ripe pears, peeled, cored, and thickly sliced
- ¾ cup dessert wine, such as Beaumes de Venise, late-harvest Riesling, or Moscato
- 2 tablespoons honey
- 6 cloves
- ½ cinnamon stick
- 1½ teaspoons fresh lemon juice

1. In a medium-size saucepan, combine the pears, wine, honey, cloves, and cinnamon and bring to a boil. Reduce the heat to low, cover, and simmer until the pears are very soft, 15 to 20 minutes. Discard the cloves and cinnamon.

2. Transfer the mixture to a blender and process until smooth. Stir in the lemon juice. Will keep, tightly covered, in the refrigerator for up to 4 days or in the freezer for several months.

MIDORI MELON COULIS

MAKES ABOUT 1½ CUPS

A PERFECTLY RIPE honeydew melon has a most lovely perfume and sweet flavor. Midori, a melon liqueur, enhances the wonderful qualities of a good melon but gives a little boost to a not-so-good one. Try tossing sliced fresh peaches or another melon with this sauce for a refreshing, low-cal summer dessert. Or double the recipe and freeze it to make melon sorbet. Served as a sauce, this is best used the day it is made.

    2 cups seeded and diced (1-inch) ripe
       honeydew melon
    ¼ cup sugar
    2 tablespoons fresh lime juice
    2 tablespoons Midori liqueur
    1 teaspoon fresh mint leaves

Put all of the ingredients in a blender and process until smooth. Refrigerate until chilled before serving.

PASSION FRUIT COULIS

MAKES ABOUT ¾ CUP

PASSION FRUIT IS one of my absolute favorite tropical fruits. It's perfumey, sweet, and tart and can be used in sweet or savory dishes. A ripe passion fruit has brown, wrinkled skin but is soft and squishy on the inside. You'll know it's ripe by shaking it—if the insides slosh, it's ripe. Use this on ice cream, custard, panna cotta, or any other creamy dessert.

    ½ pound ripe passion fruit (about 6)
    ½ cup sugar
    ¼ cup plus 2 tablespoons water
    1½ teaspoons cornstarch dissolved in
       1 tablespoon water

1. Working over a strainer set over a bowl, split the passion fruit. Using a spoon or rubber spatula, press the seeds to release as much of the juice as possible. Discard the seeds.

2. In a small saucepan, combine the sugar and water and bring to a simmer over medium heat, stirring until the sugar is dissolved. Add the cornstarch to the syrup and cook until slightly thickened and glossy, about 2 minutes. Remove from the heat, let cool, then stir in the passion fruit. Refrigerate until chilled before serving. Will keep, tightly covered, in the refrigerator for up to 2 days.

MEASUREMENT EQUIVALENTS

Please note that all conversions are approximate.

LIQUID CONVERSIONS

U.S.	METRIC
1 tsp	5 ml
1 tbs	15 ml
2 tbs	30 ml
3 tbs	45 ml
¼ cup	60 ml
⅓ cup	75 ml
⅓ cup + 1 tbs	90 ml
⅓ cup + 2 tbs	100 ml
½ cup	120 ml
⅔ cup	150 ml
¾ cup	180 ml
¾ cup + 2 tbs	200 ml
1 cup	240 ml
1 cup + 2 tbs	275 ml
1¼ cups	300 ml
1⅓ cups	325 ml
1½ cups	350 ml
1⅔ cups	375 ml
1¾ cups	400 ml
1¾ cups + 2 tbs	450 ml
2 cups (1 pint)	475 ml
2½ cups	600 ml
3 cups	720 ml
4 cups (1 quart)	945 ml
	(1,000 ml is 1 liter)

WEIGHT CONVERSIONS

U.S.	METRIC	U.S.	METRIC
½ oz	14 g	7 oz	200 g
1 oz	28 g	8 oz	227 g
1½ oz	43 g	9 oz	255 g
2 oz	57 g	10 oz	284 g
2½ oz	71 g	11 oz	312 g
3 oz	85 g	12 oz	340 g
3½ oz	100 g	13 oz	368 g
4 oz	113 g	14 oz	400 g
5 oz	142 g	15 oz	425 g
6 oz	170 g	1 lb	454 g

OVEN TEMPERATURE CONVERSIONS

°F	GAS MARK	°C
250	½	120
275	1	140
300	2	150
325	3	165
350	4	180
375	5	190
400	6	200
425	7	220
450	8	230
475	9	240
500	10	260
550	Broil	290

INTERNET AND MAIL-ORDER SUPPLIERS

Adriana's Caravan
Grand Central Terminal
Grand Central Market
New York, NY 10017
(212) 972-8804
(800) 316-0820
www.AdrianasCaravan.com
Spices, ethnic ingredients, Asian, Mediterranean, and Middle Eastern ingredients.

Citarella
(212) 874-0383
www.citarella.com
Demi-glace, specialty, and gourmet ingredients.

The CMC Company
P.O. Drawer 322
Avalon, NJ 08202
(800) CMC-2780
Fax (609) 861-3065
www.thecmccompany.com
Latin American ingredients.

D'Artagnan
280 Wilson Avenue
Newark, NJ 07105
(800) DARTAGN
Fax (973) 465-1870
www.dartagnan.com
Duck, specialty poultry, and demi-glace.

Dean & Deluca
(877) 826-9246
Fax (800) 781-4050
www.deandeluca.com
Specialty and gourmet items, spices, and chocolates.

Earthy Delights
1161 E. Clark Road/Suite 260
DeWitt, MI 48820
(800) 367-4709
Fax (517) 668-1213
www.earthy.com
Spices and ethnic ingredients.

EthnicGrocer.com
www.ethnicgrocer.com
Ethnic and specialty ingredients and spices, especially Asian.

Friske Orchards
11027 Doctor Road
Charlevoix, MI 49720
(616) 588-6185
Frozen sour cherries.

Frieda's
(800) 421-9477
www.friedas.com
Specialty produce.

Indian Rock Produce
530 California Road
Quakertown, PA 18951
(800) 882-0512
Specialty produce.

Kalustyan's
123 Lexington Avenue
New York, NY 10016
(212) 685-3451
www.kalustyans.com
Mediterranean, Middle Eastern, and Asian ingredients, spices, prepared foods, breads, grains, and beans.

Katagiri & Co.
224 East 59th Street
New York, NY 10022
(212) 755-3566
Fax (212) 752-4197
www.katagiri.com
Japanese ingredients.

Kitchen/Market
218 Eighth Avenue
New York, NY 10011
(888) HOT-4433
www.KitchenMarket.com
Latin American specialty ingredients.

The Lee Bros. Boiled Peanuts Catalogue
P.O. Box 315
Charleston, SC 29402
(843) 720-8890
www.boiledpeanuts.com
Pickles, preserves, Southern specialties and staples, and, of course, boiled fresh peanuts.

Los Chileros de Nuevo Mexico Gourmet New Mexican Foods
P.O. Box 6215
Santa Fe, NM 87502
(505) 471-6967
Fax (505) 473-7306
www.hotchilepepper.com
Latin American specialty ingredients, dried chiles, posole, cornmeal, etc.

Marché Aux Delices
New York, NY 10028
(888) 547-5471
Fax (413) 604-2789
www.auxdelices.com
Mushrooms, French specialty ingredients.

Melissa's
P.O. Box 21127
Los Angeles, CA 90021
(800) 588-0151
www.melissas.com
Specialty produce.

Penzeys Spices
P.O. Box 933
Muskego, WI 53150
(800) 741-7787
Fax (262) 785-7678
www.penzeys.com
Common and hard-to-find seasonings.

The Spanish Table
(206) 682-2827 (Seattle)
(510) 548-1383 (Berkeley, CA)
(505) 986-0243 (Santa Fe)
www.spanishtable.com
Spanish ingredients: pimenton, piquillo peppers, oils, olives, etc.

Temple of Thai
P.O. Box 112
Carroll, IA 51401
(877) 811-8773
Fax (712) 792-0698
www.templeofthai.com
Southeast Asian ingredients.

Urbani Truffles and Caviar
380 Meadowbrook Road
North Wales, PA 19454
(215) 699-8780
Fax (215) 699-3859
www.urbani.com
Mushrooms, truffles and truffle products, specialty ingredients.

SAUCE INDEX BY SUGGESTED USE

SAUCES TO SERVE WITH BREAD, TORTILLAS, CHIPS, SANDWICHES, CROUTONS, AND CRACKERS

Sauces to Serve with Bread, Tortillas, etc. (*continued*)

Roasted Sweet Pepper Salsa (page 328)
Roquefort Mayonnaise (page 305)
Roquefort-Shallot Compound Butter (page 11)
Salsa of Fire-Roasted Chiles (page 328)
Scallion-Horseradish Compound Butter (page 12)
Scallion-Macadamia Pesto (page 116)
Shrimp Butter (page 9)
Smoky Eggplant Raita (page 236)
Smoky Pan-Blackened Tomato Sauce (page 87)
Smoky Roasted Tomato and Chipotle Salsa
    (page 319)
Spicy Coconut Curry Tomato Sauce (page 226)
Spinach-Pignoli Pesto with Raisins (page 107)

Spinach Raita with Toasted Spices (page 238)
Sun-Dried Tomato Aioli (page 313)
Sun-Dried Tomato Pesto (page 113)
Sweet and Sour Tamarind Sauce (page 256)
Sweet Pea Pesto with Chive Oil (page 108)
Tahini Dressing (page 290)
Tart Lime-Ginger Mayonnaise (page 299)
Thai Nam Pla Prik (Spicy Fish Sauce with Lime)
    (page 258)
Trinidadian Hot Pepper Sauce (page 353)
Vidalia Onion Ketchup (page 340)
Wild Mushroom and Herb Pesto (page 110)
Yogurt-Lime Dressing (page 295)

SAUCES TO TOSS WITH SALADS

Anchovy Aioli (page 311)
Black Olive Tapenade Aioli (page 311)
Chipotle Mayonnaise (page 303)
Easy Anchovy Mayonnaise (page 303)
Easy Tapenade Aioli (page 312)
Garlic Confit Aioli (page 313)
Green Onion Mayonnaise (page 302)
Gribiche Sauce (page 308)
Lemon Mayonnaise (page 300)
Pesto Mayonnaise (page 302)
Pistachio Yogurt Sauce (page 243)
Quick Hazelnut Mayonnaise (page 306)

Quick Herb Mayonnaise (page 307)
Radish-Cucumber Raita (page 233)
Roasted Red Pepper Mayonnaise (page 304)
Roquefort Mayonnaise (page 305)
Sun-Dried Tomato Aioli (page 313)
Tart Lime-Ginger Mayonnaise (page 299)
Vietnamese Fish Dipping Sauce (Nuoc Cham)
    (page 258)
Vietnamese Peanut Dipping Sauce (Nuoc Leo)
    (page 259)
All of the recipes in the Vinaigrettes and Dressings
    chapter (pages 262–295)

SAUCES TO SERVE WITH EGGS

Ancho Chile and Roasted Garlic Pesto with Piñons
    (page 116)
Anchovy Aioli (page 311)
Anchovy Butter (page 7)
Béarnaise (page 20)
Black Olive Tapenade Aioli (page 311)
Caper-Shallot Compound Butter (page 8)
Charred Garlic–Tomatillo Salsa (page 321)

Classic Chinese Brown Sauce (with a Chinese omelet)
    (page 143)
Corn and Black Bean Salsa (page 322)
Crispy Shallot Pesto (page 113)
Easy Anchovy Mayonnaise (page 303)
Easy Tapenade Aioli (page 312)
Fresh Pecorino Truffle Cream Sauce (page 46)
Fresh Tomatillo Salsa Verde (page 320)

Garlic Butter (page 5)

Green Chile Tomato Sauce (page 77)

Green Goddess Dressing (page 285)

Green Tomato Salsa (page 320)

Harissa (Moroccan Chile Paste) (page 352)

Hollandaise and all its variations (pages 17–21)

Lemon Mayonnaise (page 300)

Lowfat Goat Cheese–Buttermilk Dressing (page 288)

Mexican Tomato Sauce with Sofrito (page 81)

Mornay Sauce (Cheese Sauce) (page 32)

Pico de Gallo (page 318)

Piquillo Pepper Salsa (page 326)

Poblano-Lime Dressing (page 286)

Ranch Dressing (page 289)

Roasted Garlic Compound Butter (page 5)

Roasted Pepper, Avocado, and Corn Salsa (page 325)

Roasted Red Pepper Mayonnaise (page 304)

Roasted Sweet Pepper Salsa (page 328)

Salsa of Fire-Roasted Chiles (page 328)

Shrimp Butter (page 9)

Smoked Gouda Béchamel (page 32)

Smoky Roasted Tomato and Chipotle Salsa (page 319)

Sorrel Beurre Blanc (page 16)

Sun-Dried Tomato Aioli (page 313)

Tangy Herbed White Sauce (page 31)

Tomato Cream Sauce (page 86)

Trinidadian Hot Pepper Sauce (page 353)

Wild Mushroom and Herb Pesto (page 110)

Wild Mushroom Mascarpone Cream Sauce (page 36)

SAUCES TO PAIR WITH VEGETABLES

Ancho-Garlic–Pine Nut Compound Butter (page 6)

Anchoiade (page 106)

Anchovy Aioli (page 311)

Anchovy Butter (page 7)

Anchovy-Parsley Pesto (page 105)

Avgolemono (page 22)

Balsamic Vinaigrettes I & II (pages 262–263)

Basic Vinaigrette (page 262)

Béarnaise (page 20)

Beet Vinaigrette (page 263)

Black Olive Tapenade Aioli (page 311)

Black Truffle Vinaigrette (page 264)

Blue Cheese Dressing (page 276)

Bordelaise (Red Wine Brown Sauce) (page 168)

Caesar Dressing (page 277)

Caper Brown Butter Sauce (page 13)

Caper-Shallot Compound Butter (page 8)

Carrot-Ginger Dressing (page 279)

Cherry Balsamic Vinaigrette (page 265)

Chinese Black Bean Sauce (page 145)

Chinese-Style Garlic Sauce (page 143)

Chipotle Beurre Blanc (page 15)

Chipotle Mayonnaise (page 303)

Chipotle-Cilantro Compound Butter (page 8)

Chopped Olive Vinaigrette (page 264)

Cilantro-Mint Dipping Sauce (page 246)

Citrus Vinaigrette (page 265)

Classic Chinese Brown Sauce (page 143)

Classic Coleslaw Dressing (page 280)

Classic French Dressing (page 279)

Creamy Italian Dressing (page 280)

Creamy Lemon Dressing (page 281)

Creamy Orange-Fennel Vinaigrette (page 266)

Creamy Pesto Dressing (page 283)

Creamy Sesame Vinaigrette (page 273)

Creamy Sherry Vinegar Dressing (page 284)

Coconut-Peanut Stir-Fry Sauce (page 148)

Cold Sesame Sauce (page 69)

Crispy Shallot Pesto (page 113)

Cumin-Scented Carrot Raita (page 234)

Curried Chanterelle Cream Sauce (page 38)

Curry-Roasted Pumpkin Raita (page 234)

Curry-Yogurt Sauce (page 221)

Dijon Vinaigrette (page 267)

Easy Anchovy Mayonnaise (page 303)

Easy Tapenade Aioli (page 312)

Sauces to Pair with Vegetables *(continued)*

Eggless Caesar Dressing (page 277)
Fontina Cream Sauce (page 33)
Fried Ginger Stir-Fry Sauce (page 148)
Fried Sage and Caper Pesto with Fresh Pecorino
   (page 101)
Garlic Butter (page 5)
Garlic Confit Aioli (page 313)
Ginger-Soy Dressing (page 284)
Green Curry Stir-Fry Sauce (page 150)
Green Goddess Dressing (page 285)
Green Onion Mayonnaise (page 302)
Harissa (Moroccan Chile Paste) (page 352)
Herbed Compound Butter (page 11)
Hollandaise and all its variations (pages 17–21)
Homemade Tomato Ketchup (page 337)
Indonesian Peanut Dressing (Gado Gado) (page 286)
Lemon Mayonnaise (page 300)
Lowfat Goat Cheese–Buttermilk Dressing (page 288)
Lyonnaise (Onion-Flavored Brown Sauce) (page 167)
Madras Curry Marinade (page 180)
Mascarpone Cream Sauce (page 36)
Mint, Parsley, and Scallion Pesto (page 99)
Miso-Ginger Dressing (page 288)
Mornay Sauce (Cheese Sauce) (page 32)
Moroccan Preserved Lemon Aioli (page 312)
Mixed Citrus Vinaigrette (page 266)
Mustard Béchamel (page 28)
Oven-Dried Tomato and Garlic Pesto (page 114)
Oyster Stir-Fry Sauce (page 152)
Parsley Sauce (Salsa Verde) (page 104)
Pesto Mayonnaise (page 302)
Pico de Gallo (page 318)
Pignoli-Herb Sauce (page 98)
Piquant Orange Stir-Fry Sauce (page 152)
Piquillo Pepper Salsa (page 326)
Pistachio Yogurt Sauce (page 243)
Quick Hazelnut Mayonnaise (page 306)
Quick Herb Mayonnaise (page 307)
Red Chile Brown Butter Sauce (page 13)
Roasted Garlic Compound Butter (page 5)
Roasted Garlic Vinaigrette (page 271)

Roasted Lemon Vinaigrette (page 272)
Roasted Red Pepper Mayonnaise (page 304)
Roasted Red Pepper Pesto with Pecorino Pepato (page 109)
Roasted Red Pepper Vinaigrette (page 273)
Romesco (page 120)
Roquefort-Shallot Compound Butter (page 11)
Salsina Verde (page 104)
Scallion-Horseradish Compound Butter (page 12)
Scallion-Macadamia Pesto (page 116)
Sesame-Ginger Stir-Fry Sauce (page 153)
Shallot-Soy Vinaigrette (page 274)
Skordalia I (page 123)
Smoked Gouda Béchamel (page 32)
Smoky Eggplant Raita (page 236)
Spicy Coconut Curry Tomato Sauce (page 226)
Sorrel Beurre Blanc (page 16)
Soubise (Onion Sauce) (page 28)
Soy-Ginger Beurre Blanc (page 16)
Sun-Dried Tomato Aioli (page 313)
Sweet-and-Sour Stir-Fry Sauce (page 157)
Sweet Chile-Garlic Stir-Fry Sauce (page 156)
Sweet Thai Chile Dipping Sauce (page 255)
Tahini Dressing (page 290)
Tangy Herbed White Sauce (page 31)
Tangy Mustard Cream Sauce (page 38)
Tarragon-Shallot Dressing (page 290)
Tart Lemon-Herb Dressing (page 291)
Teriyaki Grilling Sauce (page 210)
Thai Basil–Nam Pla Stir-Fry Sauce (page 156)
Thai Herb-Lime Dressing (page 292)
Toasted Bread Crumb, Rosemary, and Parmesan Pesto
   (page 99)
Tomato-Soy Beurre Blanc (page 15)
Trinidadian Hot Pepper Sauce (page 353)
Vietnamese Fish Dipping Sauce (Nuoc Cham) (page 258)
Vietnamese Peanut Dipping Sauce (Nuoc Leo)
   (page 259)
West African Spiced Curry Tomato Sauce (page 230)
Wild Mushroom and Herb Pesto (page 110)
Wild Mushroom Mascarpone Cream Sauce (page 36)
Yogurt-Lime Dressing (page 295)

SAUCES TO TOSS WITH NOODLE, GRAIN, AND RICE DISHES

American-Style Tomato Sauce (page 73)

Bordelaise (Red Wine Brown Sauce) (page 168)

Caper-Shallot Compound Butter (page 8)

Catalan Tomato, Pepper, and Eggplant Sauce (Samfaina) (page 75)

Charred Garlic-Jalapeño Pesto with Queso Fresco (page 119)

Chasseur (Mushroom Demi-Glace) (page 166)

Chunky Peanut-Chipotle Sauce (page 249)

Cilantro-Mint Dipping Sauce (page 246)

Classic Marinara (page 74)

Cold Sesame Sauce (page 69)

Crispy Shallot Pesto (page 113)

Curried Chanterelle Cream Sauce (page 38)

Curry-Yogurt Sauce (page 221)

Fontina Cream Sauce (page 33)

Fresh Indian Chile-Tomato Relish (page 345)

Garlic Butter (page 5)

Ginger Dipping Sauce (Nuoc Mam Gung) (page 249)

Gorgonzola Cream Sauce with Caramelized Onions (page 33)

Green Curry Stir-Fry Sauce (page 150)

Harissa (Moroccan Chile Paste) (page 352)

Herbed Compound Butter (page 11)

Lemongrass-Chile Vinaigrette (page 268)

Lyonnaise (Onion-Flavored Brown Sauce) (page 167)

Mango Chutney (page 343)

Mascarpone Cream Sauce (page 36)

Mornay Sauce (Cheese Sauce) (page 32)

North African Tomato Sauce with Chickpeas and Sweet Spices (page 78)

Pico de Gallo (page 318)

Pineapple Chutney with Golden Raisins (page 341)

Piquillo Pepper Salsa (page 326)

Quattro Formaggi (Four-Cheese Sauce) (page 31)

Radish-Cucumber Raita (page 233)

Roasted Garlic Compound Butter (page 5)

Roquefort-Shallot Compound Butter (page 11)

Sauce Americaine (page 170)

Sauce Newburg (page 170)

Sauce Supreme (Cream and Mushroom-Enriched Velouté) (page 168)

Seafood Cream Sauce (page 40)

Sesame-Ginger Stir-Fry Sauce (page 153)

Shrimp Butter (page 9)

Smoked Gouda Béchamel (page 32)

South Vietnamese–Style Coconut Curry Sauce (page 226)

Spicy Coconut Curry Tomato Sauce (page 226)

Spicy Lemongrass-Cilantro Dipping Sauce (page 254)

Sweet-and-Sour Peach Chutney (page 342)

Tangy Chinese Dumpling Sauce (page 256)

Thai Green Curry Coconut Sauce (page 228)

Tomato Cream Sauce (page 86)

Trinidadian Hot Pepper Sauce (page 353)

Tuscan Hare Ragu (page 62)

Veal and Wild Mushroom Ragu (page 61)

Vietnamese Fish Dipping Sauce (Nuoc Cham) (page 258)

Vietnamese Peanut Dipping Sauce (Nuoc Leo) (page 259)

West African Spiced Curry Tomato Sauce (page 230)

Western-Style Curry Sauce (page 228)

Wild Mushroom Mascarpone Cream Sauce (page 36)

Wild Mushroom Ragout (page 50)

PASTA SAUCES

American-Style Tomato Sauce (page 73)

Anchovy Butter (page 7)

Anchovy-Parsley Pesto (page 105)

Artichoke Pesto with Almonds and White Wine (page 108)

Béchamel with Manchego Cheese and Almonds (page 34)

Caper-Shallot Compound Butter (page 8)

Catalan Tomato, Pepper, and Eggplant Sauce (Samfaina) (page 75)

Pasta Sauces (*continued*)

SAUCES TO PAIR WITH POULTRY (CHICKEN, GAME HENS, TURKEY, CAPON)

Sauces to Pair with Poultry *(continued)*

Jalapeño Pepper Jelly Glaze (page 212)

Jamaican Jerk BBQ Sauce (page 207)

Jamaican Jerk Seasoning Paste (page 193)

Jicama and Cucumber Salsa with Lime (page 325)

Kansas City–Style BBQ Sauce (page 206)

Korean BBQ Sauce (Bulgogi) (page 208)

Lemon, Garlic, and Rosemary Grill Splash (page 209)

Lemon-Garlic Marinade (page 185)

Lemon-Garlic Stir-Fry Sauce (page 150)

Lemongrass-Ginger Cream Pan Sauce (page 137)

Lemon Mayonnaise (page 300)

Lemon-Walnut Pesto (page 115)

Lemony Spice Brine (page 175)

Lime-Ancho Mayonnaise (page 301)

Lime-Chile Marinade (page 179)

Lime-Honey Glaze (page 211)

Lyonnaise (Onion-Flavored Brown Sauce) (page 167)

Madeira-Raisin Glaze (page 213)

Madeira-Raisin Pan Sauce (page 136)

Madeira Sauce (page 165)

Madras Curry Marinade (page 180)

Mango Chutney (page 343)

Mango Dipping Sauce (page 250)

Maple-Chipotle BBQ Sauce (page 202)

Maple-Chipotle Marinade (page 180)

Maple-Cider Glaze (page 213)

Margarita Marinade (page 181)

Mexican Tomato Sauce with Sofrito (page 81)

Minty Mango Salsa (page 332)

Miso-Ginger Dressing (page 288)

Mole BBQ Sauce (page 200)

Mornay Sauce (Cheese Sauce) (page 32)

Moroccan Preserved Lemon Aioli (page 312)

Moroccan-Spiced Marinade (page 181)

Mustard Béchamel (page 28)

Mustard-Dill Pan Sauce (page 139)

Old Bay Brine (page 175)

Olive Salsa (page 330)

Orange-Cranberry Glaze (page 214)

Orange-Cranberry Sauce (page 349)

Oven-Dried Tomato and Garlic Pesto (page 114)

Oyster Stir-Fry Sauce (page 152)

Parsley Sauce (Salsa Verde) (page 104)

Pasilla Chile BBQ Sauce (page 204)

Pear and Prune Compote (page 351)

Perigord (Black Truffle–Flavored Brown Sauce) (page 166)

Pesto Mayonnaise (page 302)

Pico de Gallo (page 318)

Pignoli-Herb Sauce (page 98)

Piña Colada Glaze (page 214)

Pineapple Chutney with Golden Raisins (page 341)

Pineapple-Habanero Glaze (page 215)

Pineapple-Mango Ketchup (page 340)

Piquant Orange Marmalade Glaze (page 215)

Piquant Orange Stir-Fry Sauce (page 152)

Piquillo Pepper Salsa (page 326)

Pistachio Yogurt Sauce (page 243)

Plum Duck Sauce (page 253)

Provençal Fennel Tomato Sauce (page 76)

Quick Curry Mayonnaise (page 305)

Quick Hazelnut Mayonnaise (page 306)

Quince and Cranberry Compote (page 351)

Quince and Red Onion Relish (page 347)

Radish-Cucumber Raita (page 233)

Raspberry-Chile BBQ Sauce (page 203)

Ravigote (Tangy Wine-Herb Velouté) (page 169)

Roasted Corn Salsa (page 323)

Roasted Garlic Compound Butter (page 5)

Roasted Lemon Vinaigrette (page 272)

Roasted Pepper, Avocado, and Corn Salsa (page 325)

Roasted Poblano with Mango and Corn Salsa (page 326)

Roasted Red Pepper Mayonnaise (page 304)

Roasted Red Pepper Pesto with Pecorino Pepato (page 109)

Roasted Sweet Pepper Salsa (page 328)

Romesco (page 120)

Roquefort-Shallot Compound Butter (page 11)

Salmoriglio (Lemon Marinade) (page 187)

Salsa of Fire-Roasted Chiles (page 328)

Salsina Verde (page 104)

SAUCES TO PAIR WITH SHELLFISH

Sauces to Pair with Shellfish *(continued)*

Chimichurri (page 105)

Chinese Black Bean Sauce (page 145)

Chinese Ginger-Soy Dipping Sauce (page 246)

Chinese-Style Garlic Sauce (page 143)

Chipotle Beurre Blanc (page 15)

Chipotle-Cilantro Compound Butter (page 8)

Cilantro-Mint Dipping Sauce (page 246)

Cold Sesame Sauce (page 69)

Creole Spice Paste (page 190)

Cuban Mojo (page 183)

Fresh Indian Chile-Tomato Relish (page 345)

Fried Ginger Stir-Fry Sauce (page 148)

Garlic Butter (page 5)

Garlic Confit Aioli (page 313)

Ginger-Carrot Ketchup (page 339)

Ginger Dipping Sauce (Nuoc Mam Gung) (page 249)

Ginger-Lemongrass Spice Paste (page 191)

Ginger-Lemongrass Stir-Fry Sauce (page 149)

Ginger-Orange Stir-Fry Sauce (page 149)

Gingery Pineapple Salsa with Coconut and Peanuts
    (page 333)

Golden Kiwi and Pineapple Salsa with Mint (page 331)

Green Curry Stir-Fry Sauce (page 150)

Green Mango Chutney (page 343)

Green Papaya Chutney (page 344)

Gribiche Sauce (page 308)

Harissa (Moroccan Chile Paste) (page 352)

Herbed Compound Butter (page 11)

Honeydew Salsa with Lime and Hot Chiles (page 332)

Honey-Ginger Glaze (page 211)

Indonesian Peanut Dressing (Gado Gado) (page 286)

Indonesian Peanut Shrimp Dipping Sauce (page 250)

Island Pineapple Salsa with Habanero and Lime
    (page 331)

Jamaican Jerk BBQ Sauce (page 207)

Jamaican Jerk Seasoning Paste (page 193)

Korean BBQ Sauce (Bulgogi) (page 208)

Lemon-Garlic Stir-Fry Sauce (page 150)

Lemongrass-Chile Vinaigrette (page 268)

Lemongrass-Ginger Cream Pan Sauce (page 137)

Lemon Mayonnaise (page 300)

Lime-Chile Marinade (page 179)

Lime-Honey Glaze (page 211)

Madras Curry Marinade (page 180)

Mango Chutney (page 343)

Mango Dipping Sauce (page 250)

Margarita Marinade (page 181)

Minty Mango Salsa (page 332)

Miso-Ginger Dressing (page 288)

Oyster Stir-Fry Sauce (page 152)

Parsley Sauce (Salsa Verde) (page 104)

Pico de Gallo (page 318)

Pignoli-Herb Sauce (page 98)

Pineapple Chutney with Golden Raisins (page 341)

Pineapple-Habanero Glaze (page 215)

Pineapple-Mango Ketchup (page 340)

Piquillo Pepper Salsa (page 326)

Provençal Fennel Tomato Sauce (page 76)

Roasted Garlic Compound Butter (page 5)

Romesco (page 120)

Rouille I (page 314)

Saffron-Scented Tomato Sauce (page 91)

Satay Paste (page 192)

Sauce Americaine (page 170)

Scallion-Ginger Spice Paste (page 191)

Sesame-Ginger Stir-Fry Sauce (page 153)

Sesame-Lime Dipping Sauce (page 254)

Shrimp Butter (page 9)

South Vietnamese–Style Coconut Curry Sauce (page 22)

Soy-Ginger Beurre Blanc (page 16)

Spicy Lemongrass-Cilantro Dipping Sauce (page 254)

Spicy Pineapple Stir-Fry Sauce (page 153)

Sweet-and-Sour Peach Chutney (page 342)

Sweet-and-Sour Stir-Fry Sauce (page 157)

Sweet-and-Sour Tamarind Sauce (page 256)

Sweet Chile-Garlic Stir-Fry Sauce (page 156)

Sweet Sake-Soy Dumpling Sauce (page 255)

Sweet Thai Chile Dipping Sauce (page 255)

Tamarind Yogurt Sauce (page 242)

Tandoori Marinade (page 177)

Tangerine Stir-Fry Sauce (page 155)

Tangy Chinese Dumpling Sauce (page 256)

Tartar Sauce (page 308)

Tart Lime-Ginger Mayonnaise (page 299)

Teriyaki Grilling Sauce (page 210)

Thai Basil–Nam Pla Stir-Fry Sauce (page 156)

Thai Green Curry Coconut Sauce (page 228)

Thai Nam Pla Prik (Spicy Fish Sauce with Lime)
    (page 258)

Thai Red Curry Coconut Sauce (page 227)

Tomato-Soy Beurre Blanc (page 15)

Trinidadian Hot Pepper Sauce (page 353)

Velouté (page 167)

Vidalia Onion Ketchup (page 340)

Vietnamese Fish Dipping Sauce (Nuoc Cham) (page 258)

Vietnamese Garlic–Fish Sauce Marinade (page 179)

Vietnamese Peanut Dipping Sauce (Nuoc Leo) (page 259)

West African Spiced Curry Tomato Sauce (page 230)

SAUCES TO PAIR WITH FISH

Ancho-Garlic–Pine Nut Compound Butter (page 6)

Ancho, Orange, and Sweet Onion Salsa (page 327)

Anchovy Aioli (page 311)

Anchovy Butter (page 7)

Arugula Cream Sauce (page 39)

Avgolemono (page 22)

Banana-Kiwi Raita (page 239)

Béarnaise (page 20)

Béchamel with Manchego Cheese and Almonds
    (page 34)

Bercy (White Wine–Fish Velouté) (page 169)

Black Bean and Chayote Salsa (page 321)

Black Olive Tapenade Aioli (page 311)

Blood Orange Beurre Blanc (page 14)

Caper Brown Butter Sauce (page 13)

Caper-Shallot Compound Butter (page 8)

Catalan Citrus Tomato Sauce (page 75)

Catalan Tomato, Pepper, and Eggplant Sauce (Samfaina)
    (page 75)

Charmoula (page 188)

Charred Garlic–Tomatillo Salsa (page 321)

Chimichurri (page 105)

Chinese Ginger-Soy Dipping Sauce (page 246)

Chipotle Adobo BBQ Sauce (page 201)

Chipotle Beurre Blanc (page 15)

Chipotle-Cilantro Compound Butter (page 8)

Cilantro-Mint Dipping Sauce (page 246)

Citrus-Fennel Marinade (page 183)

Corn and Black Bean Salsa (page 322)

Creamy Lemon Dressing (page 281)

Creamy Orange-Fennel Vinaigrette (page 266)

Creamy Pesto Dressing (page 283)

Creole Spice Paste (page 190)

Crisp-Fried Almond and Garlic Sauce (page 69)

Crispy Shallot Pesto (page 113)

Cuban Mojo (page 183)

Curried Chanterelle Cream Sauce (page 38)

Easy Anchovy Mayonnaise (page 303)

Easy Tapenade Aioli (page 312)

Fresh Banana Chutney (page 345)

Fresh Indian Chile-Tomato Relish (page 345)

Fresh Onion-Chile Relish (page 346)

Fresh Three-Pepper Salsa (page 327)

Fresh Tomatillo Salsa Verde (page 320)

Garlic Butter (page 5)

Garlic Confit Aioli (page 313)

Ginger-Carrot Ketchup (page 339)

Ginger Dipping Sauce (Nuoc Mam Gung) (page 249)

Ginger-Lemongrass Spice Paste (page 191)

Ginger-Soy Dressing (page 284)

Gingery Pineapple Salsa with Coconut and Peanuts
    (page 333)

Golden Kiwi and Pineapple Salsa with Mint (page 331)

Green Mango Chutney (page 343)

Green Olive and Caper Berry Tomato Sauce (page 86)

Green Onion Mayonnaise (page 302)

Green Papaya Chutney (page 344)

Green Tomato Salsa (page 320)

Gribiche Sauce (page 308)

Harissa (Moroccan Chile Paste) (page 352)

Hazelnut Brown Butter Sauce (page 12)

Herbed Compound Butter (page 11)

Sauces to Pair with Fish *(continued)*

Hollandaise and all its variations (pages 17–21)

Homemade Tomato Ketchup (page 337)

Honeydew Salsa with Lime and Hot Chiles (page 332)

Honey-Ginger Glaze (page 211)

Island Pineapple Salsa with Habanero and Lime (page 331)

Jamaican Jerk BBQ Sauce (page 207)

Jamaican Jerk Seasoning Paste (page 193)

Korean BBQ Sauce (Bulgogi) (page 208)

Lemon, Garlic, and Rosemary Grill Splash (page 209)

Lemon Mayonnaise (page 300)

Lemon-Mint Vinaigrette (page 268)

Lemon-Walnut Pesto (page 115)

Lime-Ancho Mayonnaise (page 301)

Lime-Chile Marinade (page 179)

Lime-Honey Glaze (page 211)

Madras Curry Marinade (page 180)

Mango Chutney (page 343)

Mango Raita with Mint and Chiles (page 240)

Minty Mango Salsa (page 332)

Miso-Ginger Dressing (page 288)

Mixed Citrus Vinaigrette (page 266)

Mole BBQ Sauce (page 200)

Mornay Sauce (Cheese Sauce) (page 32)

Moroccan Preserved Lemon Aioli (page 312)

Moroccan-Spiced Marinade (page 181)

Mustard Béchamel (page 28)

Olive Salsa (page 330)

Parsley Sauce (Salsa Verde) (page 104)

Pico de Gallo (page 318)

Pignoli-Herb Sauce (page 98)

Piña Colada Glaze (page 214)

Pineapple Chutney with Golden Raisins (page 341)

Pineapple-Habanero Glaze (page 215)

Pineapple-Mango Ketchup (page 340)

Pistachio Yogurt Sauce (page 243)

Provençal Fennel Tomato Sauce (page 76)

Puttanesca (page 57)

Quick Herb Mayonnaise (page 307)

Roasted Corn Salsa (page 323)

Roasted Garlic Compound Butter (page 5)

Roasted Lemon Vinaigrette (page 272)

Roasted Pepper, Avocado, and Corn Salsa (page 325)

Romesco (page 120)

Rouille I (page 314)

Saffron-Scented Tomato Sauce (page 91)

Salmoriglio (Lemon Marinade) (page 187)

Salsa of Fire-Roasted Chiles (page 328)

Salsina Verde (page 104)

Sauce Americaine (page 170)

Sauce Newburg (page 170)

Scallion-Ginger Spice Paste (page 191)

Scallion-Macadamia Pesto (page 116)

Seafood Cream Sauce (page 40)

Sesame-Lime Dipping Sauce (page 254)

Shredded Beet Raita (page 237)

Shrimp Butter (page 9)

Skordalia I (page 123)

Smoky Pan-Blackened Tomato Sauce (page 87)

Smoky Roasted Tomato and Chipotle Salsa (page 319)

Sorrel Beurre Blanc (page 16)

Soy-Ginger Beurre Blanc (page 16)

Spicy Garlic-Hazelnut Sauce (page 115)

Spicy Lemongrass-Cilantro Dipping Sauce (page 254)

Spicy Sake Brine (page 176)

Sun-Dried Tomato Béchamel (page 30)

Sweet Thai Chile Dipping Sauce (page 255)

Tamarind Yogurt Sauce (page 242)

Tandoori Marinade (page 177)

Tangy Chinese Dumpling Sauce (page 256)

Tangy Herbed White Sauce (page 31)

Tartar Sauce (page 308)

Tart Lime-Ginger Mayonnaise (page 299)

Teriyaki Grilling Sauce (page 210)

Thai Green Curry Coconut Sauce (page 228)

Thai Nam Pla Prik (Spicy Fish Sauce with Lime) (page 258)

Thai Red Curry Coconut Sauce (page 227)

Tomato Cream Sauce (page 86)

Tomato-Mint Sauce (page 89)

Tomato Sauce with Olives, Raisins, and Pignoli (page 89)

Tomato-Soy Beurre Blanc (page 15)

Trinidadian Hot Pepper Sauce (page 353)
Velouté (page 167)
Vidalia Onion Ketchup (page 340)
Vietnamese Fish Dipping Sauce (Nuoc Cham) (page 258)

Vietnamese Peanut Dipping Sauce (Nuoc Leo)
  (page 259)
West African Spiced Curry Tomato Sauce (page 23)
Western-Style Curry Sauce (page 228)

SAUCES TO PAIR WITH PORK

Ancho Chile and Roasted Garlic Pesto with Piñons
  (page 116)
Ancho Chile Cream Sauce (page 37)
Ancho-Cumin Spice Paste (page 190)
Ancho-Garlic–Pine Nut Compound Butter (page 6)
Ancho, Orange, and Sweet Onion Salsa (page 327)
Anchovy Butter (page 7)
Apple-Ginger Raita (page 239)
Apple-Tamarind Ketchup (page 338)
Balsamic Pan Sauce (page 128)
Balsamic-Prune Glaze (page 210)
Banana-Kiwi Raita (page 239)
Black Bean and Chayote Salsa (page 321)
Blood Orange Beurre Blanc (page 14)
Bloody Mary Marinade (page 182)
Bulgogi Marinade (page 182)
Calvados-Cider Pan Sauce (page 129)
Caper-Shallot Compound Butter (page 8)
Catalan Tomato, Pepper, and Eggplant Sauce (Samfaina)
  (page 75)
Charmoula (page 188)
Charred Garlic-Jalapeño Pesto with Queso Fresco
  (page 119)
Charred Garlic–Tomatillo Salsa (page 321)
Chasseur (Mushroom Demi-Glace) (page 166)
Chimichurri (page 105)
Chinese Black Bean Sauce (page 145)
Chinese Ginger-Soy Dipping Sauce (page 246)
Chinese-Style Garlic Sauce (page 143)
Chipotle Adobo BBQ Sauce (page 201)
Chipotle Beurre Blanc (page 15)
Chipotle-Cilantro Compound Butter (page 8)
Chunky Peanut-Chipotle Sauce (page 249)
Cilantro-Mint Dipping Sauce (page 246)
Citrus BBQ Mop (page 209)

Classic Applesauce (page 349)
Classic Chinese Brown Sauce (page 143)
Classic Cucumber Raita (page 230)
Coconut-Peanut Stir-Fry Sauce (page 148)
Coffee BBQ Sauce (page 198)
Corn and Black Bean Salsa (page 322)
Cranberry-Port Compote (page 350)
Creamy Green Peppercorn Pan Sauce (page 132)
Creamy Sesame Vinaigrette (page 273)
Creamy Sherry Vinegar Pan Sauce (page 133)
Creole Spice Paste (page 190)
Crispy Shallot Pesto (page 113)
Cuban Mojo (page 183)
Cumberland Sauce (serve with ham) (page 348)
Cumin-Scented Carrot Raita (page 234)
Curried Applesauce (page 350)
Dried Cherry Port Glaze (page 212)
Dried Cherry–Port Reduction Pan Sauce (page 134)
Dried Fruit Chutney (page 344)
Fire-Roasted Onion Salsa (page 324)
Five-Spice Sesame Aioli (page 310)
Fragrant Riesling Marinade (page 184)
Fresh Banana Chutney (page 345)
Fresh Indian Chile-Tomato Relish (page 345)
Fresh Onion-Chile Relish (page 346)
Fresh Three-Pepper Salsa (page 327)
Fresh Tomatillo Salsa Verde (page 320)
Fried Ginger Stir-Fry Sauce (page 148)
Fried Sage and Caper Pesto with Fresh Pecorino
  (page 101)
Garlic Butter (page 5)
Garlic Confit Aioli (page 313)
Garlicky Soy BBQ Baste (page 208)
Ginger-Carrot Ketchup (page 339)
Ginger-Curry Mayonnaise (page 300)

Sauces to Pair with Pork *(continued)*

Ginger Dipping Sauce (Nuoc Mam Gung) (page 249)

Ginger-Lemongrass Stir-Fry Sauce (page 149)

Ginger-Orange Stir-Fry Sauce (page 149)

Gingery Pineapple Salsa with Coconut and Peanuts
   (page 333)

Golden Kiwi and Pineapple Salsa with Mint (page 331)

Green Chile and Scallion Pesto (page 117)

Green Mango Chutney (page 343)

Green Olive and Caper Berry Tomato Sauce (page 86)

Green Onion Mayonnaise (page 302)

Green Papaya Chutney (page 344)

Green Tomato Salsa (page 320)

Harissa (Moroccan Chile Paste) (page 352)

Herbed Compound Butter (page 11)

Hickory-Smoked BBQ Sauce (page 197)

Hoisin Five-Spice Marinade (page 184)

Homemade Tomato Ketchup (page 337)

Honeydew Salsa with Lime and Hot Chiles (page 332)

Honey-Ginger Glaze (page 211)

Honey-Mustard BBQ Sauce (page 197)

Horseradish-Cream Pan Sauce (page 135)

Indonesian Peanut Shrimp Dipping Sauce (page 250)

Jalapeño Pepper Jelly Glaze (page 212)

Jamaican Jerk BBQ Sauce (page 207)

Jamaican Jerk Seasoning Paste (page 193)

Jicama and Cucumber Salsa with Lime (page 325)

Kansas City–Style BBQ Sauce (page 206)

Korean BBQ Sauce (Bulgogi) (page 208)

Lemon, Garlic, and Rosemary Grill Splash (page 209)

Lemon-Garlic Stir-Fry Sauce (page 150)

Lemongrass-Ginger Cream Pan Sauce (page 137)

Lemon Mayonnaise (page 300)

Lemony Spice Brine (page 175)

Lime-Ancho Mayonnaise (page 301)

Lime-Chile Marinade (page 179)

Lyonnaise (Onion-Flavored Brown Sauce) (page 167)

Madeira-Raisin Glaze (page 213)

Madeira Sauce (page 165)

Madras Curry Marinade (page 180)

Mango Chutney (page 343)

Mango Dipping Sauce (page 250)

Maple-Chipotle BBQ Sauce (page 202)

Maple-Chipotle Marinade (page 180)

Maple-Cider Glaze (page 213)

Margarita Marinade (page 181)

Mexican Tomato Sauce with Sofrito (page 81)

Mint, Parsley, and Scallion Pesto (page 99)

Minty Mango Salsa (page 332)

Mole BBQ Sauce (page 200)

Moroccan Preserved Lemon Aioli (page 312)

Moroccan-Spiced Marinade (page 181)

Mustard Béchamel (page 28)

Mustard-Dill Pan Sauce (page 139)

Old Bay Brine (page 175)

Orange-Cranberry Glaze (page 214)

Orange-Cranberry Sauce (page 349)

Orange-Sherry Marinade (page 185)

Oven-Dried Tomato and Garlic Pesto (page 114)

Oyster Stir-Fry Sauce (page 152)

Parsley Sauce (Salsa Verde) (page 104)

Pasilla Chile BBQ Sauce (page 204)

Pear and Prune Compote (page 351)

Pesto Mayonnaise (page 302)

Pico de Gallo (page 318)

Pignoli-Herb Sauce (page 98)

Piña Colada Glaze (page 214)

Pineapple-Chile Marinade (page 186)

Pineapple Chutney with Golden Raisins (page 341)

Pineapple-Habanero Glaze (page 215)

Pineapple-Mango Ketchup (page 340)

Piquant Orange Marmalade Glaze (page 215)

Piquant Orange Stir-Fry Sauce (page 152)

Piquillo Pepper Salsa (page 326)

Pistachio Yogurt Sauce (page 243)

Pizzaiola (page 73)

Plum Duck Sauce (page 253)

Pomegranate Vinaigrettes I & II (page 270)

Quick Curry Mayonnaise (page 305)

Quince and Cranberry Compote (page 351)

Quince and Red Onion Relish (page 347)

Radish-Cucumber Raita (page 233)

Raspberry-Chile BBQ Sauce (page 203)

Ravigote (Tangy Wine-Herb Velouté) (page 169)
Red Chile Brown Butter Sauce (page 13)
Red Chile Tomato Sauce (Chile Colorado) (page 84)
Roasted Corn Salsa (page 323)
Roasted Garlic Compound Butter (page 5)
Roasted Pepper, Avocado, and Corn Salsa (page 325)
Roasted Poblano with Mango and Corn Salsa (page 326)
Roasted Red Pepper Mayonnaise (page 304)
Roasted Sweet Pepper Salsa (page 328)
Romesco (page 120)
Roquefort-Shallot Compound Butter (page 11)
Salmoriglio (Lemon Marinade) (page 187)
Salsa of Fire-Roasted Chiles (page 328)
Satay Paste (page 192)
Sesame-Ginger Stir-Fry Sauce (page 153)
Smoky Paprika-Garlic Paste (page 192)
Smoky Roasted Tomato and Chipotle Salsa (page 319)
Smoky Texas-Style BBQ Sauce (page 204)
Soubise (Onion Sauce) (page 28)
Spicy Garlic-Hazelnut Sauce (page 115)
Spicy Lemongrass-Cilantro Dipping Sauce (page 254)
Spicy Pineapple and Anchovy Dipping Sauce
    (Mam Nem) (page 253)
Spicy Pineapple Stir-Fry Sauce (page 153)
Spicy Sake Brine (page 176)
Spinach-Pignoli Pesto with Raisins (page 107)
Star Anise–Hoisin Stir-Fry Sauce (page 155)
Sun-Dried Tomato Aioli (page 313)
Sweet-and-Sour Stir-Fry Sauce (page 157)
Sweet-and-Sour Peach Chutney (page 342)
Sweet-and-Sour Tamarind Sauce (page 256)
Sweet Chile-Garlic Stir-Fry Sauce (page 156)

Sweet Soy–Star Anise Marinade (page 177)
Sweet Thai Chile Dipping Sauce (page 255)
Sweet Tomato-Bourbon BBQ Sauce (page 199)
Tamarind-Molasses BBQ Sauce (page 199)
Tandoori Marinade (page 177)
Tangerine Stir-Fry Sauce (page 155)
Tangy Chinese Dumpling Sauce (page 256)
Tangy Mustard Cream Sauce (page 38)
Tangy Vinegar-Chile BBQ Sauce (page 203)
Tart Cherry Raita with Scallions and Sunflower Seeds
    (page 241)
Tennessee-Style BBQ Sauce (page 206)
Teriyaki Grilling Sauce (page 210)
Thai Basil–Nam Pla Stir-Fry Sauce (page 156)
Thai Cucumber Salsa (page 323)
Thai Herb-Lime Dressing (page 292)
Thai Nam Pla Prik (Spicy Fish Sauce with Lime)
    (page 258)
Tomato, Ancho, and Pumpkin Seed Sauce (Pepian)
    (page 80)
Tomato-Soy Beurre Blanc (page 15)
Traditional Mole Negro Sauce (page 81)
Trinidadian Hot Pepper Sauce (page 353)
Turkish-Style Yogurt Marinade (page 178)
Tuscan Marinade (page 178)
Vidalia Onion Ketchup (page 340)
Vietnamese Fish Dipping Sauce (Nuoc Cham)
    (page 258)
Vietnamese Garlic–Fish Sauce Marinade (page 179)
Vietnamese Peanut Dipping Sauce (Nuoc Leo) (page 259)
Wild Mushroom Mascarpone Cream Sauce (page 36)
Yellow Mustard BBQ Sauce (page 202)

SAUCES TO PAIR WITH BEEF

Ancho Chile and Roasted Garlic Pesto with Piñons
    (page 116)
Ancho Chile Cream Sauce (page 37)
Ancho-Cumin Spice Paste (page 190)
Ancho-Garlic–Pine Nut Compound Butter (page 6)
Ancho, Orange, and Sweet Onion Salsa (page 327)
Anchovy Aioli (page 311)

Anchovy Butter (page 7)
Apple-Ginger Raita (page 239)
Apple-Tamarind Ketchup (page 338)
Balsamic Pan Sauce (page 128)
Balsamic-Prune Glaze (page 210)
Béarnaise (page 20)
Béchamel with Shallots and Morels (page 29)

Sauces to Pair with Beef *(continued)*

Black Bean and Chayote Salsa (page 321)

Black Olive Tapenade Aioli (page 311)

Bloody Mary Marinade (page 182)

Bordelaise (Red Wine Brown Sauce) (page 168)

Bread Sauce (page 41)

Bulgogi Marinade (page 182)

Caper-Shallot Compound Butter (page 8)

Catalan Tomato, Pepper, and Eggplant Sauce (Samfaina)
     (page 75)

Charmoula (page 188)

Charred Garlic-Jalapeño Pesto with Queso Fresco
     (page 119)

Charred Garlic–Tomatillo Salsa (page 321)

Chasseur (Mushroom Demi-Glace) (page 166)

Chèvre and Piquillo Pepper Pesto (page 119)

Chimichurri (page 105)

Chinese Black Bean Sauce (page 145)

Chinese-Style Garlic Sauce (page 143)

Chipotle Adobo BBQ Sauce (page 201)

Chipotle Beurre Blanc (page 15)

Chipotle-Cilantro Compound Butter (page 8)

Chunky Peanut-Chipotle Sauce (page 249)

Cilantro-Mint Dipping Sauce (page 246)

Citrus BBQ Mop (page 209)

Classic Chinese Brown Sauce (page 143)

Classic Cucumber Raita (page 230)

Coconut-Peanut Stir-Fry Sauce (page 148)

Coffee BBQ Sauce (page 198)

Corn and Black Bean Salsa (page 322)

Cranberry-Port Compote (page 350)

Creamy Green Peppercorn Pan Sauce (page 132)

Crispy Shallot Pesto (page 113)

Cuban Mojo (page 183)

Cumberland Sauce (page 348)

Cumin-Scented Carrot Raita (page 234)

Curried Applesauce (page 350)

Curried Chanterelle Cream Sauce (page 38)

Curry-Roasted Pumpkin Raita (page 234)

Dried Cherry–Port Reduction Pan Sauce (page 134)

Dried Cherry Port Glaze (page 212)

Easy Anchovy Mayonnaise (page 303)

Easy Tapenade Aioli (page 312)

Fire-Roasted Onion Salsa (page 324)

Five-Spice Sesame Aioli (page 310)

Fontina Cream Sauce (page 33)

Fresh Banana Chutney (page 345)

Fresh Indian Chile-Tomato Relish (page 345)

Fresh Onion-Chile Relish (page 346)

Fresh Pecorino Truffle Cream Sauce (page 46)

Fresh Three-Pepper Salsa (page 327)

Fresh Tomatillo Salsa Verde (page 320)

Fried Ginger Stir-Fry Sauce (page 148)

Fried Sage and Caper Pesto with Fresh Pecorino
     (page 101)

Fried Scallion–Cucumber Raita (page 237)

Garlic Butter (page 5)

Garlic Confit Aioli (page 313)

Garlicky Soy BBQ Baste (page 208)

Ginger-Carrot Ketchup (page 339)

Ginger-Lemongrass Stir-Fry Sauce (page 149)

Gingery Pineapple Salsa with Coconut and Peanuts
     (page 333)

Golden Kiwi and Pineapple Salsa with Mint (page 331)

Gorgonzola Cream Sauce with Caramelized Onions
     (page 33)

Green Chile and Scallion Pesto (page 117)

Green Mango Chutney (page 343)

Green Olive and Caper Berry Tomato Sauce (page 86)

Green Papaya Chutney (page 344)

Green Tomato Salsa (page 320)

Harissa (Moroccan Chile Paste) (page 352)

Haroset (page 348)

Hazelnut Brown Butter Sauce (page 12)

Herb Pesto with Fried Bread Crumbs (page 96)

Herbed Compound Butter (page 11)

Hickory-Smoked BBQ Sauce (page 197)

Homemade Tomato Ketchup (page 337)

Honey-Ginger Glaze (page 211)

Horseradish-Cream Pan Sauce (page 135)

Indonesian Peanut Shrimp Dipping Sauce (page 250)

Jamaican Jerk BBQ Sauce (page 207)

Jamaican Jerk Seasoning Paste (page 193)

Sauces to Pair with Beef *(continued)*

Tahini Dressing (page 290)

Tamarind-Molasses BBQ Sauce (page 199)

Tangerine Stir-Fry Sauce (page 155)

Tangy Chinese Dumpling Sauce (page 256)

Tangy Mustard Cream Sauce (page 38)

Tart Cherry Raita with Scallions and Sunflower Seeds (page 241)

Teriyaki Grilling Sauce (page 210)

Thai Basil–Nam Pla Stir-Fry Sauce (page 156)

Thai Nam Pla Prik (Spicy Fish Sauce with Lime) (page 258)

Thai Red Curry Coconut Sauce (page 227)

Toasted Bread Crumb, Rosemary, and Parmesan Pesto (page 99)

Tomato-Mint Sauce (page 89)

Tomato Sauce with Olives, Raisins, and Pignoli (page 89)

Tomato-Soy Beurre Blanc (page 15)

Trinidadian Hot Pepper Sauce (page 353)

Turkish-Style Yogurt Marinade (page 178)

Vidalia Onion Ketchup (page 340)

Vietnamese Fish Dipping Sauce (Nuoc Cham) (page 258)

Vietnamese Peanut Dipping Sauce (Nuoc Leo) (page 259)

Wild Mushroom and Herb Pesto (page 110)

Wild Mushroom Mascarpone Cream Sauce (page 36)

Vietnamese Garlic–Fish Sauce Marinade (page 179)

SAUCES TO PAIR WITH VEAL

Ancho-Garlic–Pine Nut Compound Butter (page 6)

Ancho, Orange, and Sweet Onion Salsa (page 327)

Apple-Tamarind Ketchup (page 338)

Calvados-Cider Pan Sauce (page 129)

Caper-Shallot Compound Butter (page 8)

Chasseur (Mushroom Demi-Glace) (page 166)

Chimichurri (page 105)

Chipotle Beurre Blanc (page 15)

Classic Applesauce (page 349)

Classic Gremolata (page 122)

Coffee BBQ Sauce (page 198)

Cranberry-Port Compote (page 350)

Creamy Ginger-Soy Pan Sauce (page 132)

Creamy Green Peppercorn Pan Sauce (page 132)

Creamy Sherry Vinegar Pan Sauce (page 133)

Crisp-Fried Almond and Garlic Sauce (page 69)

Crispy Shallot Pesto (page 113)

Curried Chanterelle Cream Sauce (page 38)

Dried Cherry–Port Reduction Pan Sauce (page 134)

Fontina Cream Sauce (page 33)

Fragrant Riesling Marinade (page 184)

Garlic Butter (page 5)

Garlic Confit Aioli (page 313)

Golden Kiwi and Pineapple Salsa with Mint (page 331)

Harissa (Moroccan Chile Paste) (page 352)

Herbed Compound Butter (page 11)

Hickory-Smoked BBQ Sauce (page 197)

Honey-Ginger Glaze (page 211)

Lemon, Garlic, and Rosemary Grill Splash (page 209)

Lemon-Walnut Pesto (page 115)

Lyonnaise (Onion-Flavored Brown Sauce) (page 167)

Madeira-Raisin Pan Sauce (page 136)

Madeira Sauce (page 165)

Mango Chutney (page 343)

Mustard Béchamel (page 28)

Mustard-Dill Pan Sauce (page 139)

Orange-Cranberry Sauce (page 349)

Pear and Prune Compote (page 351)

Perigord (Black Truffle–Flavored Brown Sauce) (page 166)

Pico de Gallo (page 318)

Piquillo Pepper Salsa (page 326)

Quince and Cranberry Compote (page 351)

Ravigote (Tangy Wine-Herb Velouté) (page 169)

Roasted Garlic Compound Butter (page 5)

Roasted Pepper, Avocado, and Corn Salsa (page 325)

Roasted Poblano with Mango and Corn Salsa (page 326)

Roasted Sweet Pepper Salsa (page 328)

Salmoriglio (Lemon Marinade) (page 187)

SAUCES TO PAIR WITH LAMB AND GOAT

Sauces to Pair with Lamb and Goat *(continued)*

Mint and Almond Pesto (page 102)

Mint Gremolata (page 122)

Mint, Parsley, and Scallion Pesto (page 99)

Moroccan Preserved Lemon Aioli (page 312)

Moroccan-Spiced Marinade (page 181)

North African Tomato Sauce with Chickpeas and Sweet
  Spices (page 78)

Olive, Caper, and Mint Pesto (page 102)

Olive Salsa (page 330)

Oven-Dried Tomato and Garlic Pesto (page 114)

Parsley Sauce (Salsa Verde) (page 104)

Pasilla Chile BBQ Sauce (page 204)

Pear and Prune Compote (page 351)

Pesto Mayonnaise (page 302)

Pico de Gallo (page 318)

Pignoli-Herb Sauce (page 98)

Piquillo Pepper Salsa (page 326)

Pistachio Yogurt Sauce (page 243)

Pomegranate-Mint Raita (page 241)

Pomegranate Vinaigrettes I & II (page 270)

Quince and Cranberry Compote (page 351)

Quince and Red Onion Relish (page 347)

Radish-Cucumber Raita (page 233)

Red Chile Tomato Sauce (Chile Colorado) (page 84)

Red Wine Herb Marinade (page 186)

Roasted Garlic Compound Butter (page 5)

Roasted Garlic Vinaigrette (page 271)

Roasted Lemon Vinaigrette (page 272)

Roasted Poblano with Mango and Corn Salsa (page 326)

Roasted Red Pepper Mayonnaise (page 304)

Roasted Sweet Pepper Salsa (page 328)

Romesco (page 120)

Rosemary-Balsamic Marinade (page 187)

Salmoriglio (Lemon Marinade) (page 187)

Salsa of Fire-Roasted Chiles (page 328)

Shredded Beet Raita (page 237)

Smoky Eggplant Raita (page 236)

Smoky Paprika-Garlic Paste (page 192)

Smoky Roasted Tomato and Chipotle Salsa (page 319)

Smoky Texas-Style BBQ Sauce (page 204)

Spicy Coconut Curry Tomato Sauce (page 226)

Spicy Pineapple and Anchovy Dipping Sauce (Mam
  Nem) (page 253)

Spinach-Pignoli Pesto with Raisins (page 107)

Spinach Raita with Toasted Spices (page 238)

Sun-Dried Tomato Aioli (page 313)

Tahini Dressing (page 290)

Tandoori Marinade (page 177)

Tangy Vinegar-Chile BBQ Sauce (page 203)

Tart Cherry Raita with Scallions and Sunflower Seeds
  (page 241)

Tomato, Ancho, and Pumpkin Seed Sauce (Pepian)
  (page 80)

Tomato-Mint Sauce (page 89)

Tomato Sauce with Olives, Raisins, and Pignoli (page 89)

Trinidadian Hot Pepper Sauce (page 353)

Turkish-Style Yogurt Marinade (page 178)

Vietnamese Fish Dipping Sauce (Nuoc Cham) (page 258)

West African Spiced Curry Tomato Sauce (page 230)

Yogurt-Lime Dressing (page 295)

SAUCES TO PAIR WITH GAME
(DUCK, PHEASANT, QUAIL, VENISON)

Ancho-Garlic–Pine Nut Compound Butter (page 6)

Ancho, Orange, and Sweet Onion Salsa (page 327)

Apple-Ginger Raita (page 239)

Apple-Tamarind Ketchup (page 338)

Arugula Cream Sauce (page 39)

Avgolemono (page 22)

Balsamic Pan Sauce (page 128)

Balsamic-Prune Glaze (page 210)

Béchamel with Shallots and Morels (page 29)

Black Bean and Chayote Salsa (page 321)

Bordelaise (Red Wine Brown Sauce) (page 168)

Caper-Shallot Compound Butter (page 8)

Sauces to Pair with Game *(continued)*

Sweet-and-Sour Stir-Fry Sauce (page 157)

Sweet Tomato-Bourbon BBQ Sauce (page 199)

Tamarind-Molasses BBQ Sauce (page 199)

Tangerine Stir-Fry Sauce (page 155)

Tangy Mustard Cream Sauce (page 38)

Tangy Vinegar-Chile BBQ Sauce (page 203)

Tart Cherry Raita with Scallions and Sunflower Seeds
  (page 241)

Teriyaki Grilling Sauce (page 210)

Tomato-Soy Beurre Blanc (page 15)

Trinidadian Hot Pepper Sauce (page 353)

Tuscan Marinade (page 178)

Velouté (page 167)

Vidalia Onion Ketchup (page 340)

Western-Style Curry Sauce (page 228)

Wild Mushroom Mascarpone Cream Sauce (page 36)

SAUCES TO PAIR WITH GRILLED MEATS
(RIBS, BURGERS, SAUSAGES, HOT DOGS, ETC.)

Ancho Chile and Roasted Garlic Pesto with Piñons
  (page 116)

Ancho Chile Cream Sauce (page 37)

Ancho-Garlic–Pine Nut Compound Butter (page 6)

Ancho, Orange, and Sweet Onion Salsa (page 327)

Anchovy Aioli (page 311)

Anchovy Butter (page 7)

Apple-Ginger Raita (page 239)

Apple-Tamarind Ketchup (page 338)

Balsamic-Prune Glaze (page 210)

Banana-Kiwi Raita (page 239)

Béarnaise (page 20)

Black Bean and Chayote Salsa (page 321)

Bulgogi Marinade (page 182)

Caper-Shallot Compound Butter (page 8)

Catalan Tomato, Pepper, and Eggplant Sauce (Samfaina)
  (page 75)

Charred Garlic–Jalapeño Pesto with Queso Fresco
  (page 119)

Charred Garlic-Tomatillo Salsa (page 321)

Chèvre and Piquillo Pepper Pesto (page 119)

Chimichurri (page 105)

Chinese Ginger-Soy Dipping Sauce (page 246)

Chipotle Adobo BBQ Sauce (page 201)

Chipotle Beurre Blanc (page 15)

Chipotle Mayonnaise (page 303)

Chipotle-Cilantro Compound Butter (page 8)

Chunky Peanut-Chipotle Sauce (page 249)

Cilantro-Mint Dipping Sauce (page 246)

Classic Applesauce (page 349)

Classic Cucumber Raita (page 230)

Coffee BBQ Sauce (page 198)

Corn and Black Bean Salsa (page 322)

Cranberry-Port Compote (page 350)

Crispy Shallot Pesto (page 113)

Cumin-Scented Carrot Raita (page 234)

Curried Applesauce (page 350)

Curry-Yogurt Sauce (page 221)

Dried Cherry Port Glaze (page 212)

Easy Anchovy Mayonnaise (page 303)

Fire-Roasted Onion Salsa (page 324)

Fresh Indian Chile-Tomato Relish (page 345)

Fresh Onion-Chile Relish (page 346)

Fresh Tomatillo Salsa Verde (page 320)

Fried Sage and Caper Pesto with Fresh Pecorino (page
  101)

Fried Scallion–Cucumber Raita (page 237)

Garlic Butter (page 5)

Garlic Confit Aioli (page 313)

Ginger-Carrot Ketchup (page 339)

Gingery Pineapple Salsa with Coconut and Peanuts
  (page 333)

Golden Kiwi and Pineapple Salsa with Mint (page 331)

Green Chile and Scallion Pesto (page 117)

Green Mango Chutney (page 343)

Green Papaya Chutney (page 344)

Green Tomato Salsa (page 320)

Harissa (Moroccan Chile Paste) (page 352)

SAUCES TO SERVE WITH STEWS AND CURRIES

SAUCES TO SERVE OVER CAKES, TARTS, AND BREAD PUDDINGS

Amaretto-Peach Coulis (page 381)
Balsamic Caramel Sauce (page 362)
Bay-Scented Plum Coulis (page 382)
Bourbon Hard Sauce (page 365)
Butterscotch Sauce (page 363)
Caramel Crème Anglaise (page 368)
Caramel Sauce (page 360)
Chocolate Custard Sauce (page 368)
Chocolate Sauce (page 356)
Chocolate Syrup (page 356)
Chunky Blueberry Sauce (page 375)
Coconut Crème Anglaise (page 371)
Coconut-Mango Coulis (page 383)
Crème Anglaise (page 367)
Dulce de Leche (page 363)
Espresso Crème Anglaise (page 371)
Fresh Cherry Sauce (page 377)
Ginger Crème Anglaise (page 372)

Ginger-Blueberry Coulis (page 379)
Hazelnut-Chocolate Sauce (page 358)
Hazelnut Crème Anglaise (page 374)
Honey-Pear Coulis (page 383)
Hot Fudge Sauce (page 357)
Lemon Curd Sauce (page 376)
Lemongrass Crème Anglaise (page 373)
Maple-Cider Nut Sauce (page 364)
Mint-Chocolate Sauce (page 357)
Orange-Chocolate Sauce (page 359)
Piña Colada Dessert Sauce (page 379)
Pineapple-Ginger Dessert Sauce (page 378)
Pistachio Crème Anglaise (page 369)
Raspberry Caramel Sauce (page 360)
Raspberry Coulis (page 380)
Rum-Raisin Sauce (page 366)
Strawberry Coulis (page 381)
Strawberry-Rhubarb Sauce (page 376)

SAUCES TO SERVE OVER CUSTARDS, PUDDINGS, AND ICE CREAM

Amaretto-Peach Coulis (page 381)
Balsamic Caramel Sauce (page 362)
Bay-Scented Plum Coulis (page 382)
Butterscotch Sauce (page 363)
Caramel Sauce (page 360)
Chocolate Custard Sauce (page 368)
Chocolate Sauce (page 356)
Chocolate Syrup (page 356)
Chunky Blueberry Sauce (page 375)
Coconut-Mango Coulis (page 383)
Dulce de Leche (page 363)
Fresh Cherry Sauce (page 377)
Ginger-Blueberry Coulis (page 379)
Ginger-Port Dessert Sauce (page 365)
Hazelnut-Chocolate Sauce (page 358)
Hazelnut Crème Anglaise (page 374)
Honey-Pear Coulis (page 383)

Hot Fudge Sauce (page 357)
Lemon Curd Sauce (page 376)
Lemongrass Crème Anglaise (page 373)
Maple-Cider Nut Sauce (page 364)
Midori Melon Coulis (page 384)
Mint-Chocolate Sauce (page 357)
Orange-Chocolate Sauce (page 359)
Passion Fruit Coulis (page 384)
Piña Colada Dessert Sauce (page 379)
Pineapple-Ginger Dessert Sauce (page 378)
Raspberry Caramel Sauce (page 360)
Raspberry Coulis (page 380)
Rum-Raisin Sauce (page 366)
Sour Cherry Balsamic Dessert Sauce (page 377)
Spiced Wine Dessert Sauce (page 366)
Strawberry Coulis (page 381)
Strawberry-Rhubarb Sauce (page 376)

SAUCES TO SERVE OVER FRESH OR POACHED FRUIT

Balsamic Caramel Sauce (page 362)

Beet Vinaigrette (page 263)

Caramel Crème Anglaise (page 368)

Chunky Blueberry Sauce (page 375)

Coconut Crème Anglaise (page 371)

Coconut-Mango Coulis (page 383)

Coconut-Mango Tapioca Sauce (page 378)

Crème Anglaise (page 367)

Dulce de Leche (page 363)

Fresh Cherry Sauce (page 377)

Ginger-Blueberry Coulis (page 379)

Ginger Crème Anglaise (page 372)

Ginger-Port Dessert Sauce (page 365)

Honey-Pear Coulis (page 383)

Lemon Curd Sauce (page 376)

Lemongrass Crème Anglaise (page 373)

Lemon-Mint Vinaigrette (page 268)

Lowfat Goat Cheese–Buttermilk Dressing (page 288)

Maple-Cider Nut Sauce (page 264)

Midori Melon Coulis (page 384)

Miso-Ginger Dressing (page 288)

Passion Fruit Vinaigrette (page 269)

Piña Colada Dessert Sauce (page 379)

Pineapple-Ginger Dessert Sauce (page 378)

Pistachio Crème Anglaise (page 369)

Ranch Dressing (page 289)

Raspberry Caramel Sauce (page 360)

Raspberry Coulis (page 380)

Roasted Pear–Balsamic Vinaigrette (page 271)

Sour Cherry Balsamic Dessert Sauce (page 377)

Spiced Wine Dessert Sauce (page 366)

Strawberry Coulis (page 381)

Sweet Wine Vinaigrette (page 276)

Verjus Vinaigrette (page 274)

Zabaglione (page 367)

35 RECIPES FEATURED IN THIS BOOK

Albondigas in Red Chile Tomato Sauce
(page 121)

Asian Rice Noodle Salad (page 257)

Avgolemono Soup with Greek Meatballs
(page 23)

Baked Pasta with Wild Mushrooms and Smoked
Ham (page 55)

Basic Coleslaw (page 281)

Best-Ever 20-Minute BBQ "Baked" Beans
(page 205)

Caesar Salad (page 278)

Cannelloni with Shallot-Ricotta Filling (page 112)

Chicken Mughlai Curry (page 225)

Chicken with Mushrooms, Scallions, and Black
Bean Sauce (page 144)

Classic Macaroni and Cheese (page 35)

Dry Curry Noodles (page 220)

Easy Pork Meatballs (page 252)

Fast Steamed Pork Buns (page 251)

Fast Vegetable Stew (page 224)

Juicy Southern-Style Fried Chicken (page 189)

Lasagna Bolognese (page 63)

Mussels Mariniere (page 90)

North African Lamb Stew with Chickpeas and
Raisins (page 79)

Pesto-Stuffed Chicken (page 100)

Pork Colorado (Pork in Red Chile Sauce)
(page 85)

Roasted Potatoes and Onions with Chèvre and
Piquillo Pepper Pesto (page 118)

Senegalese Chicken Curry (page 231)

Spinach and Ricotta Lasagna (page 27)

Stir-Fried Beef with Scallions and Mushrooms
(page 154)

Stir-Fried Vegetables and Udon (page 151)

Thai Green Seafood Curry (page 229)

Thai Massaman Curry (page 235)

Thai-Style Cabbage Slaw (page 293)

Turkey with Roasted Shallot–Teriyaki Gravy
(page 130)

The Ultimate Roast Beef Sandwich (page 10)

Vietnamese Seafood Curry (page 227)

Warm Lentil Salad (page 294)

Watercress and Endive Salad with Goat Cheese
and Walnuts (page 275)

West Indian Curry for Lamb or Goat (Columbo)
(page 232)

INDEX

Beurre Blanc (*continued*)
    Chipotle, 15
    Classic, 14
    preparing, tips for, 4
    Sorrel, 16
    Soy-Ginger, 16
    Tomato-Soy, 15
Black Bean(s)
    and Chayote Salsa, 321
    and Corn Salsa, 322
    fermented, about, 247
    sauce, about, 247
    Sauce, Chinese, **144,** 145
Blood Orange(s)
    Beurre Blanc, 14
    Maltaise (Blood Orange Hollandaise), 18
Bloody Mary Marinade, 182
Blueberry-Ginger Coulis, 379–80
Blueberry Sauce, Chunky, 375
Blue Cheese
    Dressing, 276
    Gorgonzola Cream Sauce with Caramelized
        Onions, 33
    Roquefort Mayonnaise, 305
    Roquefort-Shallot Compound Butter, **10,** 11
    Sun-Dried Tomato Gorgonzola Sauce, 49
Bolognese Sauce, 60–61, **63**
Bordelaise (Red Wine Brown Sauce), 168
Bourbon Hard Sauce, 365
Bourbon-Tomato BBQ Sauce, Sweet, 199
Braises, best tomato sauces for, 88
Braises, preparing, 83
Bread croutons, preparing, 117
Bread Crumb, Toasted, Rosemary, and Parmesan
    Pesto, 99
Bread Crumbs, Fried, Herb Pesto with, 96, **100**
Bread Sauce, 41
Brine
    about, 173–74
    Lemony Spice, 175
    Old Bay, 175
    Spicy Sake, 176
    working with, tips for, 174
Broccoli
    –Black Olive Sauce, 52–53
    gratin, sauces for, 37
Brown Butter Sauce
    Caper, 13

Hazelnut, 12
Red Chile, 13
Bulgogi (Korean BBQ Sauce), 208
Bulgogi Marinade, 182
Buttermilk–Goat Cheese Dressing, Lowfat, 288
Buttermilk Marinade, Spicy, 188, **189**
Butter Sauce. *See also* Beurre Blanc; Compound Butter;
    Hollandaise Sauce
    about, 3
    Brown, Caper, 13
    Brown, Hazelnut, 12
    Brown, Red Chile, 13
Butterscotch Sauce, 363

C

Caesar Dressing, 277, **278**
Caesar Dressing, Eggless, 277, **278**
Calvados-Cider Pan Sauce, 129–31
Caper(s)
    Berry and Green Olive Tomato Sauce, 86
    Brown Butter Sauce, 13
    and Fried Sage Pesto with Fresh Pecorino, **100,** 101
    Frizzled, Dressing, Warm, 293
    Olive, and Mint Pesto, **100,** 102
    Salsina Verde, 104
    -Shallot Compound Butter, 8
Caramel Crème Anglaise, 368
Caramel Sauce, 360
    Balsamic, 362
    Dulce de Leche, 363–64
    preparing, tips for, 359, 361
    Raspberry, 360–61
Carbonara, 44–45
Carrot(s)
    -Ginger Dressing, 279
    -Ginger Ketchup, 339
    Raita, Cumin-Scented, 234
    Relish, Sweet-and-Sour, 347
Catalan Citrus Tomato Sauce, 75
Catalan Tomato, Pepper, and Eggplant Sauce
    (Samfaina), 75–76
Cauliflower
    gratin, sauces for, 37
    Sauce, Sicilian, 51
Chanterelle Cream Sauce, Curried, 38–39
Charmoula, 188
Charred Garlic–Tomatillo Salsa, 321

Pumpkin, Curry-Roasted, Raita, 234, **294**
Pumpkin Seed(s)
    toasting, 364
    Tomato, and Ancho Sauce (Pepian), 80
Puttanesca, 57–58

Q

Quattro Formaggi (Four-Cheese Sauce), 31
Queso Fresco, Charred Garlic-Jalapeño Pesto with, 119–20, **121**
Quince and Cranberry Compote, 351
Quince and Red Onion Relish, 347

R

Radish-Cucumber Raita, 233, **294**
Raisin(s)
    Golden, Pineapple Chutney with, 341
    Haroset, 348–49
    -Madeira Glaze, 213
    -Madeira Pan Sauce, 136–37
    North African Tomato Sauce with Chickpeas and Sweet Spices, 78, **79**
    Olives, and Pignoli, Tomato Sauce with, 89
    -Rum Sauce, 366
    Sicilian Cauliflower Sauce, 51
    Spinach-Pignoli Pesto with, **27, 100,** 107
    Traditional Mole Negro Sauce, 81–82
Raita
    about, 218
    additional uses for, 242
    Apple-Ginger, 239
    Asian Pear, with Lime and Chiles, 240
    Banana-Kiwi, 239
    Classic Cucumber, 230–31
    Cumin-Scented Carrot, 234
    Curry-Roasted Pumpkin, 234, **294**
    Fried Scallion-Cucumber, 237
    Mango, with Mint and Chiles, 240
    Mango Chutney, Quick, 342
    pairing with curries, 238
    Pistachio Yogurt Sauce, 243, **294**
    Pomegranate-Mint, 241
    Radish-Cucumber, 233, **294**
    Shredded Beet, 237
    Smoky Eggplant, 236
    Spinach, with Toasted Spices, 238–39
    Tamarind Yogurt Sauce, 242
    Tart Cherry, with Scallions and Sunflower Seeds, 241
Ranch Dressing, 289
Raspberry-Chile BBQ Sauce, 203
Raspberry Coulis, 380
Ravigote (Tangy Wine-Herb Velouté), 169–70
Relish
    about, 335
    best, for hot dogs, 341
    cooking with, 336
    Fresh Indian Chile-Tomato, 345–46
    Fresh Onion-Chile, 346
    Quince and Red Onion, 347
    Sweet-and-Sour Carrot, 347
Remoulade Sauce, 307
Rhubarb-Strawberry Sauce, 376
Rice vinegar, about, 248
Ricotta and Fresh Tomato Sauce, 57
Riesling
    Marinade, Fragrant, 184
    Sweet Wine Vinaigrette, 276
Romesco, 120–22
Roquefort Mayonnaise, 305
Roquefort-Shallot Compound Butter, **10,** 11
Rosemary
    -Balsamic Marinade, 187
    Lemon, and Garlic Grill Splash, 209
    Toasted Bread Crumb, and Parmesan Pesto, 99
    Tuscan Marinade, 178
Rouille I, 314
Rouille II, 314
Rouille III, 315
Rum-Raisin Sauce, 366
Russian Dressing, 289

S

Saffron
    Rouille III, 315
    -Scented Tomato Sauce, **55, 90,** 91
Sage, Fried, and Caper Pesto with Fresh Pecorino, **100,** 101
Sake, 248
    Brine, Spicy, 176
    -Soy Dumpling Sauce, Sweet, 255
Salad dressing. *See* Dressing; Vinaigrette
Salads, pairing with dressings, 282